DRAMATIC CRITIC

DRAMATIC CRITIC

Selected Reviews (1922-1939)
by Charles Morgan

Selected and Edited by Roger Morgan

Introduction by Carole Bourne-Taylor

OBERON BOOKS
LONDON

WWW.OBERONBOOKS.COM

This collection first published in 2013 by Oberon Books Ltd
521 Caledonian Road, London N7 9RH
Tel: +44 (0) 20 7607 3637 / Fax: +44 (0) 20 7607 3629
e-mail: info@oberonbooks.com
www.oberonbooks.com

A catalogue record for this book is available from the British Library.

PB ISBN: 978-1-84943-135-4
E ISBN: 978-1-84943-941-1

Cover design by James Illman

Cover photo courtesy of Roger Morgan

Printed and bound by Marston Book Services, Didcot.

CONTENTS

37/6

Foreword by Roger Morgan

(Note: the cast lists have been abbreviated and the reviews in some cases cut)

Charles Morgan met A. B. Walkley, then the dramatic critic of *The Times*, in 1920 when Morgan, as President of the Oxford Union Dramatic Society, produced *Antony and Cleopatra*. In December 1921 he became Walkley's assistant, and, in 1926, succeeded him. He remained the chief dramatic critic of *The Times* until, shortly before the outbreak of war in 1939, he joined the Naval Intelligence Division of the Admiralty.

In the early Twenties he contributed weekly articles on the London theatre to the *West Sussex Gazette* under the name of "Carolus." From 1932 until 1939 he contributed signed weekly articles to *The New York Times*. His reviews, for *The Times*, mostly written overnight for the next day's paper, were unattributed, but his collection of cuttings has enabled his own reviews to be identified. This is a small selection from more than 5,000 in the collection.

Introduction

It was Charles Morgan's laudatory review of *The Old Ladies* – which he summed up as 'a slow nightmare of *macabre* genius' – that prompted Agate, the doyen of contemporary drama critics, to admit: 'When Charles is in his best form he has us all whacked', mischievously adding: '*The Times* is happy to have a critic who is, when not insisting that sows' ears shall be silk purses, indisputably first-rate.'[1] True, Morgan had a predilection for what W.A. Darlington called 'the theatre of the mind.' His polished reviews – each word exquisitely poised – were aimed at a coterie of sophisticates rather than suburban theatregoers, who would have found him a bit of a wet blanket. They certainly reveal a penchant for sublimity and aestheticism. Sustained loftiness of thought and wit were enhanced by an impeccable penmanship; he had the gift of cadence and unobtrusively precise terminology. Honesty in judgment and earnestness of purpose were the hallmarks of his criticism. It was that very brisk, at times caustic, integrity that his colleagues admired: 'telling the theatre the truth about itself – often in tones of icy austerity.'[2] Although Morgan earned his fame as a novelist and playwright, his penetrating, authoritative and finely textured reviews are testament to his meticulous craftsmanship. Within their narrow compass they include every aspect of his talent in miniature: a virtuosity of phrasing that owed much to immaculacy and lean swiftness. Morgan's favourite composer was Mozart whose symphonic idiom he somehow transposes into his dazzlingly crisp prose.

Morgan was writing at a time when the theatrical production had gained fresh momentum. The theatre was a mingling of tendencies. The enduring truths of Shakespearean drama never lost their appeal, however the West End repertory had been considerably enlarged: playwrights of consequence, such as Bernard Shaw, James Barrie, Somerset Maugham, John Galsworthy and Noël Coward were a feast upon which such an abundant critic as Morgan could exercise his acutely responsive imagination.

The versatile Coward, so skilled at navigating between revue and drama, was the embodiment of the glittering 1920s. His *Vortex* stands out in the theatrical history of the 1920s. *Tonight at 8.30* (a series of one-act plays) ran for 157 performances – the vogue for one-act plays was in full swing in the Edwardian-Georgian period. Coward's 'own swift nonsense' was at its acme in *Red Peppers*, and 'the old aspidistran sneer' in *Fumed Oak* certainly had 'an admirable comic rhythm.' It was in *Private Lives* that his 'unsurpassed gift for combining entertainment with nothingness' shone. As Morgan bestows his alliterative praise upon Amanda and Elyot, 'the fine, flippant

---

1   James Agate, *Ego 2. Being more of the Autobiography of James Agate*, London, Victor Gollancz, 1936, p. 146. Morgan also features in Agate's anthology, *The English Dramatic Critics 1660-1932* (Barker Ltd, London, 1932).
2   S.W. in *The Sunday Express*

flower of Mr. Coward's talent,' he strikes with a typical *coup de grâce*: 'Mr. Coward can pad as no one else can pad.'…

Morgan, it has to be said, was at ease with the revue – when adroit – which was imported from Paris and so popular in the first three decades of the twentieth century. The comedic entertainment of Coward and Maugham, Rattigan's lighter plays, Travers's farces, all descended from Wilde's sparkling comedy of manners. However, Morgan could hardly tolerate a play replete with melodrama with its simple yet exciting plots, stigmatising the superfluous melodramatic touch in *After the Dance* – he seems, nevertheless, to have foreseen the successful posterity of Rattigan in whom he recognised 'a serious dramatist of genuine insight', even 'a dramatist of serious consequences.' In *French Without Tears*, 'the most successful farce of modern times in London', 'the entertainment, in its own frothy kind, is beyond question', relying on 'sly, cool, and delightfully opportune dialogue.' *It's You I Want* by Maurice Braddell is so brilliant that 'the hardest-faced frowner upon farces can have delight in this performance': a confession if ever there was! A Francophile, Morgan also relished the Wigmore Hall being transformed into a café-concert through the charm of Yvette Guilbert.

But Morgan was a contributor to a broadening of aesthetic appreciation, always yearning for a theatre that would prompt thinking, hence his decrying Sardou and Dumas, and even Wilde, as being too constraining for the talent of the modern actor. There was, he felt, an exceptional crop of actors 'in need of modern pieces of the first rank.' *Children in Uniform* – with its 'quality of glowing fierceness, of tears wrung from the stone of experience, that is the mark of tragedy' – and *Musical Chairs* contrasted with the dreary commercial comedy that prevailed. A *cri du coeur* accompanies *Power and Glory* by Karel Čapek: 'at last a play on war with a mind behind it'!

Poetic drama, with its experimentation, was more than a refreshing change from drab popular entertainment. There was the magical, exotic fascination of the lyrical *Hassan*. There was also T.S. Eliot's successful passion-play, *Murder in the Cathedral*, which marked the revival of poetic drama, enthralling Morgan the *littérateur* by its 'freshness of attack': 'more mistakes are made in underestimating than in overestimating the discernment of the public.'

The foreign influences – Strindberg, Turgenev, Schnitzler, Chekhov – that had penetrated the English stage were bound to appeal to a European-minded critic who longed to be snatched from 'the stolidities of pedestrian existence.' The Ibsenian cult was well-established. A performance of his *Ghosts* brought 'the tormented delight that springs from admiration of the dramatist's power and integrity.' Chekhov's concern with the soul and obscure poetry of life was distilled into *The Cherry Orchard*, the play *par excellence*. Morgan urged his readers to go and see 'a play, admittedly of a type which they do not like, but so magnificent in its own kind that they will almost certainly be moved by it in spite of their previous opinions'. Lavish praise was bestowed upon Komisarjevsky's 'admirable' and 'memorable' production of *The Seagull* with its sober stylisation, the 'unobtrusively' or 'unforced naturalistic' interiors

transpose to ~~tare~~ era he
was writing in?

required by the measured style of Chekhov whose subtlety made him a kindred spirit. The best Chekhovian production of the time was probably *Three Sisters* (Queen's Theatre, 1938) by Michel Saint-Denis – whom Morgan credited with a 'sensitive accuracy' – unanimously hailed as a masterpiece, 'as sane and unaffected as it is beautiful.' Morgan did put his finger on its poignant beauty: 'his tragic essence [...] is not dark and stormy but has the implicit melancholy of a clear night at the end of summer.'

It was in this atmosphere of European thought that Shaw's pugnacious comic instinct thrived; it provided the stimulation Morgan craved. Here was an entertainer with a broad intellectual outlook, who brought a clear, lucid and brave mind to the study of social problems; a destroyer of illusions who was able to transcend his socialist ideals: '*Major Barbara* is very much alive, being concerned far less with the prejudices of society than with the confusions of the soul but "is it topical?" someone will ask. Well, have we not said that it is about the soul?' Morgan would approve of anything that might stir out of its apathy the English public, wary by nature of intellectual criticism. Shaw was less gifted for portrayal of characters who, often coming out of 'the Shavian slot-machine', lacked in palpability, than for the clashing expression of ideas: this he did with consummate artistry. Morgan welcomed the 'adventure in itself to find the Old Vic opening a new season with a play not by Shakespeare': as an institutional alternative, *Caesar and Cleopatra* fitted the bill, 'giv[ing] opportunity for the herald blasts upon wind instruments without which no curtain in the Waterloo Road can traditionally rise', apart from being 'the swiftest and plainest narrative in the Shavian theatre.'

Irish drama was, of course, vibrant. O'Casey was another great dramatist of that age who was 'opening up a new country of the imagination from which [...] the fashionable theatre has hitherto been shut out.' In O'Casey's poetic realism, the sympathy for Irish working-class life rings true; in the tragedy of *The Plough and the Stars* the vitality of Irish humour shines through; in *The Silver Tassie*, with its bold, if a little strained, juxtaposition of naturalistic imagination and florid language, the earthy music-hall humour makes an extravagant leap into 'a transcendental dialogue.' Despite the pathos and melodrama being a little overweighted, Morgan recognizes a visionary power when he meets one: he, too, sees tragedy and comedy as the facets of a diamond being tossed in the air until 'their flashing becomes at last one flash.'

The brightly eloquent plays in verse and prose written by Auden-and-Isherwood in the 1930s made a stir. There was an undeniable element of pamphleteering, but the satirical expressionism in *The Dog Beneath the Skin* was fused with entertainment. Morgan, predictably, deplores the lefty bias, but as long as the dramatic value of a play was not compromised, it could afford to be a little doctrinal; it was the case of a graver play by the same partnership, *The Ascent of F6*, with its satire of typical Englishmen and topical symbolism. The good critic does not care much for propagandist art: 'it is a rule common to authors, teachers, and politicians that they must not bore the audience.'

Generally conservative but above all an aesthete –

The ideal play should be 'alive in the sense that it gives life to the spectator's imagining and causes it to become the dramatist's ally.' Morgan did not care much for Griffith's doctrinaire excogitations, however it was purely as a work of art that he judged his *Red Sunday* which had been censored by the Lord Chamberlain's office. A performance ought to be a work of art, the result of 'the discipline of players to whom their art is everything': 'that is enough to say in this sorry world'…

Morgan's artistic credo was an exacting one, encompassing a firm architectural sense – that quality of 'silky smoothness', when one's 'craft ceases to be apparent except to an eye that admiringly seeks it out' – and a taste for euphony. Like any writer painstakingly devoted to his craft, Morgan had an ear for language: George Curzon's – as Captain Hook – pronunciation of the King's English was 'so extravagantly correct that he was able to discover a jest and a thrill in each separated syllable of the menacing croc-o-dile.' Edith Evans impersonated the 'upholstered voice' that 'comes from the comfortable heart of Lady Bracknell's arrogance.' Indeed, a *sine qua non* when performing *The Importance of Being Earnest* was to create the illusion that 'this fantastic language is a language naturally used by the ladies and gentleman who utter it.' No wonder any lapse was stigmatised, such as Heather Angel's slovenly enunciation definitely not fit for 'Wilde's carved periods'[3] or Peggy O'Neill's 'monotonous noise'; or Laurence Olivier's Macbeth (Old Vic, 1937), who, despite 'a rare consistency and power', failed to master 'the full music of Shakespearean verse.' How many critics these days would spot a four and a half foot pentameter?[4] As for the mistreatment of the lyricism of James Elroy Flecker's *Hassan*, it just made Morgan wince: Flecker's 'singing language', Morgan laments, 'is not allowed to sing.' But the main reason for Morgan's dismay is that an OUDS cast, surely, have got the right 'minds and voices' for learning how to declaim a language that 'sh[one]' with unique splendour': Mr. Gibson-Cowan had failed to coach his cast – it was precisely Gielgud's perfect enunciation that had made him a mentor in his OUDS production of *Romeo and Juliet*. A fierce polemic followed, the highlight of which was Morgan's rhymed venom against the directorship. This is not the only evidence of Morgan's frustration vented in rhyme, though it may be unusual for him to produce a whole criticism in that form. When that piece is doggerel, there must be subtlety. One can almost see his scribbling in the stalls, dumbfounded as the obvious plot of *Under Suspicion* unfolds. His simple scansion hints not only that the play has made little impression on him, but seems to mimic its banality: 'The story ties itself in knots/For grim and guileless men/Who wonder what the others guess/For two whole acts; and then – ' The result is actually rather clever!

Anything inimical to perfection was severely condemned, whether it was pallid sentimentality or deportment, or the actors 'blunt[ing] their sensibility in the performance of trash.' It was odd, Morgan felt, that such a work of edification as *Murder in the Cathedral* could be marred by the electric candles adorning the altar,

---

3   Cf. *The Importance of Being Earnest* at the Lyric Theatre
4   Cf. his review of *A Midsummer Night's Dream* at the Old Vic

thus introducing 'a note of toy-like naturalism which conflicts with the play's austerity of style.' Morgan is good at spotting what jars, all those so-called 'enemies of the spirit': *The Miracle*, with its 'ingenious substitutes for truth', grated on his purist's imagination, but Lady Diana Manners's Virgin somehow saved the day.

The 'violent swerve towards productionism and "mass-drama"' was certainly Morgan's *bête noire*: 'the producer's job is not to repaint the picture or daub his own signature over it, but to illumine it and give it a frame.' Such affectations, consisting in 'twisting and guying [the text] as if it were a libretto' could degenerate into 'spectacular tricks': one is reminded of Debussy's contempt for Wagner's emphatic leitmotifs, dismissed as a mere 'box of tricks.' Anyhow, 'the forcing defeats the purpose.' Only O'Casey's own particular brand of Irish eloquence could accommodate a bit of overplaying. Wilde's wit certainly needed 'no barrage of grins to prepare its coming and no winking of the eye to emphasize its advance.' If The Royal Theatre of Greece's handling of Sophocles's *Electra* was so masterful it was because the play was allowed to fulfil its destiny without 'the imposed ingenuities of stagecraft.' It was that very unforced beauty that gave a sense of 'spiritual excitement.' What a pleasure, too, when Shakespeare is allowed to have his own way, thus leaving the impression, in *The Merchant of Venice*, 'of a fairy-tale that swings to character as a beautiful ship swings to the wind': 'a performance that is not tedious in its casket-scenes is a performance indeed.'

Morgan sought in Shakespeare, whose lyricism filled him with 'a divine radiance'[5], a vindication of his own spiritualism. Hamlet's soliloquies should reveal 'the full contemplative force' of the character. Morgan was bound to be very fond of the soliloquy which he aptly defined as 'a splendid instrument [...], a beautiful weapon of the imagination', one that requires perfect tuning. The ultimate role was best performed by Gielgud, whose 1934 *Hamlet* was the major Shakespearean revival of the time, as well as a commercial triumph. A disciplinarian with polish, Gielgud was as much the artist as the actor. Morgan was unequivocal about his towering and finest performance: it provided a sense of 'complete intellectual satisfaction' that stemmed from the sense that 'everything is as decisive as the line in the pencil-drawing of a master.' His was Morgan's 'ideal performance', 'the creature of my own most secret imagination.' Godfrey Tearle's Hamlet was of a different kind: simply human, an almost refreshing change from the usual exploitation of the 'meditative subtleties and [...] introspective opportunities' of the character, however, for Morgan, a slight betrayal of 'the refinements of his mind.' Similarly, he conceded that Laurence Olivier's Hamlet was 'original in the best sense' with its alliance of intelligence and grace in the interpretation, but he was quick to spot a slight bias towards emotionalism: 'this is not an intellectually brilliant Hamlet.'

Integrity at all costs: 'timidities' were as bad as 'pretentiousness': 'Acting is not conformity to drawing-room prejudice; it is not always comfortable; it is, at its highest, a flame, a barb, a challenge, a command to the imagination; it is, as art, alive

---

5   Charles Morgan, 'Creative Imagination', in *Reflections in a Mirror*, second series, London, Macmillan, 1946, p. 88

because it is more intense than life. There is something of madness in it, the splendid, liberating madness of a dream so vital that, when we awake from it, the world's sanity seems drab and unreal.' Against the pervasive tendency towards claptrap and 'cheap applause', Morgan argued in favour of 'dramatic challenge': he was adamant that the true artist 'never play[s] for safety.' He felt that Shakespeare, as the epitome of a 'safe' theatre, was treated very much like 'a mixture between the Bank of England and a charity bazaar'! It was in the name of integrity that Morgan opposed the idea of a National Theatre: the *raison d'être* of artistic endeavours is freedom and it is in the English character to resist 'pedantic discipline.'

Sparkling irony, even sarcasm, would drive Morgan's pen to deflate the fatal farrago of cheap entertainment and pretention. His review of *Six Stokers* by Elmer L. Greensfelder is a masterpiece in the scathing genre. *Nine Sharp* by Herbert Farjeon seemed to plumb the depths of weariness with the 'inert flesh' of the pathetic showgirls, resulting in an odd mixture somewhere between 'the clean dull fun of a concert in the village hall and the dreariest exhibitionism of a second-rate Parisian review designed for Anglo-Saxon tourists.' As for *Fresh Fields*, it is, we are told, best enjoyed as 'an aggregate of absurdities' because only then will it be 'rewardingly absurd'! No wonder Morgan excelled as a mordant chronicler of disasters – it was with his customary deftness that he captured the boos and hisses of the debacle of Coward's *Sirocco* in December 1927 and the mediocre performance of Eugenie Leontovitch as Cleopatra – how could it be otherwise? She had neither English nor verse!

Morgan favoured conciseness and an art of restraint; his theatrical sense was that of a purist. The merit of Steinbeck's *Of Mice and Men* lay in its uncompromisingly plain truth about human nature. If Jean Forbes-Robertson – whom he had accused of a certain 'garish looseness' in previous parts – was praised, it was for her 'communicat[ing] passion without display' in Ibsen's *Rosmersholm*. A flaw too often encountered was the 'over-dramatic zeal' – so rife – which kills a play. He loathed histrionics, anything done for easy effect, and cacophony, of course: *The Great Romancer* (Jules Eckert Goodman) would gain from 'learn[ing] to rattle with less persistence.' Control of gesture should not be flouted: 'Everyone is so determined to exhibit the bohemian vitality of the Dumas household that everyone shouts its roof off.' Any form of otioseness, whether pomposity or mannerisms, was equally dismissed. Tyrone Guthrie's production of *The School for Scandal* (Old Vic, 1937) was, despite his former achievements, unanimously received as contrived; perplexed, Morgan hypothesises: are we watching a ballet or probably just 'an elaborately stylised musical comedy' with all the characters 'skittishly dancing' or 'mincing'? Poor Sheridan seems to have been subjected to some 'fantastication.' Such inventive 'pretty-prettiness' was more successfully applied to *A Midsummer Night's Dream* (Old Vic, 1937) because it can accommodate it. Shakespeare's universality lends itself to eccentric adaptations: he and Mendelssohn, whose music adds to the magic, inhabit 'the world of pure imagination'.

Morgan's own humour was wicked, at times waspish, so he was bound to be critical of something flimsy, typically B.C. Hilliam's *Baby Austin* exuding 'a thin atmosphere of farce without a sparkle of a wit to recommend it.' Morgan vituperates, 'a man who takes Mr. Punch with him to the first performance of a dull farce is a prophet of his needs.' *You Can't Take It With You* by George S. Kaufman and Moss Hart was abysmal: 'With the best will in the world, one can find little to commend in the play except its brevity, which the clock surprisingly proves.' Snatches of sparkling sneering pervade the review of *Six Stokers*, too. Morgan sketched idiosyncrasies skilfully in a few brush strokes: Maurice Chevalier's 'naïve sophistication' and gesticulation; Mlle Printemps's Queen Sophia (in Ben Travers's Ruritanian *O Mistress Mine*), 'ravishingly betowelled' as she runs out of her bath into a crowded drawing-room; Miss Mary Brough performing a 'positively ducal char' in '*Rookery Nook*'; Miss Ashcroft's agile performance (in Shaw's *Caesar and Cleopatra*) redeeming what Morgan perceived as a 'serious handicap': 'There is something too harshly fuzzy-wuzzy about Miss Ashcroft's Egyptian hair-dresser; until custom softens the effects of his handiwork one seems to be looking at a grotesque doll.' Thankfully, Miss Ashcroft came across as 'an engaging trickster with a spark of life fairly aglow in her.'

High standards were maintained by the 'greats' of that vintage: John Gielgud, Ralph Richardson, Laurence Olivier, Peggy Ashcroft, Marie Tempest, Sybil Thorndike, Flora Robson and Edith Evans, each of whom was dubbed. Here were the finest flowers of the stage. In the category of 'genuine artists' about whom Morgan was invariably effusive there was also the less famous Miss Rawlings with her compelling combination of 'youth and experience', as well as a deportment and diction that indicated 'devoted craftsmanship.' The 'extreme subtlety and power' of her role as Katherine O'Shea was lighted up with a mysterious and poignant beauty which sent Morgan into raptures. The two productions of *Parnell* by Elsie T. Schauffler in 1936 tackled one of his pet subjects: love as 'a single-minded passion' between – such a rare thing on the stage, Morgan laments – 'a man and a woman of intelligence and breeding.' Here were 'lovers wrapt in their own experience, not exhibitionists whose heaven is the proscenium arch.' Rawlings excelled at 'communicat[ing] the entrancement of this woman's life,' in the same way 'as a painter may enrich his monochrome with various colour until his whole canvas glows.'

Such fine intuitions were Morgan's chief gift to literature and criticism. The authority of his evaluation stemmed from a blend of imaginative engagement and fearless intellectual criticism. In its scintillating cogency, Morgan's writing enshrines several decades of dramatic history, capturing the dizzying atmosphere on the London stage and the vitality and receptivity of the English genius plugged into the international world of the arts; the changes wrought by that wide outlook initiated a new cycle in English dramatic criticism. 'Midst the reviews we find a tribute to Lilian Baylis, founder of the legendary Old Vic and Sadler's Wells companies; a record of the first TV broadcast; the opening of Sadler's Wells; the advance in the BBC's method of broadcasting plays/wireless plays; the controversy surrounding the idea of a National Theatre; the *Oberammergau Passion Play* special jubilee season hijacked by the Nazis in 1934, although Morgan seemed to have been unaware of that. On a lighter note, he had a knack of surprising his reader: who would have predicted his enjoyment of the Disney production of *Snow White and the Seven Dwarfs* (1938) with its 'roughness of humour'? True, the dwarves' chubby faces were 'designed to appeal to the easy humour of fat men in their stalls' and Snow White was, for Morgan, too much of a cover-girl, however, the entertainment worked its magic on adults and children alike and ended up being 'a work of art for the screen.'

Those years for the theatre – unsullied by forgiving or even uneducated audiences, by competition from musicals at every corner, eying tourists at the box office; computer-generated effects and blockbuster films – were golden ones; that a galaxy of real talent was to be found, in the flesh, on the stage, is the stuff of reminiscence. But as then and still now, for us, one great talent is still accessible: the pen of that unerring genius, tucked away in the stalls, Charles Morgan.

Carole Bourne-Taylor,
Brasenose College, Oxford

no despair for thtr

Peer Gynt by Henrik Ibsen

FIRST PRODUCTION IN ENGLAND

It can now no longer be effective to weigh in hand the volume which contains the text of *Peer Gynt* and to declare that such a work cannot reasonably be put upon an English stage, or that, if it were, no English audience would endure it. We confess that we were surprised by success so decisive. The Old Vic has done much in the past, but its faults seemed precisely those which might most have endangered Ibsen's dramatic poem; and though the Old Vic audiences have long displayed a better collective sense than the audiences of any other commercial theatre in London there were pardonable misgivings concerning the reception they might give to a play so unusual and so challenging. By the event, misgivings were proved unnecessary.

Last night had all the qualities of a great occasion. Before the curtain rose upon this "unproducible" play by this "unpopular" dramatist every seat and every inch of legitimate standing-room was full. And so long as men and women will stand for more than four hours to hear a great work performed – will stand, moreover, spellbound, with none of that whispering and shuffling that so often is the disgrace of more luxurious audiences – so long as it is possible for poetic drama to sweep its hearers from breathless silence into a great tumult of cheering, there need be no despair for the theatre.

Greig's music, which had been adapted and was directed by Mr. Charles Corri, is now of concern only in its relation to the action on the stage. And the more familiar one is with both the play's text and with the music in its independent renderings, the more remarkable must appear the mutual strengthening of dramatist and composer when their work is given together. There was, perhaps, no period in last night's performance when this unity was more conspicuous than in the death of Ase, and its effect was increased by the fact that Mr. Russell Thorndike and Miss Florence Buckton, with the stage to themselves, reached in this scene the height of their attainment. Peer Gynt has returned to his mother's bedside. As she in his childhood had told him amazing tales, so he now, unaware of death's approach, drives her in their magic sledge, his seat the bed-rail, his steed a chair. As Ibsen wrote it, the scene is a vast imaginative movement, an astonishing compound of the tender, the ironic, and the fantastic. The depth of its possible failure gave to its success last night the beauty of spiritual peril and escape, and we passed from it to other things with a sense that, if all else should suddenly weaken and fail, we had witnessed a great scene that would live in the memory.

...

The acting was consistently good, and it is very seldom that one felt that the laughter, which again and again was won by the play's irony, had been forced by

1

exaggeration. But the fact most remarkable is that the greater the author's poetic and imaginative demand, the greater was the response both of the actors and the audience. It is a fact happily recorded.

21 DECEMBER 1923, THE TIMES

Peter Pan by J.M. Barrie

REVIVAL AT THE ADELPHI

PETER PAN	Gladys Cooper
JAS. HOOK	Franklin Dyall
MR. DARLING	Jack Raine
WENDY	Lila Maravan
SMEE	George Shelton
SLIGHTLY	Donald Searle
NANA	Gordon Carr

Confirmed and crusty Peterists, who have unwisely allowed themselves to form fixed ideas of Peterism, pay their penalty in an annual series of shocks. At the beginning of each year's performance they are to be heard gasping. Wendy is not what they expected, Peter is too this or too that, Hook hasn't the fierceness to which they were accustomed in their youth. But, as the play proceeds, they get over it. Their gasps cease. They are overwhelmed by Peter's swagger; they lose their hearts to Wendy; they tremble before the terrible Hook. And, when they come away, they still have fixed ideas – for that is a part of their nature – but now the fixed ideas are new, and they will be the cause of fresh gasping a twelvemonth hence.

Smaller people, who see it all as a new play without prejudice, begin to enjoy themselves even before the night-lights twinkle; and continue in uninterrupted rejoicing until Peter and Wendy are waving good-bye from the tree-tops. Of course, there are anxious moments when the Pirates are defeating the Braves, or when Tinker Bell is nearly dead, or when the plank is being brought out in the pirate ship. But Mr. George Shelton, as the "lovable Smee," is always with us, and his genial placidity is proof against Hook's menace, and even against Mr. Franklin Dyall's ferocious squint. In the corner – a pleasantly conspicuous corner – is Slightly (Mr. Donald Searle), to whom nothing is surprising, and who radiates a cheerful eccentricity under a fine crop of red hair. Add to these Peter himself, who is always just in time to avert disaster, and Nana (Mr. Gordon Carr), who is the noblest of nurses and watchdogs, and terror loses all but its most delightful and least uncomfortable sting.

We confess that there were moments now and then when Miss Gladys Cooper's Peter almost found us in the ranks of the confirmed and crusty Peterists. But away with fixed ideas! Here is a Peter who is very much captain of her band, who gives her orders with an air, and pursues her adventures with amazing zest. And no Peter has reaped a richer harvest of handkerchief-waving when all was done, which proves how foolish it is to come to this play with any sort of reminiscent prejudice. We hope that many of the handkerchiefs were for Wendy, too, for Miss Lila Maravan made her a charming little lady with what seemed to our Sassenach taste a right flavour of Scotland.

14 APRIL 1924, THE TIMES

Measure for Measure
by William Shakespeare

THE FELLOWSHIP OF PLAYERS AT THE STRAND THEATRE

VINCENTIO	W. Earle Grey
ANGELO	Ernest Milton
LUCIO	Baliol Holloway
CLAUDIO	Duncan Yarrow
ISABELLA	Griselda Hervey

A few eager souls actually applauded last night when, towards the final curtain, the Duke put a crown upon his sentimental achievements by taking Isabella's hand, and it is scarcely to be wondered at, for the mechanical adjustments which bring *Measure for Measure* to an end have much in common with the last round of a musical comedy. Everyone is arbitrarily paired off, and even the luckless Mariana has to put a cheerful face upon the prospect of wedded life with Angelo. Character, antecedents, and probability are all swept aside in a universal rush for the altar. It would never have done for Isabella to have been left out in the cold. No wonder the Duke's gallantry was applauded!

The manner of the whole play has, of course, prepared us for the manner of its conclusion. From start to finish it is a mechanical affair; its coherence is the coherence of a neatly fitted story, not of a dominant and progressing theme. We find its virtue and our own entertainment in detached passages, as if, in an unsatisfactory dinner, we came now and then to an admirable dish. In no part is there an opportunity for an actor to attain the highest distinction, but almost every part presents him with a difficulty of bridging over gaps of characterisation and concealing the dramatist's most awkward twists.

The ways of such folk as Pompey and Lucio are clear enough. Play them with spirit and an easy swagger, as did Mr. Andrew Leigh and Mr. Baliol Holloway, and all is well. They are detached fantasticks; they stand apart from the plot; no one twists them into psychological contradictions. But the Duke and Claudio, even more Isabella and Mariana, are always on perilous ground, and Angelo's path is not too smooth. It is, therefore, a real credit to actors who can give to them a seeming truth and coherence. Mr. Earle Grey, Mr. Duncan Yarrow, and Miss Mary Barton all gave admirable performances.

Mr. Ernest Milton played Angelo with fiery zeal – now and then a little over-spectacular in his goings-out, but he did succeed in bringing the wretched deputy to life, in making us feel (at any rate in his presence) that he was in torment.

…

Generally seems generous, criticism is gently ironic [handwritten annotation]

17 DECEMBER 1924, THE TIMES

The Vortex by Noël Coward

ROYALTY THEATRE

PRESTON	Kathleen Blake
HELEN SAVILLE	Mary Robson
PAUNCEFORT QUENTIN	F. Kinsey Peile
CLARA HIBBERT	Millie Sim
FLORENCE LANCASTER	Lilian Braithwaite
TOM VERYAN	Alan Hollis
NICKY LANCASTER	Noël Coward
DAVID LANCASTER	A. Bromley Davenport
BUNTY MAINWARING	Molly Kerr
BRUCE FAIRLIGHT	Ivor Barnard

It has not taken Mr. Noël Coward's new play, *The Vortex*, long to come from the outskirts of London to its centre, for it is only three weeks since it was produced at Hampstead at the Everyman Theatre, and last night it was seen at The Royalty. *The Vortex*, as one of the characters points out, is "a vortex of beastliness," and Mr. Coward's study of the unpleasant was worth transplanting, not because it is a study of social rottenness, but because it is so clever and often so penetrating a study. With all its superficial cynicism there are many flashes of truth, unpleasant though they may be, but there is no beauty. All is stark ugliness, and even the final curtain seems only the prelude to more ugliness in the future.

This pervasive ugliness and the absence of beauty and pity are, however, almost the only faults in the play, which is clever from beginning to end. The characters are clever studies in the unpleasant, and the action is a clever working out of the inevitable results of their conduct. It is only a pity that we can really sympathize with none of them, if only because even the worst are unmoral rather than immoral. They seem to sin merely because it appears to them easier to do that than to be virtuous. The hero himself, who should win our sympathy, merely drifts into taking drugs.

But even where one feels least sympathy with the play one can wholeheartedly admire the brilliant acting. Miss Lilian Braithwaite has never acted better than she did last night in the part of the middle-aged woman who "refused to grow up," and Mr.

starry in own prod.

(Coward) gave a fine study of the drug-taking young hero. Miss Millie Sim presented an amusing, languid study of a perpetually exhausted young woman, and Miss Molly Kerr acted well in the part of a young girl who faced facts very clearly – when it suited her to do so. … The piece received an enthusiastic reception.

she is then old Vic ⪖ x2

27 DECEMBER 1924, THE TIMES

A Midsummer Night's Dream
by William Shakespeare

MUSIC BY MENDELSSOHN. BALLETS BY MICHEL FOKINE. DRURY LANE

LYSANDER	Mr. Leon Quartermaine
DEMETRIUS	Mr. Frank Vosper
QUINCE	Mr. Frank Cellier
SNUG	Mr. Alfred Clark
BOTTOM	Mr. Wilfred Walter
FLUTE	Mr. Clifford Mollison
SNOUT	Mr. Miles Malleson
STARVELING	Mr. H. O. Nicholson
HERMIA	Miss Athene Seyler
HELENA	Miss Edith Evans
OBERON	Mr. Robert Harris
TITANIA	Miss Gwen Ffrangçon-Davies
PUCK	Mr. D. Hay Petrie

If a man, walking through a forest, comes suddenly upon adventure, he is not, while the emotion springing from that adventure is at its height, accurately and consciously observant of the forest's architecture, or of its shadows folding and unfolding on mossy banks, or of the brilliantly changing pattern of its leaves. Meeting Titania, whether she be Shakespeare's queen or the Titania of his own imagining, he has, in that instant of encounter, no eyes but for her brightness, no ears but for the words she speaks, no thought that is not filled with her magic. Say, if you will, that he submits completely to her spell, that fairies, if they reveal themselves to him, will have all of him or none; but the implied truth extends, in fact, beyond fairyland into all the realms of imaginative discovery. Men are not and cannot be critics of the setting of their own spiritual adventure while that adventure endures. The setting produces its effect, but, so soon as the effect ceases to be subconscious, the adventure is interrupted, the dream vanishes, the spell is broken.

This is, or should be, the principle governing the stage decoration of poetic drama, particularly of Shakespeare's fairy play. No play gives to an artist a more fantastic and delightful freedom. He has a right, and, indeed, a duty, to flout those critics who, unable to escape from the library, would have an apologetic stage stripped to the neutrality of black curtains and the whole nuptial entertainment reduced to a bleak and textual reverence. He is entitled to let himself go, to subdue to his purpose all the devices of modern stage-craft. He is justified in gorgeousness, in any splendour and extravagance, so long as his extravagant splendours, enchanting us by their own beauty when first we see them, become no more than a subconscious impression when Titania speaks, no more than an atmosphere when Oberon is commanding Puck.

It is this power of withdrawal that is lacking in the decorations which now accompany the play. Often they are beautiful in themselves. The palace of Theseus, with its mounting columns and gigantic braziers, has an austerity of design and a richness of golden colouring that do honour to Miss Mary Clare's lovely Hippolyta. They are, too, an appropriate background to Bottom and his friends, who gain rather than lose by so much contrasted magnificence. Mr. Wilfred Walter, with a voice to shake the gallery, throws off in this scene the tendency to monotonous heaviness which handicaps him elsewhere; there is quick variety in the acting of Mr. H. O. Nicholson, Mr. Alfred Clark, and Mr. Miles Malleson, and there is exquisite nonsense from Mr. Cellier as Quince and Mr. Clifford Mollison as Flute.

So far the palace is in admirable accord with the courtiers and the players. But once the revels are over, the mortals gone, and the fairies afoot once more, the same palace becomes an intrusion. Puck, who should now be stealthy and full of mystery, who should have an air of whispering final secrets after the noisy world is gone, is jumping down terrace after terrace of assembled and decorative fairies. What a fine palace! you inevitably say.

There is the same scenic over-emphasis in the wood, and we need not insist upon it. The mortals hold their own, but the immortals are again and again overwhelmed by it. It is, in general, a satisfactory wood, if only we had not to meet Titania there. The lovers, dwarf-lovers properly lost on that vast stage, are the best of good fun. Helena is not Miss Edith Evans's part, but she comes very near to establishing a new Helena, sleek, sharp, and over-civilized, of her own; Mr. Leon Quartermaine as Lysander, Mr. Frank Vosper as Demetrius, and Miss Athene Seyler as a Hermia, all sting and claws, are continually planning delicate surprises for those who watch them closely enough. Once launched upon their quarrel, they are independent of the forest; they make of it a sort of mock drawing-room, and a highly diverting quarrel they have there. But there can be no drawing-room for the fairies. They have to take the forest as it is. In it are certain tall trees beautifully done, behind it on occasion are entrancing distances, and high at the back is a hill containing Titania's electric bower, of which the rocky doors open and close like a fan. In the foreground, however, is a strange, terraced structure with a rounded back. It is like no hillock, earthly or magical; it is, in fact, like nothing so much as a Tank, fitted with ledges, protectively coloured, and lacking only caterpillar wheels. It is impossible to forget it. There it stands – a platform for the fairies to dance on and for Oberon to climb. The fairies dance under the direction of

M. Fokine, and we need say no more of them at present than that we liked nothing in the play so well.

Oberon is admirably played by Mr. Robert Harris, and Miss Gwen Ffrangçon Davies, when she is not cruelly subordinated to the mechanics of her bower, is a remote, fairy-like Titania – a grave or sadly smiling queen. Mr. Hay Petrie, too has the spite which is Puck and the warmth which is Robin – a brilliant and delightful performance. Concentrate upon the acting, refuse steadily to be diverted from it, and there appears good in it everywhere. Consider the stage-craft as a thing apart and there is good in this also. But release that deliberately analytical concentration, lean back and let the play come to you as a whole, and it is not always the poet's magic that prevails.

27 DECEMBER 1924, THE TIMES

Six Cylinder Love by W. Anthony McGuire

GARRICK THEATRE

MR. BURTON	Sebastian Smith
MRS. BURTON	Sybil Arundale
PHYLLIS	Joyce Carey
BERTRAM	Ian Fleming
MARYLIN	Edna Best
DONROY	Ernest Leeman

Here, from a house at Golders Green to a humbler lodging at Islington, Miss Edna Best reads a lesson to affectionate but extravagant wives. Marylin is all smiles and foolishness when first she is discovered, providing Gilbert with undrinkable coffee and uneatable scones. A motor-car, which Gilbert is induced to buy from neighbours whom it has already ruined, is the beginning of domestic misfortune. Not that Marylin ceases to smile; she enjoys the motor-car, she likes the gay company of the friends who are eager to be entertained in it at poor Gilbert's expense, and she is, moreover, Miss Edna Best, to whom a smile is a perpetual decoration. Of course she smiles, and even the wretched Gilbert does his best. True, they no longer dine at home, a change which he finds is good for his digestion, but he reaps no other advantage from the motor-car. It drives him to mild embezzlement, to a quarrel with his affable employer, and ultimately to Islington.

Thither the Burtons, who formerly owned the accursed vehicle have preceded them. Mrs. Burton has laid aside the air of acquisitive gentility that she cultivated in Golders Green, Mr. Burton is once more solvent and happy, and Phyllis is in a fair way to becoming a contented typist. Profiting by the example which Miss Sybil Arundale and Miss Joyce Carey have set her, Marylin mends her ways. The car is sold to a night-club porter, who presumably can afford it; Gilbert is reconciled with his employer, and the moral tale is complete. There have been charming fairy-stories to point the same moral. Here, in exchange for charm, is hustle, with a glib motor-sales-man in the person of Mr. Ernest Leeman, and spanners, catch-words, and broken fences to add now and then the pleasures of pandemonium.

Mr. Bobby Howes is Gilbert, a clever study of cheerful weakness, more entertaining when he is taking his comedy quietly then when he is stuffing his pockets with Marylin's scones. Apart from his performance, and Miss Best's pretty follies, nothing in the play is so remarkable as that it starts at 6 o'clock.

8 JUNE 1925, WEST SUSSEX GAZETTE

The Cherry Orchard by Anton Tchehov

If I were to follow my general custom of giving some warning to those whose temperament and choice of a play are different from my own, I should, I suppose, say that anyone whose chief requirement in a theatre is quick, coherent action would do well to stay away from *The Cherry Orchard*. But in this instance I put caution aside, and urge everyone, no matter what their general taste, to see this play at the Lyric Theatre, Hammersmith. There are, I know, some who say, when you ask them what sort of play they like to see, that they like "a play with a good story, in which something is continually happening." Well, they will find that *The Cherry Orchard* has, in the sense in which they use the word, no "story," and that nothing physical happens in it. Nevertheless, I urge them to go, and for this reason – that they will see a play, admittedly of a type which they do not like, but so magnificent in its own kind that they will almost certainly be moved by it in spite of their previous opinions. They may, in short, be led on to make a discovery and take to a new view of the theatre.

The Cherry Orchard was produced at the Moscow Art Theatre on January 17, 1904, the last birthday of its author, Anton Tchehov. Its scene, therefore, is Russia before the Russo-Japanese war. Madame Ranevsky returns from Paris to the property which she owns – to the cherry orchard which has been hers and her family's for many generations. The place is heavily mortgaged and will soon have to be sold. Lopakhin, a rich merchant, who was once a peasant himself, and whose ancestors were serfs belonging to this very estate, urges upon Madame Ranevsky the imminence of this disaster. She hears, she understands, but she does not heed. Her brother Leonid talks vaguely about getting work in a bank, but, in fact, does nothing but talk and talk and talk and dream about billiards. Barbara, Madame Ranevsky's adopted daughter, who has charge of the house, is troubled about two things – her household economies and the fact that for years Lopakhin has been on the verge of proposing to her and will never come up to the scratch. Anya, Madame Ranevsky's daughter, is, it appears, at heart indifferent to the fate of the cherry orchard; she is a gay child, affected by the sentiment of departure, affected, too, by the curious idealism of Peter Trophimof, who has been and will always be, a student, and is incapable of decisive action or forward movement of any kind, but she is so young in mind that troubles and affections easily slide away from her, leaving her with a dominant thought of freedom and irresponsibility and escape. The inevitable happens. The cherry orchard is sold – sold without any serious attempt to save it. The Ranevsky family departs, and that is the end of the play.

Nothing, you will have observed, "happens," except that the cherry orchard is sold, as you knew at the outset it would be sold. To put it in other words, the old order, doomed, irresolute and weak, vanishes without a struggle – not because it is evil, not because it does not care, but because "everything comes to an end at last," and it has reached its end. And the play is concerned to show you the attitude of many minds towards this end as it approaches and when it comes.

"The attitude of many minds," I have said; it would have been nearer the truth to say, "the fluttering of many souls." In this difference is the whole significance of Tchehov's genius, as I understand it. He does not analyse the mind, but expose the soul. To which you may answer: "But what is the difference between mind and soul?" It is useless here to argue such a question. I am not sure that argument concerning it can ever be of very much value. A man must feel the answer for himself; he cannot be persuaded of it through his intellect alone. And I might almost sum up my chief objections to the English theatre by saying that the plays which are given make no attempt whatever to throw light upon the difference between mind and soul. Either they omit all consideration of the soul or they assume that it is something which is of concern only to those who actively practice religion. Tchehov, on the other hand, though, so far as I remember without reference to the text, he never mentions it, is writing not about outward manners, or even about the inward processes of reason, but about the soul. I do not know how many people in the theatre recognize this, but all of them, I think, must have felt that they were in an atmosphere completely strange to the English theatre, and that the strangeness depended, not as you may be tempted to imagine at first sight upon the "Russianness" as opposed to the "Englishness," not upon strange clothes or behaviour or manners that we might describe as erratic and irregular, but upon the fact that Tchehov writes upon an altogether different plane from, say, Mr. Henry Arthur Jones. He cares not a jot for "dramatic situation"; there are none of the tricks and contrivances commonly used in what we call a "well-made" play; there is no excitement of event – you are never breathlessly asking "what is going to happen next?" You are, in short, invited to consider this group of human beings, not from the point of view of a showman eager to furnish an entertainment out of their antics, but from the point of view of a being who created them and dwells within them all. They talk very often irrelevantly and at cross-purposes, nothing is cut-and-dried, nothing is arranged in a conventional pattern, but the effect is an effect of extraordinary depth and sympathy and understanding. It is not, I think, the sort of play which will ever make a pit and gallery scream itself hoarse with emotional enthusiasm, but it is a play which leaves you with a sense, now very rare, that in going to the theatre you have done something of real importance and significance. You come away with a feeling of gladness and discovery – and of deep gratitude, too, to Mr. Fagan, who produced the play, and to the actors, particularly to Miss Mary Grey, Mr. John Gielgud, and Miss Gwendolyn Evans.

14 SEPTEMBER 1925, THE TIMES

The Merchant of Venice by William Shakespeare

OLD VIC REOPENED

ANTONIO	Neil Porter
BASSANIO	Geoffrey Wardwell
SHYLOCK	Baliol Holloway
LAUNCELOT GOBBO	John Garside
THE PRINCE OF ARRAGON	Duncan Yarrow
PORTIA	Edith Evans
NERISSA	Nell Carter
JESSICA	Amy Nowell

The first night of the new season at the Old Vic has much in common with the last night of the O. U. D. S. at Oxford. There is an embarrassment of bouquets; the men, who cannot pick them up fast enough, pile them into the ladies' arms until the ladies are nearly smothered in good will. There are speeches – Miss Baylis remembering the past and welcoming the present, Mr. Andrew Leigh to make his bow as the Old Vic's new producer and gracefully to direct applause towards everyone but himself; Miss Edith Evans brief, charming, and genuinely reluctant to speak at all, and Mr. Baliol Holloway to round off the proceedings with a robust joke that makes the gallery roar. Not that another jest is needed to provoke enthusiasm. The whole audience from gallery to gangway has been cheering, with indiscriminate loyalty, since the evening began, and there would be not four but a dozen speeches if the house had its way. So be it. The meeting of friends is justification for a little eloquence, and, as Mr. Leigh said, it is pleasant to see old faces again.

To come away from such a scene and confess oneself dissatisfied by any part of a play that has caused so much pleasure is a cold and sorry task. Happier far to throw another bouquet and share the general glow! Therefore, let it be quickly done. Several performances – enough to affect the play, though only one is in a part of some importance – are distressingly bad. Some of them are bad in ways which Mr. Leigh may even now correct. There is nothing to justify actors, whose duties are little more than those of messengers, footman, or attendants, in making their words distinctively conspicuous by some wild eccentricity of voice or manner. It is as if a parlourmaid, interrupting a straightforward comedy, were to declare, in a burst of shrill rhetoric, that the carriage was at the door. It is, for example, unnecessary to tell the Court that "a messenger from the doctor" is "new come from Padua" in a tone which could only have been appropriate if St. Mark's had fallen down and the canals of Venice run suddenly dry. What is needed here and in a dozen places is a stern suppression of over-dramatic zeal – a simple remedy. Jessica is a more difficult problem which, perhaps, will largely solve itself when the actress is less nervously anxious to please than she seemed to be on Saturday night.

It is a relief to turn to recollection of what was good, particularly to Mr. Baliol Holloway's Shylock, a varied and well-considered performance which might, we felt, have been much more if it had had better encouragement in the atmosphere of the stage. Miss Edith Evans's style has a glittering artificiality which gives one aspect of Portia to perfection. That charm, not of our own drawing-rooms, which does dwell in Portia for the actress who can discover gentleness beneath her raillery, we missed sometimes; but Miss Evans's gaiety has a curious mingling of the sharp and the languid which is amusing always and has an enchantment of its own in the play's final scene. Mr. Neil Porter's Antonio is full and excellently balanced, Mr. Geoffrey Wardwell does well in the end, after an uncertain beginning, with the thankless Bassanio; Mr. Duncan Yarrow gives sudden and unexpected distinction to the Prince of Arragon; Mr. John Wyse is an admirable Gratiano; and Mr. John Garside, as well as playing Lancelot Gobbo, is responsible for the best stage design of costume and setting that we have yet seen at the Old Vic. Portia and Nerissa's entry in the last scene is a beautiful piece of grouping – two cloaked figures standing a little apart to watch the lovers at the foot of their moonlit tree.

17 NOVEMBER 1925, THE TIMES

Measure for Measure by William Shakespeare

OLD VIC

VINCENTIO	Neil Porter
ANGELO	Baliol Holloway
ESCALUS	John Garside
CLAUDIO	Duncan Yarrow
LUCIO	John Wyse
ELBOW	Allen Douglas
ISABELLA	Nell Carter
MARIANA	Edith Evans

To some, who have great joy in the tapsters, it would seem a heresy to declare that Shakespeare's fantasticks live to-day more happily than his buffoons, and indeed, it would be folly, punishable with controversy unending, to indulge in a piece of critical team-making so vague and profitless. There is nothing for it, in such a matter, but to record one's preference and there be done. If the red noses, the tankards, and the bibulous blunders please you – why, then, the tapsters, the porters, and the constables have it. If the courtly graces, or the affectation of them, amuse you better, then the fantasticks must conquer. Carry the dispute from the chorus to the principals, and who shall choose finally between Toby and Andrew? For our own part, we incline more towards Andrew than against him, and in *Measure for Measure* Lucio is for us as entertaining as Elbow is dull. The reason seems to be that the humour of Elbow is so roughly verbal that his words, like a fog, obscure rather than enlighten his character; whereas when Lucio speaks there is a man, or a recognisable caricature of a man, in his quips which gives them a comic interest independent of the turn of phrase.

However that may be – and there are many to defend Elbow and his betters in the same kind – it was Lucio who rather unexpectedly stood out from last night's performance and prompted this digression on the fantasticks. *Measure for Measure* is a play that is recommended as well by its rarity as its merits, and, in general, the Old Vic performs it well. If Miss Edith Evans was a little castaway in Mariana's colourless virtues, and if Mr. Baliol Holloway treated Angelo with rather less subtlety than is his due, there was compensation in Mr. Neil Porter and Mr. Garside as the Duke and Escalus. Miss Nell Carter, too, gave a brave performance as Isabella, which, though it lacked power for the great attacks, was admirable in the quieter passages. But it is one of the pleasures of the Old Vic to watch talent make its mark, and we offer no excuse for returning to Lucio and to Mr. John Wyse's playing of the part. A delightful fantastick he was, always within his own control, who never allowed mere extravagance to dull the edge of comedy and timed his sayings as a good swordsman times his thrusts.

18 JANUARY 1926, THE TIMES

Uncle Vanya by Anton Tchehov

TRANSLATED BY CONSTANCE GARNETT
BARNES THEATRE

ASTROV	Henry C. Hewitt
VANYA	Robert Farquharson
ALEXANDER SEREBRYAKOV	Boris Ranevsky
TELYEGIN	Ivor Barnard
SONIA	Jean Forbes-Robertson
HELENA	Dorothy Massingham

In the fretful inland sea of soured enthusiasm and self-pity which is Professor Serebryakov's household, Sonia stands like a rock. She is his daughter by his first wife and Vanya's niece. No one takes much notice of her, for they are all too busy noticing themselves. The professor, a querulous old man who, it seems, has possessed all his life a power to make women deceive themselves for his sake, is now too well occupied with his invalidism and his vanities to have any care for his daughter, unless it be as a copyist of worthless manuscripts and a carrier of cushions. Dr. Astrov, who has a spark of genius that will never spring to flame and a passion, a symbolic passion for forestry which the drudgery of medicine will never permit him to satisfy, marks Sonia so little that he is unaware that for six years she has loved him. As for Helena, Serebryakov's beautiful young wife, what does she care in her heart for her plain step-daughter? There is, it is true, a moment when, with a not ungentle patronage, she promises to hint to Astrov of Sonia's love for him and "end her uncertainty"; but when Astrov has been told, Helena forgets the girl's tragedy in the excitement – none the less pleasant because it is virtuously loyal – of repelling the declaration which her own beauty has provoked. So they all continue, floating ideas upon their inland sea as children float paper-boats in a windy pond, watching them drift a little while keelless and rudderless, borne this way and that by passionate gusts. If they care at all for their survival or direction, they make no sort of reasoned, consistent effort to guide or to preserve them. What should they care for Sonia's venture? How should they distinguish it, which is so little insistent upon itself, as a venture different in kind from their own? They will not be cruel to her or chide her. They will just leave her out of their thoughts. And because by common impulse, they thus isolate her, she appears to us who watch as a detached, illuminant figure upon a background of their confusions.

From this background Vanya emerges now and then. He loved Sonia's mother, who was his sister. Perhaps it was at first for her sake that he consented, after his sister's death, to stay on and manage the estate in return for the pittance that the hated professor allows him. Now he stays because he is in the groove. Night after night he lies awake thinking of how his life has been wasted, how age has crept upon him, how Helena would be at least a morsel for his many hungers could he but capture her. And when, in a fit of exasperation, he has tried to shoot the Professor and has missed (it was, as his fatal insight tells him, in his nature to miss), and when at last the Professor and Helena, unable to endure it longer, are leaving the estate, Vanya, hearing the bells of their departing carriage, can only return to his groove once more and, sitting down at his account books with Sonia at his side, miserably count the Professor's roubles and kopeks. His significance in this final scene is that Sonia, who has silently lost the man she loves, is at his side. His significance throughout the play is less in himself than in his relationship with her, a truth which Mr. Farquharson indicates with a hundred subtle restraints. But something of this significance is dissipated if it is not clearly suggested – and Mr. Farquharson, we felt, suggested it not clearly enough – that Vanya's loss, like Sonia's, though in a different degree, was a genuine loss – that, in short, there was once in him enough potential nobility of mind to make his longings to begin life afresh and his regrets for his squandered years not comic, as the audience was inclined to interpret them, but tragic. If we were left in no doubt of this, Vanya and Sonia would appear in their true relationship – the relationship between a life seen in old age to have been in vain and a greater tragedy of life seen to be thrown away before it is well begun. Sonia kneeling beside her uncle and promising to him and to herself the consolation of a world to come while he, not hearing or daring not to hear, stares into the emptiness of his own soul might then be a concluding scene fuller of meaning, though it could scarcely be more poignant, than it is at present.

And what of the shadows, some driving away in their carriages and some lingering on in a corner of Vanya's room, who have been Sonia's background? They are shadows only in their contrast with her light; in themselves they are vigorous enough from the Professor (Mr. Boris Ranevsky) to little Telyegin, with his smooth manner and his pock-marked face, in whom Mr. Ivor Barnard has recognized one of Tchehov's mild grotesques. Mr. Henry Hewitt, as the doctor, gives us his weakness very cleverly without losing sight of his underlying strength, and Miss Dorothy Massingham's performance combines a persuasive naturalness with a wide intellectual range. But all of them – and it is to the actors' as well as to Mr. Komisarjevsky's credit that this perspective is so consistently preserved – are contributory to Sonia. Of her we have already said enough to indicate how profound was the sympathy she created, how lively and many sided was the interest she sustained. The part is played by Miss Jean Forbes-Robertson in a way that gives the theatre new cause to be proud of her name. She stoops to none of the tricks that are supposed to beget emotion in an audience; she plays, in the moments of crisis, with a kind of stilled sincerity that demands an equal response of the heart and of the mind. There cannot have been one in the audience who did not hold his breath as she took her terrible silent farewell of Astrov, or did not bow his head with her as she sank quietly to her knees at Vanya's side. It was a performance which, if its promise is fulfilled, we shall be glad to remember as a first decisive achievement.

22 JUNE 1926, THE TIMES

Mozart by Sasha Guitry

MUSIC BY REYNALDO HAHN
THE GAIETY THEATRE

MOZART	Yvonne Printemps
GRIMM	Sasha Guitry

It is the house of Madame d'Epinay, where all is polished and all is decorated. In the long doors, which stand open upon the passage, mirrors are set so that you may, without turning your head, see who comes. The garden, you know, though little of it is visible, is full of the most shapely fountains; those who pass are all of a most formal grace; even the pictures that hang on the walls are lavishly be-ribboned. When Madame will powder her nose, her maid kneels with the puff held high upon a silver tray. It could not, you feel, be otherwise.

To this house, by the introduction of Baron Grimm, comes the boy Mozart. From it, in the end, he goes, singing his farewell to ladies silently mournful, offering them as consolation for his going the thought that, if ever they speak of his genius, they may believe, each one of them, that they have contributed to it. So, indeed, they have, with all the charm, though scarcely with all the discretion, in the world. And who shall blame them? This Mozart is irresistible. When he casts himself at the feet of Madame d'Epinay, begging that she be his instructress in the unknown art of love, is it to be wondered at that she is unwilling to be bound to theory? When, with Mlle. Printemps' perfect mingling of shyness and effrontery, he seeks another lesson from the maid, is it surprising that she falters in allegiance to her lackey? His gaiety, his smile, his absurd seriousness, his little flashes of surprised innocence – they are magic arrows. They make him invincible.

But of all conquests his is the least cruel, for his love, like the ribbons and mirrors and the fountains, is but a decoration, an exquisite game of M. Guitry's, played to the music of M. Reynaldo Hahn. ... He –, or rather, Mlle. Printemps in him– is the player; they are a contributing audience, she sings while they listen and we, listening with them, forget all else but her singing and her indescribable charm. Mozart? – perhaps not. A boy? – not that either. But a figure of extraordinary lightness and quickness, with a brilliance of attack which is ever various and ever a surprise. M. Guitry, as Baron Grimm, belongs strictly to her background. When that is his place, he is content to remain there; but now and then he emerges, sometimes with a thrust that sets the house laughing, sometimes smoothly ironical for the benefit of Mme. d'Epinay, always a portrait of such a man of insight and humour as Grimm must have been. The play, slight as it is, was received with enthusiasm – a deserved tribute to a piece of work delightful in form and in detail.

1 JULY 1926, THE TIMES

Rookery Nook by Ben Travers

ALDWYCH THEATRE

GERTRUDE TWINE	Ethel Coleridge
HAROLD TWINE	J. Robertson Hare
MRS. LEVERETT	Mary Brough
CLIVE POPKISS	Tom Walls
GERALD POPKISS	Ralph Lynn
RHODA MARLEY	Winifred Shotter
PUTZ	Griffith Humphreys

Mrs. Twine, whose habit was to be obeyed, arranged that Gerald and Clara Popkiss should return from their wedding journey to Rookery Nook. It was, if we put aside for the moment the character and proximity of Mrs. Twine herself, an exceedingly promising arrangement. Rookery Nook, as we see it on the evening of Gerald's home-coming, is a baronial place, galleried and panelled from top to toe, and Mrs. Leverett, the daily woman whom Mrs. Twine has engaged, is if we may say so with the greatest admiration for Miss Mary Brough, a positively ducal char. It is a summer's night; Gerald's old friend Clive (they were at Brighton and Bognor together) is there to meet him; an immense moon encroaches on the window-sill and the waters of Chumpton-on-Sea are not far away. Everything, except his wife, who is lingering with her mother, is assembled for Gerald's delight.

With Clive at his side he begins sedately – the adverb is to be read with Mr. Ralph Lynn's own qualifications – to unpack. When he has seen Clive off he comes in from the garden to continue his unpacking – as blameless and dutiful a husband as ever reformed himself. And there, perched on his table and industriously drying her feet with his bath wrap, is a young lady in pink pyjamas. Unable to believe his eyes, he withdraws into the garden, to make a re-entry with his eyes shut. But when he opens them there she is again. There is no doubt about it. She is, it appears, the step-daughter of a hot-tempered German named Putz, who has ejected her from his house. Will Gerald supply her with dry pyjamas to replace those that have been damaged on the dewy grass? They are provided and now, where is she to go? That question is less easily answered. Will Gerald give her protection for the night? Well, what else is Mr. Ralph Lynn, blameless and dutiful though he is, to do?

She is small, she's innocent, she is, as Miss Winifred Shotter presents her, altogether charming, but she is a difficult secret to keep. Clive finds out; Harold Twine, who, as Mrs. Twine's husband, would have been happier in ignorance, finds out, too. Mrs. Leverett makes a triumphant discovery and hurries off to spread the news. With this result, that before the end all of them, including Gerald's wife are gathered together gazing at a closed bedroom door. Gerald, in despair, plays his trump card. When his wife sees Rhoda, so charming and so innocent, surely calumny will disperse! Let her, then, come forth. The door opens and there – but that is Mr. Ben Travers's story. And after that Mr. Ralph Lynn and Mr. Tom Walls are left to explain the inexplicable, and, having failed, are yet made happy as two such droll partners deserve to be. Mr. Robertson Hare, Miss Brough, Miss Shotter, and Mr. Griffith Humphreys share their gay honours. With them and with the whole rippling foolery the audience with good reason was delighted.

5 OCTOBER 1926, THE TIMES

Love's a Terrible Thing by Frank Stayton

SAVOY THEATRE

GEOFFREY KENTON	Ernest Mainwaring
LORD WINTERLEY	O. B. Clarence
DONALD WARDEN	Clifford Mollison
ALF	Roger Livesey
MARJORIE	Peggy O'Neill

This is a play that has the appearance of having been thrown together. The method is wonderfully simple. Take the fugitive daughter of a peer, shut her up in a cottage while she establishes a residence qualification preliminary to a secret marriage, add a few tiffs, a motor-car chase, and a little mild confusion;

then hand over the whole mixture to Miss Peggy O'Neill to make what she can of it. Never mind that there are actors with the subtlety of Mr. O. B. Clarence or with the brilliant foolishness of Mr. Clifford Mollison in the cast; their talents may be wasted in caricature and empty dullness. Everything must revolve eternally around the peer's scapegrace daughter, and Miss O'Neill must be pivot, wheel and all. This must be very pleasant for those to whom Miss O'Neill's acting is a sufficient feast. They see vitality where we perceive only an uncomfortable restlessness; what we feel to be monotonous noise they recognize as assertive charm. They are to be envied, for they must have enjoyed themselves at the Savoy on Monday night.

13 DECEMBER 1926, THE TIMES

Uncle Vanya
p 12

Fellowship of Players

MISS FORBES-ROBERTSON'S JULIET

ROMEO   Lawrence Anderson
JULIET   Jean Forbes-Robertson

How strange a thing it is to write with quick pen of an experience which, we know, must so continue in the mind that thought, each time returning, shall discover new beauty in it! And yet how happy it is to tell good news while it is fresh and to record an impression of delight before it fades! Someday all of us who were at the performance given by the Fellowship of Players at the Strand Theatre may look back upon Miss Forbes-Robertson's Juliet and see in it something of history. We may see, too, aspects of it that are now hidden – foreshadowings of maturer accomplishments at which it is now possible only to guess. But we shall not see then (for the clearest of memories is drifted over here and there by mist) what is now living before us – Juliet's whole youth and fire in being, her dignity for which dignity is too heavy a word, her exquisite gentleness and grace that makes the stage a place of magic while she moves upon it. Those who saw Miss Forbes-Robertson in *Uncle Vanya* must have come to her Juliet in expectation, yet half afraid. It was a test of our hopes as well as of her quality; so much of the future seemed to hang upon it. It was performed in circumstances that it would be charitable to describe as adverse – lighting that would have ruined any balcony scene but this, a curtain that set the house laughing by premature descent, a sudden illness that caused the part of Juliet's father to be read, not acted. But this Juliet was unshaken. There can have been no hope she did not strengthen, no expectation she did not fulfil.

What is above all else remarkable is Miss Forbes-Robertson's power to make the spiritual innocence of Juliet shine through words of hers that to modern ears seem to contradict it. Has it been said that Shakespeare has made this child-woman over-eager, too swiftly passionate, too ready with a lover's tongue? Here, then, is all that eagerness and passion, brilliant in her eyes, overflowing in her speech. Even her stillness is full of it, so that when, after her first meeting with Romeo, she stands aside from the dance, we see love quickening in her, and when, after her parents have bidden her marry Paris, she stands silently again, the determination of love sweeps over her like an invisible flame. Yet there is no excess of it, no jarring of youth with knowledge; the portrait is Shakespeare's own, balanced and complete. And when sorrow is upon her, with what simple majesty she wears it, as a queen that puts on her crown! Awakening from her false death in the tomb and perceiving suddenly Romeo dead at her side, she stoops to him with an incomparable movement of tenderness and despair. Whatever else time may overcloud, that we shall not forget.

13 JANUARY 1927, THE TIMES

Astoria Theatre

OPENING PROGRAMME

The ceremonies with which large cinematograph theatres are opened demand of the audience a preliminary ritual. On these magnificent occasions it is polite to stare, to exclaim about the dimensions of the place, to notice the blue of the ceiling, the abundance of coloured marble, the Corinthian pillars, and the gilt decorations. These duties discharged everyone is ready for the business of the evening, and presently, amid muffled cries of "Now they're off," the business solemnly begins.

After the National Anthem, accompanied by a tableau of Britannia, had been sung, and the Mayor of Westminster had declared the Astoria open, the Astoria Symphony Orchestra, of a size appropriate to the building, played "1812." This was an opportunity not only for music, but for a thorough exhibition of the theatre's electrical arrangements, which interpreted Tchaikovsky by bathing the musicians in mauve, green, and stormy red. This done, the same convenient electricity, devoted now to power instead of light, fulfilled the expectations of those who were familiar with opening ceremonies by raising up from orchestral depths "Pattman at the Organ." He had time to play "Land of Hope and Glory" before being electrically removed to make way for a statement on the screen of "Our Policy." This told, among much else, of the Restaurant and the Dancing Floor, and the prices that a thousand eager dancers will pay. Information that the Astoria is a British Theatre which will look with favour upon the products of British studios was heartily cheered.

This brought us to the preliminary films. A "collation of the world's events" provided a beautiful view of H. M. S. Renown leaving Portsmouth; *The Vision* was a romantic interpretation in colour of a picture by Sir John Millais; and *The Collegians* was an American undergraduate farce. Soon after 10 o'clock began the film of the evening, *The Triumph of the Rat,* a British production, directed by Mr. Graham Cutts. The Rat will be remembered by many as an *apache* who became entangled, in an attempt to discover his better self, with aristocratic Parisian ladies not over-anxious about his soul. This is a history of his later entanglements which give Mr. Novello, Miss Jeans, and Miss Nina Vanna an opportunity to appear in a variety of decoratively luxurious scenes. Miss Vanna looks charming, and acts prettily as a lady of high degree, with whom the Rat falls honestly in love; Mr. Novello and Miss Jeans elaborate character sketches that are already familiar. It is not a very diverting story, but it is competently told.

25 NOVEMBER 1927, THE TIMES

Sirocco by Noël Coward

DALY'S

MISS JOHNSON	Miss Ada King
LUCY GRIFFIN	Miss Frances Doble
SIRIO MARSON	Mr. Ivor Novello
STEPHEN GRIFFIN	Mr. David Hawthorne

There was a fleeting moment in the first act in which it seemed possible that Mr. Coward was attempting a serious play. Lucy Griffin was saying good-bye to her dull, heavy, unimaginative husband, who was leaving their Italian hotel on a business journey to Tunis. She was begging him to take her with him, not, indeed, because she loved him, not merely because she was bored in the hotel where everyone was old while she was young, but because she had become vaguely and unreasonably afraid of herself and of the impulses, contrary to her upbringing and her knowledge of her own nature, which were stirring within her. Miss Frances Doble treated the passage quietly, timidly, but well. There was a genuine interest in this preliminary sketch of character which, in spite of the hearty clergyman and much other over-familiar stuffing, was compensation for a slow opening. If Mr. Coward is about to draw character, we thought, we will not complain of an absence of glitter. We can afford to wait.

[handwritten margin note: not a fan!]

The hope was vain. Lucy went to an Italian celebration which gave Mr. Basil Dean an opportunity for some lively stage decoration. Nothing else in her escapade was at all lively. With the assistance of a bottle of wine, a few songs, and the devastating eyes of Mr. Novello, her modest reluctance was overcome, and she consented to flee to Florence with an urgent young Italian. How that conversation faltered on and on! How dreadfully silly and cruelly solemn it became – the solemner, the sillier. There was a time when it seemed that a derisive gallery would put an end to our discomfort, but the curtain to the second act was happily quicker than their impatience.

And the third? Poor Miss Doble. She did what she could to give the studio in which Lucy found herself an appearance of tragedy, but the play was against her. When this most urgent Italian began chasing her round a table and rolling her on the floor in the urgency of his passion, we were all, profoundly relieved to see her arrive safely and alone on a sofa. Away went the Italian, hoping a little cursorily that some day they would meet again as friends. And there was Miss Doble, having put all of herself into the wretched part, left to receive and to deserve the audience's applause. They were scarcely less well-disposed towards the other warriors who had played their parts in the battle – Mr. Novello, Mr. Mather, Miss Ada King, and the rest; but, when Mr. Coward appeared, the mood of the house angrily changed. Even then the curtain was not allowed to remain down. Until Miss Doble – as if she had not already done her part nobly enough! – was thrust forward to make a speech, the hubbub continued. A more uncomfortable conclusion to an evening may we never experience. The worst of it was that Mr. Coward had indeed brought it on himself.

18 DECEMBER 1927, THE NEW YORK TIMES

London Boos a Playwright

LONDON, DEC. 1.

The first performance of Noël Coward's *Sirocco* has led to a revival of an ancient controversy. Has an audience which dislikes a play the right to express its disapproval by booing and hissing or should it decorously withdraw from the theatre in disappointed silence? The question has been asked before and will be asked again, but there will never be a final answer to it. Probably we should all prefer to avoid such a scene as greeted the fall of the curtain at Daly's theatre. There is always something embarrassing and painful in finding one's self in the presence of an angry mob, however much reason the mob may have for its anger; and to see actors and actresses trying to smile in face of a storm that must be a torment to them is too like witnessing a public execution to be comfortable. And yet it is hard to say that a crowd which has paid for its seats and has waited for long hours in a queue, and which has come prepared to applaud good entertainment, has no right to express its annoyance if, in its opinion, the entertainment is bad. Of course, if there is an organized conspiracy to hiss a play, not on its own merits but on some personal grounds, that is another question. Conspiracy of that kind is cruel and indefensible. But I'm convinced that in my own mind that there was no conspiracy against Mr. Coward.

At the beginning of the evening the audience seemed willing and even eager to be amused. The scene opened in the lounge of an Italian hotel, and we listened to the chatter of the English visitors. It was not very good chatter, but Miss Ada King, who has a genius for the character of elderly spinsters, spoke her part of it so well that the gallery rippled with generous laughter. It then appeared that Lucy Griffin, an ordinary, well-brought-up and extremely beautiful girl of 26, was annoyed because her dull husband was leaving for Tunis on a business journey and was not taking her with him. She begged him to take her. Why? Not because she loved him so passionately that she could not bear to be parted from him, but because she had begun to be afraid in her heart of how she might be tempted to behave in his absence.

Her instinct was to be a loyal and faithful wife, but she was dreadfully bored in this hotel and she did not trust herself. The appearance of a handsome young Italian, Sirio, had caused her to trust herself less, even though she had abruptly checked his advances. Therefore, she begged her husband to remove her to the comparative safety of Tunis.

Her entreaty and his stubborn refusal were the best of the play and perhaps provide an indication of Mr. Coward's general purpose. He seems to have wished to discuss serious matters of emotion and character, and in this part of his first act the emotion, though tentative, was sincere, and the sketches of character, though slight as yet, were good enough to have been used later as the groundwork of interesting portraits. Now it is to be observed that, though there was in the interval a little grumbling that the act was "dull" and had none of Mr. Coward's accustomed wit, this opening was received quietly by the gallery. There was not a sign of "organized conspiracy" so long as the play held together and gave promise of intelligence to come.

In Act II, after the departure of Lucy's husband, we watched the English from the hotel visit a local Italian carnival. Here all the Italians were in fancy dress and inclined to be cheerfully riotous. The humours of a facetious English clergyman and of the hotel spinsters scarcely succeeded in filling the first half of the act. The drama was making no progress; the revellers, though decorative, were becoming tedious; and we were all heartily glad when Lucy, going home with her respectable friends, promised Sirio that she would secretly rejoin him and finish the carnival in his company. Anything, we felt, may happen now; and again the audience, though a little restless, suspended judgment.

But what happened was extremely obvious, extremely solemn, and hopelessly absurd. After long preliminaries and a bottle of sparkling Asti, Sirio suggested that Lucy should run away with him. She was shocked and refused. He urged her again; once more she was shocked (but tempted) and rose to say good-bye to him. Whereupon he kissed her vigorously, not once but often, and she completely lost her head. She loved him! She would go to Florence with him! Not content with this, he stood or knelt at her side, and improved the passionate occasion with a stilted speech on youth and love. What was Mr. Coward thinking of? Had all his humour and all his stagecraft deserted him? Here were Ivor Novello and Frances Doble, as handsome a pair of lovers as you could wish for on the stage, condemned to a scene which steadily became more ridiculous as they strove to make it more serious. The audience were tittering. The actors had a derisive house against them. The curtain to the second act came down just in time.

"A week later" we were in Sirio's studio in Florence. Lucy was disillusioned, and Sirio, revealed as a lazy, worthless cad, was tired of her. Here again it was probably Mr. Coward's intention to be serious – to indicate the tragedy of hasty passion that

used for Times too

springs from a bottle of sparkling Asti; and again, in spite of all the actors could do, the sublime became the ridiculous. Lucy's husband appeared, offered to take her back in order to hush up the scandal of her behaviour, and was made the object of a tirade on the falseness and selfishness of himself which, though well justified, had the effect of mock-heroics because he was so obviously a farcical puppet and his indignant wife no less obviously the mouthpiece of high-sounding platitude. When he was gone, Lucy realised finally that she had made a complete mess of her adventure – and this was, I suppose, the moral of Mr. Coward's play.

Sirio was tired of her; she would therefore leave Sirio and henceforward go alone through the world. At the thought of her going, Sirio's passion once more became inflamed. He would teach her, as he taught her once before, to be haughty and cold and aloof! Once more with his kisses he would make the blood flow within her! Once more he would prove to this well-brought-up English lady what an animal she was! But this time she was too quick for him and we were presented with the undignified spectacle, which was intended to be thrilling but which was agonisingly absurd. ...

29 JANUARY 1928, THE NEW YORK TIMES

Thomas Hardy

LONDON, JAN. 12

This morning before I sat down to write there came news of the death of Thomas Hardy, in his eighty-eighth year. He was the greatest writer of his time, and his greatest work, *The Dynasts*, though he did not intend it for the stage, was written in dramatic form. After the storms of the nineties, when *Tess of the D'Urbervilles* and *Jude the Obscure* were fiercely attacked, and he was, in his own words, "cured of his interest in novel-writing," he returned to poetry, which was his earliest love, and became in his late life a pre--eminent figure in English literature and English life. Nowhere in his own country was his supremacy questioned. That in Europe other writers in English were preferred before him and were offered literary prizes not given to him caused Englishmen to smile at the oddity of foreign taste, but never to doubt their own judgment.

No one who met him during his last years will cease to treasure recollection of the meeting. The opportunity came to me early in 1920, when I was an undergraduate at Oxford. The Oxford University Dramatic Society, having been reorganized after the war by Maurice Colbourne, had sought for a play that should mark its rebirth. I had suggested *The Dynasts*, partly because its subject – the struggle with Napoleon – seemed appropriate to the time, partly because it seemed fitting that a society, whose activities were generally confined to Greek and Shakespearean plays, should, when it turned to the work of living writers, choose Hardy's great epic. But we doubted Hardy's consent; he might well have objected to a performance by undergraduates of chosen scenes from his work. We asked for his permission and he gave it, not grudgingly but with extraordinary graciousness. He was, it seemed, genuinely pleased that young men should wish to perform his work, and consented to leave his home at Dorchester and make a Winter journey to Oxford that he might see our attempt.

I met him at the railway station. Before driving to the house where he was to stay he insisted on making a tour of Oxford and looked out eagerly on the streets long ago familiar to him. Then, as we drove on, he produced from a little bag several slender volumes of verse. They were, he said, the work of young men, and had been sent to him by the authors, and he spoke of the gifts, not with irritation or aloofness but with pride and pleasure, as if he read in them a tribute that was delightful to receive. He began then to speak of modern poetry until I, with an undergraduate's ingenuous rashness, asked him whether there was any chance that he might write another novel. A less generous man would have snubbed me mercilessly. Instead, Hardy answered very simply: "No, I think not. There are two reasons. First, I am interested now in the writing of verse and have not written fiction for many years. Secondly it is so long now since a novel of mine appeared that a new work of that kind could scarcely be received with much interest. The memory of readers is very short." I have reproduced his words as nearly as I can remember them. Knowing with what excitement a new novel by Hardy would be received wherever English is spoken, I found his speech almost incredible then; it seems now easier to understand. He was both aware and strangely unaware of his own pre-eminence. He was at once greatly proud and astonishingly humble.

In November, 1922, I saw him again. I had gone to Dorchester to see a performance by the Hardy Players of *Desperate Remedies*, and was invited to tea at Max Gate. After tea we sat by the fire, talking chiefly of the theatre, of which, as a young man, Hardy had been fond. He told me how he used to go to Shakespearean plays and sit in the front row, so that, while the play proceeded, enough light might fall upon the book which he held in his hand to enable him to follow the text. He told me, too, how many years ago he came to write a dramatic version of *Tess of the D'Urbervilles*, which had never been performed. I remember the shock with which I realized that, while we spoke, there was lying somewhere in a drawer an unproduced play written by Hardy at the height of his powers – the play which was afterward performed with Gwen Ffrangcon Davies as Tess. When the time came for me to go I tried to prevent Hardy from coming beyond the door of his house into the wintry night. But he lighted a lantern and came with me through the dark trees of his garden to the road, talking, I remember of *The Return of the Native*. As I turned away towards Dorchester I saw him standing in the road with the lantern held above his head. From a little distance I watched him return through his garden until the light vanished. I could not help thinking that this, in all probability, was the last I should ever see of him. With him ends a tradition. He was the last of the great Victorians, and he wore his greatness with a wistful quietness and dignity rare in the present age.

...

Young Woodley by John Van Druten

STAGE SOCIETY

COPE	Tony Halfpenny
VINING	Henry Mollison
AINGER	Jack Hawkins
MILNER	Derek de Marney
WOODLEY	Frank Lawton
LAURA SIMMONS	Kathleen O'Regan
SIMMONS	David Horne

This is a study of the first love of a schoolboy of eighteen. It is a subject that cannot easily be treated of within the limitations of colloquial speech that the modern stage imposes. All the pain and rapture that dwells in it cannot be expressed except in poetry or in a prose that is not withheld from subjective analysis, for a boy's love does not stand upon his lips but is part of a secret, the key to which he himself is perpetually seeking. Young Woodley is inarticulate; in a play that is a representation of an aspect of contemporary life he could, within the bounds of truth, be nothing else. He is a House Prefect and the woman he loves is his housemaster's wife. What is told must be told in the language of the prefects' room or of the housemaster's drawing-room; all else must be imagined, and the dramatist can do nothing openly, being tied by the "truth" of natural conversation, to lead imagination beyond the boundaries of his representative scene. Yet how much of his subject lies beyond them and how far imagination must travel with little aid from him but his first prompting! Because this is a play written in to-day's convention, how much, we think continually, is being denied us of all that the writer has it in him to tell.

This is the regret – that the artist's chosen medium is unsuited to the fullest expansion of his subject; but from the regret proceeds wonder that he has yet been able to tell so much. His play is limited, but, within its limits, is beautiful and true, having sentiment that does the word honour, and a freshness which, in the sordid squalor that besets a great part of the theatre, is like a spring wind. There may be some, not knowing the play, who will declare that the love of a prefect for his housemaster's wife is "morbid," is "abnormal," is opposed to a dozen healthy traditions. That was the housemaster's view. He could see them only as prefect and housemaster's wife; that they were boy and woman he was incapable of understanding. There was, he had lately perceived, a "bad tone" in the school, and, when he discovered Woodley kissing Laura for the first time, he saw neither the idealism of the one nor the bitter tragedy of the other. On that score he dared not have Woodley expelled, but watched him and dogged him until he found a less scandalous excuse. That is the end of this episode in the boy's life. We see him take his farewell of Laura and, still very young, set out for the world. We see her, bidding him go, turn to face again the marriage into which she has been trapped. Though they are guilty of nothing but their single kiss, it has illuminated his future and hers, showing to him, in his youth, life's fruitful spaces, and to her its enclosures of despair.

Their tale is introduced very simply. Laura asks the boy to tea with her and is kind to him because he is strange and lonely. Suddenly he rises to go, says he must not come again, confesses at last why he dare not come. Here, for once, his inarticulateness says all there is to be said, and Mr. Frank Lawton, whose whole performance is distinguished by insight and control, conveys in his stumbling gesture and intonation the delight and agony of the boy's mind. The rest follows quietly and inevitably. Miss Kathleen O'Regan is too young in her appearance to give full weight to that part of Laura's tragedy which springs from youth departed; she seems scarcely older than, and fully as vigorous as, the boy himself. But she plays her part, though not always to its depths, with an enchanting grace, and gives to this love, which is like sunlight moving on water, her share of its loveliness. As a background to the lovers is the school. The drawing of the housemaster is sometimes too harshly strained by the dramatist, and Mr. David Horne can but follow his plan; but the boys are very carefully distinguished studies, and Mr. Henry Mollison gives an extremely persuasive sketch of the callow cynicism which is chiefly responsible for the school's "bad tone." From the fag (Mr. Tony Halfpenny) to the captain of the House (Mr. Jack Hawkins), the school is alive, and is the basis of a piece of work so delicate and sincere that it is hard to believe that it has been refused the Censor's license. Mr. Basil Dean produced it on Sunday for the Stage Society at the New Theatre, and it will be performed throughout this week at the Arts Theatre Club. It deserves a far wider audience than it can at present receive.

means can't be put in mainstream thtr?

27 MARCH 1928, THE TIMES

An Enemy of the People by Henrik Ibsen

WYNDHAM'S THEATRE

DR THOMAS STOCKMANN	Rupert Harvey
MRS. STOCKMANN	May Agate
PETER STOCKMANN	Hubert Harben
HORSTER	B. A. Pittar
ASLAKSEN	Philip Wade

*A*n Enemy of the People, Ghosts, and The Wild Duck have been chosen to celebrate the centenary of Ibsen's birth in a series of afternoon performances at Wyndham's Theatre this week. There are good arguments for the choice of Ghosts as representing an aspect of the dramatist's purpose; there are even better reasons, and these aesthetic, for giving The Wild Duck; but why, we wonder, was An Enemy of *the People* chosen and let us say, *The Master Builder* rejected? The principal organizer of these performances is Mr. J. T. Grein, who, we may be sure, does not make such a choice lightly; it is natural, therefore, to turn for an explanation to the prefatory note that he has written for the programme. Here he speaks boldly of two plays in particular as Ibsen's masterpieces – *An Enemy of the People* and *Brand*. The second choice is unconventional, but so perceptive that we are not at all inclined to combat it, but the first is extremely odd. Mr. Grein's critical opinion is always entitled to respect and never to more respect than when he speaks on the subject of Ibsen, and, the longer we watched this play, the more respectfully we struggled to obtain his point of view upon it – and struggled in vain.

It is a piece of deep sincerity. It exhibits a brilliantly satirical insight into characters widely different. It is remarkable in the sureness of its control of successive incidents that illuminate and contribute to its central theme. It has, too, a humour, sometimes almost boisterous, which gives to a great part of it liveliness of a kind exceptional in Ibsen's social studies. But it has an air of artificiality, of having been forced into shape, of which other and, as we believe, greater plays are free. The chief flaw seems to be in Ibsen's refusal to allow Dr. Stockmann, knowing himself to be right, to make full use of his knowledge as an instrument of battle. He knew that the supply of water to the municipal baths was poisoned; he knew that, however tightly the Burgomaster and the townspeople might shut their eyes to this truth for the sake of their present advantage, the poison would at last bring ruin to them and justification to himself. If he had made this clear to the Burgomaster, or if the Burgomaster, who was no fool, had been allowed by Ibsen to perceive it himself, the dispositions of the struggle would inevitably have been changed. It is true that the moral symbolism of the play would not have been affected, but that is the more reason for criticising what seems to have been a turning away from a structural difficulty which might, by facing it, have been overcome.

There is another possible charge against the play. In stating his main argument that the "majority is always wrong," Ibsen neglected to distinguish between the subjects upon which a majority may express its opinion; for, though it may be nearly true that the majority is wrong on questions of what may, for convenience, be called originating thought, it is by no means so obviously true that it always errs in estimates of its own present interest. The story of the play provides a natural opportunity to discuss this distinction and, because Ibsen has missed it, Dr. Stockmann's famous speech in the fourth act is marred by seeming avoidances. For these reasons it is permissible to differ from Mr. Grein's choice while being grateful for his initiative and for the performance that the play is given…

...

Ghosts by Henrik Ibsen

WYNDHAM'S THEATRE

MRS. HELEN ALVING	Mrs. Patrick Campbell
OSWALD ALVING	John Gielgud
PASTOR MANDERS	Fewlass Llewellyn
JACOB ENGSTRAND	Frederick Lloyd
REGINA ENGSTRAND	Margot Sieveking

It is customary to say of Ibsen's social plays, and may generally be said with a measure of truth, that time and the success of their own persuasions have taken something from them. We can all, if we will, pat one another on the back and say that we have moved beyond Nora's doll's house, and have at least changed the poisonous source of Dr. Stockmann's municipal baths. But we have not escaped from the influence of heredity that darkens Mrs. Alving's country house. Time has taken nothing from *Ghosts*; time has, indeed, by exhibiting the unchanging nature of its tragedy, added to the intolerable pressure of its truth.

It is the most unrelenting of plays, and must be performed, as it has been written, without an attempt to soften or make transferable the blows that it inflicts. It is one of the very few plays that are altogether without delight except the tormented delight that springs from admiration of the dramatist's power and integrity. Never for an instant is there pleasure in the company of any of the people who appear in it; there is no laughter to share, no smile which is not an anticipation of weeping, no hope that contains any promise but of its own disaster. No light touches Mrs. Alving's room except the light of burning, and no sunshine enters it until sunshine itself is a herald of madness. These are the conditions of spiritual death which, in performance, have to be charged with dramatic life. To perform other plays badly may be to make them tedious; to perform this play weakly or falsely would be to make torture of it.

The performance yesterday afternoon, though not faultless, had that quality of courage which is necessary above all else to support the burden of this play in the theatre. Mr. Fewlass Llewellyn betrayed now and then a tendency to stray into irrelevant humour; but his wanderings in this direction were happily brief and did not seriously damage a firm study of Pastor Manders, though that study seemed to be on the whole rather gentler than Ibsen's probable intention. Mr. Frederick Lloyd played Jacob Engstrand on the right lines, lacking only a certain fierceness of portraiture appropriate to this exceptionally base coward. Regina Engstrand, greedy, passionate, morally uncertain, lived brilliantly from the first moment of encounter. She is a conspicuous example of Ibsen's use of accumulated fragments in the development of minor character, a method that makes a heavy demand on the actors who are his collaborators; and Miss Margot Sieveking collaborated with so vital an imagination that Regina became a genuine portrait, rich and full, entitled to take rank with Mr. John Gielgud's more elaborate and beautifully restrained study of Oswald Alving. At the centre of the play Mrs. Alving, gathering the past and the future of herself, continuously exhibits the present in their light. Mrs. Patrick Campbell's performance was received with an enthusiasm that was a just tribute to it. There were moments when the vision of extending tragedy somehow failed to match, in this Mrs. Alving's eyes, the discoveries of which she spoke – surprising moments, at the end of the first act, for example, or when Regina went out "to her ruin," in which, to use a conventional phrase, Mrs. Campbell seemed not to be living in her part. But these were passing weaknesses in the midst of great dignity and strength. While she listened in silence to the Pastor's recital of the past, then, indeed, her own knowledge of it lived in her eyes. While she heard Oswald's final confession, how imagining of the future burned in her! And to watch Mrs. Campbell's slow gestures, graceful and charged with meaning; to see her move on the stage with a significance in bodily movement that is nowadays almost forgotten – this is an experience which alone would make a performance memorable.

6 JULY 1928, THE TIMES

Six Stokers by Elmer L. Greensfelder

GATE THEATRE

CENTRO	Robert Speaight
ETCETERO	Norman Shelley

The full title of this dismal piece is *Six Stokers Who Own the Bloomin' Earth*, a name which, in its would-be humorous brutality, has at least the merit of matching the play. The stokers represent the nations of the world, and, lest we should remain unaware of the symbolic significance of their quarrels, a magic lantern throws upon a sheet behind them such legends as "Mobilization," "War Imminent," "World Cataclysm," and "Locarno." Lest they should stray for a moment into that human variety, that distinguishing of character from character without which drama is not, they have a uniform appearance and babble their silly dialogue in a uniformly raucous voice. Lest we should be tempted to suppose that we are witnessing an attempt, however unsuccessful, of a dramatist to express himself in dramatic form, Mr. Greensfelder frequently abandons speech altogether and relies upon a cinematographic exhibition of rotating omnibuses and waving legs. And lest, in the midst of so much that is well calculated to torment those of us who have not achieved the relief of coma, an element of sensuousness should be missing, there are several ladies who, clad principally in head-dresses of talc and *caleçons* of mackintosh sheeting, leap in uncomfortable representation of the spirit of jazz. At least we suppose that this was their purpose, for at the outset of the evening Mr. Peter Godfrey announced his intention of "jazzing everything."

He said, too, that this was an entertainment. It is to be hoped that he was entertained, for there can be no other excuse for a hoax so empty and pretentious. It scarcely mends matters to discover, by re-reading the programme, that the ladies in mackintosh-sheeting were "angels," wearing costumes designed by C. Denis Freeman. We had supposed them to be a cabaret chorus equipped for a rainy day.

11 DECEMBER 1928, THE TIMES

Journey's End by R.C. Sherriff

THE STAGE SOCIETY

CAPTAIN HARDY	David Horne
LIEUTENANT OSBORNE	George Zucco
PRIVATE MASON	Alexander Field
2ND LIEUTENANT RALEIGH	Maurice Evans
CAPTAIN STANHOPE	Laurence Olivier
2ND LIEUTENANT TROTTER	Melville Cooper
2ND LIEUTENANT HIBBERT	Robert Speaight
THE COMPANY SERGEANT-MAJOR	Percy Walsh
THE COLONEL	H. G. Stoker

This is not story-telling, for there is neither beginning nor middle nor end, nor any formal progress of narrative, nor convergence of selected incident. It is not story-telling, and if, 50 years hence, an audience, watching it unmoved, says: "This is a historical document, but not a work of art," there is no doubt that they will be able to discover in it good reasons for their opinion. We, who have not their detachment from St. Quentin and the month of March, 1918, cannot afford their aesthetic didacticism. If we must risk an opinion, it is that Mr. Sherriff's study of the front line, though it comes as near as the stage may ever come to precise representation of life in a dug-out, is not a work of art with any prospect of endurance. It has the poignancy, the accuracy, the revealing brilliance of many letters that were sent home in those days, but like them it needs a naturally responsive audience which the passing of a few years will take away, and like them, even the best of them, it is sharply localized and confined by narrow circumstance. Within its own boundaries, which seem, like the boundaries of personal experience imposed upon the letter writers, to have been drawn by wasteful and haphazard chance rather than by an artist's deliberate selectiveness, it is true and deep, but it has little power to expand beyond these boundaries; with this almost contradictory result – born of the distinction between tragedy proper and the accurate recounting of events which are the raw material of tragedy – that you experience, while watching the play, a hot, cloudy, unstable emotion, but await in vain that poetic leap from things observed to universal truth apprehended which yields tragedy's own exultation, not hot though flaming, not cloudy but serene.

What Mr. Sherriff has done is to take away one earthen wall of a dug-out and exhibit for a few days the life within. There is a raid, led by the second-in-command of the company, who does not return; there is an opening of the enemy's offensive and the death of a young officer fresh from England. This is the trickle of narrative that comes to us and, like the fragmentary narratives of the War, it seems to have no source, no direction. The play's substance is in an aggregate of portraits – first of Captain Hardy, whose casual slackness in turning over to his reliefs is very cleverly shown by Mr. David Horne to be but his way of breathing again now that his spell of duty is ended; then of his successors. Stanhope, the company commander, is drinking steadily that fear may not break the spirit in him; Osborne, an older man, a schoolmaster, is a beautifully familiar example of unspectacular loyalty; Hibbert is a youth whose terror is greater than his control; Raleigh has come from school in all the gravity of illusion and hero-worship; Trotter, risen from the ranks, is an imperturbable horticulturist, with nerves like the rest of them, but none exposed; the mess-servant uses in self-protection the sharp backchat of omnibuses; and the colonel has a dry precision and sympathy which are given remarkable authenticity by Mr. H. G. Stoker's quiet performance. His is a piece of acting which, small in itself, may well serve as a standard by which to judge the rest. Mr. Zucco, bringing the same merit to a larger portrait, gives a beautiful impression of character and of the background of character; his Lieutenant Osborne towers above the others. Mr. Laurence Olivier gives an extremely able performance, vital, eager, rich in understanding, and Mr. Speaight and Mr. Maurice Evans control admirably very difficult and subtle emotions; but all three of them splash their colour now and then, sacrificing to the theatre the truth that Mr. Zucco and Mr. Stoker so rigidly observe. Mr. Field, Mr. Walsh, and Mr. Melville Cooper, having plainer tasks, discharge them with judgment and humour. All these men are alive; they draw their audience into communion with their suffering and their concealments of it; the patch of life which we see is justly and poignantly remembered. That it is a patch and not a core of life matters not very much now, but it will matter more and more as the play and the observation to which it is keyed sink into the past.

6 MARCH 1929 , THE TIMES

Major Barbara by George Bernard Shaw

WYNDHAM'S THEATRE

LADY BRITOMART	Margaret Scudamore
STEPHEN	Eric Portman
MAJOR BARBARA	Sybil Thorndike
ADOLPHUS CUSINS	Lewis Casson
CHARLES LOMAX	Wilfred Fletcher
ANDREW UNDERSHAFT	Baliol Holloway
SNOBBY PRICE	Harold Scott
JENNY HILL	Elizabeth Colls
PETER SHIRLEY	Wilfred Shine
BILL WALKER	Gordon Harker

It don't matter at all that Charles Lomax, though wearing the costume of to-day, says "don't it?" instead of "doesn't it?" and has other peculiarities of foppish speech which were current 20 years ago, for this play stands or falls as a morality, and the moralities, fortunately or unfortunately, though they change their symbols and add a flying-battleship to their list of properties, do not date. This does not prevent certain farcical decorations, which may once have been welcomed as a sugar-coating to the social pill, from dating very badly or from making the first act of Mr. Shaw's play flounder in its old humours; but anyone who imagines that the Shavian theatre is dying because so many of the abuses it attacks have been "reformed" may rest assured that *Major Barbara* is very much alive, being concerned far less with the prejudices of society than with the confusions of the soul. But "is it topical?" Someone will ask. Well, have we not said that it is about the soul? And, if the soul is not topical enough shall we add that it is about Versailles and Geneva and Locarno and the Kellogg Pact – about every factor in an analysis of power. The faith of an armourer, as expressed by Undershaft, comes indeed as a refreshing gale in an atmosphere that has become a little clogged by nobly phrased aspirations. The first act, as we have said, seems to be a little too eager to placate those who came to the theatre 20 years ago to have a good laugh. Miss Margaret Scudamore makes of Lady Brit a monument to the morality of personal convenience, and Mr. Wilfred Fletcher, perceiving that he is a farcical trimming and that his character is to be taken away to make a Shavian holiday, does all that mortal man can do with a concertina; but – the laughter of 20 years ago, though it was indeed to be heard at Wyndham's last night, refused to rise up for our own delight. The second act, in the Salvation Army shelter, was a great advance. Miss Clare Greet, Mr. Gordon Harker, Mr. Wilfred Shine all distinguish themselves; drama and character deepened, and we began to perceive in Miss Thorndike's Major Barbara, a part that suits her as well as any she has played, one of the few women in Mr. Shaw's theatre for whom he seems to have felt a genuine affection; and, above all, Mr. Lewis Casson emerged from behind the big drum as a very shrewd critic of Undershaft.

But the enduring life of the play is in the final scene in Undershaft's munition factory. What a sermon! What a group of sermons! Long? Yes, indeed, for you know who wrote them; but how brilliantly their breadth and depth justify their length. Mr. Baliol Holloway, who has here the honour of leading the attack, leads it with speed, lucidity, and insight – a performance of splendid vigour and humour. Miss Thorndike is at her best, eager, alive, quick in apprehension, and Mr. Casson's drawing of Cusins increases with every phrase in richness and subtlety. What questions does the sermon answer? None, finally. It has been said – or should have been – that the merit of philosophy is not in its answers but in its questioning; the absence of finality in reason being the compulsion of reason towards faith. We add our own question: what would the play have been if Major Barbara, instead of falling into her too convenient acquiescence, had broken from the confusions of reason and reform to lead a contemplative life? Well, it would not have been this play, and Mr. Shaw 24 years ago would not have written it. But now? It is good to encounter a piece so full of life that it sends you away asking rash, excited questions near the end of the fourth hour and beyond the end of the second decade.

28 MARCH 1929, THE TIMES

Wake Up and Dream by John Hastings Turner

LYRICS AND MUSIC BY COLE PORTER
LONDON PAVILION

Mr. Cochran may be trusted to be master of an occasion. His first-night audiences have an air. They do not sit in professional mournfulness; they are alive, they expect pleasure, they graciously buzz their anticipations. Such is prestige; and blessings be upon it, for it is an assurance of a lively evening, the mood of an audience being at least half the battle of a *revue*. When the curtain rose last night, the theatre was already wide awake and prepared eagerly to dream. What good promise there was in the title! To awaken us from the stolidities of pedestrian existence into a sustained fantasy of music and dance, to carry us away from earth on the winds of unfettered imagination, to buffet us hither and thither with puffs of nonsense and gales of extravagance, to throw upon us such a spell as would give to inconsequent entertainment the quality, the miraculous unity, of a veritable dream – would not this have been an idea for a *revue*? For a little while we supposed it to be the idea of this *revue*. There was a scene called "The Dream," which, though it was itself a trifle weak in composition, might well have been a prelude to a leap from earth; but that, alas, was the end of the dream and the end of the idea and a last farewell to the title; thereafter we were on firm and familiar ground, watching a lavish variety entertainment amid a traditional scent of cigars.

On the whole it is a very pleasant entertainment. It has no great pretensions to wit; its humour, when humorous, makes – shall we say – a rather harsh bid for the raising of an eyebrow over a knowing eye; and its music, except when it borrows in passing from the gayer masters, though cheerful enough is strangely characterless. But the dancing is admirable; the *décor* is abundant, ingenious, and, on occasions, beautiful; and Mr. Cochran's Young Ladies seemed a very good reason for the opera glasses of the connoisseur who sat nearby. Where to begin less general expressions of gratitude it is hard to know – perhaps with Mr. Oliver Messel, who proves himself an artist in design, or with Miss Tilly Losch, who dances superbly and is a choreographist of high merit, or with Miss Tina Meller, who is an actress as well as dancer and has a hard, flashing manner that is a genuine style. She commands the stage as much by the power of mind as by that of movement. Miss Jessie Matthews sings with a wicked charm; Miss Margie Finlay has a brilliant vitality and Miss Laurie Devine a lovely, slow grace; Mr. Lance Lister, Mr. William Stephens, and Mr. Douglas Byng variously distinguish themselves; and Mr. Sonnie Hale, who is in the van of the battle, wins a famous victory as the dispenser of operatic pills. To arrange the scenes in an order of merit is beyond the wit of man, but the encounter between Ruskin and Mr. Noël Coward is a little jewel; *Coppelia* (seen from the wings of the old Empire) is delightful; and there is an idol, with an accompanying dance, almost good enough to be compensation for the lugubrious song that heralds it. Now and then the tension slackens, and certainly the dream is no dream, but the entertainment is in general swift and gay, good to the eye, though less good to the ear. The gentleman with opera-glasses knew what he was about.

11 APRIL 1929, WEST SUSSEX GAZETTE

Lights of London

I am unfortunately compelled to dispatch this article two or three days before the production of *Porgy* at His Majesty's. I can, therefore, do no more than call your attention to it in advance. Some years ago, during a brief period in which I was a reviewer of books, a batch of novels was sent to me. I read five without much encouragement. The sixth appeared to be a book about negroes by an American unknown, and I opened it with little hope, for neither the style of American writers nor the subject of "colour" often pleases me. But what a relief that book was – a sensitive, passionate, perceptive book, with a genuine power to discover emotion within the rhythm of words. Here at last, I said, is something I may praise, and ever since I have retained a feeling of gratitude to DuBose Heyward. *Porgy* was greatly successful as a novel. Then DuBose Heyward, in collaboration with Dorothy Heyward, made of it a play that was performed by the Theatre Guild in New York, and has run for over a year. Now it comes to England with the American negro cast little changed. Whether I shall or shall not like it in the theatre, I do not know; ...

Porgy by DuBose and Dorothy Heyward

HIS MAJESTY'S THEATRE

SPORTING LIFE	Percy Verwayne
SERENA	Rose MacClendon
PORGY	Frank Wilson
CROWN	Jack Carter
CROWN'S BESS	Evelyn Ellis

Beyond the gate of Catfish Row is the sea, and above the roof of the gaunt buildings that straddle the gate is the sky – the hot burdened sky of a summer in Charleston. You feel the weight of the sky, as if it were a lid clapped on to the courtyard, and, looking at the houses by which the yard is enclosed, you know, as if by a miracle, the swelter, the smell, the crowded darkness within. Porgy, a crippled beggar, does indeed emerge from the crowd as the principal figure. The story is his story, telling how he was happy with Crown's Bess when Crown, having killed a man, was a fugitive; how the shadow of Crown hung over his happiness, threatening to take Bess from him; how Crown, who was a bully and a giant, returned during a hurricane and vanished; how he returned again and was strangled by the cripple's hands; and how, by the cruelty of a trick, Porgy lost his Bess after all. Porgy emerges, a creature of heroic gentleness and humour; Crown's brutality, Bess's mingling of weakness and loyalty and passion, the rough kindliness of the cookshop-keeper, the meanness and guile of Sporting Life, who tricks Bess with his lies and his "happy dust" – all these stand out in their due proportion; the narrative is simple and clear. But never do they stand out so far from the general scene as to drive Catfish Row into an insignificant background. They remain part of Catfish Row as the figures in a landscape remain part of the picture's composition. Their lives spring, not from the theatrical manipulation of hero, heroine, and villain, but from the life of a community, and the life of that community is the life of the play.

It is a wild, violent, turbulent life, charged with extreme passions and extreme ecstasies, but Mr. Rueben Mamoulian, whose production for the Theatre Guild of New York has been transported to London, is not content with the opportunities of violence. It would have been easy, with this play as material, to shock and stun a white audience with a parade of savage discords and to throw out to them sops of negro humour. Mr. Mamoulian has done much more and much better than this. He and his actors, whose performance has a composite rhythm so elaborate and perfected that there is no need for a catalogue of names, have aimed at, and have attained, the sort of orchestration of the life they have to represent, an orchestration not of sound only, but of movement and of light. In Serena's room, there is a mourning for a dead man, and the great pattern of shadows on the wall is all one with the sway of bodies, the throbbing of voices. In Serena's room again, an assembly cowers from the hurricane, desperately chanting prayers for the men at sea. Crown enters, a naked giant in their midst, and instantly his body is a focus, not of eyes only, but of emotion, so that the whole scene is gathered up in him.

The exteriors have no less of magic in them. Catfish Row is familiar and intimate; its gaiety, its fatalism, its superstition become a part of the air you breathe; stretch out your hand, and you will feel the burning of its walls. Its songs, its weeping, its laughter, even the clatter of its hammers and its pots and pans, seem a continuous music, intricate and profound. And all this from a tale not of great depth in its treatment of separate characters. The emotion is the emotion of the people, and it floods the theatre like a wave.

28 JUNE 1929 , THE TIMES

Red Sunday by Hubert Griffith

ARTS THEATRE

BRONSTEIN (TROTSKY)	John Gielgud
ALEXANDRA LVOVNA	Lydia Sherwood
LENIN	Robert Farquharson
PRINCE YUSSOUPOV	Denys Blakelock
PURISHKEVITCH	Eugene Leahy
RASPUTIN	George Merritt
THE CZARINA	Athene Seyler

The play produced by Komisarjevsky

There is a host of prejudices with which criticism of this play must contend. First, there are political prejudices which tempt you into aesthetically irrelevant objections to its propaganda: secondly – and this is more difficult to overcome – there is a hot and indignant prejudice against the exploitation of this tragedy while it is still the personal tragedy of men still living. But however profoundly we may differ from the taste of Mr. Griffith as a man, we are not now concerned with it but with his quality as an artist. We are bound, so far as may be possible, to think of his work as a work of imagination and not as either a revolutionary pamphlet or an offence against good manners.

The tale he has to tell is that of the revolution in Russia. It is told in a series of incidents that give no hint of evil or the possibility of evil in the enemies of the *ancien régime*. Trotsky is seen as a young man in Odessa in 1906. He is a high-minded though as yet an uninstructed idealist. Lenin appears, gives him a brief lesson in self-help, and witnesses his arrest. A scene in Siberia follows. Here Trotsky is living very comfortably with his wife and children, employing an "intensive leisure" in revolutionary scholarship. He escapes and we see him again with Lenin at Geneva in 1916 and yet again, after his triumph, collaborating in Lenin's rule. The great chief is shot by an assassin; the doctor says that he will in consequence be paralysed for life; Trotsky asks: "Who will save the Revolution now?" And the curtain falls on a note of ecstasy.

Meanwhile, having gone to the Soviets for the morals, Mr. Griffith has sought among the Royalists for the high colour of his drama. We watch the murder of Rasputin and are invited to contrast the uxoriousness and irresolution of the Tsar with the noble vigour of his betrayers. The murder of the Tsar and his family is not mentioned, which, though the play is thereby falsified and its pretended impartiality brought to nothing, is perhaps as well, for, if he had not omitted it altogether, Mr. Griffith could scarcely have resisted a temptation to portray the scene of butchery.

This, then, is the course of the narrative. We shall not judge it by what of history it has told and what rejected. The one question is – does it live dramatically, and, if so, what is the quality of its dramatic life? It does live. Except when it is so ingenuous as to become tiresome, it holds the stage. The murder of Rasputin is a bold and successful piece of melodrama; the scene in which the Tsar takes the oath to his people would be a good scene if the solemnities of our ambassador were not allowed to make its conclusion ridiculous; and the early sketches of Trotsky have a pleasant, lively straightforwardness.

Mr. Griffith can, in brief, order dramatic action and can draw men and women so long as they have nothing of genius in them. But Lenin had the genius of fanaticism and without it he is nothing. It was his personality, his idea, reflected in an artist's criticism of it, that might have held the nine scenes together in a dramatic unity. Mr. Robert Farquharson with flashing eye and eager gesture does what can be done for him, and Lenin seems to be a great man until he speaks. Thereafter he is a mediocre man acting greatness and the truth is not in him. Rasputin is correspondingly a failure; he is a figure in melodrama but he is no more. Similarly, what Mr. Griffith has lost in the Tsar is his mysticism, and a brilliant performance by Mr. Hannen just fails for lack of material.

The smaller sketches, that demand less of the fire of the spirit, are much happier, Mr. Gielgud, Miss Sherwood, Mr. Leahy, and Miss Seyler all distinguishing themselves within Mr. Griffith's range. So long as the play is an observation of highly dramatic scenes, it is alive, but it lacks the force and cohesion that nothing but genius itself could give to a work on a canvas so vast.

3 JULY 1929, THE TIMES

The First Mrs. Fraser by St. John Ervine

HAYMARKET THEATRE

NINIAN FRASER	Mr. Robert Andrews
JAMES FRASER	Mr. Henry Ainley
JANET FRASER	Miss Marie Tempest
ALICE FRASER	Miss Margaretta Scott
ELSIE FRASER	Miss Ursula Jeans

Here, by the grace of all the ladies and gentleman whose names appear above, is comedy: not farcical comedy or fantastic comedy or whimsical comedy, not spiteful or "smart" or scandalous comedy, but comedy that needs no prefix but good. Here, too, is a new Mr. Ervine. By his early work we learned to know him as one of the first tragic dramatists of our time. His later experiments in farce were uncomfortable, for, though fancy and invention were in them, the strength of Mr. Ervine's mind was not. Now, again taking himself seriously as an artist, he has written a comedy of genuine substance, firmly rooted in character from which humour and feeling spring with natural ease, and decorated with a wit, never forced and never ugly, that continually sends laughter rippling through the attentive silences of the house.

Mr. Fraser was a Scot, a man of business, who lived happily with his Janet for 20 years. Then, as men of business will, he began to pine for youth – for his own youth in theory, for Elsie's in divorce court practice. We see him, after five years' experience of Elsie, a sadder but (and there's the truth of him) a not much wiser man. She, cruel, arrogant little beast that she is, has had what she could get from him. She has had his jewels, his money, and, it may be presumed, her independent pleasures. She has sniggered behind his back when he has made an ass of himself by pretending at night-clubs that he is young, and now, to be brief, she is sniggering in his face, is conducting a secret intrigue with a professional dancer and openly setting her cap at a nincompoop peer. To crown it all, she expects poor Fraser to allow her to divorce him. She is a woman and young; he is a man and is becoming old. What does he matter? Besides, isn't he a gentleman, and isn't it the duty of a gentleman to aid a selfish wife to be a cad?

Well, Fraser may not be wise, but he is commendably stubborn. He comes to Janet's drawing room to ask her advice, and Janet, being Miss Tempest, gives him, not advice only, but active alliance. She discovers the secret of Elsie's adventure in the fishing inn; she stands by the telephone, a flash in her eye and an A. B. C. in her hand, while Elsie commits herself to an elopement; and she quietly awaits the return of her Scotsman when his decree *nisi* is granted. And now, of course, all the too-knowing playgoers settle down for the conventional scene of sentimental reunion with which Miss Tempest and Mr. Ainley shall round off the play. They settle down – and suddenly they sit up again. Mr. Ervine still has a surprise up his sleeve.

These battles between the two Mrs. Frasers, the skill and triumph of the one and the sneers and capitulation of the other, might very easily have been the fireworks of theatricalism; the exchanges, half-laughing, half-solemn, between Janet and her Scott might easily have become the contrivances of sentimentality; and Janet's old friend Philip and her sons and her servant and her daughter-in-law might have been well satisfied with a ripple of supplementary and detached epigrams. But that is not Mr. Ervine's way. He has given to Miss Tempest a part that exhibits the force and integrity of her acting as well as the nimbleness of her wit; to Mr. Ainley an opportunity to show how brilliant and perceptive an artist the stage would have lost if he had not returned to it; to Miss Ursula Jeans a chance to draw a swift and persuasive portrait of an unpleasant woman; and to the rest character enough to make them as necessary as they are entertaining. There is not a moment during the evening in which the play sags or in which Mr. Ervine loses command of it. In writing and performance it is a beautiful piece of workmanship. Not to rejoice in it, as the Haymarket audience unanimously rejoiced, would be to have lost all sense of the strength and *finesse* of English comedy in its lighter, but still serious moods.

20 AUGUST 1929, THE TIMES

The Apple Cart by George Bernard Shaw

MR. SHAW'S NEW PLAY

BOANERGES (President of the Board of Trade)	Matthew Boulton
MAGNUS (King of England)	Cedric Hardwicke
PROTEUS (Prime Minister)	Charles Carson
ORINTHIA	Edith Evans
AMANDA (Postmistress – General)	Dorothy Holmes-Gore
LYSISTRATA (Powermistress – General)	Eileen Beldon
MR. VANHATTAN (American Ambassador)	James Carew

(From Our Dramatic Critic) Malvern, August 19

Mr. Shaw appears to have discovered England. Who would have thought, in another August 15 years ago, that a Shavian mouthpiece would ever tell, except with tongue in cheek, of "this little gem set in the silver sea"? The jewel may not, indeed, be quite of the same water as the "precious stone" preferred by another patriotic dramatist, but is it not gratifying to find the author of "Common Sense about the War" even roughly in agreement with John of Gaunt? It is true that King Magnus of England is hard-driven to his little emotional quotation. The American Ambassador has announced to him the decision of the United States to enter (or, as the King sees it, to annex) the British Commonwealth. The unhappy monarch is in despair, feeling that American penetration of his realm has already gone far enough. Our rocky shore may beat "back the envious siege of watery Neptune," but not of American ideas and American money. "We live" – it is a pretty Shavianism – "in a world of wops." Hence the unexpected Lancastrian outburst, which leaves us to wonder why, in the matter of annexation, it should have needed an American threat to convert Mr. Shaw.

But he is evidently, for the purposes of this play, converted, and not to patriotism alone. Democracy, King Magnus declares, instead of establishing a responsible government, has abolished it, and all the best of the play is a dialogue with this text. In the first and last acts the King is seen giving audience to his Cabinet. They are a queer lot. One of the ladies looks and behaves as if her place were in a music-hall and Miss Holmes-Gore does it admirably. The other looks, but does not behave, like a woman undergraduate in a Gilbert and Sullivan opera. The men are all jobbers or nonentities except Boanerges, a hearty republican whom a little flattery twists round the royal finger, and Prime Minister Proteus, a caricature of adroit political insincerity. The time is vaguely in the future. They are one of a long series of Labour Governments, for politics has become a despised profession and there is little competition for their dismal duties. Every one of intelligence has "gone into the City"; not more than 7 per cent of the electorate trouble to vote; poverty and hardship have been abolished, and England, principally devoted to the manufacture of chocolate creams, lives, as a vast *rentier*, on the sweated labour of other peoples. No protection against the very rich and no safeguard against corrupt legislation exist except in the royal veto. The King, in a public speech, has said as much, and here are his Cabinet to protest. Henceforth they will have a dumb King. They have brought a charter for Magnus to sign. Either he must make a "rubber stamp" of himself or – heaven knows, and the Ministers certainly do not know, what they will do if he refuses.

Seven men and two women sit down to debate the position. Their debate is twice interrupted – by the coming of the American Ambassador with his message, the delivery of which by Mr. James Carew is a highly entertaining piece of serious farce; and by another interlude, occupying the whole of the second act, which is so dull and pointless that it is hard to imagine what persuaded Mr. Shaw to write it. Magnus, during this unhappy passage, is in the boudoir of a lady, Orinthia, with whom his relations (we give the phrase for what it may be worth) are "strangely innocent." She parades the room, elaborating her own vanity; she talks and talks about her excessively tedious self; when the King wishes to go, she retains him by force, and ends by rolling on the floor with him. What is this interlude, which gives Miss Edith Evans no chance? Is it a skit on puffed-up courtesans? "You are beautiful! You are divine! You are gloriously amusing!" exclaims Magnus, quite seriously. Can Mr. Shaw have believed it?

It is better to keep our noses to the political grindstone, for this does grind ideas and make the sparks fly. There is an essay, delivered by Magnus, on the uses of royalty when democracy has proceeded to its logical conclusion which is as ingenious a piece of dialectic as Mr. Shaw has written. There is another essay, on the impossibility of honestly governing a corrupted plutocracy, to which Miss Eileen Beldon, though handicapped by her fantastic costume, gives a persuasive seriousness. Mr. Charles Carson's Prime Minister is a genuinely wily hypocrite, and Mr. Matthew Boulton's republicanism is excellently good humoured. At the centre of their discussions is King Magnus, and Mr. Cedric Hardwicke, except in the boudoir where nothing but cardboard could live, exhibits in him a quick intellect, a quiet humour, and a rich store of good nonsense that, in the best Shavian manner, isn't nonsense at all. When the King is orating or abdicating or beguiling his Ministers all is well. There may be no dramatic illusion; you may not care a snap of the fingers whether all these people live or die; but their argument is, so to speak, "good to read." It is prophecy sharpened by satire, backed by reason and, though damaged now and then by buffoonery, undistorted by prejudice. It is, moreover, extremely well delivered, and holds the stage as much by its easy and brilliant manner as by the solidity of the matter contained in it.

The audience at the Malvern Theatre, where the play was performed privately on Sunday and again to-night, received it well. Except in rhetorical fragments it is not Mr. Shaw at his full range; in one section, which is independent of the others, it is Mr. Shaw at his worst; but the first and last acts, taken together, are good entertainment and make up a pamphlet on democracy which may silence many a catchword and charm away many a pious delusion.

8 SEPTEMBER 1929, THE NEW YORK TIMES

More about Mr. Shaw's Play

MALVERN, ENGLAND, AUGUST 20

After an earlier performance in Polish at Warsaw, Bernard Shaw's new play, *The Apple Cart*, was given in English at Malvern last night. The circumstances are unusual. The town of Great Malvern, which lies on the eastern slopes of the Malvern Hills, is not of great size or importance, but it is a pleasant place embedded in one of the most beautiful of English countrysides. "The valleys of the Severn, the Wye, the Teme and Shakespeare's Avon, with their towns and villages, their cathedrals, abbeys, churches and castles, all lie within a day's motoring distance, and for those whose inclination keeps them nearer home it is no exaggeration to say that from the hilltops these places lie at their feet." So says the official pamphlet of the Malvern Festival, and it speaks the truth. For my own part, though I might well return to London now that Shaw's new play has been performed, I purpose to stay here a week, not in devotion to *Back to Methuselah*, *Heartbreak House*, and *Caesar and Cleopatra*, but because I like the air, the water, the great expanse of sunlit valleys as yet uncontaminated by industrialism.

It is evidently the intention of Sir Barry Jackson to make the Malvern Dramatic Festival an annual affair if he can. I hope he succeeds, for there could not be a more charming place for a week's leisurely play-going. Whether he succeeds or not will depend, I presume, very much upon the support of American visitors.

Will Americans be favourably impressed by *The Apple Cart*? It is a question that an Englishman cannot – and certainly will not – attempt to answer. If you enjoy being criticized, and criticized with slashing severity under the general show of good humour, you will enjoy the last act of *The Apple Cart*. If you are interested in a criticism of democracy – not American democracy only but the whole principle of so-called democratic government – you will be interested by the first as well as by the last act. How anyone of any nationality or taste can enjoy the second act I cannot conceive. It is not concerned with democracy or with America. It seems to have been intended as light humorous relief in the midst of serious argument. When it is done you wonder why on earth it was done at all. While it is in progress you are made uncomfortable by the dawning discovery that in it Mr. Shaw is trying to be funny and is lamentably failing. Let me put this unhappy subject aside for a moment and return to consideration of the play's main substance, which is contained in the first act and the last.

The time is the future. The place is London. England is ruled, at least in name, by a Parliament, a Cabinet and a constitutional King. King Magnus is giving audience to his ministers, who have called upon him with an ultimatum demanding that he speak no more in public and that no reference be made again to the royal power to veto legislation. The King, who is an astute politician, sidetracks their demands and leads them into general debate.

England, it appears, is now greatly prosperous. Wages are high, hardship and poverty have been abolished, the principal manufactures are Christmas crackers and chocolate creams, and the greater part of the country subsists upon the sweated labour of foreigners in lands where English money is invested. The real rulers of the country are a plutocracy who, by control of the press and by intimidation of the government, turn all policy to their own financial advantage. The profession of politics has deteriorated. "Men of genius despise it as dirty work"; every one of intelligence has gone into business, and the electorate care so little for parliamentary government, or have so far realized the unreality of it, that not more than 7 per cent of them trouble to record their votes. The Crown alone, says the King in a long speech that is as brilliant an argument as Mr. Shaw has ever written, is not overawed by the plutocracy. Democracy, instead of establishing responsible government, has destroyed it; the Crown remains. The royal veto alone stands between the people and corrupt legislation.

Do the ministers really wish to destroy their only genuine and incorruptible ally against the force of plutocracy that makes puppets of them? The ministers are shaken, but stick to their point. The King must sign their ultimatum. Very well, says he, I will give you my answer at 5 o'clock. The first act ends. The debate, having lasted nearly an hour and a half, is adjourned.

The disastrous second act is relatively brief. It is an uninterrupted duologue between the King and Orinthia, his favourite. Mr. Shaw's suggestion appears to be that this woman is the King's intellectual companion, for "he has never really possessed her" and the relation between them is "strangely innocent." However this may be, she is a mountain of chattering vanity. She explains her divinity, her brilliance, her superiority to other women, her glorious artificiality. When the king most pardonably refuses to make her his Queen and yet more pardonably tries to get away to his tea, she retains him by force, and the proceedings are enlivened by their rolling together on the floor. The trouble is not only that the scene is pointless but that it is deadly dull. Let us say that it is a Shavian squib that has failed to go off and, with relief, pass on.

At about 5 o'clock the King, with his Queen, is on a terrace overlooking the palace gardens. Enter the American Ambassador, dressed in a fantastic costume of stars and stripes and bursting with excitement and good-will. He has news to impart such as there has never been in the history of the world. He may say that the Atlantic Ocean has been submerged in the British Empire. He may add that the Prodigal, great with riches, has now returned to his ancestral home. "You don't mean –", says the King in horror. "Yes, I do," replies the Ambassador. "The Declaration of Independence has been cancelled. The treaties depending upon it have been torn up. The United States has become again a part of the British Commonwealth. I shall have the honour to present myself to you soon not as the Ambassador of a foreign country but as the High Commissioner of the greatest of your Dominions." "The devil you will," says the King.

The royal misgivings are Mr. Shaw's criticism of the Americanization of the world. This new move, inspired as he perceives by big business, means the annexation of England. Oh, I shouldn't put it that way, says the Ambassador in effect. You English won't be annexed; you will "merge" into the universal American tradition into which everything is "merged." "Did you say merged or submerged?" asks the King. But it is impossible in this article to pursue the argument. It is full of truth for Englishmen as well as for Americans; it is brilliantly amusing; it must be for Americans as well as for Englishmen extremely and bitterly painful. At any rate it ought to be.

When the Ambassador is gone, the Cabinet returns with its ultimatum and the debate on democracy takes a new turn. The King announces that he will abdicate, enter politics himself and become the leader of a party. By the prospect of an honest and able man entering into competition with themselves, the Ministers are so alarmed that they tear up the ultimatum and are content that the old game should be played as it has always been. So the piece ends.

Except for the second act it is – well, not a good play, but a good piece of Shavianism. Mr. Shaw has ceased to aim at what is ordinarily understood by dramatic illusion.

We remain consciously the auditors of a debate, and, though the King himself is an extremely able and lively puppet represented with excellent judgment by Cedric Hardwicke, there is never any question about identifying ourselves with any character or feeling any sympathy with it. I state fact; I do not complain of it; when Mr. Shaw is in pamphleteering mood, there is nothing to do but to enjoy pamphlets. And this is an interesting, and amusing, and, above all, a revealing pamphlet.

Those who look for socialistic consistency in Mr. Shaw will find in the play a suggestion, made in passing, that socialization of industry would be a remedy for some of the evils of plutocracy, but the work as a whole is much more a High Tory than a Socialist document. I do not wish to imply that Mr. Shaw has become a member of the Conservative Party; he has gone far beyond that; he has developed what is, in the noblest sense, a new traditionalism. He has the courage to mock at what his American Ambassador calls "progress." He has delivered an unrelenting attack on the fallacies, the absurdities and the corruption of the so-called representative system. A few years ago he would not have been made sad by the prospect of the removal of Ely Cathedral to America and its replacement by a structure of reinforced concrete. A few years ago he would scarcely have allowed any stage character, clearly representative of his own views, to quote with serious sentiment John of Gaunt's speech in Act II, Scene I, of *Richard II* and, when English tradition was threatened, to speak of "This precious stone set in the silver sea." In fact, he (or it may be Mr. Hardwicke) misquotes it, but even "this little gem set in the silver sea" is evidence enough that Mr. Shaw is beginning at last to love the country which has for so long been the object of his ridicule and it has often seemed, of his hatred.

but is patriotic

24 SEPTEMBER 1929, THE TIMES

The Merchant of Venice by William Shakespeare

LITTLE THEATRE

ANTONIO	Reyner Barton
SALARINO	Cecil Trouncer
BASSANIO	Tristan Rawson
GRATIANO	Frederic Sargent
SHYLOCK	Lucille La Verne
LANCELOT GOBBO KEEP	Andrew Leigh
PORTIA	Virginia Pemberton
JESSICA	Dorothy Dunkels

By what standard is a feminine Shylock to be judged? By the same standard inevitably as any other Shylock, or we should do discourtesy to an actress in compliment to a lady. Moreover, to discuss whether womanhood is successfully disguised by a beard and whiskers would be a dismal occupation of criticism. Let us

add to screen

X ¶o.

say, then, briefly, that Miss Lucille La Verne's disguise is extremely good, though, in her walk and certain movements of her head, imperfect, but that we devoutly hope she will not set a fashion. Say what you will, a feminine Shylock is an uncomfortable thing and a most unnecessary twister of judgment.

The next observation to be made in this difficult analysis is that Miss La Verne is a very accomplished actress. She has thought about Shylock and can interpret her thought. She has control of speed and inflexion, and discovers an impetus not an impediment, in verse. She can, too, reach out to high emotion, and might, but for the twist in judgment, the bar to response, have succeeded in communicating it. The truth is that, having set herself an impossible task, she has made a creditable attempt to perform it; but why any actress should so handicap herself, heaven knows.

Nor can her performance, skilful though it is, be compensation for accompanying distresses. Mr. Reyner Barton's Antonio is a sound piece of work: so is the Bassanio of Mr. Rawson. Mr. Sargent's Gratiano has spirit; Mr. Andrew Leigh does what a man can do to pretend that Lancelot Gobbo is funny; the casket scene has at least the recommendation of having been drastically cut. But the grace which is needed to cover the deficiencies of this limping story is entirely absent. Belmont seems to be a city in the United States where Portia is taught to recite her pentameters with a regular and native accent on the second, fourth, sixth, eighth, and tenth syllables. Miss Virginia Pemberton repeated her lesson with an accuracy to dream about. You would never have believed, except in this dream, that William Shakespeare's thought, or the professional theatre of London, ran so continuously to the tune: Te-tum, te-tum, te-tum, te-tumty-tum.

12 OCTOBER 1929, THE TIMES

The Silver Tassie: A Tragi-Comedy by Sean O'Casey

APOLLO THEATRE

SYLVESTER HEEGAN	Barry Fitzgerald
SIMON NORTON	Sidney Morgan
SUSIE MONICAN	Beatrix Lehmann
MRS. FORAN	Una O'Connor
THE CROUCHER	Leonard Shepherd
TEDDY FORAN	Ian Hunter
HARRY HEEGAN	Charles Laughton
THE TRUMPETER	Emlyn Williams
1ST CASUALTY	Clive Morton

Many years may pass before Mr. O'Casey's art ceases to produce confusion in the mind of an audience accustomed by long theatrical usage to consistency of mood. Hitherto it has commonly been demanded of a play that it be tragic, or that it be comic, or, if by profession a tragi-comedy, that the contrasted elements should remain distinct, the one appearing as a "relief" to the other. This theory Mr. O'Casey has definitely abandoned, and has substituted for it another, still very unfamiliar in the theatre, though having its now recognized counterpart in the novels of Mr. Aldous Huxley. We are no longer invited to give attention to one aspect of life and to consider it dominant for the time being. The unity of the work of art is no longer to depend upon the consistency of its material. Instead, as if some diamond were being rolled over and tossed in the air before our eyes, we are so to observe its facets of tragedy, comedy, and open farce that their flashing becomes at last one flash and perhaps, by imaginative and symbolic transition, one spiritual light. Unity is to spring from diversity. The elements of drama are to be compounded – not separated, not mixed.

Mr. O'Casey's experimental practice of this theory is of absorbing interest, and it is no less interesting because he has not perfected it. And of even greater value is his attempt to break free from the bonds of naturalism by the bold use of verse. Anyone in this history of a footballer who was maimed in the War may break into verse at any moment. A group of soldiers, resting at night from their labours, fall into a rhythmical chanting which has no relation with the matter or manner of naturalistic speech. Another group joins them, and all, falling upon their knees, send up a bitter prayer to a gun raised against the skyline. Above them, like a figure of Death itself, crouches the solitary figure of a man, chanting – and Mr. Leonard Shepherd does it magnificently – a terrible parody of the Valley of Dry Bones. The whole scene is almost a masterpiece. Mr. Augustus John's setting is its background. Mr. Raymond Massey's direction of the stage – his assembling of the soldiers in closely packed groups and his disposition of them so that they have continuously the quality of great sculpture – marks him as a producer who is also a poet.

Mr. O'Casey's attempt to make his play take wings from naturalistic earth succeeds; we move in a new plane of imagination. Yet the scene is not a masterpiece. The elements are not truly compounded. There appear two farcical figures of a Staff Wallah and a Visitor whose coming shatters the illusion and momentarily reduces Mr. O'Casey's irony to the level of a mean, silly, and irrelevant sneer. And more important and more disastrous is the discovery, which we begin to make as the scene advances, that the greater part of its effect springs from the setting, the leaning crucifix, the shadowy gun, the grouping of men, and the rhythm of language – the rhythm of language, not the substance of it. Though the use of poetry has lifted the play from earth to dream, the poetry itself has not force enough to sustain so great a suspense. The scene is filled with a kind of wonder. It is, in the theatre, a new wonder; it is exciting and, at intervals, moving; but little proceeds from it. Mr. O'Casey has not been able to give a full answer to his own challenge.

The other acts are more limited in their range. They are not, as the second act is, a brilliant failure that might have been the core of a masterpiece. But in them also Mr. O'Casey is working at his proper experiment, twirling his diamond, leaping suddenly from a music-hall turn at a telephone to a transcendental dialogue between a blind man and a cripple, giving to a dance at a football club an extraordinarily tragic significance, matching a poem with a waltz, wringing a new intensity from a scene in a hospital ward which does not hesitate to continue the broad and delightful fooling of Mr. Barry Fitzgerald and Mr. Sidney Morgan. This method of compression does not and cannot yield the full, naturalistic portraits that arise from drama of a different kind. Miss Beatrix Lehmann plays with a fierce concentration admirably directed; Miss Una O'Connor, gives life to a shrewd, hard sketch; Mr. Charles Laughton passes with remarkable skill from footballer to poet, becoming at last a pursuing conscience in a wheeled chair; and there is a beautifully controlled study by Mr. Ian Hunter. But the method and not the drawing of character is the central interest of this play. It is rash; it is extravagant; it fails sometimes with a great stumbling failure. But it is a method with a future.

19 NOVEMBER 1929, THE TIMES

Richard II by William Shakespeare

OLD VIC

KING RICHARD II	John Gielgud
JOHN OF GAUNT	Brember Wills
HENRY BOLINGBROKE	Gyles Isham
THOMAS MOWBRAY	Donald Wolfit
QUEEN ISABELLA	Martita Hunt
DUKE OF YORK	Eric Adeney

The performance cannot now be blamed, as some performances at the Old Vic have been blamed during the present season, for excessive haste. The speed is lively, but reasonable, and no actor can say that he is not given time enough to speak his lines. All have their opportunity, and the trouble evidently is that too few of them are capable of taking it. Something seems to have befallen the Old Vic. We do not look, and have never looked, for highly finished performances from top to bottom of the cast; there has always been an air of experiment in the lesser nobles and the sixth and seventh murderers; but in the past the experiments were good to watch, if not for their accomplishment, then for their promise, there being generally a good voice to redeem a clumsy movement or a feeling for the rhythm of verse as compensation for an undramatic stiffness.

It is useless to pretend now, even for the sake of old loyalties, that there is joy in the mass of the experiment. Many of the parts, and many far above the rank of the grooms and servants, are played badly and, what is worse, listlessly, the words being so minced and mumbled that even Shakespeare is not permitted to save the actors from themselves. Mr. Brember Wills, as Gaunt, is not listless; on the contrary, he is so continuously active that you cannot forbear to watch, with miserable fascination, the twistings of his hands, the tossings of his head, the wrigglings of his body, and to forget that once there was magic in the words he was speaking. Is there not majesty in Gaunt's death? Is there not a mounting and swelling rhythm in his speech of England? Then let us have stillness sometimes; let us have firmness and splendour, not the nervous, bubbling senility of a dotard. And if we were to descend a little in the social scale – but it is a weary business to be demonstrator of errors.

We will look rather where we may praise – to Miss Martita Hunt, who gave a clear outline to a dull little part; to Mr. Eric Adeney, who had the character, if not all the speech, of Gloucester; to a Bolingbroke by Mr. Gyles Isham, which had steady insight and a refreshing vigour of speech; and to a Richard who did indeed serve to remind us that this, of all the histories, is the loveliest, the poet in Shakespeare triumphing most often over the chronicler, and the deliberate humorist troubling us not at all. Mr. John Gielgud has always been an actor of sensitive imagination, his danger being that his sensitiveness stood sometimes very near to affectation. But there is no affectation now; strength and firmness have increased. Richard's pride is as persuasive as his weakness; the King with Edward's blood in him looks out through the dreamer's dreams. There are lines whose emphasis Mr. Gielgud betrays; there are middling passages whose plain meaning he clouds a little by a monotony of rhythm; but his performance as a whole is a work of genuine distinction, not only in its grasp of character, but in its control of language.

1 DECEMBER 1929, THE NEW YORK TIMES

A National Theatre

PRESENTING BOTH SIDES OF THE MATTER
ONCE MORE ON ENGLAND'S MIND

For many years there has been in England a hope that someday a national theatre will be built and endowed. The realization of that hope is still far distant, but recent events have brought it appreciably nearer. Various Ministers have spoken sympathetically of the idea, the British Drama League, which represents a considerable body of opinion, has passed a resolution in its favour, and the Home Secretary has gone so far – but it is not, perhaps, so very far after all – as to invite the supporters of a national theatre to submit an agreed scheme to him. The time seems to have come to give the subject serious consideration.

The first thing to decide is whether we want a national theatre at all. There is much to be said against it and the objections must be faced. That other countries have theatres that are nationally endowed and that we ourselves spend public money on the support of other arts is not necessarily a valid argument in favour of the English theatrical scheme. We are, or were, a nation which, though possessed by an overruling passion for law and order in so far as law and order affect and preserve personal liberty, hates any official attempt to govern our tastes. We dislike being told what we ought to like and think and believe. We are naturally suspicious of professors, schoolmasters, critics and pundits of all kinds; they may by their skill persuade us, but the moment they begin to tell us ex cathedra what we must think and believe our fingers itch to tip them out of their chairs.

The first objection to a national theatre is, then, that it is alien to us. Just as no academy of letters could presume in England to occupy the position held by the Académie Française without being laughed out of court, so a national theatre, whatever its merit or demerit, would stir up among us an instinctive hostility. We might reason ourselves out of this hostility. Seeing good work done, we should, I hope, praise it and not grudge our praise. But there is no escaping the fact that we should more readily and happily praise the same good work if it appeared under less formal, less official auspices.

There is a second danger, not generally recognized. The idea of building a national theatre has arisen out of the idea of erecting a memorial to Shakespeare. A large sum of money, amounting, I believe to about £70,000 was contributed to the latter project by one donor, and a few other subscriptions have trickled in. This happened years ago. The money has accumulated, and the idea of a national theatre has been grafted onto the idea of a Shakespeare Memorial. Now nothing is more evident than that the English do not care enough for a memorial to Shakespeare to be willing to pay for it on a large scale. Why? Not because they are unaware of Shakespeare's pre-eminence or ungrateful for his genius, but because they are sick to death of having him thrust down their throats, in school and out of school, as if he were the law and the prophets. And this is what a national theatre is in supreme danger of doing. Urged on by the abominable company of bardolators, inspired by a foolish notion that Shakespeare is a "national poet", it may continue to make the English think of him as they think of a tax-gatherer. Through no fault of his own, the poor man has become "official" – the most cruel fate that any poet can suffer. It is hard to believe that a national theatre will not add weight to his fetters.

A third objection to a national theatre is financial. This disappears if the money is privately subscribed; indeed, if the theatre, though endowed, were not nationally endowed, the principal objections to it would all disappear, and even Shakespeare might escape the final doom of canonization by Lords and Commons. But the existing project, as I understand it, is to get money or at least a site, which is money's equivalent, out of the government. I admit that public money is being spent every day in worse causes; our taxation for "social expenditure," some of which goes in betterment of the people's condition, but much more in an indirect attempt to influence votes, is higher than that of any other country in the world. We are paying, or have paid, in unproductive and, as I think, unwise subsidies money enough to build and endow fifty national theatres.

Much as many of us may hate this expenditure, we are powerless to check it, for we are outvoted by those who, themselves paying no taxes, care nothing for national thrift. But if we believe that the national expenditure is greater than the nation can afford, we are bound to resist any addition to it, however much we may desire that addition. A national theatre might have many advantages, but at the present time I think we cannot and ought not to afford it. A theatre privately endowed is a different proposition.

Let us assume, however, that the financial difficulties are overcome. The next question we have to decide is: what is to be the point of view of the national theatre? Is it to be aristocratic or democratic? I assume that its aim will not be simply to please the greatest number. But is it to aim at producing what someone considers "good" for the people? Is it, in brief, to seek the same ends as the education acts, though by a different means? Or is it to exist for the sake of giving expression to the works of great artists, whatever their immediate effect may be on the audience?

Of course, it will be said that, in the long run, the two purposes are identical, for there is no nobler education than a work of art. This is true, but it does not solve the problem. It does not tell us whether the first consideration in the mind of the director of the theatre is to be the artist or the general public. If the first consideration is to be the "public good," we all know what will happen. Experiment will be barred, controversy will be avoided, the theatre will be Shakespeare ridden, for Shakespeare is an artist who is "safe." If, on the other hand, the theatre's point of view is to be genuinely aristocratic, if its choice of dramatists and actors and producers is to be governed by considerations of art only, then I suggest that it is fantastic to expect to run such a theatre successfully so long as the director is responsible for his conduct to the House of Commons, and so indirectly to the mob. A privately endowed theatre might be genuinely aristocratic; a nationalized theatre cannot be.

And yet there is no doubt that we are in need of an economically-independent theatre, and ought to make great sacrifices to obtain it. We need a privileged group of endowed actors who are subjected to a rigid training for a period of years and are not allowed to blunt their sensibility in the performance of trash. We need even more a theatre for which artists will be encouraged to write works of art with no thought of their commercial value. Such an organization would best spring from private endowment preferably by a capitalist who, being dead, would not be tempted to interfere. Failing this, it might spring from a single gift from the public funds, which, having been made, could not be withdrawn and which would not be subject, like an annual subsidy, to continual parliamentary debate. In the artistic control of the theatre, one man should be absolute. There should be a committee with power to dismiss him once in three years, but with no other power to influence him.

Thus good might come, though so vilely is our theatre ridden by the twin fetishes of Shakespeare and "productionism" that my faith in any national theatre, as an aristocratic and artistic implement, is weak. But the risk is, I think, worth taking, though not at present, worth paying for out of public funds.

10 DECEMBER 1929, THE TIMES

A Midsummer Night's Dream
by William Shakespeare

THE OLD VIC

HERMIA	Margaret Webster
DEMETRIUS	Donald Wolfit
LYSANDER	Francis James
HELENA	Martita Hunt
QUINCE	Brember Wills
BOTTOM	Gyles Isham
PUCK	Leslie French
OBERON	John Gielgud
TITANIA	Adele Dixon

A blessing nowadays must rest on *A Midsummer Night's Dream* that is not burdened and weighed down with the producer's affectations but is allowed to be played simply and gaily, reliant on its own nonsense, its own poetry. So it is played at the Old Vic. The dresses and the setting are not masterpieces, but they are pleasant and appropriate, making no attempt to proclaim themselves by some wild eccentricity to be more important than the play, and Mr. Harcourt Williams has devoted himself to the text, not with the purpose of twisting and guying it as if it were a libretto, but of enlivening it with a comic perception that is legitimate and his own. Here, then, is a performance which, though it can sometimes be a little slovenly in its verse and does not make all there is to be made of the Pyramus interlude, is a straightforward, good-humoured interpretation of the play and a very comfortable entertainment.

The Pyramus interlude is odd. Some will declare it to be impossible, but the truth is that the playing, particularly at rehearsal, is too broad – so broad that the characters of Bottom and his fellows, which should give its edge to the fun, are overlaid by horseplay and unable to define themselves. Mr. Isham is a good bovine Bottom, looking and sounding (of course, when unenchanted) astonishingly like a caricature of Mr. Sam Livesey; Mr. Brember Wills is a tricksy Quince, looking and sounding very like an amusing caricature of Mr. Brember Wills in more solemn parts; but neither they nor their companions quite succeed in establishing their characters in the English village from which they came, and their farcical humour is left, in consequence, a little in the air.

There is a charming Titania by Miss Dixon, and Mr. Gielgud's Oberon knows exceptionally well how to be a monarch and a poet with a discreet tongue in his cheek and a twinkle in his eye. Mr. Leslie French, as Puck, is sharp and clear, and wonderfully swift with a graceful, not an extravagant, swiftness. The four lovers, let it be confessed, are unevenly matched, for, in spite of evidence that Mr. Francis James has an ear for Shakespearean music, the women outplay the men. Miss Margaret Webster is uncertain and seemed nervous in her opening scene, but her best is very good, even the highest wrath of Hermia failing to rob her of her lucidity or of the humour that sounds deliciously in her voice; while Miss Martita Hunt's Helena has an artist's care for little things. "How happy some o'er other some can be! Through Athens I am thought as fair as she" – Miss Hunt can speak a couplet, and care to speak 20 couplets, with a brilliant gaiety and preciseness. But even she can afterwards say: "To bait me with this foul derision" as if there were but nine syllables in the line, a surprising lapse in her who is generally a model for others.

8 JULY 1930, THE TIMES

The Importance of Being Earnest
by Oscar Wilde

LYRIC THEATRE, HAMMERSMITH

JOHN WORTHING	John Gielgud
ALGERNON MONCRIEFF	Anthony Ireland
REV. CANON CHASUBLE, D. D.	Charles Staite
MERRIMAN	Scott Russell
LADY BRACKNELL	Mabel Terry-Lewis
HON. GWENDOLYN FAIRFAX	Iris Baker
CICELY CARDEW	Heather Angel
MISS PRISM	Jean Cadell

What little flaws there are in this superb comedy it would now be tedious to discuss. It is not perfect, and that is the worst that can be said of it. As *Lady Windermere's Fan* is stained with ancient melodrama, so is *The Importance of Being Earnest* coloured here and there, and particularly in the second act, with ancient farce; it stiffens for a moment, it ceases to be Wilde's own, it becomes a little strident and so a little dull. But such moments are few; the play is, in its own kind, almost flawless – consistently trivial to the last. The question that remains is of its performance.

How should it be performed? In costume, certainly; but should the costume be naturalistic of its period, or should it be "stylised" as it is at Hammersmith so that the stage and the dresses become a pretty Beardsleyesque dream in black and white and silver? In the first place Beardsley is a dangerous man to imitate; the stage is not capable of his spacing and cannot maintain the firmness and fluency of his line. In the second place, to fantasticate Wilde is to be in peril of burlesquing him, and to burlesque him is to apologize for him, and to apologize for a masterpiece is to be ridiculous. Pleasing to the eye though it often is, and very beautiful though some of the dresses certainly are, this artificial decor is more often at war with the play than in accord with it.

And how should Wilde be played? There is one simple answer, that he should be played as Miss Mabel Terry-Lewis plays Lady Bracknell. Her dry, incisive, unforced wit; her proud carriage; the exquisite precision of her emphasis; above all, her personal dignity that preserves a great lady in one who might have been a butt – these things make of her acting a standard by which other acting in this piece may be judged. Mr. John Gielgud conforms to it. His phrasing is quick; he maintains the tension of the dialogue; he discovers the music of this astonishing artificiality. Only in the second act does he falter, allowing the burden of farce to slacken the pace of comedy. Mr. Anthony Ireland and Miss Iris Baker give admirable performances, but they have not quite his ease, Mr. Ireland being sometimes too casual and Miss Baker – how shall we say it? – too consciously la-di-da. There is a gay, spirited performance by Miss Angel, but she, too, is driven into exaggerations by the will to be artificial and she has not the enunciation for Wilde's carved periods. Miss Prism is a good though ancient joke, and Miss Cadell makes the most of it, though the Beardsley obsession has had the confusing effect of making her look like Mr. Robey in all but eyebrows. The best of the acting is always to be seen where burlesque is most carefully avoided. Mr. Gielgud and Miss Terry-Lewis together are brilliant. They have what the others collectively lack – the rhythm of the play, for it is very like a piece of formal music; and they have the supreme grace of always allowing Wilde to speak for himself in his own voice and not in the voice of a modern imitator.

15 JULY 1930, THE TIMES

The Man with the Flower in His Mouth
by Luigi Pirandello

THE FIRST PLAY BY TELEVISION
B. B. C. AND BAIRD EXPERIMENT

THE MAN	Earle Grey
THE CUSTOMER	Lionel Millard
THE WOMAN	Gladys Young
PRODUCER	L. de G. Sieveking

The Baird system of television was yesterday applied, for the first time in England, to a public, though still experimental, broadcasting of a play. The piece chosen – and, having regard for all the circumstances, very perceptively chosen – by Mr. Val Gielgud, the director of productions for the B. B. C., was

Pirandello's *The Man with a Flower in His Mouth*. It is a forbidding study of emotion in the shadow of death, which the B.B.C. might not ordinarily choose as part of an afternoon's programme, but its qualifications as a subject for the present experiment are overwhelming, for where else shall we find a play that is almost without action, that demands no depth of perspective, and that can be performed without grave loss though but one actor (and then only his head and shoulders) is to be seen at a time?

Let it be admitted at once that plays by television are as yet a subject for men of science, not for critics of the finer points of acting. The visual transmission is far from perfect; you feel yourself to be prying through a keyhole at some swaying, dazzling exhibition of the first film ever made. But if the process has still a long way to go before every subscriber to the B.B.C. is fully satisfied by seeing and hearing plays in his own library, the difficulties that have already been overcome are many and remarkable. Imagine the conditions that govern the performance of the play itself. The space in which the actors have their being (to say "in which the actors move" would be to suggest too great a freedom) is a half of a small cube, sliced through on its diagonal. Even the full beam of the light-projector is not theirs to play in, for the effective plane of the photo-electric cells cuts it diagonally and cuts off the actors' retreat. They must stay very close to the projector. Each of them, as his turn comes to speak, must thrust his shoulders into the imaginary half-cube that is his stage. Once there, he plays his part like a man with his head in a band-box. When he moves, he must move slowly and deliberately, for a swift movement will perturb the whole delicate affair and blur the screened image. When another actor's turn comes a chequered screen must be passed across the face of the occupant of the band-box while he withdraws and his colleague takes his place. When a little scenery is necessary one of Mr. Nevinson's drawings is substituted for the chequered screen. When – as does once happen in the present performance – we see the face of The Man and, at the same time, the back of The Customer's head, the two actors are, we understand, within a few inches of each other. These are conditions such as the most intimate of intimate theatres have never dreamt of. Mr. L. de G. Sieveking, the producer, working in inches where other producers work in yards has made an extremely ingenious use of his material. His chequered fadeouts are cleverly timed and accompanied by music. He has thought, as he was bound to think, in fragments of dialogue, and, greatly assisted by the clearness and variety of Mr. Earle Grey's speech, has given coherence to the play within the limits prescribed by the apparatus.

So much for the actor's part in the experiment. What the audience sees in the televisor is an image of about the size of a postcard. The clearness of the image greatly and rapidly varies. At its best it allows slow gesture, such as the moving of the man's hand to his mouth, to make its effect, and even admits the more striking changes of expression. At its worst, when the apparatus appears to have temporarily taken leave of its senses, the whole world of television leaps into the air and the actor oscillates violently between the room above and the cellars beneath, not deigning to pause in the little rectangle on which our attention is fixed. Perhaps, you think as you watch this dazzling battle between scientific virtue and natural vice, the fellow would behave more discreetly on a larger screen. In this hope, and because a play on a postcard has its limitations as an amusement, we went unofficially onto the roof. Here – an experiment within an experiment – a larger screen, about 10 square feet in area, was being used so privately that it must not at present be criticized; but it is perhaps permissible to say that, coming out of the long, low tent at the end of which the apparatus was set up, we did feel, as one does not feel in the same degree when looking at the television post-card, that we had been watching a cinema of the future. Not that on the large screen the image is clearer or steadier than on the small; indeed the lighted rectangles of which the image is composed are larger, and there is a certain loss of intensity. But all these things will pass, and the use of the large screen, even with its present imperfections, did suggest that this afternoon on the roof of 133, Long Acre, will prove to be a memorable one. Much lies ahead – the clarifying and steadying of the image; the intensifying of detail so that an ear ceases to be a gleam of gold and a nose a smudge of sepia; above all, the extension of the width and depth of the "stage." How far off these improvements are only Mr. Baird and his men of science can judge. Men of the theatre may meanwhile rest in peace. The time for interest and curiosity is come, but the time for the serious criticism of television plays, as plays, is not yet.

19 AUGUST 1930, THE TIMES

Let Us Be Gay by Rachel Crothers

LYRIC THEATRE

KITTY BROWN	Tallulah Bankhead
BOB BROWN	Arthur Margetson
MRS. BOUCICAULT	Helen Haye
DEIDRE LESSING	Joan Matheson
TOWNLEY TOWN	Francis Lister
MADGE LIVINGSTON	Cecily Byrne
STRUTHERS	Walter Fitzgerald
WALLACE GRANGER	Eric Cowley

They loved each other. They really and truly did. When he slipped, he apologized, but, when he apologized, she fairly howled. His slip, he protested in despair, was of a kind that did not affect the truth and reality of his love for her, his wife. Would she not forgive him? She would not. All her ideals were shattered. Never, never, would she believe anything again. And by the time he had gone out into the passage forever and she had flung herself down again on her desolate bed, we knew that for the duration of this play we were doomed to share her unbelief.

Not that, as things turned out, there was much to believe or disbelieve. Three years later they met by chance in a country house, where the story of their marriage and divorce was unknown even to Grannie, all-knowing Edwardian though she was. Her plan was to use Kitty Brown as a means to lure Bob Brown away from her inexperienced but eager granddaughter Deidre. Bob, though the three years had been a fickle interval for him, followed Kitty about (as in prologue), lavishing truth and reality upon her. Kitty, who had spent her three years in a gay pretence of fickleness, called up her ancient battery of shattered ideals. She would not allow him to hurt her so again. She would not take the risk – even for their children's sake. And yet she loved him. Why wouldn't she say so? For no other reason so good as that a little squeal of rapturous yielding had to be reserved to get the curtain down on the fifth scene.

Meanwhile, the struggle of the evening was to find excuses for keeping the curtain up. There was a trio for male voices about a place called Paree (Miss Bankhead at the piano), and a solo for Bob (Miss Bankhead still at the piano), and what, since we seemed to have wandered into a harsh and somnolent talkie, had better be called an exterior shot of two bedrooms (Miss Bankhead on the communicating balcony). Mr. Margetson was Bob quietly, a self-righteous rake; Mr. Eric Cowley and Miss Cecily Byrne were attendant decorations; Miss Matheson, as a young girl condemned to drunken humiliation, suffered with discretion, and Miss Bankhead, though her heart was breaking, was gay. Seeming to believe himself to be in a *milieu* wherein sensitive acting would produce its reward, Mr. Francis Lister played comedy and was lost; and Miss Helen Haye, whose business was to be rough-tongued and dictatorial, was useful in solving the authoress's difficulty in getting people on or off the stage. She just shouted at them and they moved, like a marine sentry bitten by a dog. It is, in the theatre, a tedious method of egress. However, if they had not gone in that manner, they might have been there still.

10 SEPTEMBER 1930, THE TIMES

Street Scene by Elmer Rice

GLOBE THEATRE

ABRAHAM KAPLAN	Abraham Sofaer
GRETA FIORENTINO	Grace Mills
EMMA JONES	Margaret Moffat
ANNA MAURRANT	Mary Servoss
FRANK MAURRANT	David Landau
ROSE MAURRANT	Erin O'Brien-Moore
AGNES CUSHING	Miriam Elliott
MRS. JONES	Millicent Green

A hot day in a mean street of New York with every detail that Mr. Rice's ingenuity can summon up to make your imagination blink and gasp and sweat. He is a master in the selective accumulation of little things; his play is an ant-heap of urban observations; and his method of suggesting the sickening inferno of bricks and paving-stones is the same method that he applies to the lives of human beings. There are certain things, scarcely noticed when the weather is cool, which acquire significance as the temperature rises – ices, bought from a barrow and carried in cardboard containers by a hand which (you remember suddenly) must be meltingly hot; dustbins, which lose their menace in the winter; humanity which, in mass, establishes during a heat-wave its identity with meat; milk, small babies, flies – all these speak of the sun that has become a curse. Nothing here is omitted – nothing but the flies, which are, indeed, not easily dramatizable; but it can be done, and such is Mr. Rice's skill and thoroughness that we refuse to believe that the flies were forgotten. New York must be exempt from them.

Observe, then, this dramatic method applied to the inhabitants of a "walk-up" apartment-house. We never enter their rooms, though sometimes we have glimpses of them through their windows, where they may be seen washing their hair or reading a newspaper or murdering someone. They come out on to the steps and talk; they shout down from storey to storey; they go out shopping or revelling, and sometimes they return with odd companions, who make love to them and drift away, or, making love, happen to be murdered. When the last curtain falls you remember it all in the plural; "they," you say, not "he" and "she." It is true that some of them are, in action, a trifle more prominent than others, but the prominence has an air of having been permitted almost with reluctance. Mrs. Maurrant is a weak, hopeless, half-tragic figure, whose sick eagerness for the colour of life is cleverly indicated by Miss Mary Servoss; her husband's stern, suspicious, chilling nature is suggested by Mr. David Landau with a judgment that rightly wins the audience's pity; and Miss Erin O'Brien-Moore draws a portrait, firm, sensitive, and distinguished by its emotional control, of their bewildered daughter.

But there are a dozen other figures almost as important as these and without whom these would lose their meaning. A young poet, intended to be weak, is in performance weaker than he need be; his love-scenes with Rose allow attention to wander from them, but they are almost the only fragment in Mr. Rice's ant-heap that is not what he intended it to be. A fat, jovial Italian, a revolutionary Jew, a girl most brilliantly intoxicated by Miss Millicent Green, the lovers who come and go, the women (Miss Moffat and Miss Grace Mills) whose comments lead the worldly chorus, are all – well, what are they? People who make up the composite life of an apartment house on a hot day in New York, where beauty consists in a rare, faint, ineffectual revolt from ugliness, where there may or may not be a murder between breakfast and dinner, and where, because Mr. Rice has done so well what he set out to do, urban civilization goes on and on like the noises in a deaf man's head.

15 SEPTEMBER 1930, THE TIMES

Henry IV (Part I) by William Shakespeare

OLD VIC

KING HENRY IV	Alfred Sangster
HENRY, PRINCE OF WALES	Ralph Richardson
SIR JOHN FALSTAFF	Henry Wolston
POINS	Leslie French
EARL OF WORCESTER	George Howe
EARL OF NORTHUMBERLAND	Valentine Dyall
HOTSPUR	John Gielgud
LADY PERCY	Dorothy Green
OWEN GLENDOWER	Powell Lloyd

The Old Vic, during the season which opened on Saturday, will be a necessity to discriminating playgoers and particularly to those who pride themselves upon storing in their minds recollections of Shakespearean acting in which they allow no serious gaps. The performances may not always be collectively of the first rank; the circumstances of the theatre forbid it; but Mr. Harcourt Williams is a producer to whom a production is generally a fresh adventure and never a piece of tedious routine, the costumes and settings of Mr. Owen Smyth are, as was proved in the beautiful opening tableau of *Henry IV*, a pleasing balance between courage and discretion, and, above all, the presence in the cast of Miss Dorothy Green and Mr. John Gielgud is a compulsion to the Waterloo-road. Mr. Gielgud's Hamlet is everywhere remembered; his Richard II, is yet more memorable; he has a poet's stillness and fire. And if a producer were told to choose a permanent company, with no more precise direction to guide his choice than that it was to appear in plays, ancient or modern, by English writers of genius, Miss Green's name would spring to his mind. She is unfit for nothing except dull-minded triviality. She can hear laughter in a tavern or harps in the air. The full music of tragic verse, the wit and raillery of a drawing-room, the lively strength of unspectacular passages of persuasion or narrative, are all within her command. Even in Hotspur's wife she discovers a little gem of tender, smiling comedy with an aspect of woman in every facet of it.

But we shall have to wait for other plays than the first part of *Henry IV* to exhibit her powers – and Mr. Gielgud's. Hotspur dwells too long and too loudly on one note to be a musician's piece. Mr. Gielgud's attack is brilliant; the thrill of it runs through the theatre. He has been standing unnoticed, his back to the council table, while the King, whose solid dignity Mr. Sangster admirably represents, has poured out reproofs. When Worcester has been dismissed and Northumberland has spoken, Hotspur rounds like a tiger in his own defence.

My liege, I did deny no prisoners.

But I remember, when the fight was done –
The forty lines of passionate, glowing narrative so leap from him that you are unaware of accumulated description. The popinjay, "so like a waiting gentlewoman," and Hotspur himself, "pester'd ... made mad... all smarting," appear before you. A scene and a character are in the speech and Mr. Gielgud achieves a superb concentration of his forces. But unhappily when Hotspur has said this, though he has still abundant reserves of splendid words, he has of himself little more to tell, and, lively though the invention is which here relieves the warrior's monotony, the part is not one that draws out Mr. Gielgud's power to reveal phrase by phrase and cadence by cadence the innermost secrets of men.

...

25 SEPTEMBER 1930, THE TIMES

Private Lives by Noël Coward

PHOENIX THEATRE

SYBIL CHASE	Adrianne Allen
ELYOT CHASE	Noël Coward
VICTOR PRYNNE	Laurence Olivier
AMANDA PRYNNE	Gertrude Lawrence
LOUISE (a maid)	Everley Gregg

On the adjoining balconies of a French hotel are two couples married this morning – Amanda with Victor, Sybil with Elyot. Now, it happens that five years ago Elyot and Amanda were divorced because they loved each other so much that they were for ever quarrelling. They meet on the balcony; they discuss two champagne cocktails and the spouses to whom they were this morning linked; they dither, embrace, and flee. That is the first act, an omelette relatively rich in eggs. In Paris they quarrel, and that is the second act. Next morning Sybil and Victor, having breakfasted, quarrel likewise, and that is the third. And yet what an entertaining play it is! Mr. Coward has an unsurpassed gift for combining entertainment with nothingness.

And he does it with two characters, though there appear to be four; for he depends scarcely at all on Victor and Sybil, and has, indeed, spent so little of his wit on them that, until at last they sit down to an irresistibly droll breakfast party, Mr. Olivier and Miss Allen have their work cut out to prevent two people, intended to be dull in life, from being dull on the stage. The evening thus consists in three scenes – a love-scene on the balcony; a bicker and a free fight on a sofa; and another fight (breakfast included) among the debris of the previous engagement. Marvellously, they are enough. Amanda and Elyot are the fine, flippant flower of Mr. Coward's talent. What would happen if the parts were indifferently well played we tremble to think, but Miss Gertrude Lawrence has a brilliant sparkle and an extraordinary skill in embellishing speech with silence, Mr. Coward's wayward mannerisms have here their most fitting background, and the dialogue which might seem in print a trickle of inanities becomes in the theatre a perfectly timed and directed interplay of nonsense.

There are moments when even Mr. Coward falters. Before the quarrel reaches its climax the play, because there is nothing else to happen and the author's patter is exhausted, is temporarily converted into a concert party; and again, before breakfast, the patter nearly peters out. But Mr. Coward can pad as no one else can pad; he has made of dramatic upholstery an art and provides a delightful support for our utmost laziness. Someday, perhaps, he will invite us to more austere pleasure; we must be content to await the passing of his determination to be defiantly young. "Let's be superficial and pity the poor Philosophers," says Elyot in a moment of solemnity. "Let's blow trumpets and squeakers and enjoy the party as much as we can... Come and kiss me darling, before your body rots, and worms pop in and out of your eye sockets." If there were people who spoke like that about the time of the Peace of Versailles, have they not since grown up?

1 OCTOBER 1930, THE TIMES

The Breadwinner by W. Somerset Maugham

VAUDEVILLE THEATRE

PATRICK BATTLE	Jack Hawkins
JUDY BATTLE	Peggy Ashcroft
DIANA GRANGER	Margaret Hood
TIMOTHY GRANGER	William Fox
MARGERY BATTLE	Marie Lohr
DOROTHY GRANGER	Dorothy Dix
ALFRED GRANGER	Evelyn Roberts
CHARLES BATTLE	Ronald Squire

It is the pleasing, and sometimes critically instructive, habit of those who write *revues* to show us how the idea informing a famous play would have been treated by a dramatist other than the play's own author – how, for example, Shaw would have written *Quality Street* or Barrie *St. Joan,* and how *Charlie's Aunt* would have appeared if she had emerged from Norway or the Celtic twilight instead of from Brazil. Now at the Vaudeville Theatre Mr. Somerset Maugham adroitly shows how *The Father* of Strindberg might have been written, in complete independence of Strindberg's influence, by Mr. Somerset Maugham.

Of course, in Mr. Maugham's piece, Mr. Ronald Squire is the father. No one else's smile could so charmingly persist beneath the persecutions of the Battle family; no one else could carry off with such an air of comedy the revolt which Strindberg would have made tragic and frustrate. Mr. Maugham is fully alive to the tragedy. He is willing even to admit – *sotto voce*, and a little too apologetically – that Charles Battle's revolt is a spiritual one. Charles is a stockbroker of unblemished repute, one of whose clients fails and shoots himself. The settlement approaches; at the last moment, after heroic struggles, he obtains credit enough to preserve, not indeed his private fortune, but his firm's solvency. Hurrah, he thinks at breakfast, my position is saved, my wife and children are saved, I shall not be hammered this afternoon. I can continue to work and build up my fortunes again. But as he approaches the tube station at Golders Green, prepared to press his honourable nose to the solvent grindstone, his mood changes. His wife, his children, his firm, his repute may all be saved – but he is not. He is a slave. He is a slave to arrogant and selfish children, to a wife who does not love him and whom he has ceased to love, to work that bores him, to a monotonous drudgery of self-deception. By Jove, he exclaims, women have gone their own way and lived their own lives and slammed symbolic doors ever since Ibsen wrote *A Doll's House*. Why shouldn't a man live his own life for once? And so he keeps in his pocket the cheque that would have saved him, walks on Hampstead Heath instead of going to the City, is hammered at 3 p.m., and returns home with Mr. Squire's irresistible smile to tell his family that they are all but ruined, that he is bored with them, and that he is going off alone to find his soul (though he doesn't mention his soul) on five pounds a week.

8 NOVEMBER 1930, THE TIMES

The Only Way
by Freeman Wills and Frederick Langbridge

SAVOY THEATRE

SIDNEY CARTON	Martin Harvey
ERNEST DEFARGE	James Dale
LUCIE MANETTE	Margaret Marsh
CHARLES DARNAY	George Thirlwell
PUBLIC PROSECUTOR	John Garside
MIMI	N. De Silva

When playgoers now playgoing sit down to write their theatrical memoirs, there will be a sad gap in the index that has not an entry: "Harvey, Martin, in *The Only Way*" – such a gap, indeed, as will cause the reader to exclaim, "But this fellow can't have been a real playgoer at all – just a *dilettante*, no more." For whatever the chilly intellect may have to say of the piece, Sir John's performance is a memorable thing, a necessary link in the chain of theatrical history.

He has the rare gift of making you feel that you are present at an occasion. When Sidney Carton is discovered asleep among his wine-bottles; when with light shining about his head he delivers his oration to the revolutionary tribunal at the trial of Charles Darnay, formerly Marquis de St. Evremonde; when he stoops to kiss, for the first and last time, the girl for whose sake he is about to sacrifice his life; when at last, in a bath of illumination with a ruddy Parisian sky in streaks behind him, he tells himself that this is a far, far better thing that he does now than he has ever done – you may not altogether suspend your disbelief in Sidney or deny yourself a smile now and then at his heroic expense, but you do perceive that here is an actor whose individuality makes itself felt from stalls to gallery, a man who feels his audience and has the theatre in his blood.

How easy, and how foolish, to pull *The Only Way* to pieces! It has a glamour that is compensation for all its absurdities and is, indeed, partly made up of them. Why Lucie loved Charles Darnay no one will ever know. What a kitten and what a self-righteous prig! And yet there they are, decoratively represented by Miss Margaret Marsh and Mr. George Thirlwell and looking for all the world as if their whole spiritual inheritance were a garden-seat by Marcus Stone, and we, the bewitched audience, are prepared without a tremor – except the tremors appropriate to so sacrificial an occasion – to see Sidney perish for their sakes. And Mimi, the faithful maiden with auburn hair and tricolour ribbons, whose hopeless passion throbs in the voice of Miss de Silva, why is she not in the theatre the stick she ought in reason to be? Because the glamour of the piece is on her also, and the audience is touched even by her prolonged drooping against a wall. Perceive, too, with what fierceness Mr. James Dale and Mr. John Garside attack our friends and with what tender humility Mr. John Garside supports the sufferings of Dr. Manette. In cold blood, what would these things be? But no blood in Sir John Martin-Harvey's theatre runs cold – except when he means it to – for he can be serious without solemnity and solemn without absurdity. And when he soliloquizes and a hushed audience is eager for his lightest tone, then one asks oneself what this Ibsenish convention is that has stolen our soliloquies. Melodrama of the glamorous sort would be lost without them. Who will ever forget how Sidney Carton, wrapping a wet towel around his head, meditated aloud on the sweet nature of Lucie Manette? And without a soliloquy what would be the point of the scaffold and the blood-red sky?

Antony and Cleopatra by William Shakespeare

OLD VIC

CLEOPATRA	Dorothy Green
ANTONY	John Gielgud
ENOBARBUS	Ralph Richardson
OCTAVIUS CAESAR	George Howe
A MESSENGER	Harcourt Williams
EROS	Leslie French
A CLOWN	Harcourt Williams

The objections raised to this play by Johnson and other critics, though varied in form, may generally be traced to a common origin – the impression, which all who witness it must receive, that Shakespeare's innermost self was not in it. Evidently it is not only a play of action but a prodigious exercise in that form; the quality of secret meditation, which won from Shakespeare his most personal music, which lighted *Richard II*, was Hamlet's whole being, and filled the air of Prospero's island with confessions and prophecies, is not found in this Rome or this Egypt. The poet's orchestra is without its beloved instrument, and all his genius, though it give to the resulting music supreme richness and colour and depth, cannot make it, with the final intimacy of his greatest tragedies, his own. We observe with his eyes and are shown marvels; hear with his ears and receive a thousand enchantments; move in the train of his invention, and are born in unceasing expectancy from scene to scene; but though with him, we are not here within him. The world moves past, and he tells us of it.

But what a triumph of objective writing! The more we consider that the method and the theme were, in a sense, self-imposed and, in the dramatist, unique, the more brilliantly does the triumph shine. Why he, who knew so well how to sweep technical obstructions aside, allowed Proculeius and Dolabella so long to weary his climax and afterwards dissipated its effect in the dullness of Caesar's final intervention, even this production of Mr. Harcourt Williams's cannot make clear; but all else is illuminated by it and the play moves and burns with rare swiftness and fire. Mr. Gielgud, perhaps because in a first performance his judgment misled him, used too soon and too often the utmost range of his voice and exhausted its reserves while yet there was need of them. With this reservation, he gave a performance of great energy and insight and power, being at his best when Antony is most in peril of confusion – in the breakdown of reason, the extravagant romanticism, that is the cause of Enobarbus's desertion. Mr. George Howe discovers all the subtlety and weakness and stubbornness of Caesar; Mr. Harcourt Williams as the bringer of evil tidings and as the countryman who gives Cleopatra the asp doubly distinguishes himself; Mr. Ralph Richardson plays his best part as Enobarbus, in rhythm and in character continuously alive. But if there is one performance which, more than all others, makes this production memorable, it is Miss Dorothy Green's Cleopatra. What evil there is in the woman, gathered scene by scene as one might gather flowers, and what superb and dreadful tenderness when the asp is at the breast! The whole spirit is understood and revealed; the twisting of that variable mind is never for an instant obscure; and through it all the great verse is spoken, not with the empty boast of rhetoric, but with cunning and with majesty, the meaning and the music running intertwined, like the mingled currents of some deep and powerful stream.

2 DECEMBER 1930, THE TIMES

M. Maurice Chevalier

DOMINION THEATRE

Not long after 10 o'clock patience, tolerance, and hope – all the less exhilarating virtues with which a polite audience may support boredom for an hour and a half – were rewarded. Until then the grace of Veloz and Yolanda had been the only strong encouragement in a sad mixture of symphonic bands, prancing girls, and oriental tushery, diversified by a contortionist or two and a mule. If the purpose of the preliminary entertainment had been to compel a sigh of relief when M. Maurice Chevalier appeared it could hardly have been better planned.

But how soon he had his audience in good humour! Prestige is much, but to banish the accumulated apathy of 90 minutes, prestige alone would not have sufficed. M. Chevalier came in, so to speak, to stop the rot; if he had played nervously, or had attempted to stone-wall, what a disaster there might have been! Happily he began at once, as the wise men of the pavilion say, to see the ball, and played with brilliant confidence. His style is a winning one that joyfully combines impudence and humility. Before he sings a song in French he tells the story of it in English. Whoever attempts to "tell the story" of any popular ditty that springs to his mind will perceive the awful difficulty of the task. But awe is not among M. Chevalier's emotions. "I will explain you," he cries. "It is in me a vice"; and he explains the love-story of the two elephants in "Mon P'tit Tom" or the pathetic history of "Valentine" with the same naive sophistication that is the salt of the songs themselves. "Ma Régulière" being one of those songs least easily explained, M. Chevalier makes it an occasion for a diverting essay on *apaches*, and "Dîtes-Moi Ma Mère" becomes beneath the new hats that he gathers from the wings a serial comment on the ages of man. As for the American songs, let us leave them to the talkies, which are their natural instrument, adding only that M. Chevalier does sing them with a blessed speed and zest. He enables you to forget their words by watching his eyes, his hands, his absurdly expressive mouth. But charming entertainer though he is, he cannot carry a whole evening on his back.

23 DECEMBER 1930, THE TIMES

Peter Pan by J.M. Barrie

THE PALLADIUM

PETER PAN	Jean Forbes-Robertson
CAPTAIN HOOK	George Curzon
MR. DARLING	George Curzon
MRS. DARLING	Stella Patrick Campbell
WENDY	Mary Casson
JOHN NAPOLEON DARLING	Freddie Springett
NANA	George Elliston
SMEE	James C. Wilton

A playgoer who goes season after season to *Peter Pan* may as well give up any hope of being consistent. This year one scene, next year another, will claim his preference, leaving in his mind a confusion of judgments. But after prolonged experience he generally finds himself established in one of the two chief critical camps – he's either a Darling, whose principal delight is in Nanas and nurseries and mother-love, or, shivering a little over that embarrassing business of thimbles and kisses and tragic perambulators, he is a Pirate and plumps for Hook. Fortunately, Peter Pan himself is a liaison officer between the two camps. We piratical fellows come into our own when his triumphal battle with Hook leaves him sitting on the place once occupied by a tub, and the Darlings of this world are free to take their pleasure in the polite domesticity of the Home under the Ground. How anyone can be quite comfortable when Peter, coming clean out of the play's illusion, asks us to clap our hands if we believe in fairies remains a mystery, but certainly small voices are uplifted in spontaneous response, and in such a play as this one small voice outvotes a multitude of sceptics.

There is, then, not a fragment of the piece that has not its eager partisans, and the entertainment consequently remains alive. This year the nursery is at a disadvantage, the vast spaces of the Palladium stage robbing it of some of its intimacy. Poor Nana's emphatic and protestant paw has an air of being waved in a wilderness, and the quiet charm which Miss Stella Patrick Campbell brings to her part has to struggle for its effect. But the size of the stage is elsewhere a gain, particularly in the Mermaids' lagoon, where Peter and Wendy have an ocean – and a very ingenious ocean it is – to swim in, and Peter is rescued from the vanishing island beneath a sky full of sweeping clouds, perilous to mariners. And the children have more room than ever for flying and fighting. Mr. Freddie Springett never misses an opportunity to command the stage; he has a superb contempt for pirates and is Hook's master with but a third of his inches. Mr. James Wilton is a benign and mellow Smee; Miss Mary Casson's prim discretion gives a saving humour to Wendy's maternal solemnities; and Miss Forbes-

Robertson's Peter is as quick and fiery as in the past – a beautiful performance, at once lively and mysterious, that saves Peter in his moments of silliness and exalts him when his author's imagination is moving in strength. Mr. George Curzon, having satisfied the Darlings, in the nursery, afterwards proves himself a genuine champion in the piratical camp. There have been Hooks who communicated more alarm for the rending of their breeches; for some reason, perhaps of timing, that good joke fell a trifle flat; but in all else this Hook excelled, his education at Eton and Baliol having yielded him a pronunciation of the King's English so extravagantly correct that he was able to discover a jest and a thrill in each separated syllable of the menacing Croc-o-dile, and what appeared to be a natural joy in the part being rewarded by a power to imply a wink in even the darkest and most blood-curdling passages of villainy. In brief, a highly cultivated scoundrel who, in the noblest tradition of the Hook family, had evidently taken to piracy in the spirit of a connoisseur of adventure.

7 JANUARY 1931, THE TIMES

Twelfth Night by William Shakespeare

SADLER'S WELLS

ORSINO	Godfrey Kenton
VIOLA	Dorothy Green
SIR TOBY BELCH	Ralph Richardson
MARIA	Elsa Palmer
SIR ANDREW AGUECHEEK	George Howe
FESTE	Leslie French
OLIVIA	Joan Harben
MALVOLIO	John Gielgud
ANTONIO	Henry Wolston
SEBASTIAN	Antony Hawtrey
FABIAN	Richard Riddle

One may always know that theatrical history is being made when no one, having entered the theatre, sits. At Sadler's Wells the audience stood and gazed, the stalls at the gallery and the gallery at the stalls, perhaps examining the new playhouse, which is spacious and beautiful, perhaps looking for faces or remembering ghosts. When the curtain rose and the anthem had been sung, still there were ghosts, not indeed on this stage where the Mayor of Finsbury was in the chair and the helpers of the Sadler's Wells fund were solidly represented, but in remembrance of another stage in this place where, as Sir Johnston Forbes-Robertson reminded us in a brief and moving speech, Phelps, "his master," worked for many years. The Mayor of Finsbury welcomed the new theatre that is to work in conjunction with the Old Vic, Sir Johnston declared it open, Dame Madge Kendal smiled on it, and Miss Lilian Baylis quietly and modestly surveyed her kingdom. Then, lest we should complacently suppose that all the work was done, Mr. Rowe, who has done so great a part of it, gently told us that Sadler's Wells still needed £21,000 and the Old Vic £7,000 to free them of debt.

Whereupon, cameras having flashed their blessing upon speakers so admirably brief and straightforward, the company began to prove in a performance of *Twelfth Night* that few debts are better worth the lifting. Mr. Godfrey Kenton, in his opening, proved the quality of the cast. This Orsino, Duke of Illyria, the love-sick sender of messengers who at last turns from Olivia to Viola as lightly as another man would turn a penny in his pocket, is an impossible fellow, but he has one supreme merit – his tongue's music – and Mr. Kenton can play it. And, not to pass too swiftly to the giants, how good to hear the songs sung as Mr. Leslie French sings them, holding the audience under a spell of natural grace and feeling, and how refreshing to have a Sebastian as firm as Mr. Hawtrey's and a Fabian and Maria as full of life as Mr. Riddle's and Miss Palmer's. Fabian's eyes seemed to be coming out of his head with joy in the Malvolio hunt – a joy that gave a flash of genuine colour to what may easily be a dull part.

So to the immortals. Sir Toby and Sir Andrew are a pretty pair, Mr. Richardson having the uncommon virtue of remembering, even in his cups, that Toby is no pot-house brawler but Olivia's kinsman, and Mr. George Howe treating Sir Andrew with a corresponding lightness and discretion. Comedy, in brief, not a shouting-match, and comedy with an edge. Mr. Gielgud's Malvolio was handicapped in prison by the sound-proof qualities of the queer sentry-box to which he had been condemned, but elsewhere we were more fortunate. His seriousness is better than his fooling, there being now and then something a little too deliberate in his manner to carry the illusion of unconscious self-mockery, but even that nonsense is good and the cruel conclusion is brilliantly done. With Olivia and Viola, Sadler's Wells has varied a tradition of some strength but questionable value. Olivia is now little more than a child, not a creature of almost Royal dignity, and Miss Joan Harben shows very prettily that Olivia's eager wooing chimes more easily with youthful impulse than with an older discretion. To such an Olivia Miss Dorothy Green's Viola is an admirable complement, light, graceful, but commanding too, and with a sharpness in her scorn. What is most delightful in it is that the woman is ever present in the boy. You perceive the feminine mind more in each phrase. Uncaptivated by her disguise, Miss Green has thought with Shakespeare scene by scene and line by line; there is a new vitality in such close companionship.

4 FEBRUARY 1931, THE TIMES

Strange Interlude by Eugene O'Neill

LYRIC THEATRE

NINA LEEDS	Mary Ellis
CHARLES MARSDEN	Ralph Morgan

It is unfortunate that the "mystic premonitions" of Mr. O'Neill's ninth act should add their weight to the sixth hour, for they are an encouragement to those who will say that five hours and more of playgoing are necessarily too many. They are not too many for the treatment of a theme that demands them, and it is right to say at once that Mr. O'Neill's work has too much substance and challenge in it, and keeps the mind too continuously occupied, ever to become an inconvenient weariness of the flesh. He is telling the history of a woman's emotional life from the girlhood in which her being was centred in her father, through the vicissitudes of marriage, passion and motherhood, until the late age in which, desire having failed, she reverts to the man, Charles Marsden, who has become in her mind her dead father's representative and substitute. Nine acts are not too many for a history of the seven ages of woman.

The question is whether Mr. O'Neill has made the best use of so generous a canvas. Not content to submit to the limitations of dramatic dialogue which, since Ibsen, most dramatists have observed, he has taken up again the old instrument of soliloquy. A splendid instrument it is, a beautiful weapon of the imagination, not to be despised as it has been, but the man who uses it must submit himself to a new discipline as strict as that which he has overthrown. Mr. O'Neill has not commanded himself by any perceptible rule. Sometimes the actors are speaking what others hear, sometimes they are speaking their thoughts; this is clear and legitimate; but a closer examination of the soliloquies shows that they themselves are not always on the same plane, and that, whereas some of them enrich the dramatic illusion, many are but wordy impediments to it. What is the distinction? It seems to be this – that those soliloquies which admit us into the secret thoughts of the speakers are valuable, but those others (and they are many) which either criticize the external dialogue or, worse still, are used as a convenient way of informing the audience of external fact, are often dull and sometimes destructive. Some of the plunges into Marsden's and Nina's minds are brilliantly illuminating; they enable us to perceive directly what the ordinary dramatic method could have revealed only by prolonged divagation: but Mr. O'Neill does not distinguish, and will often take the natural speed from a good scene by holding up the dialogue with soliloquy which, if not positively barren, yields nothing but information that might be better conveyed by other means at other times. It is easy to lay too much emphasis on this aspect of *Strange Interlude* for no better reason than it is new. There is no new principle, but extended soliloquy has not elsewhere been used on the same scale. It would, however, be a real misfortune if discussion of the technical apparatus were allowed to obscure the merits of the play. Until the last act, where drama wanders off in purple clouds and "mystical premonitions" are extremely uncomfortable, the story moves with the sweep and vigour that overcome all but the most stubborn technical obstacles. Nina and the men who influence her life appear as a composed group; the episodes of the tale hold together in a tragic unity; you are continuously aware, in spite of every extravagance of language and clumsiness of emphasis, that an eager and fruitful mind is expressing itself on the stage. When that is true, five hours are not too many. And the performance of the Theatre Guild is at once closely knit and highly sensitive to each phase of Mr. O'Neill's emotion. Mr. Basil Sydney gives a carefully developed study of the lover who is deprived of his son; Mr. Ralph Morgan's portrait of Marsden is one of the fullest and most consistent pieces of biographical acting we have seen on the stage; and Miss Mary Ellis exhibits the cruelty and tenderness and pitiable egoism of Nina with a beautiful control of emotional values.

18 FEBRUARY 1931, THE TIMES

Hassan by James Elroy Flecker

MUSIC BY DELIUS
O.U.D.S.

HASSAN	G. W. Playfair (Merton)
CALIPH	G. A. C. Devine (Wadham)
RAFI	R. M. Raikes (Exeter)
ISHACK	W. G. Devlin (Merton)
MASRUR	P. D. Howard (Wadham)
HERALD	P. McLaughlin (Worcester)
PERVANEH	Peggy Ashcroft
YASMIN	Thea Holme

Flecker's play is a song, a great lamentation for the cruelty of fate, or it is nothing. A few scenes are maintained by the tension of narrative, but they are very few. That in which the Caliph, in high divan, bids the lovers, Rafi and Pervaneh, choose between life in separation and death in torment after a day of love stands as plain drama, independently of its language; the scene of choosing, though it had not been written by a poet of Flecker's quality, would have stood likewise, and the coming of the disguised Caliph into the house of the King of the Beggars has the same intrinsic strength. But, considered as a whole, the play is one that has a tendency to halt in the division of its interests. Flecker's attempt to conceal this by calling his work *Hassan* and stringing diverse themes on the thread of the meditative confectioner's adventure in the company of Haroun-al-Rashid does not succeed, and what binds the play together, making of it – for all its theatrical defects – a great work of art, is its language which, enriched by the music of Delius, shines with unique splendour in the theatre of our time.

When *Hassan* was performed in London several years ago, Mr. Basil Dean overloaded it with the magnificence of productionism. The Oxford University Dramatic Society's performance, produced by Mr. Gibson-Cowan under Mr. Dean's direction, is at least innocent of that mistake. The settings – though the use of steps and platforms, particularly in the Procession of Protracted Death, might have been more judicious – have been designed by Mr. Richard Oke with the admirable purpose of revealing, not of adorning, the action, and his costumes, drawn from Persian sources with a justified disregard of particular period, are a very brilliant use of limited material. Here and there a hat is over-elongated in the cause of humour, and there are details – such as the formalized torches too closely resembling sliced grapefruit on the ends of poles – which insist over-much on themselves, but generally Mr. Oke's designs combine invention with restraint and deserve more space and better grouping than has been given them. Mr. Bernard Naylor's conduct of his orchestra has the same effect of genuine collaboration with Flecker, not of self-assertion against him, and Mr. Mark Fawdry has very ingeniously, and with evident care, contrived his ballet in a small space that for a great part of the time is inconveniently littered with bodies. All this to the good; the splendour of Flecker's language, one would say, is to be given its chance to appear. But either Mr. Gibson-Cowan has no ear for it or he is incapable of persuading amateur actors to accept his guidance. And where, in any case, is that "personal supervision" of Mr. Dean which is given more prominence in the programme than the names of Flecker and Delius? It is true that the men of the cast are amateurs, but it is not to be believed, remembering O. U. D. S. productions in the past, that they are unteachable. On the contrary, Flecker's flexible and patterned rhythms are precisely what young men with minds and voices may be taught. It can only be assumed that Mr. Gibson-Cowan is deaf to his own failure; that he has not taught because he himself has not heard.

The strongest evidence is in Mr. G. W. Playfair's Hassan, because of the men's performances his is the best and its lapses are for this reason the more conspicuous. He has a strong and lively voice; and though he is extravagantly young for the part, he has a genuine sense of character and a genuine power to communicate it. At his best he is very good, and even his invocation of Yasmin, at its best, is very good, particularly in its dramatic quality. So little was needed to show him that the opening of each phrase of that poem cannot bear the same emphasis of attack or to persuade him to carry in the sweep of a heightened voice the one tawdry line in it,

But when the deep red eye of day is level with the lone highway,
is followed by –
And some to Mecca turn to pray, and I toward thy bed, Yasmin, and the trite impediments of that "lone highway" can and ought to be transcended by the mounting rhythm of what follows it. It is fatally easy to expose Flecker's weaknesses by applying to his monosyllables the regular stress of a barrel organ – a truth of which Mr. Playfair himself is evidently aware, for he often successfully applies it. It was the

producer's business to see that he and others applied it consistently. But there appear to be no lutes in Mr. Gibson-Cowan's orchestra of verse and prose, and he has allowed his production to thud and stutter – a fate that always befalls a singing language that is not allowed to sing.

Mr. Devine's Caliph, which may be allowed to depend more than the other parts on character and less on language itself, is a careful, intelligent study; Mr. Devlin's Ishack, though slow in spirit, has a promise of subtleties that needed only a little teaching to be fulfilled; and though in the cell Mr. Raikes's Rafi is beyond all teaching, lifeless in rhythm and emotionally unperceptive and confused, he gives an acceptable performance in *The House of the Moving Walls*. Some of the lesser parts are good fun. Mr. P. D. Howard's negro executioner is superbly statuesque and a gigantic contrast with Yasmin's frailty, though the statue crumbles a little when it is required to speak; and Mr. McLaughlin's Herald, rolling off titles in high divan, has an accomplished eloquence. But the gap between amateur and professional performances has seldom appeared to be wider than in this production. Miss Thea Holme may not have Yasmin's evil when she cries: "I laughed to see them writhe – I laughed, I laughed, as I watched behind the curtain." But she has beauty and vitality and, above all, decision and flexibility of speech. Here at last, one exclaims, is acting with an edge! And to observe Miss Peggy Ashcroft in the cell is to cease to be greatly troubled by poor Rafi. "Hark! Hark! – down through the spheres – the Trumpeter of Immortality! Die, lest I be shamed, lovers. Die, lest I be shamed!" Pervaneh is in her own secret ecstasy, and a cast of undergraduates whose merits have not been given their chance cannot now disturb her. Here at the close of the fourth act is Flecker, the poet, given at last his instrument.

23 FEBRUARY 1931, THE TIMES

Hassan at Oxford

TO THE EDITOR OF THE TIMES

Sir, – The anonymous Dramatic Critic of *The Times* – who is known to all the world – in one more of his interesting critiques, this time on the O. U. D. S. production of *Hassan*, has a reference or two to the teaching of actors.

He is displeased with Mr. Gibson-Cowan and Mr. Basil Dean. He thinks that Mr. Gibson-Cowan, the producer, and Mr. Dean, the director, might have taught the actors, although they were amateurs, how to speak properly. He says: – "Either Mr. Gibson-Cowan has no ear for the splendour of Flecker's language, or he is incapable of persuading amateur actors to accept his guidance." Further on he says: – "It is true that the men of the cast are amateurs, but it is not to be believed, remembering O. U. D. S. productions in the past that they are unteachable."

Now what does this mean? How long does it take any of us to learn anything difficult to learn, yet worth learning? Of course, it all depends: if we are inspired amateurs, or inspired professionals, we learn pretty quickly – we learn so quickly that they tell us to the end of time that we are greatly inspired, but sadly deficient in technique. All the great actors have had this hurled at them – until their days came to an end, the stoning did not end. "Inspired, untaught genius." That is because he taught himself.

Then we come to the uninspired geniuses, who can be taught. Let us suppose that the O. U. D. S. is full of these – clever men, keen about the theatre, willing to work. How many years does anyone suppose it takes to train such men to speak the verse of Shakespeare and Flecker, the divine prose of Synge and James Stephens, and the other prose plays? It is my belief that it will take five or six years to bring a group of men working together to perfection in this craft. If they already know a very great deal about it, perhaps they might speak their lines perfectly in two or three years. But your Dramatic Critic seems to suggest, Sir, that, in the few weeks or months that the O. U. D. S. had for preparing *Hassan*, the commonplace, bird-or snail-like speech that is the usage of to-day could be transformed into something very beautiful.

How long is it going to take to get some of these notions out of everybody's head? I should think I had made a very stupid blunder if I ever supposed that any part of the immense work of journalism could be learned perfectly in a hurry. Now why does not journalism pay those of us who are artists, and practice some art or craft, the great compliment of knowing that our work is as serious as journalism, and cannot be learned a scrap quicker?

Yours faithfully,

GORDON CRAIG, Georgian House, Bury Street, St. James's, Feb. 19.

24 FEBRUARY 1931, THE TIMES

Hassan at Oxford

TO THE EDITOR OF THE TIMES

Sir, – It is true, as Mr. Gordon Craig has discovered, that art is long, but no less true – though he has a unique power to forget it – that critics and producers must, unless they are to be sterile, reckon with life's brevity. Six years may be needed to perfect the art of speaking, but whoever has, as an amateur, worked with the O. U. D. S., or, as a critic, observed the methods of William Poel, will know that six weeks is time enough for a few preliminary miracles. It was the absence of these, not of the ethereal perfections of Rapallo, that saddened an observer of the Oxford performance of Hassan, and would, perhaps, have saddened Mr. Craig if he had seen the play before writing of it.

Blest, who can unconcern'dly find
Hours, days and years slide soft away,
Leaving but promises behind,
      And yet can say –
Thank God, my Art is long and vague,
And pupils die before they're taught
What none can teach to Gordon Craig –
      That life is short.
      I am, &c.,

YOUR DRAMATIC CRITIC.

28 FEBRUARY 1931, THE TIMES
MR. CHAPLIN'S NEW FILM

City Lights at The Dominion
Written, Directed, and Produced by Charles Chaplin

A small grey man, pleased but seemingly less excited by the occasion than his audience, walked to his place in the front of the dress-circle, and, having bowed his acknowledgements and sat down, remained seated with modest determination. A battery of cameras had some difficulty in persuading him to pose on the balustrade. He had evidently come to see a film and at last now allowed to see it. Meanwhile the crowd in Tottenham Court-road was probably still facing the police and the deluge.

After Krazy Kat and a couple of Chicago politicians had contributed to the evening's entertainment, there appeared upon the screen a statue, waiting to be unveiled. The lady and gentleman charged with its unveiling chattered a charmingly incoherent satire on the talkies and pulled the string. In the lap of Peace lay the Tramp who had been sheltering there for the night. All eyes were turned upon his grotesque figure. What could be easier than to clamber down and escape? But it is not so easy when your breeches become impaled on a symbolic and statuesque sword. You can of course take your hat off when a misguided band plays the Star Spangled Banner, but even the most earnest gesture of reverence loses dignity when you are suspended in mid-air.

Down he comes at last and, wandering vaguely round a corner, encounters the romance of his life, a blind girl selling flowers. Now we offer up for the first time our thanks, to be repeated again and again throughout the evening, that this is not a talking film but a return to genius in pantomime. If that blind girl had begun to hoot lugubrious sentimentalities, all would have been lost; if Mr. Chaplin himself had begun to stutter his adoration there would have been little left in this film worth waiting for. As it is, adoration dawns upon his face and we are bound in his enchantment. In the time that it would have taken a talkie to utter a few discordant yelps he has fallen in love and has vanished like a penguin. Like a penguin – is that debated bird the model for this superb pedestrianism? The same stateliness, the same courtesy, the same miraculous compromise between caution and progress, the same angle of the haughty head, the same expressiveness of the empathic feet, the same wisdom – certainly it is a being with an abundance of penguin attributes that rules this City of Lights.

There follows a swift succession of penguin adventures. Mr. Chaplin falls in with a millionaire who, when drunk, welcomes him, and, when sober, fails to recognize his companion of the night before. Meanwhile the flower-girl is in distress and Mr. Chaplin sets out to earn the money she needs and to prevent her from discovering that he is not the dollar-prince she supposes him to be. But he is not a successful wage-earner. When he tries to clean the streets, he is thwarted by travelling menageries; when he ventures into the prize-ring he becomes entangled in the string of the gong and rings his own knell. Fortunately the millionaire is drunk at the next encounter. Hoping for $22, the blind girl's rent, Mr. Chaplin achieves $1000, which will cure her of her blindness. "Then I shall be able to see you!" says she silently. And when you do see me, the tramp thinks, will you love me as you love me now? The penguin vanishes for a moment. Doubt and joy, hope for her and profound misgiving for himself, pass and repass over Mr. Chaplin's face, grown serious. It is a masterly piece of acting, poised on the very edge of a sentimental morass into which dialogue, and above all the delays of dialogue, would have certainly hurled it.

The money having been obtained and handed on, Mr. Chaplin goes into prison with a joyful and defiant flourish of his hind leg. Observe that hind leg – with what accuracy of timing it kicks a cigarette into the air. The little scrap of detail is one of a thousand that are composed into this tapestry of humour and character. At one of the millionaire's parties Mr. Chaplin is unable to hiccough without whistling; the taxis flow and the dogs bound to him; nothing is lacking but the birds. At the girl's home, when he presents her with a plucked duck, he puts a ghostly gun to his shoulder and goes through the motions of a Tartarin after game. There is no end to his inventiveness. And when at last, emerging from prison, he strolls in rags past his princess's flower-shop and finds her with her sight restored, he abstains once more from that touch of over-emphasis that would have ruined his story. Here is no ecstatic reunion fading into unqualified bliss. The tattered little man gazes with delight at the girl; the girl having expected a dazzling cavalier, gazes with confusion at this grotesque who has been her benefactor; then, while we are still wondering how she will reconcile reality with dream, while his face is still full of agonized expectation and hers of baffled tenderness, the film ends. Mr. Chaplin deserved the welcome the audience gave him and he thanked them in a short speech, so pleasantly spoken that if ever he does fall to the talkies we may still have hope. Certainly he must, in his own phrase, "la-la" the music for them. His music fits his acting like a glove.

Tell England

A BRITISH INSTRUCTIONAL FILM FROM THE BOOK BY ERNEST RAYMOND
DIRECTED BY ANTONY ASQUITH AND GEOFFREY BARKAS

RUPERT RAY	Tony Bruce
EDGAR DOE	Carl Harbord
CAPTAIN HARDY	Frederick Lloyd
MRS. DOE	Fay Compton

This film, which was shown privately on Monday evening, cannot be coldly discussed as an entertainment or as an exercise in cinematography. Parts of it are profoundly, almost intolerably, moving; the audience, knowing the event, is yet held in attention higher than the tension of excitement; no man of imagination can witness it without suffering. All this is plain. But he would be a bold critic who declared that he could with assurance distinguish between the emotions proper to the film itself and those springing from his own memory and sentiment. The story is of the Gallipoli landings and evacuation – a story which, when told with the screen's approach to naturalism, cannot yet be considered with detachment.

It is remarkable that the illusion created by the film is always most powerful where Mr. Asquith and Mr. Barkas have either abstained from dialogue or have used it, not to convey information or to illustrate character, but impressionistically as a form of supplementary sound. Partly for this reason, the opening is very weak. The two men, Ray and Doe, who are afterwards to serve in the same company in Gallipoli, are here shown as senior schoolboys in the spring and early summer of 1914. The intention is to emphasize their friendship and their youth, to offer a peaceful contrast with the scenes that are to follow, and, we are afraid, to provide a part for Miss Fay Compton as the mother of one of them. Some of this may be necessary, but how much better it would be if these scenes of swimming and delight were run together in a swift sequence, a unified impression, instead of being treated as a formal narrative in which, after all, Miss Compton, whose voice is very harshly and gustily reproduced, can produce little effect. Not until her son has gone and she, herself silent, hears with her ears the vain chatter of a visitor but with her mind the music, the cheering, the blasts of sirens that accompanied his going, does Miss Compton influence her audience and Mr. Asquith enter into the true use of his medium. The strength of this little scene is a comment on what has preceded it.

It is a relief to be away to the Mediterranean. The personal story of Ray and Doe is skilfully interwoven with the general movement. After an illustration of the Anzac landing and the attack by the 29th Division, the action is localized to a section of trench occupied by Ray's men, with Doe as second-in-command. It is threatened by a trench mortar, which after many weeks, the company is ordered to take. Doe succeeds in his particular duty, but is mortally wounded. The Peninsular is evacuated, and the last scene is an inspection by German and Turkish officers of his grave

The course of events – the failure of one man's nerve and a raid in which he redeems himself and dies – is not unfamiliar in fiction of the War, but this story is told with an exceptional discretion and is backed by scenes of attack that have been admirably produced and selected. Mr. Tony Bruce represents with persuasive care a young officer not deeply imaginative but quietly determined to do his job; Mr. Carl Harbord points a contrast in nervous, highly strung idealism; and there is a shrewd sketch of a Company Commander by Mr. Frederick Lloyd. The cutting leaves an impression of having been sometimes less skilful than the production. Not only the English scenes but those in which Doe is dying need reorganization, and there are passages in the trenches which lack fluidity. But the film, as a whole, has an outstanding merit that distinguishes it from many of its own kind – that its austerities are deliberate and do not spring from fear of sentiment. Though it does not shirk the terror of war, it is never a whine of defeatists. It recognises heroism as a thing of beauty which, even when frustrate, is not vain. But we could wish that it were not described as a "Great Romance of Glorious Youth." It is well able to speak for itself.

4 MARCH 1931, THE TIMES

Hamlet by William Shakespeare

THE HAYMARKET THEATRE

CLAUDIUS	Malcolm Keen
HAMLET	Godfrey Tearle
HORATIO	Dennis Hoey
POLONIUS	Herbert Waring
LAERTES	Tristan Rawson
ROSENCRANTZ	Henry Hewitt
GUILDENSTERN	Patrick Waddington
OSRIC	Robert Speaight
GHOST	Baliol Holloway
PLAYER QUEEN	Margaretta Scott
GERTRUDE	Irene Vanbrugh
OPHELIA	Fay Compton

No Hamlet ever had a warmer heart, a gentler or more winning humanity than Mr. Godfrey Tearle's. Before heaven, a very likeable man – one to choose as a friend, to honour as a prince. And to feel for Hamlet the liking, the almost unswerving affection, that we do feel at the Haymarket is implicitly to criticize Mr. Tearle's performance. See his welcome of Horatio from which the impression of friendship springs instantly; observe with what warmth, what eagerness and good sense, he treats the players; listen to his converse with the gravedigger, which is never twisted to an extravagant humour and is the more touching, and the more valuable as a retrospective comment, because held in so careful a simplicity. All this enables us to know – or, shall we say, to feel – a virtue in the man that more highly-strung and seemingly more sensitive performances had often obscured. The same merit is preserved even among the demerits of Mr. Tearle's soliloquies. They are clean of theatrical affectation; they are never mouthed or ranted, but spoken always with a kind of modesty that draws us to the speaker; and when, beside her grave, Hamlet says that he loved Ophelia, his love is plain and his grief directly communicated. A loving man, an honest, struggling, loyal man, held back from his active purpose by weaknesses in his character, but not, as some Hamlets have been, a neurosis on legs or an actor wallowing in a great part.

For all this a blessing on Mr. Tearle, but gratitude cannot conceal that the portrait he draws is incomplete. Two instances will serve. First, the soliloquies; they are clear, reasonable arguments, but they are never what the soliloquies should be – a trickle, a flow, a torrent of apprehension passing through the mind into the soul, as rain passes into thirsty ground. Second, the scene in which Hamlet comes upon the King at prayer and abstains from killing him lest, if the body die upon its knees, the spirit be carried to heaven. This is a fiend's abstention; this carrying of revenge into eternity is an act of devilish imagination of which Mr. Tearle's loving and honest man, so little troubled by the subtleties of the Renaissance, would have been altogether incapable. The defect is a damaging one. Not only is this particular scene, psychologically as important as any in the play, robbed of its effect, but the failure of it makes clear what Mr. Tearle's portrait lacks. He succeeded Mr. Ainley very recently in the part; as the evenings pass his performance will certainly be enriched, perhaps beyond our criticism of it. It is already an extremely able piece of acting, full of life, particularly in the early scenes, and rich in those human attributes which more spectacular playing has often concealed.

...

5 MARCH 1931, THE TIMES
HAMLET IN LONDON

Acting Traditions

TO THE EDITOR OF THE TIMES

Sir, – In common with a large multitude of Mr. Ainley's friends, or, as in my case, his friendly acquaintances, I deeply deplore the sudden loss of voice which at the last moment deprived him of realizing what must have been the ambition of his life – to play Hamlet in London with a company of great actors and actresses behind him. But I do not think that within the spacious limits of the generous republic of true art this natural regret should deprive me of the joy of congratulating, with you, the fine actor who at short notice took his place on the conspicuous success he achieved, and, particularly on the words of noble praise with which *The Times* has recorded it.

In the years that are now long past I spent much time in reading and, I think, closely studying nearly all that was best in the criticism of *Hamlet* by the greatest writers both in this and in foreign countries, and I cannot remember that in any of them, whether Hazlitt or Coleridge or even Goethe, I ever found anything that was more true to the character of its subject than is implicit in your article published this morning – that he was a friend to love and a prince to honour, a simple, natural, human soul, an honest, struggling, loyal man held back from his active purpose by his one infirmity of will. And that Mr. Tearle realized this in his performance last night, and that your critic has said so in words of such noble praise, seems to me sufficient reward for the work of a lifetime.

But there are just two remembrances to which you may, I trust, be able to allow me to give expression within the limits of my short letter. At the risk of seeming to have acquired the character of a literary Rip Van Winkle, I will say that I knew Mr. Tearle's father, and that that fact gives me half the joy with which I have read of the son's great success. We were boys together before we had reached our teens and friends when he had just launched himself into the career of an actor. At his best (he was not always at his best, being beset by many of the troubles of life) he, too, was a great actor and Hamlet was his greatest performance. I doubt if he ever played the part in London, but he had been brought up on the traditions, and in the companionship, of some of the greatest actors of the near past – Phelps and others – and now I, being, perhaps the last of his friends surviving, ask you to allow me to tell the public that all you say of Mr. Godfrey Tearle's Hamlet might have been said of his father's at its best.

Finally, I ask you to allow me to offer a word of reply to the only qualification of your praise. Forgive me if I am mistaken when I say that in the scene in which Hamlet comes upon the King at prayer and abstains from killing him, lest, if the body dies on his knees the spirit will be carried to heaven, this impulse of a fiend is inconsistent with Mr. Tearle's representation of a gentle, honest, and loving man. But is it the poet's intention to carry Hamlet's revenge into eternity? I think not. That idea was first promulgated in Germany (I cannot at the moment remember where) before the critics of that country had made their magnificent contribution to the appreciation of the greatest of our poets. But it was wrong to the poet and wrong to the character. When Hamlet conquers that devilish imagination he is acting solely and only out of the weakness of his will, which both then and at all times prevents him from doing anything at all by the deliberate exercise of intention.

Yours very truly,

HALL CAINE, Greeba Castle, Isle of Man. March 4

London, Too, Has An All-Star Hamlet Revival

LONDON, MARCH 4

I have never had great sympathy with those who hold up their hands in pious horror and say that Shakespeare is neglected in this land of his birth, and I have still less sympathy with those who organize leagues and societies to rescue him from neglect. Shakespeare's misfortune is not that he is outcast and despised, but that he is treated too much as though he were a mixture between the Bank of England and a charity bazaar. Men whose habit is an uncritical subservience to established institutions pay lip-service to him and treat an adverse critic as they would treat a man who shot a fox or cheated at cards. Women given to good works plead for him as they would plead for a hospital for mental incurables. The consequence is that for every Englishman who thinks of Shakespeare as a poet and entertainer there are a dozen who regard him as a duty and a bore.

It is this more than anything else that keeps his work out of the fashionable theatres. If you will go by omnibus or underground railway into outlying quarters of London, you will find Shakespeare at the end of the journey. If you will go to places where seats are hard and cheap and no one wears evening dress, again you will find Shakespeare. If you will go to playhouses supported by little leagues or charitably aided by financiers who believe in the educational value of the drama, you may have Shakespeare in abundance, but not in those parts of London where, having dined, people go in festive search of entertainment. Why? Because, it is said, Shakespeare doesn't pay on the West End. And why is that? Because nine people out of ten have had his plays thrust upon them as a school subject and inflicted upon them as an object for charity. Far from neglecting the poor man, we have strangled him with our idolatry and embalmed him with our reverence.

All this by way of preface to the fact – in England a remarkable one – that "Hamlet," which was given a special performance to celebrate Shakespeare's birthday last Spring, has now been put on for a run at the Haymarket. The Haymarket is a theatre of ancient, honourable and catholic tradition, but in recent years it has been chiefly associated with polite and romantic comedy. It is the place above all others to which people go after a good dinner in quest of light entertainment of some distinction. That "Hamlet" should appear for a run on the Haymarket stage is important.

Horace Watson, to whose courage this enterprise is due, was doubtless inspired to it by the success of last year's special performance. He employs what is called with justice an "all-star" cast. The light of stars who dazzle us here does not always carry across the Atlantic, and I shall not burden this article with a list of names. If I say that Godfrey Tearle, having taken Henry Ainley's place at the last moment, is Hamlet; that Malcolm Keen is the King and Irene Vanbrugh the Queen; that Fay Compton is Ophelia, and that such small parts as those of Rosencrantz and the Player Queen are taken by Henry Hewitt and Margaretta Scott, who are accustomed to play leads, it will be plain that this is the kind of cast not ordinarily assembled except on a gala occasion and by royal command. It is not a perfect cast. An English Shakespearean cast cannot be perfect that omits John Gielgud and Dorothy Green. But it is a cast of the highest distinction.

Two performances are of outstanding interest – Miss Compton's Ophelia and Mr. Tearle's Hamlet. Superficial criticism would say at once that Miss Compton could no longer have the childlike qualities and appearance of Ophelia and that Mr. Tearle's methods were too masculine and too direct for Hamlet. It is true that in her scene with Hamlet that is overheard by Polonius and the King, Miss Compton seems miscast, but I do not hope to see Ophelia's madness better done. She carries no flowers; her rue and rosemary are all of her imagination: and her performance is full of ghosts. What we see is not one girl lost utterly in a fog of insanity, but two girls, one mad and approaching, the other sane and receding, who, as they pass, perceives their identity with a shuddering but not unhappy recognition. Madness is often an ugly thing to watch, a thing associated with deadness and decay, and it is the peculiar quality of Ophelia's madness that it has the appearance not of a disease but of a spiritual liberation and is not ugly but beautiful. This is the quality of Miss Compton's interpretation. Her Ophelia is a creature who is shedding the illusions that we call reality and who is already half-possessed by profounder apprehensions not less happy than those she is forsaking.

Godfrey Tearle's Hamlet lays emphasis on an aspect of the character that it has become a habit to pass over too lightly. Many actors, preoccupied by Hamlet's meditative subtleties and by the introspective opportunities they afford, fail to make clear what is abundantly clear in the text – that to Shakespeare the Prince was human and lovable, a friend to whom Horatio was deeply attached, a man whom even those silken courtiers Rosencrantz and Guildenstern hesitated to betray. Mr. Tearle restores the balance. No Hamlet has ever seemed a gentler, more honourable or a saner a man than his. His treatment of the players is full of wisdom, balance and good comradeship. His persuasions of his mother are the persuasions of a son who, even in the most bitter resentment, can never forget his former love. His conversation with the grave-digger has an ease and humour which put it beyond doubt that at the end of the play Hamlet was as fully master of his own mind as at the beginning of it.

Mr. Tearle's performance has, however, the defect of his special merit. Hamlet was sane and lovable and this he shows, but Hamlet was also an introspective philosopher, whose action was paralyzed by the refinements of his mind. And though Mr. Tearle shows the paralysis in effect, he does not enable his audience to enter fully into the causes of it. Watching his Hamlet, one is always inclined to say: "But this man would have acted! I don't see what is holding him back!" The truth is that Mr. Tearle does not communicate the full contemplative force of the soliloquies or discover illumination in that deeply subtle and revealing scene in which Hamlet abstains from killing the

King at prayer; but the performance as a whole is a welcome departure from the custom of representing Hamlet as a timid neurotic with no health in him.

15 MAY 1931, THE TIMES

The Good Companions
by J.B. Priestley and Edward Knoblock

MUSIC BY RICHARD ADDINSELL
HIS MAJESTY'S THEATRE

LEONARD OAKROYD	Clive Morton
JESS OAKROYD	Edward Chapman
ELIZABETH TRANT	Edith Sharpe
INDIGO JOLLIFANT	John Gielgud
FAUNTLEY	Deering Wells
SUSIE DEAN	Adele Dixon
JOBY JACKSON	Alexander Field
LADY PARTLIT	Margaret Yarde
RIDVERS	William Heilbronn
MR. PITZNER	Alexander Field

No one will complain here of a dull and mumbling sub-naturalism. This is the theatre all out, and thank heaven for it, there was never a better occasion for a strong whiff of grease-paint, an abundance of wise barnstorming and music to taste. His Majesty's is a big playhouse and *The Good Companions* is a whale of a play. To have treated it as a polite and elegant goldfish in a domestic bowl would have been to make nonsense of it, and dull nonsense too. Play it with gusto, play it rantingly by gold-fish standards; remember the glamorous days of snow and limelight – recall the spirit of them; plunge from scene to scene violently, give Mr. Gielgud his head, allow Miss Adèle Dixon to dash at her part with eyes sparkling and colours flying, persuade Mr. Edward Chapman – by way of contrast – to discover a brilliant theatrical stolidity in Jess Oakroyd; in brief, sound the trumpet, advance to the charge, and you will have the audience at your mercy. Mr. Julian Wylie has found a play to suit his method and it is highly improbable that he will have this season to find another.

From this it must not be supposed that the play is all sound and fury. On the contrary, it is a firm, rapid narrative of the fortunes of Mr. Priestley's famous concert party, beginning with the evening on which Oakroyd lost his job and took to the road, and ending – a conspicuously well-chosen ending – with his marching up the gangway of the ship that is to take him to Canada. All of the book could not be crowded into the intervening space, but how much there is and with how little effect of congestion! Miss Trant is something of a miniature, but Miss Edith Sharpe defines her so clearly and gives her so much life within her restricted range that she fits admirably into her place. Mr. Priestley and Mr. Knoblock have applied an equally selective economy to their minor characters. Joby Jackson, with Mr. Alexander Field to increase the temptation, might well have led them to waste space, but they use him for what he is worth to their general scheme and no more. They are as wise and as a ruthless with Ridvers and Lady Partlit and Fauntley the schoolmaster, sketching them with a few decisive strokes, giving to Mr. Heilbronn or Miss Margaret Yarde or Mr. Deering Wells a complete though slight opportunity, and passing on swiftly to the main story and main characters. None of the character drawing can be very subtle; it is largely an affair of highlights and dark masses; but we shall not complain of that in a picture as lively, as brilliantly coloured, and as glamorous as this. The play lives by such scenes as that on the stage of the Gatford Hippodrome where The Good Companions, with their backs to us, are "given the bird" by an audience that is to our eyes a black, riotous gulf beyond the footlights. This is the moment of all moments for Inigo and Susie to fall into each other's arms; their excitement is ours and the more theatrical their emotion the better we are pleased. This does not happen to be one of Mr. Chapman's scenes; his northern sentiment and discretion appear better in Susie's dressing-room or in his own home in Bruddersford, where he establishes Oakroyd as a fine, vigorous, lovable being whose adventure it is good to share. The fine flowers of theatricalism are left to Mr. Gielgud and Miss Dixon. This Susie Dean is full of spirit; you feel her ambition quivering in her; you believe her when she says that if she doesn't get on she will burst. And what fun it is to see Mr. Gielgud, as the composer of Mr. Richard Addinsell's very beautiful tunes, apply the romantic tradition to a modern part and so set the key of the whole production. It is a dashing piece of *bravura*, designed with courage and discretion, sparklingly right in its romantic place.

7 JULY 1931, THE TIMES

Measure for Measure by William Shakespeare

FORTUNE THEATRE

THE DUKE	Henry Oscar
ANGELO	Baliol Holloway
CLAUDIO	Sebastian Shaw
ISABELLA	Jean Forbes-Robertson

The gods themselves, visiting the stage, could not make this play persuasive or advance a better reason for performing it than the pedant's reason – that it is seldom performed. The whole dramatic structure is flawed by the tricky contrivance of the Duke's pretended departure and by the extravagant artificiality of

Angelo's enforcement of the law. A piece so begun could but proceed from falseness to falseness, floundering through wooings by compulsion, disguises that could deceive no one, and that sorriest of stage-conventions – the assumption that a lover does not recognize his own bed-fellow. And a play so long dependent on these things could but end as this play ends-with a "discovery scene" so crude that one gasps at the careless effrontery of the man who wrote it.

The common objection to the story – that Isabella's preference of her own chastity to her brother's life is against nature and a condemnation of her – seems to us invalid. Isabella's choice is consistent with the tradition of her age, her calling, and her faith, and certainly Miss Forbes-Robertson's austere presentment of it establishes it as a part of the character. This has evidently been her central purpose, and for its sake she has turned away from the fireworks of "Fie! Fie! Fie!" and "Justice! Justice! Justice!" upon which other actresses might have relied to give a theatrical brilliance to the part. What she has cared for is to make Isabella credible; in this she has succeeded as far as one may succeed; but nothing can ultimately save a novice who, at the bidding of the Duke whom she has known for five minutes, abandons the religious calling that has hitherto been the basis of her action and enters into marriage as easily as other women pass through a drawing-room door when it is opened to them.

Mr. Baliol Holloway plays Angelo as well as we hope to see him played; the detail is careful, the action vigorous, the thought lively – but what a man! The Duke, who will seem to many more dismal because more given to moralizing, has the advantage of never seriously pretending to be more than a decoration, and Mr. Henry Oscar makes the decoration an elegant one.

...

13 JULY 1931, THE TIMES

Disturbance by Cyril Campion

GRAFTON THEATRE

HELEN WESTDRAKE   Nora Swinburne
SIR HOWARD WESTDRAKE, K. C. B.   Felix Aylmer

The value of this play is not in its story, which is commonplace and sometimes a little stiff, but in its portrait of Lady Westdrake and her husband. In the two young men it was hard to be greatly interested. One, an erratic and passionate youth, killed himself in Lady Westdrake's room; the other, though he became her lover in Sir Howard's absence, was a slightly ridiculous sinner, so strong and silent was his conscience. As for the scandal threatened by Julian's death and the too elaborate means by which it was hushed up, they were the ordinary small change of the stage; but Helen and Howard Westdrake, as represented by Miss Nora Swinburne and Mr. Felix Aylmer, were well worth a hot evening in the theatre.

Helen is more than a minx and more than a player with fire. Vanity and hot blood are so mingled in her that it is hard to distinguish their effects. In a bad play or in a film, she would have been so evidently a vamp that her influence upon men would have been incomprehensible to a man of taste, but here that influence is not at all incomprehensible, and Miss Swinburne plays the part with such charm and gaiety that one is left with only one regret – that she did not make prouder conquests than the suicidal painter and the strong and silent conscience. Against Mr. Felix Aylmer, too, there is but one complaint – that he does not appear in the second act. His performance has, as always, a brilliant precision and grace; his humour and his seriousness are faultless in timing and emphasis. What a likeable man! you say of Sir Howard and – too rare in the theatre – what a genuinely distinguished one! To watch Mr. Aylmer with a critical eye is to perceive careful judgment in every movement and intonation of his; to lean back and, turning from detail, yield to the general effect of his performance is to receive an impression of natural ease. It must be delightful to be so good a craftsman that your craft ceases to be apparent except to an eye that admiringly seeks it out.

23 AUGUST 1931, THE NEW YORK TIMES

As a Business and a Profession the Theatre is Undergoing Changes, but the Public Remains Loyal

LONDON, AUG. 8

The interval between seasons has given an opportunity for a renewal of the old discussion about the prosperity of the theatre. C. B. Cochran in a letter to *The Times* has vigorously contradicted those who declare that the theatre is exceptionally depressed, and my own observation tells me that his arguments are justified. It is true that many theatres are closed, but that is always true at this time of year, and enough of those that remain are doing good business to prove that, far from being exceptionally unfortunate, the theatrical trade is suffering less than most of its rivals from what the Chancellor of the Exchequer has described as the "economic blizzard." The rivalry of the cinemas, which many of a nervous temperament so greatly feared, has done little in London, though something in the provinces, to affect the fortunes of legitimate theatres. Indeed, there are strong reasons to believe that the popularity of the "talkies" has definitely waned and that playgoers who were for their sake temporarily disloyal to their old allegiance are fast returning to it.

It is, however, plain to any careful observer that we are passing through an anxious period of transition. The theatrical trade and the acting profession are alike taking on new forms and no one yet knows how complete the revolution will be. A great number of managers still cling as far as possible to the old ways, edging nervously from time to time toward momentary fashions for spectacle or for plays dealing with particular subjects, such as the subject of war. They rely upon their knowledge that in London there is always an experimental public for plays which are "different" and at the first hint of the success of a "different" fashion they rush in with imitations in order that they may have a share of the profits. They too often fail to observe that to imitate a "different" play is to produce an entertainment that is already beginning to be stale. More losses spring from this sheep-like tendency than from any other single cause.

But the dully commercial and imitative managers, though formidable, by no means represent the whole theatrical life of England. Side-by-side with them are growing up managers of a different sort, whose purpose is to back their own judgment and to persuade the public to follow them, while outside London there are increasing evidences of new life in the vigour of the amateur and repertory movements. Add to this the fact that published plays are steadily establishing themselves among the reading public as younger sisters of the novel and it will be plain that Mr. Cochran's confidence in the vitality of the theatre has very solid foundations.

The change that is taking place may perhaps be best considered in relation to the profession of acting. In England the profession is as yet imperfectly organized, as was proved by the strong differences of opinion expressed by rival professional bodies when the question of opening theatres on Sundays was being discussed in Parliament. But organization is increasing in strength and will year by year exercise a stronger influence on the destiny of actors. To many the change in the actor's status since the days of the giants that were before Irving seems a matter for romantic regret. The old spirit of adventurous Bohemianism is gone, and so far as they are able to do so actors are moving toward the established professional positions occupied by lawyers and architects. A consequence of this is a decay of spectacular personality, and it is this decay that the romantic conservatives chiefly deplore; but it is part of the changing conditions of the theatre itself, and cannot by any means be stayed. The whole tendency of modern producers and dramatists is to treat a play not as an opportunity for an individual display, but as a subject for regulated team-work. Except in classical revivals and on rare modern occasions the individuality of one actor is becoming of less and less importance. It follows that the power of professional organization is greatly increased, for the majority of actors can no longer be treated as an indifferent stage army of mercenaries to be dragged in at the heels of one famous chief.

In this, as in all else, we are still in a transitional period. The profession is weak in safeguarding its own interests because it is overcrowded and has as yet evolved no effective means of protecting itself from unqualified competition. A manager who wishes to do so can still neglect the claims of trained men and women, and if he is prepared to spend enough money on artificial publicity can exalt a girl who is virtually an amateur to the position of a star. Her stardom does not last long; the public awakes at last from the hypnotism of advertisement, recognises incompetence and rejects it. But meanwhile good actors and actresses are left out in the cold – actors and actresses who, if they had won for themselves a corresponding position in any other profession, would be assured of at least a regular living by their achievements and repute. What we are moving toward, and shall certainly have before many years have passed, is a system that requires of any performer certain recognised qualifications of experience and training before he or she can receive a London engagement.

A professional organization which was able to insist upon this preliminary safeguard would soon gather power to make war upon the salaries of stars, which are now universally acknowledged to be exorbitant. Many good plays fail and hundreds of actors are thrown out of work every year because the salaries of one or two performers make it impossible for managers to keep pieces on the stage which do not instantly fill the theatre.

The natural changes in the actors' profession and in theatrical business will, I think, eventually combine to produce a system with three distinguishing features. First, there will be in London, as well as in the provinces, many theatres with a consistent policy and a stock company able to be supplemented. Second, many actors will be employed on the basis of an annual retainer plus fees, and during their employment will be co-partners in the theatre in which they work. In brief, they will cease to live from hand to mouth, and their position will approximate more closely than in the past to that of professional men employed, maintained and, in accordance with their merit, regularly promoted in other businesses. Third, the profession will thus cease to be dependent upon voluntary charity for benefits given in sickness or misfortune, and will be enabled at least in some degree to provide for the future of its own members.

A change so revolutionary means that much of the old glamour and adventure will go from the stage. But they are already going. Actors have long ago become "respectable"; they dress and behave as other men; they desire, as their Bohemian predecessors probably did not, a regular and assured existence. We could not, even if it were desirable, put back the clock to the days of the mummers. Let us then recognize and stabilize the revolution, and have the advantages as well as the disadvantages of the new system.

Counsel's Opinion by Gilbert Wakefield

STRAND THEATRE

LOGAN	Owen Nares
LESLIE	Isabel Jeans
SLADE	Ronald Simpson
WILLCOCK	Morton Selten
LORD MERE	Alan Aynesworth
GEORGE	Cyril Smith

Mr. Nares has a vast overcoat, which Miss Jeans, if she had paused to talk about it, would probably have called woofy; but she did not pause to talk – she commandeered it, and his eiderdown, and the sitting-room in his suite; and not content with his sitting-room as a place in which to spend the night, she commandeered his bed (reluctantly vacated), his dressing-gown, and his heart. In the morning, being a barrister with practice in the divorce courts, he returned to Chambers, where his opinion was sought by Lord Mere. Lord Mere required a divorce from his young and pretty wife. Why? Well, partly because she was too young and too pretty for the old gentleman to keep in order, and partly because last night, having gone to a fancy dress ball in Restoration costume, she had been cut off by the fog, had spent the night in the Royal Parks hotel, and had occupied a room from which a man had been seen to emerge. Now Miss Jeans, before she began to commandeer overcoats and hearts and beds and dressing-gowns, had been wearing a Restoration costume in the Royal Parks hotel. Poor Mr. Nares, so gallant and so innocent, doomed, unless he can succeed in extricating himself, to be at once counsel and co-respondent in the same divorce case!

How he would extricate himself, or be extricated, was fairly plain to all of us, and that was a weakness in the play, for very little except an amusing butler by Mr. Cyril Smith and some not very dazzling dialogue was left for the last act. We all guessed, for example, that Mr. Alan Aynesworth and Miss Jeans were – but why should we betray our guesses? It is enough to say that the story is not the strongest part of what remains in spite of it a very gay and light-hearted entertainment. Miss Jeans's performance is full of good things – dash, coquetry, and sparkle; but they would be better things if they were toned down a little or, shall we say, exhibited in a more natural illumination; it is possible to overlight a jeweller's show-case and to over-act a farce. Observe Mr. Alan Aynesworth in this as in all things, for precision of stress and perfection of balance. His study of Lord Mere is a classical piece of fooling, and Mr. Morton Selten, though his attack is less brilliantly formal, is extremely good fun. The solemnity of Mr. Ronald Simpson is a light in Mr. Nares's chambers, and Mr. Nares himself, from the moment in which he surrenders his coat, his bed, and his heart until the achievement of his romantic purpose, rides a temperamental horse with admirable judgment. He has, like the barrister whom he represents, a *flair*. He knows intuitively when the dialogue is sagging, and correspondingly increases his pace; he knows, too, when the scene is offering him opportunities, and proceeds at leisure to avail himself of them. And he has an unfailing air of adventure which, when ladies commandeer your bed, is a very useful affectation and more than half the retreat – *pour mieux sauter.*

11 FEBRUARY 1932, THE TIMES
O. U. D. S.

Romeo and Juliet by William Shakespeare

NEW THEATRE, OXFORD

CAPULET	M. W. Bennitt (Trinity)
ROMEO	C. V. Hassell (Wadham)
MERCUTIO	G. A. C. Devine (Wadham)
JULIET	Peggy Ashcroft
NURSE	Edith Evans
Producer	John Gielgud

The Oxford University Dramatic Society, who began on Tuesday night their performances of *Romeo and Juliet* at the New Theatre, Oxford, have cared to speak verse again, and have learned to speak it. By this their work is transformed. As first consequence, they have their poet as their ally, not their enemy; as second consequence, Shakespeare being now in their support, they survive collectively their individual errors, are never swept off the stage by the professional actresses who accompany them there, and give their best balanced and most satisfying performance of recent years. No one will pretend that Mr. Hassell is in all things fitted for the part of Romeo. In the give and take of rapid dialogue his thought lags behind his words; he is, on these occasions, lacking in spontaneity; his attack is too smooth, and there is always a peril of his allowing Romeo to become genteel, which that rash young man certainly was not. But his performance is evidently one to which he has given the utmost care, for he has elaborately and successfully developed the qualities natural in him. He is not yet, and perhaps would never be, as good an actor as Mr. Devine, but the contrast between the two is extremely interesting. Mr. Devine, whose Mercutio makes not very much of Queen Mab, does not shine in his set-speeches, but give him dialogue and action and feeling directly responsive to action, and he will vitalize the stage with them, his treatment of Mercutio's death being particularly distinguished. Mr. Hassell on the contrary, though slow in the discovery of character in action, has a good voice and has learned how to cultivate the purple patch. To the great scenes he contributes his share with modesty and judgment – Juliet's subordinate certainly, but never a drag on her.

A triple-arched setting by Miss Molly McArthur provides at once a pleasant frame to the action and an opportunity for swift progress from scene to scene; the costumes, by designers who conceal themselves under the collective name Motley, have the double virtue of being separately delightful and of resolving themselves continually, under the influence of Mr. Gielgud's grouping, into pictures glowing with a composed richness of colour; and the impression given by the whole production, in spite of one accidental delay on the first night, is never of a play being dragged or driven across the stage but of natural urgency and eagerness.

The society, being this year gratefully fortunate, have had the art, the wit, and the discipline to avail themselves of their good fortune. The steady, unaffected integrity of Miss Edith Evans has given them confidence; the flashing lightness of Miss Ashcroft has given them impetus.

...

It happens again and again in this production that one seems to hear Mr. Gielgud's voice on the stage – which means, not that the undergraduates are slavish imitators, but simply that they are indeed learning to speak verse and are sensitive enough to recognize a master when they hear him. Mr. Gielgud's individuality impregnates the performance, not by self-assertion or any of the tricks of productionism, but by the force that dwells in full knowledge and profound love of the play. One does not feel: "Here is a man doing his weary best with a mixed team of undergraduates and professional actresses," but rather: "Here is an artist, honoured by his task and devoted to it, whose imagination is fired by *Romeo and Juliet*, and who is so far skilled in the theatre that he can give to the acted play the unity, the pulse, the excitement of his inward imagining of it."

The production is, moreover, given exceptional interest by the appearance in it of Miss Edith Evans and Miss Peggy Ashcroft. We have all known for some time that Miss Ashcroft ought to be given the opportunity of Juliet, but it was Mr. Gielgud's private discernment that saw the Nurse in Miss Edith Evans. The discipline of players to whom their art is everything unites the two performances. Miss Ashcroft's Juliet is the youngest and freshest that we remember. What faults it has spring from a too plaintive over-straining of the voice in the passages of tragic despair. "Oh, break my heart!" had not the dreadful composure of grief, not because Miss Ashcroft herself had not profoundly considered and apprehended the emotion of that scene, but because she had taken its climax too early and her voice would yield no more. But her balcony scene shines with all its magic. "Well, do not swear..."; the superb farewell that follows it can never have been spoken with a lovelier gravity; and the scene in which Juliet is impatient for her Nurse's news – a scene of teasing and charged excitement – is brilliant in its zest and invention, proving that in comedy Miss Ashcroft may well go where she pleases. And, above all, this Juliet is in love – not rehearsing phrases but passionately in love. The high music of that love's despair sometimes tests her too far, but its melancholy is a rapture and its delights are delight itself.

Miss Evans meanwhile is busy with a contributory masterpiece. She has the walk of an old woman; the hands of a sly one; and all the Nurse's experience of ribaldry and affection are in the curious tortoise-like movements of her head. If Mr. Bennitt, whose Capulet is so funny (now deliberately, now unconsciously) that it threatens scenes that cannot endure nonsense from Capulet, would learn how to direct humour within tragedy, he has only to watch Miss Evans. Never a strain, never an affectation; laughter proceeding naturally from character and all controlled; in movement, in speech, in the light of the eye, above all in restraint, masterly. In brief, Juliet's Nurse. Not to see Miss Evans and Miss Ashcroft together in the fifth scene of Act II. ("Do you not see that I am out of breath?"), not to hear Miss Ashcroft's farewells to Romeo or Miss Evans's lovely tenderness over the girl who seems to be dead is to miss a part of the history of this play.

14 MARCH 1932, THE TIMES

Othello by William Shakespeare

BROADCAST PLAY

OTHELLO	Henry Ainley
IAGO	John Gielgud
DESDEMONA	Peggy Ashcroft
RODERIGO	Leslie French
EMILIA	Gwendolyn Evans

The B.B.C. have made great advance in their method of broadcasting plays, and the performance of an abbreviated *Othello*, which was sent out from Savoy-hill yesterday afternoon, was rich in evidences of that advance. The sounds of which the performance was composed were being gathered in from seven separate studios – if "echo studios" be included – and it was thus possible, by the exercise of a central control, to do with voice and bells and music and the sound of water what a conductor can do with the instruments of his orchestra, softening too strong an insistence in one, increasing the emphasis of another, bringing all into accord with the balance in the producer's mind. It is true that if one voice began to come through too powerfully, Mr. Val Gielgud could do little to check it without depressing too far other voices in the same studio, but the control of "effects" is absolute, and the relative sound-emphasis between dialogue and, let us say, the striking of a clock can be adjusted from moment to moment. This gives to a producer for wireless a control, while the performance is in progress, denied to a producer for the stage. He can, so to speak, *play* his piece as an organist plays his music, using what stops he will.

The difficulty is to choose material that gives scope to the B.B.C.' s special powers and is gentle with its limitations. On the face of it, *Othello* does not seem to have been a wise choice. It is true that the force and beauty of its language give it support. One may have pleasure in its sound apart from the continuity of its narrative, and, if the attention wanders, in sections of it apart from the whole. To hear Mr. Ainley say: –

O Desdemona! Desdemona! Dead!

Oh! Oh! Oh!

is to discover, as one might not on the stage, new subtlety and new emotion in the dying fall of the human voice. Miss Peggy Ashcroft's steadfast pleading before Desdemona's death is spoken beautifully enough to lift the hearer's blindness and to recreate the scene; Mr. John Gielgud's Iago is particularly good in its passages of intimate self-revelation, and is proof that in soliloquy lies one of the principal sources from which wireless plays may draw their strength; and Miss Gwendolyn Evans has the excellent virtue of possessing an individuality which expresses itself fluently in her tone and a voice that is flexible, good to hear, and instantly distinguishable as coming from Emelia and none other. These pleasures and the great interest there is in considering the play as a technical experiment prevent the performance from being for a moment tedious, but they cannot persuade us that *Othello* was well chosen.

A wireless play should be structurally simple, not shifting continually from scene to scene; it should be written in such a way that the speakers in each section of dialogue swiftly reintroduce themselves, for, though actors may soon be identified by their voices, "soon" is not soon enough, and there is always a delay, an effort of recognition that blunts attack. No important twist of its narrative should depend upon things seen, for then that twist will be lost to the listener, as, we are sure, Desdemona's handkerchief and much depending on it must have been lost yesterday to anyone not closely familiar with the Shakespearean text. Above all, a wireless play should make abundant use of audible "effects," and Othello gives little scope to them. Everything possible has been done to apply the resources of the B.B.C. to the play. "The woman falls; sure, he hath kill'd his wife," has been rightly changed to: "The woman falls; Iago hath killed his wife." Echo has been most skilfully used to give volume to certain speeches and to suggest the resounding alarm in Brabantio's house when Iago and Roderigo summon him by night. But Mr. Val Gielgud's gallant attempt has been made upon the impossible. *Othello* is not a play for broadcasting – if only because, even when abbreviated, it lasts more than two hours, and two hours is a long sitting to a blind playgoer. Joan and Betty's Bible Story from Cardiff ought not to have been so long postponed.

5 APRIL 1932, THE TIMES

Othello by William Shakespeare

ST. JAMES'S THEATRE

OTHELLO	Ernest Milton
IAGO	Henry Oscar
RODERIGO	George Thirlwell
BRABANTIO	Frederick Culley
CASIO	Nicholas Hannen
DESDEMONA	Lydia Sherwood
EMILIA	Athene Seyler
BIANCA	Flora Robson

This is as bold and challenging a production of *Othello* as has been seen in our time, and will stir up inevitably all the fires of controversy. Mr. Ernest Milton is a man who, being at root an artist, has never played for safety; now, as producer and actor, he takes every imaginable risk. There will be voices to say that as an actor he has failed, and this we shall presently discuss, preferring meanwhile to say only that he does by certain extravagances of gesture, of manner, and voice prejudice the virtues, let us call them rather than the splendours, of his own performance. Judgment of his acting will depend upon the emphasis that we lay upon these extravagances – whether they appear to us as superficial faults of manner or as errors of spirit, corrupting the interpretation of character itself. This is what is in debate. Let us consider meanwhile what is certain.

First, the production, for which Mr. Milton himself is responsible, is vital and ardent. In its opening scene appear the two actors whose success is beyond question – Mr. George Thirlwell, who saves Roderigo from being a fantastick and makes him a creature lively with comic spirit, and Mr. Henry Oscar, whose Iago is a remarkably complete and satisfying treatment of the part. From that opening the play moves forward with excellent clearness and vigour, maintaining always the story's shape, laying emphasis where emphasis points the narrative and not where the producer bethought him of a producer's trick. Mr. McKnight Kauffer's designs have beauty when one seeks them out; they have also the greater dramatic merit of allowing themselves to be forgotten in the play. Mr. Hannen's Casio, rich in humour, various in mood, is an admirable portrait; Miss Athene Seyler's Emilia, never forced, never grasping for effect, reveals all the natural merits of a part that abounds in them; several of the lesser parts – Mr. Culley's Brabantio, for example, and Miss Flora Robson's Bianca – are exceptionally well played. The whole piece holds together, moves, is alive. Of this there can be no doubt. And though Mr. Henry Oscar, by definitely rejecting the Satanic interpretation of Iago, may provoke those who prefer it, he does establish his own view of this man – not as a giant of evil, but as a mean, thwarted, tormented creature, seeking his revenge upon life for what life – perhaps in his relations with women – has bitterly denied him. It is, on the material plane, supremely well done, and so the audience at curtain-fall had evidently decided. Of Mr. Oscar at least there was probably but one opinion.

Now let us face the controversy. First, the minor controversy of Desdemona, who seemed to us, by her appearance, miscast, but will not have seemed so to all. Her performance, weak and a trifle querulous at the outset, greatly improved towards the end, gathering balance and strength. Mr. Milton himself is a deeper problem. If any thought that an actor of his elaborate sensitiveness must fail in the soldierly splendours of the Moor, they were mistaken. When he is still, when dignity is his quest, when he is defending himself in Venice or reproving Casio's outbreak on the night of triumph, he is magnificent. Fire gleams in him then as in some dark, smouldering jewel. It is in his rages of jealousy and in his love for Desdemona that the difficult challenge comes. He fawns upon Desdemona sometimes with the fawning of a weak man not of Othello's weakness, and in his rage he yields himself to gestures, to a rolling of the eyeballs, to a circular movement of the head that are in peril of bringing his passion into ridicule. These extreme manifestations of feeling have possible justifications in the text; Desdemona herself speaks of the eyeballs; and in an age less accustomed to naturalism in acting they would seem less extravagant than they do to-day. But they are perilous. If Mr. Milton would moderate them, the fire, the emotional brilliance, the imaginative range of his performance would not be impaired, and he would be protected from the effects of the uneasiness, the embarrassment, which is created in parts of his audience by hearing an actor uttering the cries of a tormented animal and seeing him fling himself, almost with relish, into the physical distortions of an epilepsy. The thing can be justified; it is the product of courage, of a passionate adherence to a great tradition of acting; but we believe it to be an error of judgment and, in its effect, a confusion of Mr. Milton's performance.

11 APRIL 1932, THE TIMES

The Miracle by Carl Vollmoeller

MUSIC BY ENGELBERT HUMPERDINCK AND OTHERS
LYCEUM THEATRE

THE NUN	Tilly Losch
THE ABBESS	Maud Allan
A CRIPPLE	Glen Byam Shaw
THE SPIELMANN	Leonide Massine
MADONNA	Diana Manners

Herr Reinhardt's production of *The Miracle* appeared, under the auspices of Mr. Cochran, at the Lyceum Theatre on Saturday night. As they will remember who saw it years ago in a yet more spacious setting, *The Miracle* is a mime play, expressing in pageantry, music, and dance the story of a young Nun who was lured from her vows by the temptations of a Spielmann. Before setting out upon her adventures in the world she snatches the Christ-child from the miraculous image of the Virgin that stands in the cathedral served by her convent. The Christ-child vanishes; the Virgin, coming down from her pedestal and leaving only her empty robe to mark where the image stood, assumes the duties of the errant nun; but when the Nun, broken and penitent, returns from her wanderings, the Virgin becomes an image again, standing with empty arms. The penitent's dead baby supplies this emptiness and is miraculously transformed into the original image of the infant Jesus. That, with the Nun's carnal progress to provide unecclesiastical interludes, is the story, which may be interpreted as you please.

It is told in a playhouse which has been converted to look as much like a cathedral as possible. Even by those who feel that this particular effort was inevitably made in vain it will be acknowledged that the conversion has been well done. The architectural detail is often beautiful; the stone looks solid and has the texture of stone; and if the presence of our alien selves, the interruption to design of a rectangular proscenium opening, and, above all, a pervasive sense of something strained and false and theatrical, removes this cathedral farther from the Gothic aspiration than the Lyceum unadorned might have been, that is not the fault of the fibrous plaster manufacturers. And it is true that these tricks played with the auditorium add to the interest of the affair regarded as a spectacular pageant. As such it is best to regard it, for so – by ruling out spiritual values from consideration – we may freely praise it. Mr. Messel's costumes have an extraordinary splendour; the scenery, designed by Professor Strnad, though sometimes prejudiced by a weak employment of transparencies, generally combines richness of colour with imaginative dignity of form; the processional crowds and the whole movement and grouping of the stage have been skilfully used by Herr Reinhardt to express the course of the narrative. With what effect a crowd can be used and how masterly is Herr Reinhardt's timing of emotional emphasis may be observed when a cripple, brought into the cathedral on a litter, draws all eyes – and the inclination of all bodies – to him as he miraculously receives his strength. A great part of the credit for that scene is Mr. Glen Byam Shaw's, but he owes to Herr Reinhardt and Mr. Messel a brilliantly regulated background.

Mr. Leonide Massine's choreography is seen at its best when its mood has gaiety and light – for example, at the opening of a scene in a forest, before it takes on a tragic colour; and his own dancing as the Spielmann has a genuine power to excite which fails only when, being used in excess, it is dissipated in violence. Miss Tilly Losch is a lovely dancer and is uniformly successful except when what is demanded of her lies outside her temperament. In the vocation of her Nun it was never possible to believe. The world was in her eye, in the carriage of her head, and in her vital, springing walk from the moment of her first entrance, and her penitent return to the cathedral was scarcely more persuasive. Her strength like that of the play itself, lies in the world. In the robes of a nun, she is "dressed up"; out of them, she is a creature of natural brilliance and fire – a glittering decoration of the pageant.

A pageant *The Miracle* is, and one could praise its splendours with a less divided mind if it claimed to be no more. But it does lay claim to a spiritual beauty not of this world, and the claim is false. The cathedral is impressive if we forget cathedrals; the ceremonies if we forget their original; the music if, yielding to the solemnities of its organ or rejoicing in the contrasted gaiety of its pipes, we do not remember how, by the chanting of male voices unaccompanied, it might be reduced to emotional insignificance. The play is full of ingenious substitutes for truth which, like the electric bulbs that do service for candles, are enemies of the spirit while decorative of the substance. Its attitude seems to be that of one who chiefly values the life of the cloister as a pale background to the action of the world, and it is always in danger – as in the Nun's scourging and crucifixion – of throwing out hysterical challenges not to be sustained. One thing stands apart from and above it: the Lady Diana's representation of the Virgin. There are long passages during which a wise man will look at nothing but this glowing stillness, this superb passivity in which all action is gathered up and transcended. It is as if coming in from a hot, turbulent street, one rested coolly before the picture of a master.

27 JUNE 1932, THE TIMES
ARTS THEATRE CLUB

Richard of Bordeaux by Gordon Daviot

NEW THEATRE

RICHARD II	John Gielgud
ANNE OF BOHEMIA	Gwen Ffrangçon-Davies
DUKE OF GLOUCESTER	Sam Livesey
MICHAEL DE LA POLE, Chancellor	H. R. Hignett
ROBERT DE VERE, Earl of Oxford	Robert Harris
THOMAS MOWBRAY	Anthony Ireland
AUMERLE	Anthony Quayle
ARCHBISHOP OF CANTERBURY	Reyner Barton

By virtue of its subject, which is material for great tragedy, and of the seriousness with which that subject is treated, this play, which was performed at the New Theatre last night and will be repeated there next Sunday, can justly claim the attention of playgoers who are weary of nothingness in the theatre and eager for dramatic challenge to an adult mind. Such plays are now so rare, and provide, even in their faults, a pleasure so much greater than any to be wrung out of mechanical clap-trap that there is a temptation to accept the will for the achievement and write only of the good in them. But the author, whose name must now be given as Gordon Daviot, is evidently not of a quality to require that kind of leniency. The whole claim of the work is to serious criticism, which by its own merits it is abundantly entitled to receive.

Its purpose is no less than to give a new interpretation of the most mysterious and subtle of the Shakespearean Kings. Mr. Gielgud, whose representation of Richard II in another play presides over the present stage like a beautiful ghost, represents him again – first as an idealist for peace, allied in vision with Anne, his Queen; then, after the destruction of his early friends, as a man grown fiercer and more vigorous, but held to his ideal and restrained from rashness by Anne's influence; finally, after her death, as a King who, partly because the vanity of rule appeals to him but chiefly because her influence is gone, gives rein to vindictive arrogance and rides to disaster. The interpretation is, in a work of art, legitimate whether or not we believe that, in history, Anne played the part assigned to her on the stage. There are indications in the dialogue that the author imagines in the King a view of the Constitution that he can scarcely have had. "The Constitution says that the king is law," does not sound like Richard's claim to absolutism. Let it pass. Nor shall we complain of colloquialism, for it is used plainly and easily, not for the tricky purpose of winning anachronistic guffaws. "If only I could trust them, Anne, like I trust you," is a little hard to bear, but bearable. There are, in brief, details that need amendment, but the play is broken by the need.

It has three general disadvantages. First it struggles on from scene to scene, and is sometimes betrayed, conspicuously in the Council Chamber, by what, in terms of dramatic effect, are repetitions. Second that, if we are to accept Anne's death as the turning-point in Richard's life, Anne must be more than the clinging, affectionate creature which is all she can become within the scope of Miss Ffrangçon-Davies's opportunity. Third, that Richard himself, though the outline of his character is firmly drawn and the chief stages of its development are clearly marked, does not go deep enough. Here the Shakespearean challenge is destructive. We may, indeed, differ from Shakespeare, but plain statement will not serve as a sufficient weapon. Mr. Gielgud plays the part richly and brilliantly, but he has no chance to get far below the visible surface of Richard's changing moods. His weariness of government, his philosophic perception of the vanity of power is briefly spoken of; it is not searched or communicated; it is not felt; and for that reason Richard is more interesting in his actions – his contest with Mr. Livesey's rough Gloucester, his gentleness to Mr. Hignett's gentle de la Pole, his fierceness against Mr. Harris's repentant Oxford when Oxford has betrayed him – than in his thought. And yet it is true in history, and is implied even in the play itself, that the core of Richard was in his mind. This is the cause of the impression of incompleteness, of something intended but not expressed, which one receives from the evening; but the evening, in spite of this defect, is worth a year of frivolous avoidances.

Loyalties by John Galsworthy

GARRICK THEATRE

CHARLES WINSOR	A. R. Whatmore
FERDINAND DE LEVIS	Oliver Raphael
GENERAL CANYNGE	Cecil Ramage
MARGARET ORME	Cathleen Nesbitt
CAPTAIN RONALD DANCY	Colin Clive
AUGUSTUS BORRING	Jack Minster
LORD ST. ERTH	Paul Gill
JACOB TWISDEN	Lawrence Hanray

It is not impossible that, in the distant future, when they have ceased to play *Money* with an all-star cast at the nobler charity *matinées*, they may promote *Loyalties* to its place. It deserves a happier fate, for, in spite of a certain stiffness that the years reveal, it is free of the elaborate air of impartiality that causes some of Mr. Galsworthy's work to resemble a scolding by too just a parent, and it tells a good story with economy and precision. But its very virtues mark it down for the splendid massacre of the *matinées*, its cast being a team without a tail. They can all score, even down to the club footman with his news of – was it the Cambridgeshire? Old Sir Timothy Tompkins, still the darling of the gods in 1982 though his voice doesn't reach them, will appear with impressive modesty as Treisure the butler, and Dame Daisy Deadwood, who entered the chorus in 1932, will play – well, they will have to provide Mabel Dancy with an ancient nurse to hold her hand, for Mr. Galsworthy has made no provision for old ladies. And perhaps 50 years hence there will still be someone in the stalls who will lean across to his neighbour and say that the original cast of *Loyalties* was one of the best ever seen in London, adding that Mr. Ernest Milton's De Levis –. It is a little hard on those who come after him that, whoever plays De Levis, Mr. Milton will always receive good notices next morning.

Discussion of *Loyalties* has, in brief, come to mean a discussion of the acting, which, on this occasion, is a mixed benefit. This Jew who, with right on his side, finds himself opposed to the clannishness of a society determined to protect one of its members is, it is true, necessarily theatricalized by his isolation, but Mr. Oliver Raphael represents him with the wrong kind of theatricalism, making him puffed up and extravagant, but failing altogether to suggest the tragic and formidable dignity of the man. This De Levis is always at a disadvantage. Whether it be in the country house or in the card-room or at his last entrance, he is struggling to assert himself without an inner consciousness of power. This upsets the play's balance, and good performances by Mr. Paul Gill, Mr. Whatmore (whose words are sometimes indistinct), Mr. Cecil Ramage, and Miss Cathleen Nesbitt do not serve to restore it. The best of the play, though

Mr. Colin Clive's performance is an admirable one, is to be seen in the lawyer's office aside from the main battle. Mr. Frederick Piper is here a welcome invasion; Mr. Jack Minster is a pleasantly discreet young lawyer (except when he covers the earpiece of a telephone to prevent his conversation in the room from being overheard); and Mr. Laurence Hanray, as the senior partner, is full of shrewd, quiet persuasive humour. In him his profession and his humanity are charmingly combined. You feel that he would intuitively cover the mouthpiece; and you hope that he enjoyed his tea the more for being drunk from a saucer.

20 SEPTEMBER 1932, THE TIMES

Caesar and Cleopatra by George Bernard Shaw

OLD VIC

A PERSIAN	Marius Goring
JULIUS CAESAR	Malcolm Keen
CLEOPATRA	Peggy Ashcroft
POTHINUS	Alistair Sim
ACHILLAS	Antony Quayle
RUFIO	Roger Livesey
BRITANNUS	Geoffrey Wincott
LUCIUS SEPTIMIUS	George Devine
APOLLODORUS	William Fox

It is almost an adventure in itself to find the Old Vic opening a new season with a play not by Shakespeare. Having chosen Mr. Shaw as an institutional alternative, the management have chosen well the piece to represent him. Not only does *Caesar and Cleopatra* give opportunity for the herald blasts upon wind instruments without which no curtain in the Waterloo Road can traditionally rise, but it is the swiftest and plainest narrative in the Shavian theatre. Even without its distinctively Shavian fal-lals, which happen to be few and good, it would stand by its power of story-telling and the continuously developed interest of its character-drawing. Britannus, it is true, comes out of the Shavian slot-machine, but even he, because Mr. Geoffrey Wincott, holding back from extravagant pomposity, has allowed him to be a human being as well as a butt, has now a lightness as welcome as it is unexpected. Indeed, Mr. Wincott had a good evening. He spoke the prologue of the god, Ra, with excellently serious wit, and his Britannus marvellously abstained from being a bore and became an entertainment instead.

A pardonable misjudgment, either in the actor himself or in Mr. Harcourt William's vigorous production, halted Julius Caesar, at his first entry, too far upstage, with the consequence that his preliminary address to Cleopatra's pet sphinx was in great part inaudible, but as soon as Mr. Malcolm Keen could be heard he began steadily, and without forcing, to draw out the humour in his part, presenting to us very clearly that identity between Caesar's wit and wisdom which is the essence of the man. There is something too harshly fuzzy-wuzzy about Miss Ashcroft's Egyptian hair-dresser; until custom softens the effects of his handiwork one seems to be looking at a grotesque doll; but the handicap – for it is a serious handicap, is overcome by the mental agility of Miss Ashcroft's performance. This is no doll when you get to know her, but a petulant child quick to her immediate advantage, shallow in long judgment, cruel as a kitten, dangerous in her follies. Not, let us say at once, a pleasant child, for she would have been at home in the highest Jamaican wind, but an engaging trickster with a spark of life fairly aglow in her.

These leading performances have support in the clear sketch of the time-serving Lucius Septimius by Mr. George Devine, a pleasant liveliness in Mr. William Fox's drawing of Apollodorus, and a performance of uncommon warmth and solidity by Mr. Roger Livesey as that loyal Rufio who, when Caesar promoted him, calling him his shield, asked of what use the shield would be if it were worn no longer upon Caesar's arm.

...

27 SEPTEMBER 1932, THE TIMES

The Left Bank by Elmer Rice

AMBASSADORS THEATRE

CLAIRE SHELBY	Mary Grew
JOHN SHELBY	Vernon Kelso
CLAUDE	Hugh E. Wright
SUSIE LYNDE	Sunday Wilshin
WALDO LYNDE	Martin Walker

It is, unfortunately, not possible for the English to burn their hearts for Claire Shelby who, being an American expatriate in Paris, yearned passionately to grow – unless our memory betrays the State or the vegetable – turnips in Kentucky. Our insular detachment from Mr. Rice's problem makes it difficult not to yawn unjustly at his play, which, if we could care a brass farthing whether Claire's husband lived on the left bank of the Seine or in Greenwich Village, would unquestionably reveal merits now obscure. For the clash between foreign and domestic ideals is not all the battle. There is a quadri-lateral exchange of wives and husbands to give encouragement to three Acts in a bedroom; there is a fourteenth of July celebration to enable Mr. Rice to show how sadly gay his countrymen may become in mass, in exile, and in drink; and there is a decrepit *valet de chambre* by Mr. Hugh E. Wright who is among the happier interruptions of the evening.

But Mr. Rice is not always blessed in his interpreters. Shelby is intended to be an ironic study of a vain and disappointed man, but Mr. Vernon Kelso, having begun well in that vein, drags him, and Miss Sunday Wilshin with him, away from irony towards farce. Miss Grew's emotional attack on the turnips was, for our taste, too strenuous and her gentler endearment too arch. Not, therefore, a well-balanced evening, though Mr. Martin Walker's performance, as a plain, shy, straightforward American to whom turnips were never a cause of rhetoric, had all the virtues elsewhere lacking – precise judgment of emotional transition, a genuine power to create interest in the character he represented, and, above all, an unerring sense of the difference between Mr. Elmer Rice and Dumas *fils*.

8 OCTOBER 1932, THE TIMES

Children in Uniform by Christa Winsloe

DUCHESS THEATRE

FRÄULEIN VON NORDECK, Headmistress	Cathleen Nesbitt
FRÄULEIN VON BERNBURG	Joyce Bland
MANUELA	Jessica Tandy
FRAU ALDEN, Dancing Mistress	Katie Johnson

Night after night, month after month, through all the sops and timidities and pretentiousness that are turning men and women of quality away from the theatre, one waits for such an evening as this, holding back from the carpentry that is without design, the flaccid, trumped-up passion that is without feeling, the glitter that is without warmth or fire. Holding back so long from the daily chorus of praises that one begins to ask if one's own faculty of delight is perished. But the reward, when it comes, is worth the vigil, and it came last night.

Children in Uniform springs from the same German source as the film, *Mädchen in Uniform*. Its scene is a boarding school for girls who are the daughters of noblemen and officers of the old regime. Germany will have need of the mothers of soldiers; they must submit to discipline now that in the days to come they may know how to suffer and to command. Under the rule of Fräulein von Nordeck they are being made into women of iron. Watching them at their drill, observing the brief, agonized delight of their recreation, seeing how, in common room and dormitory, all human tenderness has become for them intolerably precious and rare, one seems to be looking at flowers that are being slowly petrified by some dreadful spell.

The personal tragedy of Manuela is not personal only; it is the core of the tragedy of an idea. Her love for Fräulein von Bernburg, this young mistress's love for her, the ruin that befalls them both in an organization where all individual distinctions are forbidden – these happenings, ending in the child's death, are as beautiful as they are terrible, but their significance is not in themselves alone. They speak the tragedy of a school, of a tradition, of an ideal; and that this ideal, which causes suffering so profound, is neither mean nor petty but endowed with the splendours of loyalty and self-discipline gives to the play a poignancy that reaches far beyond the range of dramatic anecdote.

It is not easy to praise the acting as it deserves to be praised, for Frau Sagan has, without trick or affectation, made an orchestra of her cast, and its excellence consists not chiefly in personal performances but in its collective power to communicate the unity of a work of art. Miss Cathleen Nesbitt, while exhibiting the harshness, interprets the reason of the headmistress. As the girl, Miss Jessica Tandy, though she has not the spiritual intensity that might pour the whole life of Manuela into a few scenes, gives a performance remarkable at once for the vitality of its impulse and the order of its emotional ascent. The wonder of a child and the first discoveries of a woman do not make perfect contact in this girl's portrait as Miss Tandy draws it, for she falls back now and then upon "type," seeming to lack, neither the energy nor the intelligence, but the poetry that must go to the full creation of this tormented child. Miss Joyce Bland's study of the young schoolmistress with her imprisoned tenderness and her very soul ridden on the curb is, on the contrary, flawless. But the emotion of the play does not depend on any one or on all three of these performances. It rises naturally and continuously from a source very deep in the theme and the form. Only to those who know its outline without having discovered its spirit can this story seem morbid or hysterical. It has that quality of glowing fierceness, of tears wrung from the stone of experience, that is the mark of tragedy. It has too much wisdom to be bitter, and too much beauty to be cruel.

29 NOVEMBER 1932, THE TIMES

A Kiss in Spring
by Julius Brammer and Alfred Grünwald

DANCES AND BALLET BY FREDERICK ASHTON
THE ALHAMBRA

Leaders of the Ballet

Alicia Markova
Harold Turner
Prudence Hyman
Walter Gore

The discreet will visit the Alhambra after a very late dinner, arriving in time for a brief, preliminary entrance of the ballet near the end of the second act. They will then possess themselves in patience during the opening of Act

III, and be abundantly rewarded when the ballet, led now by Mme. Markova and Mr. Harold, Turner comes into its own in the penultimate scene. All else in this lamentable tale of three artists, the street-singer, and a model is unspeakably dull – the music commonplace, the dialogue pointless, and the narrative a gush of pallid sentimentality.

But the ballet is genuine ballet, not the grotesque acrobatics that are too often substituted for it, and is a pleasure to watch. Not that, among ballets, this one is a masterpiece. Mr. Frederick Ashton's design and Mr. Herbert Griffith's music have had to conform in some degree to their setting, and the emotion that their work can produce is limited by circumstance. But within these limitations they have discovered a thing of minor beauty, decorative, charming, lively, and excellently well performed. Mme. Markova and Mr. Harold Turner bring the evening suddenly to life, fulfilling the promise of the ballet's first appearance, which was like a drop of rain in drought; and *the corps de ballet* itself has a grace and assurance that are plainly the outcome of a real devotion to its art. Even before the dance begins, while the revolving stage is conducting us from the Green Room to the front of the house, a glimpse of a few dancers waiting in the wings and framed by a door of plain yellow brick has in it the thrill of a Dégas. The dancers themselves may fall short of that thrill, being a trifle too conciliatory in their attack, but they are the work of artists, and that is enough to say in this sorry world.

6 JANUARY 1933, THE TIMES

Fresh Fields by Ivor Novello

CRITERION THEATRE

LADY LILIAN BEDWORTHY	Lilian Braithwaite
LADY MARY CRABBE	Ellis Jeffreys
MRS. PIDGEON	Minnie Rayner
UNA PIDGEON	Eileen Peel
TOM LARCOMB	Fred Groves
LADY STRAWHOLME	Martita Hunt

This piece justifies the surprising originality of its title by refusing firmly, and with entertaining consequences, to see the wood for the trees. As wood, field or pasture, as a unity of any sort, it is flagrantly unpersuasive, but as an aggregate of absurdities it is rewardingly absurd. Mr. Novello, in brief, having taken an irresponsible holiday, has had the wit to communicate his enjoyment of it.

Everything has appeared to him to be more than life size: the vulgarians who come from overseas to enjoy a London season, the pair of ducal daughters who receive them in their house, the clumsiness of the antipodean maiden who breaks the china and kicks over the what-nots, the rapidity of aversion's change to love, the heartiness with which aristocracy and democracy fraternize at the final curtain. And when once Mr. Novello has said that the farcical extremes of Brisbane and Belgravia may be amusingly exhibited under a single roof, he has said all he has to say. For this reason the scene in which the statement is first made is to be preferred to those that follow it, and if one were foolish enough to meditate on the thinness of the theme one might fear a tiresome evening. But the evening is not tiresome. The wood, as a wood, may not be either satisfying or various, but there are some cheerful trees to be encountered by the way. There is, for example, a little piece of elaborated misunderstanding between the maiden, who has broken a statuette, and the sympathetic lady who misinterprets her confession; there is another piece of elaborately mocked sentiment between an icy aristocrat and a rough, impetuous lover who is determined to melt the ice; and there are other fragments of the same kind. They are verbally dextrous and theatrically effective; there are enough of them to provoke an audience to good, and often to boisterous, humour.

Moreover each performer plays his or her particular stroke with an admirable combination of lightness and energy. Miss Braithwaite and Miss Jeffreys, with Miss Martita Hunt's assistance, play for the aristocrats and play with style; Mr. Fred Groves exhibits, with gracious roughness, a heart of gold; Miss Minnie Rayner bounces her jokes with enthusiasm, and Miss Eileen Peel is charming among the fragments of porcelain.

7 JANUARY 1933, THE TIMES

Dinner at Eight
by George S. Kaufman and Edna Ferber

PALACE THEATRE

MILLICENT JORDAN	Irene Vanbrugh
DORA	Jane Baxter
GUSTAVE	Ivan Brandt
OLIVER JORDAN	Tristan Rawson
PAULA JORDAN	Margaret Vines
CARLOTTA VANCE	Laura Cowie
DAN PACKARD	Lyn Harding
KITTY PACKARD	Carol Goodner
LARRY RENAULT	Basil Sydney

Has Miss Irene Vanbrugh ever before been thus accelerated? If any are in doubt of the value of craftsmanship to an artist, here is their answer. Miss Vanbrugh responds brilliantly to the producer's pedal; her acceleration is smooth and faultless; one hears every word, and, if a leisurely English mind could jump fast enough, one would understand every word she speaks. As it is, Mr. Kaufman having his foot on the gas, one leans back and hopes for the best. Miss Vanbrugh, an American hostess, is inviting guests to attend a dinner-party a week hence. In the final scene they assemble, making the conglomerate noise of dinner-parties assembling. Meanwhile, with the eye of the cinematographic camera, we peer swiftly and curiously into their private lives. The pace, set by Miss Vanbrugh at the originating telephone, never slackens. Click, click, click – how we admired this method when it was first applied to detective drama! In serious investigations of the soul, it is magnificent but a little comfortless. To speak seriously, Mr. Kaufman has produced his play, in England and for England, just 20% too fast. It is not pleasing to bolt good wine.

And the wines are good. The glimpse we have of the kitchen, where Miss Baxter, Mr. Brandt, and Mr. Leslie Perrins pursue their detached, triangular passion, is an illuminating one. In the doctor's consulting-room, where his wife comprehends his straying affections, Mr. Martin Lewis gives an ingenious sketch of the man, and Miss Susan Richmond, with yet scantier material, a yet more satisfying portrait of the woman. Miss Vanbrugh is, thank heaven, Miss Vanbrugh, and never has she performed a more rapid or more successful adaptation of her qualities: while Mr. Tristan Rawson, a man of business shadowed by the depression, is pleasantly depressed. Miss Laura Cowie, too, represents with dash and colour an actress in flamboyant decay. But the life of the play is in two scenic groups. One has its centre in Mr. Basil Sydney, a film star in decline, with whom Miss Margaret Vines is vainly and passionately in love. The core of the other is the conjugal quarrel conducted by Mr. Lyn Harding and Miss Carol Goodner.

Mr. Sydney, drunk or sober, communicates Larry Renault's disillusionment with bitter intensity. Miss Vines, having a part with a sharp edge to it, uses it as a knife with which to strike to the heart of her scenes. Mr. Harding and Miss Goodner develop a bicker into a fight, and a fight into a tumult, with a passion and a control of passion that are equally to their credit. While these are on the stage, the play is progressive and alive. When they are not, the play is still violently progressive. One is in an express train. The scenes flash past. "Stop," one cries, "that was beautiful!" or "Stop, let us know more!" "Nonsense," Mr. Kaufman answers. "This speed, this rocking violence, this incompleteness, is the rhythm of the life I seek to represent." Perhaps he is right.

Modern Acting

I. Ahead of the Authors

A NEW TURN FROM TRADITION

" When I was young," wrote Swift, "I thought all the world, as well as myself, was wholly taken up in discoursing upon the last new play" – a delightful error, for it is a good world that talks of art, not of wars and money, and one into which it may soon be possible to fall again. A few years ago it had ceased to be a custom to use the theatre as text in the discussion of ideas, the stage having lost touch with contemporary thought. To go to a play was a diversion for a dull dinner-party unfitted for bridge, and after the play came supper, not debate. Next day the evening's entertainment was forgotten, never more to be spoken of, though at luncheon there might well be warm discussion of a novel or a film. The theatre, in brief, had lost caste; few of the better imaginative writers gave much thought to it; and the youthful Swifts of the twentieth century – the young men and women naturally critical of contemporary life and of the arts that might express it – did not discourse upon the last new play at all. Indeed, until it had run 100 nights and they were taken to it by an aunt who had preserved a habit of playgoing, they did not know it had been performed.

To-day conversation and dramatists are returning to the theatre. It is still very far from being in the intellectual foreground, but it is perceptibly advancing. In the recent past, when a good play did appear, all the noise of criticism would often fail to draw an audience to it in time; it would die of high rents before it found the discriminating support that should have saved it. Intelligent audiences had been bitten so often that they were shy even to despair; it seemed that they had put the theatre out of their lives and were no more watchful even for what might please them. They are shy still, but they are awake – awake enough to bring such a piece as Chlumberg's *Miracle at Verdun* from the Embassy to central London, to fill the drawing-rooms with talk of *Le Viol de Lucrèce*, and to turn into a popular success *Children in Uniform*, which has neither love story nor happy ending nor greatly fashionable star, which has indeed nothing to recommend it except that it is a profoundly moving tragedy, beautifully performed and produced. Here at last are plays to "discourse upon." So, gradually, the theatre is resuming its place. A new dramatist of the first rank who arose now would be met with challenge, not indifference. For a few nights there might be hesitation; his audience is still a little remote and cautious; but it is alive again and watchful; it would fill his theatre in time to hold his play.

But the English, it is said, have always been more interested in acting than in plays. Were there not decades in Queen Victoria's time during which, though actors flourished whose names still endure, there were almost no plays of quality but Shakespeare's, and these garbled? So barren was the dramatist's patch, so dusty with adaptation and burlesque, that even Tom Robertson, who was no great master, had, when he appeared, the freshness and the welcome of rain after drought. Does it not follow, then, the argument proceeds, that, if the theatre languishes in our own time, the fault is in the acting? "If there were an Irving or a Terry, the theatre would be alive enough!" And they tell us mournfully that to cry out for dramatists is to cry in vain, for, they say, of what use would a dramatist be with this set of mumbling players to interpret him? "There's not a great personality anywhere – not one man of them all that can send a thrill through the house as Irving did."

That is the indictment, and it is because I believe it to be false, and false for a special reason connected with the art of playwriting, that I have prefaced this discourse upon contemporary acting with a preliminary discourse upon plays and the prestige of the theatre. It is true that Irving could produce his peculiar effect with material no better than *The Bells* or *The Lyons Mail*, but it does not follow that, because no one to-day can do likewise, modern actors are to be condemned. There are men on the stage now who pursue the Irving tradition. Though they may not be Irvings, they would have been thought greatly more of in his day than they are in ours, for we are inclined to think of them as ranters and limelight men who commit, or struggle to commit, the crime, which was once a virtue, of violent self-assertion in season and out. Such an actor would break down the whole composition of *The Cherry Orchard* or of any play written and produced in obedience to the collective, the unifying principle that Stanislavsky has established, and it is as well to recognize – though some may regret – that the same principle, though it cannot cancel out the pre-eminence of the Prince of Denmark, as a powerful influence on modern productions of *Hamlet*. Whether we like it or not, the art of acting has become more contributory than it was, and the light of genius is to be displayed not in dazzling an audience, but in its power to diffuse itself throughout the stage and, by its subtle transcendence, to illumine the whole play, the collective histrionic act. This, of course, is true neither of the actress who is called upon to die in *La Dame Aux Caméllias* nor of the actor who finds himself the hero of the polite melodramas that are deliberately written round a star part. Here it is necessary to be a romantic individualist or nothing. But such plays are outside the main current of dramatic advance, not at all because modern theatrical technique is superior to that of the past, but because the contemporary world has ceased to think in terms of heroic individualism

LIMITING THE ACTOR

It is within this frame of circumstance that modern acting must represent and interpret the twentieth century, and it is useless to cry out: "An Irving, a man of genius would break the frame if it suited him! An artist creates his own circumstances." Writers may, painters may, but not actors. Nothing but pen and ink stands between a writer and the expression of what is in him; there are no rules he may not break, no prejudices he may not overcome, for he chooses his own material. An actor does not. Though he own a theatre, he must play what he can find; generally, he must play what he is told. And if, as I believe, a modern actor cannot, and ought not to, revert, except on rare occasions, to the spectacular individualism of the past, if he must diffuse his light throughout a whole work of art instead of turning it, like the beam of an electric torch, upon his own face, it follows that there must be something for him to illumine.

It is precisely for this reason that Shakespeare can be played in the modern manner and Henry Arthur Jones cannot. In Shakespeare there is something to illumine which such an actor as Mr. Gielgud can discover to us by the use of his own style, not by the surrender of it; but in Jones there is little but an opportunity to let off fireworks of the Jones design. The misfortune of our stage for several years has not been a deterioration of acting, but of an ill-adjustment between the development of acting and of English dramatic authorship. The majority of modern plays offered to actors as commercial material have been degenerate inheritors, with an admixture of American blood, from Sardou or Dumas or Wilde. To these the best of young modern acting is unsuited. Miss Edith Evans by a brilliant transition can leap farther back – to Congreve and his Millamant; Mr. Coward and Miss Gertrude Lawrence could presumably play Wilde if Mr. Allan Aynesworth were there to insist upon the importance of being blandly unconscious of one's own epigrams; modern actors are by no means incapable of historical *tours de force*. But the theatres of Sardou and Dumas and all that they begat, though modern acting will live in them if need be, are not the soil in which contemporary interpretive genius can flourish.

I take leave to differ from the sad gentlemen who don't know what modern acting is coming to and whose lamentations for the past prevent them from discovering good in the present and future. No lesson is more vigorously rubbed into a regular playgoer than that modern acting, though sometimes disgracefully dilute with fashionable amateurism is in advance of its material. To show that it is prepared to take the opportunity which may now be coming to it, to criticize its defects and examine its range and principles, above all to suggest its merits with modern instances, shall be the purpose of the article that follows.

Modern Acting

II. A Clash of Styles

"STAGE CENTRE" AND "WHOLE STAGE"

If it be true, as was suggested in an earlier article, that the present tendency of English acting is away from heroic and romantic individualism towards a style that defuses itself throughout the play, it is true also that this tendency is by no means universal, and cannot be, as long as many dramatists and a large section of the public that loves the domination of a star remain opposed to it. The position is, therefore, one of conflict between two styles which may, perhaps, be best defined as the style that concentrates on the Stage Centre and the style that is based upon a continuous imagining of the Whole Stage. To actors of the former school, a play divides itself into a rapid succession of scenes in which first one actor, then another, "has the stage." To actors of the Whole Stage school, a play is a unity, a continuous process, a chain whose strength depends not on its strongest but on all its links.

To say that this divergence of styles is a plain conflict between self-assertion and contributory team-work would be to give a false impression of its nature and to substitute for criticism an uncomprehending sneer. None but a fool in a coterie sneers at Irving or scorns him as a "selfish" player; as well sneer at the "selfishness" of Mr. Ernest Milton's superb entrance and mounting of the throne in *Enrico Quattro*, or at Miss Compton's Ophelia, so lovely in madness that the whole play of Hamlet stands still for her, or to Miss Dorothy Green when she walks through the night of Lady Macbeth. There are occasions when the Stage Centre cries out for brilliant, concentrated illumination; there is a legitimate, a magnificent style – Irving's, if you will – that seeks those occasions and, finding not enough, creates them. Nor is it at all true to say of many of the adherents of the old-style that they are selfish; on the contrary, they are often enabled by their superior technical equipment to build up a scene by joint action more successfully than their younger rivals.

TEAM AND TALENT

Miss Irene Vanbrugh is an actress with a flawless technical equipment; a critic, and particularly a critic young enough to incline towards the Whole Stage school, does well to correct his standards by her, for her acting is like cut crystal, as clear and as decisive. In brief, she takes the centre of the comic stage with a dazzling grace. But, like all the leading players of her own school – like Du Maurier, Aynesworth, Cellier, Aylmer, to mention but four of those who, differing in all else, are at one in technical precision – she is a team-worker in the special sense that she contributes to a scene continually, when all but the professional sections of the audience are least aware of her, by the unobtrusive accuracy of what was once called deportment – the minor arts of sitting down, of standing up, of giving or receiving a cup of tea, above all of being still, which are nowadays too little cared for. When young Miss X sits down on the sofa to wait, it is ten to one that she will draw attention to herself and away from the key action of the scene by some ungainliness in her attitude or by fiddling with her cigarette. Miss Vanbrugh will never do that; Miss Tempest, though she knows all there is to be known about the Stage Centre, will never do it except with naughtiness aforethought and the licence of genius; Miss X does it because she knows no better.

For this reason a young actor declares nothing but his own ignorance who, because his own aesthetic purpose is not the same with Cellier's or Aynesworth's, says that these actors, even at their best, have nothing to teach him. He is as the heathen are who, dabbling piously, hope to paint like Cézanne for no better reason than they cannot draw like Ingres. All masterly acting in whatever style teaches acting to them that have ears to hear and eyes to see. From Miss Haidee Wright's nurse in Strindberg's *The Father,* a performance so charged with pity and terror that it wrote Aristotle's phrase anew for our generation, what might not a young actress have learnt of attack and restraint, of pathos, tenderness, and cruelty, of the head's carriage and the voice's control – lessons applicable not to Strindberg's tragedy only but, in differing degrees, to the whole range of an actor's art?

MR. SEYMOUR HICKS

There are, no doubt, playgoers who, not having thought very much, think lightly of Mr. Seymour Hicks. Is he proposed as a model in the dramatic schools, except to the young gentleman seeking a diploma in farce? How much more he is than a buffoon may be seen by comparing him with a multitude of actors, some good, some bad, whose receding chins and foreheads are their principal fortune. He has a power, now exceedingly rare, to establish himself at once. "There's Hicks!" – and instantly the stage is aglow. Sometimes he gets the bit between his teeth; we know that he is improvising, and lean back in alarm and delight; it is not on these occasions that he is to be recommended to candidates for gold medals. But the greater part of his acting – if for no other reason than that his timing is the most perilous and faultless in the contemporary theatre – will teach tragedy and comedy as well as farce if the student is not too intoxicated by the risk to enjoy the perfection. Even in a stupid play a Hicks performance at its best has the thrill of a dance on the edge of a chasm; he seems to be enjoying himself too much to remember the abyss. In a moment, you say, he will be lost! But he is safe, being Hicks, for, like Sasha Guitry, he can, if necessary, dance upon the air.

To turn from these long-established leaders of the stage without speaking of more than the few who have already been discussed would be impossible without unreason in any formal analysis of the English theatre. There are a dozen others – Miss Thorndike, Mr. Ainley, Mr. Loraine, Mr. Nicholas Hannen. Mr. Baliol Holloway, Mr. Godfrey Tearle – upon whose various art an essay might profitably be written. That none may suppose me to be compiling a private order of merit, I have said nothing of Mrs. Patrick Campbell, and shall, in discussing a generation younger than hers, say nothing of Miss Ffrangçon-Davies or of Mr. Marshall and Miss Edna Best. Names have been used to illustrate general arguments, not in the selection of a representative team. So I shall continue to use them.

It is a little late to speak of Mr. Cedric Hardwicke and Mr. Leslie Banks as though they were newcomers, but their art is so progressive, so alive to new ideas and influences, that one inevitably thinks of the quickness of their minds rather than of the solidity of their fame. They are, like Mr. Hannen, invaluable instances of command in both styles. Give Mr. Hardwicke the centre of the stage and he can dominate his audience as he did in *The Apple Cart*, but even when to dominate is his purpose his method is always persuasive and intellectual rather than declamatory; he creates illusion by undermining our disbelief, not by overwhelming it in spectacular emotional assault, and so proves that, even when the fluid, whole-stage tradition of Tchehov has made more headway among our dramatists than it has at present, his name will still be among the first to be hopefully written down by the selector of any permanent company of actors. Mr. Banks has a lighter touch, but his introspective acting is even more subtle than Mr. Hardwicke's.

MISS EDITH EVANS

Miss Edith Evans may not inspire the same solid confidence as these two, but almost the worst that can be said of her is that, unlike Mr. Hardwicke, who moves comfortably from Shakespeare's grave-digger to Shaw's Caesar, she may easily be miscast. Her Millamant is unlikely to be surpassed in our time; her study of Lady Utterword in *Heartbreak House*, Mr. Shaw's contribution to the Russian drama, stakes her claim in the whole-stage theatre; and she has what is rarer in her own than in a writer's profession – the genius of revision and self-teaching. There was a time when an intonation of mannered elegance, brilliantly successful in plays of the Restoration, threatened her elsewhere, but she is now fully mistress of it, using and rejecting it at will. At Oxford last year it twisted her opening phrases; then, suddenly, she threw it off and played Juliet's Nurse with an entrancing power to lose and newly find herself in the character she represented.

Many of the younger players of high accomplishment are hard to follow critically. Some are lost to sight for months in a box-office comedy; others vanish into Hollywood's remote glory. Mr. Charles Laughton, who, in *The Silver Tassie*, confirmed his place in the theatre of the future and has an imaginative intensity too rare to squander on the macabre, has done with Nero and is soon to be on the stage again. Miss Diana Wynyard also is returning from America, and a wise choice of parts – they are now hers to choose so far as they exist – may be of genuine importance to the theatre. Though she has, among her near contemporaries, an unrivalled equipment in looks, physique, and experience, she has not yet, in London, been greatly tested. No discerning playgoer who has watched her in polite comedy, in which she has established herself as a popular actress and a leader of the fashionable stage, has doubted that it is very far within her range. The time has now come for her to look beyond it.

The more one studies the younger generation of actors, the more one is persuaded that what holds them back, or drives them to the film studios, is a lack of plays to give their merit continuously developing opportunity. To the great majority of playgoers Mr. Robert Donat is probably little known, but in a couple of performances sometime ago – since when he has vanished – he made so distinguished a mark that there is no very young actor with a future of greater interest. Mr. Robert Douglas, Miss Marie Ney, Miss Ashcroft, Miss Alison Leggatt, Miss Jean Forbes-Robertson, Mr. Ralph Richardson, Miss Margaret Vines, Miss Fabia Drake, and Mr. Maurice Evans have all done something more than seize the chances that have been given them; they have proved themselves imaginative and creative actors who stand in need of modern pieces of the first rank that shall give them scope.

REVEALING PLAYS

One such play, *Children in Uniform,* written in the fluid, contributory style, has been enough to establish the names of two actresses – Miss Joyce Bland and Miss Jessica Tandy – whose quality might otherwise have been long unrecognized, and to enrich the repute of a third, Miss Cathleen Nesbitt. *Musical Chairs,* whose author's early death has robbed the theatre of a brilliant expectation, threw new light on Mr. Frank Vosper and Miss Carol Goodner. If more chances such as these were substituted for the dreary round of commercial comedy and farce there would be no outcry against modern acting. Nine-tenths of the pieces that are produced in London are not, and do not pretend to be, any better than the routine stories in the magazine that one tosses aside during a railway journey. They are not written with an artist's purpose and cannot supply material to artists.

Miss Flora Robson's opportunities have begun to come to her, rather in Mr. Priestley's play than elsewhere, for Mr. Priestley has his finger on the collective nerve; but her great opportunity, which should be modern, is still before her. Meanwhile, having proved, even in burlesque, that she can use her hands, in slow gesture, as no other actress on the stage can use them, she might freeze the blood in *The Cenci* or *Macbeth.* But can she speak verse? We do not know. Can Miss Wynyard speak verse? We do not know that either. Of how perilously few young actors we know it! There are Miss Ashcroft and Miss Forbes-Robertson. There is Mr. Abraham Sofaer, whose whole personality is lighted and transformed by verse and who sends up one's hands again to the volume containing *The Cenci,* which, so far as the theatre is concerned, comes down so seldom from its shelf. And there is Mr. John Gielgud, who is a representative of so much in the youth of the theatre that all sins of omission may find pardon in an essay that ends on his name. He had mannerisms and has overcome them. He has natural genius which he reinforces continually with fresh accomplishment. To the centre of the stage, if the dramatist requires him to take it, he can summon all the glamour of tradition, but if the play is of a different sort, if it is not Shakespeare's Richard II, but *Musical Chairs*, he can discover a new emotional rhythm in it.

MR. GIELGUD'S EXAMPLE

While he is on the stage, employing either of two styles and marvellously reconciling them in one style that is his own, we need not lament for the past or fear for the future. His merit appears in nothing more conspicuously than in his ready understanding of the principles of the Left Wing and his steady avoidance of their errors in practice. Many of them fall into tiresome affectations of which he is free, for the Left Wing is an invitation to amateurs who will make a virtue of scorning the Stage Centre because they are incapable of holding it, and there are others, actors of genuine quality, who hate limelight and rhetoric so much that they have chosen, as bitter alternative, to mumble on a darkened stage.

To see and hear are the first requirements of an audience; a technique is valueless that does not satisfy them. Cherry Orchard acting, pure and undefiled, can be intolerably dreary unless the play itself is a work of genius – unless it has, like *The Cherry Orchard* itself, the effect of opposite mirrors reflecting themselves and their images in endlessly deepening repetition. Of such plays, applied to an interpretation of contemporary life, modern acting stands desperately in need. By them, through a poetic compression in which *The Silver Tassie* was an experiment, we may be led at last to discover a new aspect of romanticism, without which, in one or other of its many forms, the art of acting can never be in health.

14 MARCH 1933, THE TIMES

All God's Chillun Got Wings by Eugene O'Neill

EMBASSY THEATRE

JIM HARRIS	Paul Robeson
ELLA DOWNEY	Flora Robson

Mr. Eugene O'Neill's study of the marriage of a white woman with a negro, though not in itself among the best of his plays, gives high emotional opportunity to those who perform its principal parts. That its opening movements are slow and hesitant and that its strength, when strength comes, is not cumulative but violent and uneven, does not prevent it from being an extremely well-chosen piece to exhibit the powers of Mr. Paul Robeson and Miss Flora Robson.

Jim has an almost religious devotion to the woman he has married. For her sake he will endure all things – the alienation of his family, the breakdown of his ambition, even her madness in which love for the man and abhorrence of his colour emerge in direct opposition. The part requires not tragic acting of the first rank, for Mr. O'Neill's play is rather a series of brilliant notes for tragedy than tragedy developed and sustained, but a profound pathos. This Mr. Robeson is able to supply, having the simplicity that gives pathos its depth and the dignity that saves it from becoming hysterical declamation.

Miss Flora Robson's Ella is, as it must be, a more elaborate portrait. It exhibits with uncommon subtlety the many planes on which the girl's mind travels – the planes of affection and tenderness, of the instinctive contempt that begets fierceness, of the self-condemnation that will give her no peace – and it produces the effect of madness, through which recollections of sanity arise, by exhibiting these planes, not in turn but simultaneously. Miss Robson has power to turn this wretched woman's mind into glass so that the whole truth of her is visible, and to stain the glass with the changing colours of her longing, her suffering, and her insane escape.

13 MAY 1933, THE TIMES

The Day I Forgot
by Elsie Schauffler, from a novel by Mrs. Henry Dudeney

GLOBE THEATRE

ANDREW MCSHON	Sebastian Shaw
PENELOPE WILSON	Dorothy Hall
SIR JOHN MCKENZIE	Frank Cellier
AUNT GRACE	Charlotte Granville

The lady in this lamentable case was educated, or at any rate brought up, in America, betrothed in Coblenz, and, in the period intervening, scared out of her senses, or most of them, by an exceedingly unfortunate experience on Brighton beach. It was at Brighton, when she was 16 years old, that Penelope, having girlishly escaped from the panelled drawing-room through which her stupendous aunt was accustomed to stalk, went, still girlishly, to a supper party with two indubitable swells; of whom the first, Jacko, became benignly protective when he perceived how very girlish she was, while the second, Bobskie, did not. He knocked out Jacko with one hand, covered the lady's mouth with the other, and carried her off to the shingle, where, less girlishly, she plucked out the bowie knife which this military swell so surprisingly wore with a belt in evening dress, and slaughtered him.

Aunt Mabel, who seems to have heartily disliked the girl, persuaded Penelope that she had committed a crime that would stand between her and all possibility of happiness. She persuaded her also to forget the circumstances of her adventure, so that Penelope developed as she grew older an aunt-complex, a Brighton-complex, and other psychological embarrassments. This was her condition at Coblenz. On the verge of marriage with Andrew she was full of nameless dreads. Well, said the wise Sir John, you must go to Brighton and face them, and Andrew must go with you.

So there she is again in the panelled drawing-room all agog for Aunt Mabel's spectre in a red wig. She has a fit – or something more elegant but as effective – and, in it, carries us through gauze curtains into the past. Now and then, just to keep the present in tune, the gauzes disappear, and Andrew, kneeling by her couch, attempts to win her from her trance by protestations of love or snatches of Scottish song. Miss Dorothy Hall takes it all as seriously as can be, and, except when she had to exclaim, "I knew that to go to Brighton meant death," the audience on Friday night were for her sake more than tolerant. Mr. Frank Cellier and Mr. Sebastian Shaw did what England expects every man to do when he finds himself cast in a play that might have been written in a slightly Freudian dream by Little Lord Fauntleroy after a visit to *Mary Rose.*

16 JUNE 1933, THE TIMES
O.U.D.S.

Mid-Summer Night's Dream

PROFESSOR REINHARDT AS PRODUCER

HIPPOLYTA	Sanchia Robertson
HERMIA	Mary Gaskell
HELENA	Joan Maude
TITANIA	Oriel Ross
FIRST FAERY	Nini Theilade

Forsaking college gardens that Professor Max Reinhardt's production may have full range, the Oxford University Dramatic Society has chosen as the setting of its play a great meadow at Southbank, Headington. At the foot of the audience a bank rises sharply for some 20 yards, set with elm and beach and may. Beyond the great trees the incline is less. The prospect widens and flattens into what appears as a vast circle of grass, set about with distant woods.

In such a theatre there is nothing the faeries may not do. Puck may mock his victims from branches above their heads or from the swift invisibility offered him by a hole in the ground; Oberon's troop and Titania's, advancing from opposite woods, may meet by sudden chance and vanish, when their encounter is over, like the legions of a dream; from faraway, while the lovers in the foreground are disputing the confusions of the night, a solitary faery may come through the late dusk, come for no reason of ours and depart beyond our knowledge, having miraculous business of her own.

The customary emphasis of the play has thus been changed. No longer is it a story of mortals in this world behind whom an enchantment has arisen; it is a tale of sprites and goblins pursuing the natural life of their own dwelling place, into which men and women have blindly wandered. That it has been Professor Reinhardt's purpose to enforce this emphasis to create an illusion of immortal intimacy becomes increasingly clear as the evening passes and his lighting, which is masterly in its restraint and its gentle use of foliage, begins to have its full effect. At first there is an inclination to be over-jealous of the text, not because Bottom and his friends are too lavish in their amendment of it, for clowns must have license to gag, but because a passage of verse is gone that one misses, or because the virtue of Titania, and not of Titania alone, is in her movement and appearance rather than in the music of her words, and it remains conspicuously true to the end that individuals have been subordinated to the mass.

Miss Sanchia Robertson is a charming Hippolyta; Miss Mary Gaskell and Miss Joan Maude are allowed the opportunity of their quarrel; the men speak well and act lively. ... but still it is to the mass that one returns. The only outstanding individual is Miss Nini Theilade, and she is the first faery and the chief of all the dancers.

Through her and her companions, through Mendelssohn and his music, through the meadow and its woods and the glow of the concealed lights on the underbranches of giant trees, Professor Reinhardt exercises his influence. *A Midsummer Night's Dream* has never been more lovely to the eye, nor has it ever partaken more fully of the nature of a dream. The panic of his friends at the sight of Bottom translated has a superb flash of terror in it; the advance of the faeries when the sleeping lovers await their reconciliation is a brilliant enchantment. It would be childish to cavil at a line lost or a line added. The play has not been sacrificed to mere productionism. It has been freshly seen, freshly interpreted, and performed in accordance with its woodland circumstance and an artist's dominating idea. It is not flawless; the spoken poetry is sometimes weak, and the clowns have been dangerously given their heads; but at its peaks it is a production to take the breath away.

15 SEPTEMBER 1933, THE TIMES

Sheppey by W. Somerset Maugham

WYNDHAM'S THEATRE

ALBERT	Clive Morton
MISS GRANGE	Dorothy Hamilton
SHEPPEY	Ralph Richardson
BESSIE LEGROS	Laura Cowie
MRS. MILLER	Cecily Oates
FLORRIE	Angela Baddeley
ERNEST TURNER	Eric Portman
DR. JERVIS	Walter Fitzgerald

What would you have of the theatre? To see a dramatist not given to sentimentality, a master of his craft not clouded by the mists of the third floor-back, undertake a theme than which there is none greater – the pattern of Jesus in the contemporary world? There is no more that anyone may ask, and for an instant richer in expectation than any that the stage has yielded for many years it seemed that Mr. Somerset Maugham was to make this supreme attempt.

The craftsmanship of the first act was not in doubt. It told only that Sheppey, a hairdresser's assistant, had won £8,500 in the Irish sweepstake and that, overcome by excitement, he fainted or suffered some kind of stroke; but it established his character, it made him comprehensible and lovable, a good tradesman, a genial and honest man, no crank, no fool. And on the first act the second suddenly cast a fresh light. Sheppey, in his own home, took a new view of his wealth. He would not provide his wife with a housemaid, nor his daughter with a honeymoon in Paris, nor himself with the house he had so long coveted. He would not fulfil his worldly ambition by accepting a partnership in the barber's shop in Jermyn Street. Instead he would take into his house the harlot from the streets and the thief from the gutter and give all that he had to the poor. He had seen "a white light"; he looked now, in spite of the intellectual persuasions of his prospective son-in-law and the wild protests of his daughter, with an absolute simplicity to the Kingdom of Heaven. It looked as if the stroke that had fallen upon Sheppey in Jermyn Street had found him and Mr. Maugham on the road to Damascus.

But Mr. Maugham, having now but one act in which to discuss so prodigious a subject, turned into a by-path and took a shortcut home. His subject became not the life of the Gospel, nor a criticism of Sheppey's interpretation of it, but an ironic study of his family's self-protective resistance. The ironic study is, in all truth, bitter and brilliant – swerving now and then towards caricature in its treatment of the doctor who is to certify this giver away of wealth and guilty of an ugly twist towards dramatic hysteria (or over-compression) when the daughter, wringing her hands, runs about the room offering to forego sugar and cinemas if God will make the doctors "say that father is potty," but still a shrewd and terrible study of callous blindness, moving in its passionate indignation.

From the fate that the world has prepared for him Sheppey is rescued by death, and even his dialogue with this grey lady is written with so skilled a restraint and played with so quiet a dignity by Miss Cowie that it holds the stage. This, and Miss Cecily Oates's betrayal of her husband with a kiss, are scenes as perilous as any that a dramatist may risk, and Mr. Maugham's tact does not fail him. As a *tour de force* the play is from first to last astonishing. The hairdresser's shop gives sparkling opportunity to Miss Dorothy Hamilton; Miss Cowie, who represents the harlot as well as the lady in grey, supplies colour to the one as carefully as she withholds it from the other; Miss Baddeley and Mr. Eric Portman give hard, cruel sketches of two aspects of the world's resistance; except in the momentary hysteria of which we have spoken the play, as a piece for the theatre, does not waver.

But Sheppey and Mr. Richardson's performance of the part are the test of the play as something more than astute craftsmanship. Mr. Richardson with an artist's patience builds up little by little a character in whom the miracle of conversion is acceptable, a saint with his feet on earth. If we had been permitted to see the influence of this fool of God upon those whose lives had contact with his, if Mr. Maugham himself had stood firm for his sanity instead of giving loopholes to doubt, if the dramatic initiative had remained with Sheppey in his imitation of Christ, what a play this might have been! Mr. Richardson would have been equal to it; as it is, his performance is masterly. But Mr. Maugham has not written a play about a saint; he has written a play about the world's reluctance to part with its money, and has written it with fluency, judgment, and wit – with everything, indeed, except the supreme devotion that might have exchanged success for a masterpiece.

29 SEPTEMBER 1933, THE TIMES

Before Sunset by Gerhart Hauptmann

ENGLISH ADAPTATION BY MILES MALLESON
THE SHAFTESBURY THEATRE

PROFESSOR GEIGER	O. B. Clarence
BETTINA CLAUSEN	Joyce Bland
ERICH KLAMROTH	Charles Mortimer
HANNEFELTD	Felix Aylmer
MATTHEW CLAUSEN	Werner Krauss
INKEN PETERS	Peggy Ashcroft
MRS. PETERS	Clare Harris

It took a little time ... to recognize that Hauptmann's play is written in a convention to which the English theatre has become strange. Mr. Miles Malleson has done something to lighten the dialogue, but he has preserved, and rightly preserved, the essence of the dramatist's style. The play has in consequence a kind of emotional pomp and solemn intensity which need special treatment in performance, and this treatment is given in the lavishly passionate acting of Herr Krauss. In a climax he has a violence without modern parallel. The words pour from him; the stage and the theatre are flooded with sound; the noise itself, to leave aside for the moment every other consideration, is a shock. But the noise is regulated and deliberate. Sometimes the attack is a little too steep and Herr Krauss, having, so to speak, hit the roof too soon, can ascend no further; but for the most part his performance is remarkable for its power to lift the action onto a plane of theatrical emotion greatly higher than any to which we are accustomed, and to sustain it there without that sacrifice of inflexion and variety which is rant.

The tale is of an old man, Matthew Clausen, who discovers renascence in his love for a girl, Inken, his social inferior. His family are desperate in their opposition. Treating him not as an independent human being but as their possession, they refuse to speak with the girl or eat with her, and, when their father defies them, they seek to put him under restraint. In face of this threat, he dies. The theme has something in common with the theme of Strindberg's *The Father*. Obviously it might have been treated as a closely naturalistic psychological study, in which case the acting would have depended for its effects upon the strengths of understatement. Hauptmann, like Strindberg, has chosen otherwise. He has used the whole theatrical orchestra. Now and then the result comes perilously near to the ridiculous. If this German family of eight had continued a moment longer to drink soup in a passionate silence of hatred the tension would have broken. But the soup was an introduction to Herr Krauss's first climax of indignation and the danger passed. So it was throughout the play. For a moment it would seem to droop, weighed down with its solemnities; then suddenly a storm of emotion would arise so fascinating as a spectacle that the action was rescued, the audience held.

No scene was more persuasive than that, in which Mr. Felix Aylmer, as an intermediary who loathed his task, came to tell Clausen that he was to be considered mad. The dry, nervous intensity of Mr. Aylmer's acting, seen in contrast with Mr. Krauss's heavy wonder and dawning rage, was more moving than anything else in the evening. Miss Ashcroft suggested the girl's devotion and innocence and hero-worship with a beautiful discretion, giving the part its warmth and saving it from weak prettiness; Mr. O. B. Clarence lent distinction to Clausen's oldest friend; Miss Joyce Bland discovered a brilliant, hard subtlety in his daughter; and there were admirable performances by Mr. Mortimer and Miss Clare Harris. But the play is to be judged rather as an emotional spectacle, with Herr Krauss at its centre, than as a narrative that compels the spectator to be lost in its illusion. One hears and watches, feeling very little; admiring always, but always with detachment.

The Tempest by William Shakespeare

SADLER'S WELLS

ALONSO	Marius Goring
ANTONIO	Dennis Arundell
FERDINAND	Clifford Evans
GONZALO	Evan John
MIRANDA	Ursula Jeans
PROSPERO	Charles Laughton
ARIEL	Elsa Lanchester
CALIBAN	Roger Livesey
CERES	Flora Robson

A quarrel in one's mind with scenery or costume on Prospero's island is a misfortune to be avoided at all costs, but there are forms of decoration that defy indifference and cry out against peace. Prospero and Miranda are discovered on a pile of logs which, if they were like nothing on earth, might plead symbolism or what not, but do in fact so closely resemble abundant roles of mauve and lamentable linoleum that when Ferdinand, in discharge of his task, begins to carry them about, one feels that in a moment he will spread them at Miranda's feet while Ariel tinkles the celestial cash-register. Among the dancers the dogs, who seem to be wearing gas-masks, are perhaps a pardonable eccentricity, but when the nymphs, with hairs screwed up in top-knots, are evidently the 'tweenies from one pantomime, while the reapers, with yellow sunhats, turn out to be six Aladdins from another, one almost ceases to care whether Juno, Ceres, and Iris are mounted on Prospero's pyramidal sandcastle or whether poor Miranda, just to prove that the more substantial pageants do leave a wrack behind, is perched on her linoleum dangling a cluster of witch-balls given her by the goddesses as a wedding-present. It is sometimes extremely difficult to save *The Tempest*'s magic from its more ardent friends.

But it is at Sadler's Wells very often and very beautifully saved. In the first place Miss Elsa Lanchester's Ariel is a rare creature with extreme swiftness, lightness, vitality, grace, such a translation of airy imagination to bodily form as the stage is seldom blessed with. Trinculo and Stefano are deadly slow, but so is their material unless whipped with uncommon ingenuity. Mr. Roger Livesey's Caliban, though without that yearning for humanity which is the edge of Caliban's tragedy, is grossly animal and slavish, like a snarling, fawning dog. There is an exceptionally neat Gonzalo by Mr. Evan John and a clear individuality in Mr. Arundell's Milan. Miss Jeans Miranda has not the full light of wonder about her; she knows her world, new or old, a trifle too well; but, with this reservation, the performance is admirably clear and fresh, good to see and to hear. Neither she nor Ferdinand has the ultimate courage of a great speech. Perhaps of their own will, perhaps in conformity with Mr. Guthrie's, they have a tendency to "naturalize" the high music of verse, but Mr. Clifford Evans and Miss Jeans do find in their method the compensation presumably looked for – simplicity, directness, feeling expressed at ease. It is not the equivalent of exaltation, but it is much, and Mr. Laughton carries the same method yet further. His Prospero is genuinely a very old man, wearying of his power. His delivery is unforced, his manner unspectacular. His great verse does not challenge the heavens, but it does impress and persuade the mind. And, except when insistent 'tweenies and linoleum will permit no influence but their own, Mr. Guthrie knows how to enchant the stage. To his production belongs a part of this Ariel's credit, this Prospero's dignity. He times his movements beautifully; he manoeuvres space; he composes and holds his groups – particularly (and here with assistance from Mr. John Armstrong's simpler costumes) a group of men, bowed and with uplifted hands, gazing spellbound at the thin air whence from our eyes Ariel has vanished.

8 FEBRUARY 1934, THE TIMES

Within the Gates by Sean O'Casey

ROYALTY THEATRE

DREAMER	Basil Bartlett
BISHOP	Douglas Jefferies
FIRST NURSEMAID	Isobel Scaife
ATHEIST	Richard Caldicott
FIRST CHAIR ATTENDANT	Walter Herbage
SECOND CHAIR ATTENDANT	Jack Twyman
YOUNG WHORE	Marjorie Mars
OLD WOMAN	Marie Ault

Mr. O'Casey's fierce play is that very rare thing – a modern morality that is not a pamphlet, but a work of art. In substance it is a violent attack on the whole fabric of civilization, which Mr. O'Casey represents as a tottering edifice with its foundations in hypocrisy, false compromise, and fear. The Bishop, seeking credit for mixing with the common people, fails at the first challenge to give help to a young harlot, and when at last, learning that she is his daughter, he is driven by his conscience to pursuit of her, he has no counsel or hope for her but that she accept what the dramatist evidently regards as the living death of a convent. Behind all the actors in the public park which, for Mr. O'Casey, represents the world is the same menace – expressed in the chorus of the Down-and-Outs; and in them all is the same poison of negation, the same refusal of life. Even the Dreamer and Janice, the young harlot, though in them there is a flash of an opposite philosophy, rejoice and sing, not in wide-eyed joy, but in blind defiance of despair.

A little writer, impelled to this theme, would have fallen inevitably into shrill and bitter screaming, and there are moments when Mr. O'Casey himself weakens; but except on these rare occasions his art purges the dross from his controversy. The play ... is a high challenge to the contemporary theatre, and in the present performance, though it is here and there badly miscast and presented in a way that drops its essential rhythm, it survives – whatever one's view may be of its opinion – as a work that may well mark a period in dramatic development. For it restores to the theatre the compression and vitality of poetry, not only in its declared lyrics accompanied by music, but in passages that have the shape of prose. It is here that the defects of Mr. McDermott's courageous production appear. He has permitted – or his actors have insisted upon – a naturalistic emphasis in many passages which cannot accept it. The Chorus of the Down-and-Outs (except that it should be, on the stage, not a group of individuals but a compact mass pressed together) is beautifully managed; its approaches, its distant song, the beat of its drums have a just spiritual menace; it is genuinely universalized; it is much more than a group of unemployed.

But the persons of the drama are universals also, not particular instances merely, and so they should speak, their dialogue falling upon the ear not with conversational accent, but with the calms, the rare tempests, above all the underlying evenness of a ritual moving towards its climax in the harlot's death.

Miss Marjorie Mars plays her part with so much understanding and so little vanity that one hesitates to suggest a failing in her difficult experiment; but there can be little doubt that if she spoke with less deliberate expression the splendour of Mr. O'Casey's language would more strongly appear. Sir Basil Bartlett's Dreamer is too elegant, and has not inward fire enough; Miss Marie Ault's Old Woman, to whom some of the most brilliant passages of the play are given, is too weakly naturalistic to carry them; and there is a gardener who seems to have strolled indeterminately out of a pale musical comedy. Several of the lesser parts are well played by Miss Isobel Scaife, Mr. Richard Caldicott, Mr. Herbage, and Mr. Twyman, but all of them except Mr. Caldicott, who is altogether admirable, have the general tendency to chatter rather than to orchestrate. Mr. Douglas Jefferies gives, as the Bishop, a solid and rightly unspectacular performance which allows irony to appear unforced. All this work, good and less good, is, it should be remembered, experimental. Except in Strindberg and the early O'Neill there are no precedents for Mr. O'Casey. He is opening up a new country of the imagination from which, by its rigid photography, the fashionable theatre has hitherto been shut out.

17 FEBRUARY 1934, THE TIMES

Conversation Piece by Noël Coward

HIS MAJESTY'S THEATRE

SOPHIE OTFORD	Heather Thatcher
PAUL, DUC DE CHAUCIGNY-VARENNES	Noël Coward
MELANIE	Yvonne Printemps
THE MARQUIS OF SHEERE	Louis Hayward
THE EARL OF HARRINGFORD	George Sanders
THE DUKE OF BENEDEN	Athole Stewart
LADY JULIA CHARTERIS	Irene Browne

Fortunately it was in the year 1811 that Paul, a fugitive and impoverished French aristocrat, brought Mélanie to Brighton. Fortunately because, in that year, if you were, – like Mr. Coward's story – slim but not scraggy, frail but gracefully rounded, it was wonderful what costume could do to conceal the inconsequence of your character by revealing and decorating your charms.

As for Paul and Mélanie, nothing in their history became them quite so well as their dresses. Paul had found her singing in a café. Observing, with the shrewdness of Mr. Noël Coward, that her talent was no less than that of Mlle. Yvonne Printemps, he entered into a business partnership with her, brought her to England, passed her off as the daughter of a nobleman, and set about finding her a rich husband, upon whom he was to receive a commission. Need the anecdote be pursued? Mélanie, while pretending to be a woman of business, "followed her Secret Heart" – and a very pretty song it is when Mlle. Printemps sings it. Paul was her secret heart, but it was not until very late in the play that he discovered it – almost too late, for Mr. Coward had to make his emotional transitions positively skip in his determination to persuade the right wedding bells to ring down his final curtain. Never mind. This is an entertainment, not a psychological analysis of romantic love, and an entertainment it certainly is.

Mlle. Printemps is enchanting. That we did not sooner guess the secret of her secret heart must have been our own fault, for in all else, in every detail of mockery and feeling, she is brilliantly explicit, throwing a glitter of laughing criticism over every scene in which she appears and carrying off (in French) that passionate revelation which, if she had not been there to take it at a glamorous gallop, might have been an awkward business. Mr. Coward too, grave, middle-aged, and owl-like, gives Paul all his chances, while Mr. Athole Stewart, Mr. Louis Hayward, and Miss Irene Browne push forward with skill the rather ungrateful plot. And then there are the trimmings, and better trimmings there have seldom been to a musical piece. The songs, which have verbal point and lively rhythm, are sung, particularly by Miss Heather Thatcher and Mlle. Printemps herself, with a charming air. But one returns to the dresses, the scenery, the furniture, the whole *décor*. What a relief to see a musical piece genuinely designed! Much of the honour of the evening goes to Mrs. Calthrop and to the blessed furniture-makers of the Regency who are her graceful collaborators. The play is amusing, the playing is often brilliant, but the decoration is delightful from first to last.

25 MARCH 1934, THE NEW YORK TIMES

On Learning How to Act

Every country has, I suppose, its own queer, illogical customs. Foreign observers never tire of pointing out how odd is that when two schools, Eton and Harrow, play their annual cricket match, all the fashionable ladies of England should put on their most beautiful frocks to watch the game, while businessmen and grave statesman leave their businesses and the affairs of state to look after themselves for a little while. An even stranger annual event is the matinee given by the students who learn how to act under the directorship of Kenneth Barnes at the Royal Academy of Dramatic Art.

They perform in groups – one group giving a scene from *Children in Uniform*, another group appearing in an excerpt from *Musical Chairs*, another choosing a piece of Molière or Shakespeare. They are all amateurs; there is no novelty in the plays they perform; the occasion, one would have supposed, was not of great public interest. And yet, just as Eton and Harrow play their match at Lord's Cricket Ground, so is this matinee given at the premiere London theatre – the Haymarket; and it is attended not only by all the leading critics, but by the theatrical profession itself.

This year the three appointed judges, who awarded the Bancroft Gold medal (which was formally won by Charles Laughton in his student days) and the Academy's silver and bronze medals, were Sir Nigel Playfair, Mary Ellis and W. A. Darlington, dramatic critic of *The Daily Telegraph*. Last year I, myself, was a judge, sharing the task with Irene Vanbrugh and Owen Nares, and I know how great the difficulties of the judges are. Whether their decision ever receives the general approval of the audience is very doubtful. The audience is highly critical and highly specialized. All the leaders of the stage assemble – managers looking out for new talent, actors and actresses on the watch for new collaborators and, perhaps, for new rivals. A student who gives an outstanding performance at this matinee establishes himself immediately and is almost certain of employment.

The extreme difficulty of making a just award leads me to think that perhaps the principle on which the awards are made needs re-examination, and such re-examination opens up the whole question of an actor's training. For my own part, I am extremely distrustful of collective training in any of the arts.

It is certainly of the utmost importance that an artist should be drilled in his craft; nearly all the troubles of modern painting and writing spring from the fact that young men begin to paint who have not learned to draw, and young women pour out novels who have served none of Flaubert's blessed apprenticeship to the waste-paper basket. They must be disciplined in their craft – but how? The answer almost certainly is: by individual apprenticeship to a great master. Leonardo learned in Verrocchio's studio, not at an art school; Irving learned on the stage itself, not in an academy. The difficulty now is that, though there is beginning to be a revival of repertory theatres in the provinces, the stock companies, in which actors of an earlier generation learned their job, no longer exist.

Granted the academic principle, is it wise to spend much time in rehearsing selected casts in selected scenes with an eye to public performance on the Haymarket stage? The disadvantage of this method is that a girl of genius once chained to an insignificant part may have no chance to develop or exhibit her particular powers, while another of moderate talent, given an easy and spectacular opportunity, may carry off the Bancroft Gold medal.

It is one of the rules that the judges must make their reward on what they see before them and not on what they imagine. Thus the judges at this year's matinee gave the highest prize to Jacqueline Clarke. She is a young girl who appeared as an old woman in a one-act play which but for her appearance would have been entirely without interest. She took her theatrical opportunity well and gave laughter to an audience tired by a long afternoon. For this she is entitled to credit, but her part seemed to me to be one which more or less "played itself." This, the judges are entitled to answer, was not their concern. She made her effect and their award must be made on effect. Presumably for this reason they preferred her to another girl, Marjorie Kirby, who appeared in the much more exacting part of Manuela in *Children in Uniform*.

By the rule they were perhaps right, for Miss Kirby's performance was more faulty than Miss Clarke's, although there were imaginative passages in Miss Kirby's playing which seemed to me to place her, as a potential artist, in a class apart. If the judges were right by the rule, then the rule was wrong, and if the rule was wrong then there is a defect in the academic system of examination which necessitates this particular rule. It seems to be clear that the purpose of training should not be simply a finished performance in one part but the discovery and development of that rare quality which is the spark and genius of the theatre. No doubt, training for this particular matinee is but a part of the Royal Academy's curriculum; but an immense importance is attached to it, employment springs from it, and it seems that the principles underlying its awards might well be reconsidered.

4 MAY 1934, THE TIMES

The Voisey Inheritance
by Harley Granville-Barker

SADLER'S WELLS

MR. VOISEY	Felix Aylmer
MRS. VOISEY	May Witty
TRENCHARD VOISEY, K. C.	Harcourt Williams
MAJOR BOOTH VOISEY	Archibald Batty
EDWARD VOISEY	Maurice Evans
HUGH VOISEY	Marius Goring
MRS. HUGH VOISEY (BEATRICE)	Joyce Bland
ETHEL VOISEY	Hermione Hannen
ALICE MAITLAND	Beatrix Thomson
MR. GEORGE BOOTH	O. B. Clarence
PEACEY	Frank Napier

For four of its five acts *The Voisey Inheritance* holds the stage as it is held by very few pieces nowadays. There are minor disappointments: Mr. Archibald Batty overdoes the strident assertiveness of Booth Voisey, and Mr. Marius Goring gives a too theatrical fantasy to Hugh; their individualities lack the Voisey veneer. It is a little sad, too, that Mr. Granville-Barker has thought it necessary to move the date of his scene forward by 30 years, but that, in this instance, is admittedly a matter of prejudice, not of criticism, for the substance of the play does not "date." The story is brilliantly alive, and the characterization will maintain its truth as long as there is in England anything that may be called "an upper middle-class." Not indeed that everyone behaves as Mr. Voisey behaved, but, granted a solid, genial, respected solicitor who has been using trust funds for private speculation, the Voisey group gives a remarkably fair suggestion of how his family might meet the crisis.

After Mr. Felix Aylmer has drawn a portrait of Mr. Voisey, accurate, discreetly entertaining, and lacking only the geniality of a buccaneer, we see the burden of the inheritance fall upon his son Edward. Mr. Maurice Evans gives an extremely sensitive and illuminating study of him, enabling us to watch him change and grow from a priggish rectitude to a genuine courage. Every contact deepens knowledge of him – his duel with the blackmailing clerk brilliantly sketched by Mr. Frank Napier; his timid love for Alice who, until the disastrous fifth act, is made continuously interesting by Miss Beatrix Thomson; his encounter with the old client who threatens disaster – a faultless and delightful piece of acting by Mr. O. B. Clarence. Minor persons in the abundant family are given vitality by Miss Joyce Bland, Mr. Harcourt Williams, and Dame May Witty. All this is not enough to save the fifth act, though it can be saved very simply by reversion to the original text, or, perhaps, by a drastic blue pencil. Mr. Granville-Barker has redrafted it; its dryness has gone; rhetoric and an over-elaborated sentiment have entered in. Worst of all, it has lost its shape, and until a quarter of an hour before midnight there was no assurance that it would ever end. But let it be forgotten, for it will inevitably be changed. Apart from it, there is, in the evening, the rare pleasure of story naturally and steadily developing, of acting that is for the most part first rate, and of a production, devised by Mr. Harcourt Williams and by Mr. Granville-Barker himself, which has a care for detail and an absence of affectation that give it uncommon distinction.

18 MAY 1934, THE TIMES
OBERAMMERGAU PLAY

Modernism and Tradition

A COMPROMISE IN STAGECRAFT

Little in the village of Oberammergau and nothing in the *Passion Play* has been affected by the changed conditions of Germany. The tercentenary performance, though it is strangely spoken of in the official preface to the text as being peculiarly appropriate in "these days of the suppression of the anti-Christian powers in our Fatherland," is completely free from the political distortions rumoured in England. If any attempt was made to introduce them the Oberammergauers have resisted it, and their play survives the storms of to-day as it survived the decrees of suppression which threatened its existence in the last decades of the eighteenth century. There are in the streets formal evidences of the new regime, a salute now and then, a flag here and there, but a more peaceful and friendly place would be hard to find in Europe.

Last night Oberammergau began to fill, and to-day, until rain began in the afternoon, it wore an air of festival, but two evenings ago the little train from Murnau set down its few passengers not in a town greedily expectant of tourists but in a long rambling village whose inhabitants quietly pursued their ordinary trades. Yesterday the village was as undisturbed. The long hair of men and boys was the only sign of what was to come. Beside the road to Ettal a workman, stripped to the waist, stood up to his spade and shook back a great golden mane as he greeted the passers-by. In the little paths among the meadows boys with hair to their shoulders, whose faces were given a special serene intensity by this unaccustomed frame, walked with that grave and happy ease which is characteristic of the Bavarian country-people.

In the morning newspapers were brought from door-to-door by an angel on a bicycle. Near sunset, when the rays slanting from the west had given to the green hills their last sudden brilliance and the streams flowing through the village were dark between banks still shining with flowers, two patriarchs stood to gossip on a bridge as they returned from their day's work. Their trade was the carpenter's; one carried on his shoulder a bag containing his tools. Both would appear in the play to-morrow, but not in any of the leading parts. They looked as they said good-night as if they might have worked in "The Carpenter's shop" of Millais.

The great monastery of Ettal, through which the original text of the Passion Play probably came, lay at noon very still in the sun. There was no movement within, one monk only was to be seen and the church was empty. In Oberammergau itself even the theatre was almost deserted, the only evidence of last-minute preparations being in a room where a dozen women, themselves performers unless some were excluded by the tradition which forbids matrons to act, were putting the finishing touches to their eight weeks' task of preparing costumes.

RESOURCES OF THEATRE

Vast though the theatre is when seen from without, its extent, its resources and its character do not appear except to a visitor given access to the stage itself. A fore-stage, 150 feet wide, has six entrances, two down steps from the Houses of Pilate and the High Priest, two which open upon the streets of Jerusalem, and two which admit the chorus. In the midst, set back from the orchestra by nine yards, is a curtained proscenium opening, behind which, on stages 50 feet deep, interior scenes are revealed as the chorus divides. The fore-stage is open to the weather; above the proscenium arch appears a great curve, not of tinted cloth, but of open sky and mountains whose aspect changes as the day's performance continues. Over the interior stage is a glass roof fitted with sliding white curtains. These are used with extraordinary judgment and skill to procure, in a theatre that depends on natural light alone, an illumination as various and accurately directed as may be obtained from the most elaborate electrical installation.

But nothing in this unique theatre was more impressive, on the day preceding a production that was to include 1,000 performers, than the ordered simplicity of the dressing-room. Here, in wide airy spaces, scented by scrubbed wood, hung the costumes of each player – his shoes, his stockings, his armour or his embroidered robe. The angels' dresses, each with its golden circlet, shone in the sun against the landscape background of great windows. In the place allotted to children was a cupboard, full of toys and games with which to pass away the long intervals of their service. There was something in this empty theatre which, combined with the absence of excitement or theatricalism in the village itself, answered, before to-day's performance began, the question so often asked – what is the attitude of the people of Oberammergau towards their Passion Play? The answer was confirmed early this morning when, in the eighteenth-century rococo church, which with its domed tower is among the most remarkable country churches in Bavaria, the people attended Mass before going to their dressing-rooms.

OPENING SCENE

The performance itself began at 8 a.m. With the entrance of the chorus, four dozen singers, uniformly dressed in grey cloaks and white under-robes, with Herr

Anton Lang, a splendid and dignified Prologue, at their head. When their opening song had been sung, the story of the life of Jesus began with His entry into Jerusalem and His cleansing of the Temple. This scene, the most beautiful of the play, is the earliest proof that Oberammergau has created for itself a peculiar stagecraft. In the dressing of the immense crowd there is no visible sign of a consciously organized colour scheme: certainly there is none of the deliberate simplification and massing of colour which, though successful in some of the tableaux, gives to others an angry clash.

Instead, the concourse of people surrounding Jesus as He rides upon an ass wear dresses many of which date far back in the history of the Passion Play. Organization of colour has not been attempted, but a natural organization results from the numbers and the astonishing vitality of this vast crowd. A modernistic producer would have ordered every movement. One would have been able to perceive his touch in the coming and going of distinguishable groups. Herr Georg Johann Lang's method, whenever he uses the full crowd, most brilliantly conceals itself. The people of Jerusalem give no appearance of having been regimented for the stage. They pour through the streets a living and burning crowd; their colour and the simplicity of their gestures are the colour and the simplicity of the illustration in a child's Bible, but their fervour is the fervour of the text. This alliance of naivety with faith expressed in action is irresistible. The scene finds its response at once in the spectator's memory and in his imagination.

From this point the play moves steadily onwards during the morning towards its first climax in the Garden of Gethsemane, and during the rest of the day towards its culmination of the Cross and the Resurrection. Each act has a choral prelude illustrated by carefully designed Old Testament tableaux, the Agony in the Garden, for example, being preceded by a beautiful representation of Adam earning his bread by the sweat of his brow. The least successful New Testament scenes are invariably those in which Jesus Himself does not appear and in which the text has been able to borrow but little dialogue directly from the Gospels. Herr Hugo Rutz gives a fiery portrait of Caiaphas and the Judas of Herr Hans Zwink has a quiet distinction, but they cannot altogether save from dullness the prolonged wrangling of the accusers of Christ.

THEME OF VENGEANCE

Daisenberger's text, instead of discovering the motive of the Passion in the mind of Jesus alone and in the fulfilment of a preordained purpose, lays elaborate emphasis on the sustained enmity of the money changers and the bitterness of the Pharisees. So considered, the drama of the Passion loses a part of its splendour and the scenes which are dominated by this theme of vengeance weaken the general structure. The strength of the play lies first in its crowd and, secondly, in those passages in the life of Christ Himself which the Gospels have made most familiar. The Agony, though often weighed down by a monotony of intonation, is in general surprisingly accomplished if the narrowness of the community's resources be taken into account. Nor would it be right to judge the performance by the standards of naturalism, for it often happens that several actors speak in formal unison or that, while some important action is in progress, the washing of the Disciples' feet or the counting by Judas of his 30 pieces of silver, the company on the stage is left without a word to speak.

Herr Georg Lang, the producer, has not altogether avoided an impression that the Passion Play, as it is now performed, is a slightly uneasy compromise between traditionalism represented by the text, the old dresses, and the introductory choral passages, and a modern technique which finds lively expression in the stage itself and in the uniform severity of the singers' robes, but has gone either too far or not far enough in the painted backgrounds to some of the interior scenes. What appears above all to be needed is a bold choice between symbolic and representational scenery. As it is, many of the tableaux and some of the active scenes themselves are damaged by a mixing of styles.

THE PLAYERS

...

Herr Alois Lang, who has played the part of Jesus before, plays it now, not with professional accomplishment, but with a simple humility that suffices except in one of the greatest scenes. The Agony in the Garden, though supported by all the power of association, is not as moving as one expects it to be partly because Herr Lang has not the means with which to communicate its spiritual urgency, partly because it is one of those scenes of which the design is a compromise of styles. But Herr Lang gives a vivid representation of the patience and indomitable strengths of Jesus during His trial, and when this evening the Crucifixion was reached at last the unspectacular reticence of Herr Lang justifies itself. In this scene over-insistence on physical torment is carefully avoided. Though it fails to suggest the full passage of time it is moving in its almost ritual calm and deliberation.

The Passion Play remains what it has always been, a tragedy from which a spectator may take away what he is by temperament equipped to discover in it. To look for a finished work of art is to risk disappointment; but whoever, remembering the play's origin, is prepared to yield himself to the influence of a community's devotional act will be rewarded.

I. – The Munich Theatre

NEW ASPECTS OF KULTUR

In the past, however confused the state of Europe and however narrow the political systems under which men have lived, the liberal arts and the enterprise of independent thought have somehow continued. That they continue to-day and will emerge again as an international influence is not to be doubted. Meanwhile little is heard of them; artists have gone to earth; frontiers have sprung up everywhere against the traffic of intellect; and there are many who assume that, because the emphasis of foreign news is nowadays political, nothing but politics exists. It is rashly said that in Germany, since the Jewish exodus, there is "no more art," that Vienna is unproductive and Salzburg threatened, that in Prague, once a city of theatrical experiment, enterprise has languished, and that even Paris is politically obsessed. An unpolitical journey and an attempt to re-establish touch, however briefly, with the work and thought of men whose ideas do not necessarily march in column of fours may prove a useful corrective.

It was perhaps unfortunate that such a journey should have had its prelude at Oberammergau, for the peace and friendliness of that mountainous village are misleading. Whoever goes there must pass through Munich, and Munich, named as the future cultural capital of the Reich, is harsh, tense, and watchful. A profound solemnity pervades it. Though a foreigner is unmolested, his freedom is as conspicuous and as little comfortable as that of a civilian who should find himself with a permit in the midst of a camp. Any question, even on what would appear in England to be the most innocent subject of aesthetics, may be greeted by prolonged, cautious silence, and a playgoer who wanders out onto the steps of the theatre during an interval may hear the tramp of horse and foot at the end of the street. Torches appear. A procession passes, with banners that proclaim the propaganda of the Saar.

GERMAN REVALUATION

In these circumstances it becomes clear that the first duty of an English observer is to recognize that, the German world having accepted values fundamentally different from his own, these values are for that reason to be the more patiently investigated. Everything in Munich, and presumably throughout Germany, is dominated by one word, *Weltanschauung*, which may mean one's "idea of life" or "world-attitude," but is not easily translatable into English. Not to understand the German *Weltanschauung* is to miss the underlying motive of those who seek now, in the theatre and in every department of life, to give a new significance to the word *Kultur*. It is to miss also the

---

1. These are from Morgan's visit to Germany, Austria, Czechoslovakia and France.

strength and the irreconcilable nature of the German challenge to what not we alone but Germans themselves have hitherto regarded as civilization.

An understanding of the new *Weltanschauung* may well be approached through the particular instance of the theatre. Here the guiding truths appear. Though in one sense the new movement is new indeed, so new that its constructive elements are improvised from day to day, in another it is not new at all but a passionate reaction, an attempt to eradicate the influences which made themselves felt after 1918 and to revert to the historical or mythical glories of the past. This conflict of purpose appears in the vigour of the new regime's negative attitude towards the theatre and the vagueness of its constructive policy. What is undesirable is abundantly clear; what is desired cannot be stated except in the most general terms. Fortunately music, except opera, is inoffensively wordless, and may be left alone unless its authorship is non-Aryan or it contains those unvirile elements of the "grotesque" or the "expressionistic" which relate it to the fatal period 1918 – 33. Fortunately, too, Wagner's material is of the heroic sort which gains him ready admittance to the party. The great classical poets present a sterner problem. On the one hand they are national assets not likely to be repudiated; on the other, they had an embarrassing taste in subversiveness and internationalism. They had, too, genius's irritating habit of seeing more than one side of a question. ...

AN OPPORTUNITY WAITING

... What is required of the potential dramatist, whose fortune would be made by a lack of rivals, is that he affirm the Nazi *Weltanschauung,* that he keep in touch with the people and respect ancient customs, and that his work have that mysterious thing *Formwille*, a will to form, which has nothing to do with aesthetic form as we individualists understand it, but is – or would be if it existed – a dramatic expression of that desire for collective discipline which is implied in group-holidays, group play-going or a column of Brown Shirts on the march. It is said the Dietrich Eckart achieved this difficult symbolism, but Eckart died in 1923 and is without successor.

Meanwhile the Nazi theatre falls back upon classical plays and mystery plays, racially or historically connected with contemporary ideals; upon stories of peasant life which, though they have long been characteristic of the Bavarian stage, are now particularly honoured because they express (without ridicule) the ideals of racial purity and peasant virtue embodied in the phrase *Blut und Boden*; and, finally, upon pieces which, though they may have few other merits, are at any rate harmless. The consequent dullness is remarkable.

....

AUDIENCE-FODDER

The truth to be grasped is not only that the new Germany is as yet artistically barren but that its governors have set their face against individual creation and experiment. The drama has always been regarded in Germany as directly educational. Hence the subsidized playhouses in so many cities. Until a few weeks ago subsidies were paid, not by the Reich, but by States and Municipalities. Now the Reich is beginning to assume a part of the burden, and the idea of the theatre as an educational instrument is being given a fresh emphasis. Dramatists, actors, and producers are henceforth to be considered valuable not for the ideas which they themselves beget – all necessary ideas having been conclusively begotten – not as entertainers and not even as originating teachers, but as lesson-rehearsers or audience-fodder. The audience, not the artist, is what interests Germany, and it is now being organized as even German audiences have never been organized in the past. There are three principal organiszations. *Kraft durch Freude*, Strength through Joy, has much more than a theatrical influence. .... It arranges group holidays as well as cheap play-going, and generally contributes to the formation of a new theatrical audience – not the proletarian audience which sprang up after 1918 but an audience based upon the little *bourgeoisie* whose support is the chief strengths of the *Dritte Reich*. ...

Nor is there now an absolute ban on foreign imports as long as they may be regarded, like Shakespeare's historical plays or Mr. Shaw's latest work, as a contribution to the "mental rearmament" of Germany. But for the most part the German audience must live still on its native ration of propaganda and on plays which, if they discuss fighting, do nothing to bring that heroic exercise into hatred, ridicule, or contempt. Those who discuss the present condition of the theatre in Germany like to suggest a parallel between it and the romantic movement of the early nineteenth century, in which they discover the same attraction to history and legend, the same interest in folk-lore, and the ancient customs of the people. But the comparison remains essentially false. One of the keys to the romantic movement was an exaltation of personal love, and love stories, though it is gravely explained that they are not banned, are considered, if not precisely undesirable, at any rate a waste of time. They invite a man to think of himself as an individual; they are not affirmations of the prescribed *Weltanschauung*. In the theatre and elsewhere a woman must think of herself as the mother of Aryans and a man must hold one thought continuously – that he has no real existence except as a member of a community, united and pure, which is being led. To what he is being led it is neither his nor a dramatist's business to inquire, for life in Germany is become a headline without a text.

II. –Vienna and Salzburg

REMEMBERED GREATNESS

Vienna, though not "gay" as those who think of it in terms of musical comedy imagine it to be, has a special grace and charm. A certain melancholy broods over it, the melancholy of greatness remembered. The streets, uncrowded by day, are almost empty at night. Plays begin at such an hour that an unaccustomed Englishman, having failed to take his food with him in a paper bag, finds himself, soon after 10 o'clock, looking eagerly for supper. This is in itself an instructive adventure. You wander into a restaurant to discover a little orchestra playing to perhaps two couples among an archipelago of empty tables. Discouraged, you turn again towards the door, expecting to be frowned upon by the head waiter, stranded among his smiles. But the smiles continue. He is of your own opinion – one cannot sup *à la* Crusoe. Perhaps another evening? Sometimes the Viennese are a little sad, but they are not importunate or angry or glum. Even in misfortune they have the detachment of a people not inexperienced in fortune's changes.

...

From this it is a long step to consideration of the achievements of the State theatres. Nothing in this journey has been more reassuring than the courage and the elasticity of the Austrians' artistic policy. The country is passing through a period of political complexity, but the great theatres are used for the production of works of art on their merits, while a consistent and successful attempt is made to reduce the financial burden by economies and by organization of the audience into "theatre communities."

...

But the pleasures of Vienna are by no means confined to its theatres. Its special merit as a city is that the country is within a stone's throw. After a supper party, a taxi will take you briefly to Kobenzl at dawn. There, suddenly, is a fresh, glistening, wooded hill; on one side the extremity of the Alps, on the other a pearly Vienna; in the wood, squirrels and fawns; everywhere the sweet smell of tree and grass and flower. It is Sunday morning and Sunday in Vienna is not to be missed. In the Spanish Riding School of the Hofburg, the Lipizaners of the State Stud will perform before luncheon. A more expert performance or one more flattering to a conservative mind is not to be imagined. These white, dancing stallions have survived everything. ... The young horses come first, exhibiting their 'prentice skill to music of Chopin. Then, "turn" by "turn" we mount the degrees of experience, watching horses assume with astonishing grace those "impossible" positions ordinarily associated with prancing tin soldiery. Now the camera has told us that these things cannot be done – the Levade, the Mezair, the brilliant Capriole – and here they all are on Sunday morning in the white riding-school with beautiful ladies looking down from the galleries or drawing back into the window-embrasures to chatter with their friends.

SUNDAY AFTERNOON

On Sunday afternoon one goes to the Theatre an der Wien to see an operetta, in this instance *The Yellow Lily*, to music by Krasinay-Krausz. There is as much of history in the Theatre an der Wien as in the Spanish Riding School. Here, in 1805, Fidelio was first performed, presumably to an unconversational audience. Here, too, hang the playbills of innumerable operettes, including that which celebrated the hundredth performance of the *Merry Widow*, and here Herr Hubert Marischka still presides over the fortunes of all that we understand by Viennese musical comedy. The Viennese manner of production is certainly a revelation. *The Yellow Lily*, in which Herr Marischka himself plays the leading part, is a cheerful piece of nonsense about a young man who falls in love with a lady beneath his royal station, greatly assisted by a gypsy band which trails after him in his serenades. The point of the production – and its difference from the English kind – is that it is not stately or spectacular, but intimate. Except when Fräulein Friedel Schuster is singing (and even in Vienna we take seriously the romantic charm of our leading lady), it has a delicious air of mocking itself. Herr Marischka knows precisely how to hover between romanticism and burlesque; as a producer of work in this *genre* he evidently begins where other men leave off; ...

And in the evening? To the Prater inevitably, to sup off the little sausages that are carried round in cauldrons shoulder high; to watch the "confirmation children" drive up in their white robes and flowery wreaths, seated in carriages smothered by flowers; to visit, at a respectful distance, the side-shows, and to wonder whether the timeless leisure of the Great Wheel is in any way connected with the Viennese art of flirtation. Probably not, for flirtation in Vienna is a genuine art, requiring an audience. The cabins of the great wheel, lifted heavenward, would be too dark, too solitary. Better, on Sunday evenings, one of those little restaurants where the people go to dance and, between dances, to sit out in open loose boxes like family pews. The pews are doorless; the light, though discreet, is sufficient; the mutual entertainment is charming as it is ardent. There is no word for it in English or American. It is the respectable Viennese equivalent of "walking out." After all, when one is born into a nation whose every shop girl dances like a dryad and whose every bank clerk has a string orchestra at his feet, why should not the dance continue between dances? It is precisely that, as pretty, as amusing, as unembarrassed as the Lippizaners' quadrille.

IV. –The Mission of France

TWO WAYS OF LIFE

To an Englishman who cares above all else for the integrity of art and individual liberty within the rule of law, arrival in Paris from Germany and Central Europe is almost a home-coming. "Have you seen the Chinese bronzes in the Orangerie?" is the first question asked, and to hear such a question, to know that there still exists a profoundly pacific nation interested in civilization for its own sake, is to breathe again; for the truth, little understood in England, to which every experience of this journey points is that what is at stake in Europe is not boundaries, armaments, and political systems only, not even peace and war as they have been formerly understood, but the freedom or the conscription of the mind.

...

A CRITICAL PEOPLE

In France, moreover, it is still not perilous to talk. Without consideration of party, a Frenchman may say what he likes of Racine, and there is a blessed understanding, as between brothers, that he may, without "humiliating" his English guest, say of Shakespeare precisely what he pleases. That he is intensely critical and so suspicious of *l'enthousiasme* that enthusiasm, even in the English sense, is rarely his, gives weight to his praise and accuracy to his conversation, but it does not make of him, collectively, an encouraging theatrical audience. Every night in a Parisian theatre is too much like a first night in London to be very comfortable for those on the stage. When one French player said to me that, from an actor's point of view, an English audience was the best in the world, I dismissed the saying as an habitual compliment. But the verdict was repeated and repeated again: the English come to enjoy themselves; the French to sit in judgment. Perhaps it is true. Certainly the French are not passive playgoers. They make themselves heard. Their seats tip and they tip them like musketry throughout the first act, though it start at nine or later. In the intervals (and between the intervals) their comments are more caustic than gentle. It is often said that what we need in England is a more critical, less gullible and acquiescent audience. Here it is. A play that survives in Paris survives something.

...

IBSEN IN PARIS

The Pitöeffs have done nothing better and nothing stranger than Ibsen's *The Wild Duck*. Whoever looks at the *Théâtre du Vieux Colombier* for a preconceived Norwegian phlegm will not find it. The Pitöeffs are little troubled for stoves and domestic atmosphere. They strike for the play's spirit and set it on the stage, flaming. Mme. Ludmilla Pitöeff, though her Hedwig has an astonishing impact, does not, even here, altogether banish the impression often given by her acting – that it is, in a limiting sense, an "impersonation." One swerves from the illusion of Hedwig to exclaim with admiration, but with admiration momentarily detached: "What a clever impersonation of a child!" M. Pitöeff on the contrary, permits no swerving. His Hjalmar Ekdal is, one would wager, a more mercurial creature than Ibsen's, but he establishes his interpretation. Even more remarkable is M. Lugné-Poë's Old Ekdal, a genuine masterpiece of character and technique, who, even when he snores, snores with his soul.

At the top of another technical ladder ... is M. Sasha Guitry with a little nonsense piece, *Mon Double et Ma Moitié*, in which as fast as Maurice (Sasha) hurries out his double (also Sasha) hurries in, with the conjugal consequences to be expected. ...

...

And there was Jean Cocteau's *La Machine Infernale*, a fresh treatment of the story of Oedipus. French admiration is, I gather, tempered by the criticism, typically French in its logical tenacity, that the final scene is technically encumbered by explanations, admittedly necessary to one ignorant of the Oedipus story, but superfluous to our prescience. What does it matter? May we not have a little patience? And, in any case, ought not a work of art to be complete in itself? And *La Machine Infernale* is a work of art. The make-up of the young men, with their white faces, their blue-rimmed eyes, their whole air of lounge-bar, Beardsley, and beauty-parlour leads one to expect only spineless affectation. But the play, which has a genuinely beautiful decor by Christian Bérard, transcends its fashionable follies. ...

This is the whole lesson of the journey now ended: that the Rhine has become a rough frontier between two ways of life, mutually exclusive; to the West, to think for oneself is a virtue; to the East, if the violence sprung from an inferiority complex ultimately prevail over the surviving opposition, there will be created from Strasbourg to Vladivostok a prison of the mind. The greatest service that France might do to the world would be to produce another Voltaire; ours to hear him. Ferney and Weimar are empty; only Geneva is full.

9 SEPTEMBER 1934, THE NEW YORK TIMES

The Late Sir Nigel Playfair

...

He has died at the age of 60. No one expected him to die; a few weeks ago he was acting in the Open Air Theatre in Regents Park; there was no actor more alive, more cheerful, fuller of eagerness and ideas. Until his death forced us to look up dates, very few of us can have been aware that he was 60 years old.

It was, in the theatre, an unusual life, with little of the heavy plodding which is called "going through the mill." Not that Playfair did not serve his apprenticeship, but he can never have been poor, and he preserved always the love of experiment and the light-heartedness of an amateur. The son of a fashionable doctor, he was educated at Harrow and Oxford. At the University he gave his time to the Oxford University Dramatic Society, and when, ceasing to be an undergraduate, he became a barrister, amateur acting, with such famous clubs as the Old Stagers and the Windsor Strollers, was still his diversion. He became a professional at the age of 28.

Always round and cheerful, without classical features and with indeed a noteworthy comic expression, he had no chance in tragic parts. Clowns and grave-diggers were what Tree gave him, but he won his way from farce to comedy, played well for Pinero and extremely well for Shaw, whose *Doctor's Dilemma* has not had a better Cutler Walpole. Playfair's reputation steadily grew; audiences liked him; he had tricks of absurdity that made them laugh as soon as he came onto the stage; but a great actor he was not, and no one knew it more modestly than himself. What made his fame and gave him his special niche in the history of the modern stage was his control of the Lyric Theatre, Hammersmith.

Hammersmith is a remote suburb and London playgoers are a very conservative people. They will endure any amount of nonsense in the theatres which lie within a mile of Charing Cross and ten minutes of their dinner table; but they will not make inconvenient and laborious journeys for the sake of all the dramatic masterpieces in the world. A few enthusiasts will toil out, but the people with money will not. To make a distant theatre fashionable is an impossible task – in which Playfair succeeded. He started, with little money behind him, a month after the armistice. Early in the following year he produced John Drinkwater's *Abraham Lincoln* and the public of 1919 was full of hopeful idealism and very eager to hear about Lincoln. The play ran for a year and set the theatre on its feet. But still it was not fashionable in the ordinary sense. It needed *The Beggar's Opera* to bring the Rolls-Royces to Hammersmith. All London, from the errand boys who could whistle to the smart young women who could not, were caught in its tunes. Lovat Fraser's designs gave a new mannerism to the stage. The piece ran to 1,463 performances.

For my own part, I hated it. Not being a critic in those days but an undergraduate, I was fortunately not called upon to say so. The piece was harmless enough, and gay enough if you went to it in a receptive spirit, and that it offended me by its special mingling of frivolity, brutality and baseness and by its veneer of prettiness has nothing to do with the case. I thought of it as a stale and poisonous cake covered with sugar-icing, but England thought otherwise and to Playfair the way was open. Until 1932 he held the Lyric together, his speciality being the revival of classical plays such as *The Way of the World*, *She Stoops to Conquer* or *The Beaux Stratagem*. With these were mingled revues and skits, many of them from the pen of A. P. Herbert.

The man fitted his time, and a more lovable man there has not been in the theatre. He was not a wit, but he had a sense of fun. He made no parade of charity, but he had an extraordinary kindness of heart. As an undergraduate, I knew him when he came to Oxford to produce *As You like It* for the O.U.D.S. of which I was then a member. Undergraduates, like most amateurs, can be very solemn and laborious; he saved us from ourselves and he made us work. Afterward I knew him well. There was not a room or a theatre that was not a happier place for his being in it. That he was, as actor or producer, one of the great leaders of the English stage no one will pretend, but he brought back the classics when no one else could, and he maintained a theatre for fourteen years in a part of London in which, everyone else would have assumed, it was doomed to failure.

14 SEPTEMBER 1934, THE TIMES

Treasure Island

A FILM DIRECTED BY VICTOR FLEMING FROM STEVENSON'S STORY
EMPIRE THEATRE

If English stories are in future to be interpreted in Hollywood with even this degree of faithfulness, film-going will lose many of its terrors and the prestige of American studios be greatly increased. It is not necessary to be a fanatical stickler for Stevenson's text to be in trouble now and then. Long John Silver says "No sirree!" in a moment of enthusiasm and Jim Hawkins's accent must at times have been an embarrassment to his mother. More serious is the twist given to the story by Jim's personal attachment to Silver, which leads to his setting the rascal free on the homeward voyage and to a blubbering parting between the two as Silver drops over the side. Of this there is a simple explanation. "A vast audience," we are told, "awaits Wallace Beery, Jackie Cooper invoking again the tear-dimmed sentiment of their previous triumph in *The Champ*. A little blubbering was therefore commercially desirable, but, even in this matter, we have been let off very light.

In all else the film is remarkably faithful to the original. Mr. Beery is at the outset less smoothly hypocritical than the Silver who made a fool of Stevenson's Squire Trelawney, and afterwards, in preparation for tear-dimmed sentiment, he is a softer monster than the sea-cook of our dreams. Mr. Cooper has a more self-confident humour than Jim of the Admiral Benbow, and lacks that spice of priggishness which was the distinguishing and, oddly enough, the endearing quality of all heroes of the Stevensonian era whether they searched for treasure in fiction or built empires in fact. But on their own lines both performances are lively, reasonable, and consistent. Mr. Nigel Bruce's Squire is as affable, as foolish, and as English as can be.

...

This is, then, on the whole a straight-forward version of the story. The ship is beautiful under sail; the famous scene in the apple-barrel is almost as good on the screen as in the book; and such intelligent use is always made of the masts and rigging that, in the duel of knife and pistol in the shrouds, the honours are with the film. The director's interest in the fauna of the island has, perhaps, made of the place rather too lavish a zoo, but the fighting ashore is first-rate. The merit of the film is in its being for the most part content to translate the story without embellishing it. On the voyage out, not a luxury liner is encountered; on all Treasure Island there is not a cabaret, a woman, or a wise-crack. In brief, an honest and well-constructed film of adventure.

14 SEPTEMBER 1934, THE TIMES

Eden End by J.B. Priestley

DUCHESS THEATRE

WILFRED KIRBY	John Teed
SARAH	Nellie Bowman
LILLIAN KIRBY	Alison Leggatt
DR. KIRBY	Edward Irwin
STELLA KIRBY	Beatrix Lehman
GEOFFREY FARRANT	Franklyn Bellamy
CHARLES APPLEBY	Ralph Richardson

This is the point at which criticism gives itself a conscientious pinch. Has coma set in? Has the natural power of response died? Or is this play, though written by a man who has proved himself to have a finger on the theatrical pulse, as immobile as it seems? If so, why?

Let it be approached, if possible, from Mr. Priestley's point of departure. What he has set out to describe is a few days in the house of Dr. Kirby in a remote country district in the North. Lillian, his unmarried daughter, is unexpressively in love with a neighbouring landowner, Farrant, one of those blunt men who confess, with embarrassing modesty, that for them poetry is Kipling but are prepared, when roused by quotation, to "tackle" Wordsworth. Such men exist; they shoot birds which worse men eat; they are preferable in their porous tweeds to many more spectacular gentlemen for whom Kipling is not poetry and for whom Wordsworth – but, never mind; they exist, and that is Mr. Priestley's first point, for, unless we misinterpret him, what Mr. Priestley is feeling for is a new kind of naturalism.

To continue the Kirby's history. There is a young son home from British West Africa who is yet too young to have outgrown the romance of barmaids – a crude puppy who sayings are as flannel to the teeth; he is represented not at all crudely by Mr. John Teed, who has the insight that recommends Wilfred to mercy. The domestic circle is peaceful and dull. Into it comes Stella, a prodigal sister to Lilian and Wilfred. She ran away some years ago to be an actress and has failed. Mild complications, with Wordsworth's assistance, between Stella and Farrant; appearance of Stella's husband, Charles, an actor not yet positively seedy; discussions between the sisters, discussions between father and daughter, a little drunkenness by Charles and Wilfred – and, farewell. Stella and her husband, with a pale flicker of dead romance, are on the road again. Eden End settles down to its routine.

What Mr. Priestley seems to have said to himself is that life is not patient of "plots"; he has, therefore, eliminated, or almost eliminated, fable. There is no spectacular untying because nothing has been artificially tied. These, Mr. Priestley would seem to claim, are not "characters" in "a piece for the theatre"; they are ordinary people leading ordinary lives; therefore a dose of the humdrum is not only permissible, but necessary. To write such a play is a very interesting ambition; to perceive the author's experimental purpose and give him credit for it is the first duty of criticism. No one wants a play to be jerked into motion by the mechanism of plot. But if it does not move in action, it must move in idea. It must move or die, and *Eden End* is static.

The reason seems to be that the naturalism is not naturalistic or fluid enough. Miss Alison Leggatt keeps Lillian on the right plane, suggesting the years she has lived in this place and their effect on her; from her imagination does receive impulse. But everyone else, partly because the performances are too slow, too expectant, too aware of the audience, and partly because there are patches of theatrical dialogue clean out of the naturalistic convention, is doomed again and again to check the naturalistic flow. Miss Beatrix Lehman seems to be arguing her way towards a climax that does not come; Mr. Edward Irwin and the old maidservant belong to a piece of more decorative sentiment; and even Mr. Ralph Richardson, though he is too good an actor not to entertain an audience in a scene with the decanter, is given no chance to get below the surface of Charles's mind. It is all extremely unfortunate. Mr. Priestley's experiment is worth making, but the new convention that he seeks is not yet "pure." He is feeling towards a fluid, unassertive, undeclamatory style – a play not of crashing emotion but of accumulating perceptions. A blessing upon his labours! But in this play they are but beginning.

20 SEPTEMBER 1934, THE TIMES

Moonlight is Silver by Clemence Dane

QUEEN'S THEATRE

DAME AGNES RONSARD	Helen Haye
GILBERT MERLE	Cecil Parker
STEPHEN	Douglas Fairbanks, jun.
JOSEPHINE	Gertrude Lawrence
BARBARA DAWE	Martita Hunt
CHARLES LANKASTER	Barry Jones

Who will may argue of the probabilities – an unrewarding task, human creatures being as unaccountable as they are. Would any woman that loved her husband confess to an unfaithfulness of which she was not guilty? Would any husband that loved his wife drive her to this confession by his tormented doubts, his insane jealousy, his wild incapacity to believe the innocent truth? They are useless and, at root, uncritical questions. To answer "Yes, perhaps" to the first, and "No" to the second, is but to say that Miss Clemence Dane draws her women more persuasively than her men. There can be no arbitrary ruling about what men and women will or will not do. What concerns us is whether what they do on the stage seems to spring from their individualities and circumstance or from the dramatist's command. That is the difference between drama and theatricalism.

In the present play, which for a dozen reasons is a delightful and absorbing entertainment, there is only one flaw, which Mr. Douglas Fairbanks, the younger, though his performance is pleasant and attractive, has not the guile to conceal. It is that Miss Dane commands Stephen too much. One feels that, having made up her mind at the outset that he is to be abnormally suspicious and lacking in self-confidence, she has, so to speak, tied these labels round his neck and sent him as a parcel, denying to him that illusion of free-will on which the truth of dramatic characterization rests. But, Stephen being granted, all is well. If he was what he is represented as being, the rest follows – even the scene in which Josephine, terrified by his jealousy, gives him the confession by which alone he can be satisfied. The rest follows – unless one is to assume that the girl, instead of pursuing the scene to a swooning curtain, rings for a reasonable glass of cold water and goes to bed.

But this after all is a play, and too good a play to have cold water poured upon it. The first act is enchanting. Stephen comes home from abroad, and Miss Gertrude Lawrence's welcome of him is enough to make doubt impossible in any mind but Stephen's own. One observes first a white frock so genuinely beautiful that not to comment on it is to miss one of the pleasures of the evening; then that Miss Lawrence is within it; then that she is acting with a grace and tenderness and vivacity new even in her. She is not playing with this man; she loves him, and the sparkle she gives to her dialogue is not the harsh tinsel of the stage but the brilliance of happiness itself. When it is discovered that she is about to be dragged into a divorce case by the wife of a neighbour, Charles Lankaster, she is at first incredulous, then laughs. With Charles! Charles is a dear, a nice, solid, friendly creature – but to be accused of having been unfaithful with Charles, that is too much! If Stephen had watched her he might have been reassured. But he had retired to his gloomy, suspicious corner, from which two acts were needed to extract him.

And the two acts, however actively one may desire a glass of water for Stephen, are worth watching. The faithful Charles, upon whom faithfulness is a mildly ridiculous burden, is given an excellent edge by Mr. Barry Jones; Mr. Cecil Parker, a gently pompous brother, Miss Martita Hunt, an intelligent friend with a shrewd eye to cold water, and Miss Helen Haye, a grandmother unobtrusively faultless, are admirable; and though it may be true that Miss Lawrence, in high emotion, has not the perfect control that distinguishes her gentler moods, it is true also that she is compelled by the nature of her part to force the emotional pace. It is possible to prefer the earlier to the later passages of her performance, but only because her first act is so lovely a piece of comedy that whatever follows is imperilled by the memory of it.

26 SEPTEMBER 1934, THE TIMES

Josephine
from the German of Hermann Bahr by Emlyn Williams

HIS MAJESTY'S THEATRE

JOSEPHINE	Mary Ellis
NAPOLEON BONAPARTE	Frank Vosper
EUGENE BEAUHARNAIS	Emlyn Williams
AN ORDERLY	Donald Wolfit
MADAME LAROSE	Lady Tree
TALMA	George Grossmith

Though Josephine, in conversation with Barras, had given fair warning that Bonaparte was like a tiger, Mr. Frank Vosper's conduct of the first act was a surprise. It is one thing to enter a drawing-room as though you had come out of a cage; it is another and a slightly ridiculous thing to prowl and snarl continuously as though only cages existed. It is, moreover, one thing to be a tiger, with the tigerish virtues of swiftness, decision, courage, and another to be a creature full of mewing and swearing, but with no higher ambition than to retire to Corsica with Josephine. This in 1796. It may be very satisfactory to guy great men and very reasonable to criticize them, but he that wishes to persuade us that Napoleon was silly, contemptible, pompous, of no account, needs to be a more subtle illusionist than Herr Hermann Bahr.

Even before Lodi, where it is true that Bonaparte's military genius was not at its highest, he is shown as a man to whom his army was nothing and the Paris courier everything. There he sits, deaf to news of battle, consulting fortune-tellers and mewing for Josephine. Lady Tree is the fortune-teller and to see her in militarily uniform is worth a wilderness of tigers; there is a good breathless orderly by Mr. Donald Wolfit, a comfortable old soldier by Mr. Lyn Harding, and a lively, quick-witted Eugene by Mr. Emlyn Williams; but for all their help in passing it, the time is long until at last Bonaparte does something – in brief, goes out. After that, the only remaining encouragement is Mr. Vincent Korda's *décor* for the palace to which Josephine is brought in Milan. The play itself becomes one of those things at which it would be kind to laugh. Miss Mary Ellis, compelled to a tourist's vulgarity which, for all her faults, was not Josephine's, does all that may be done to give personal sparkle to nonsense about nightdresses, and to grumblings, in the Tuileries, about the pomp that stands between her and the man she loves. But this Josephine is so mean a creature, so awkward and silly a minx, that one wonders whether Herr Bahr can have supposed her to have been a peasant and whether this is his idea of a peasant dressed up. Bonaparte himself is treated correspondingly; he's never shown at work; Mr. Vosper is given not a spark of talent to play with; and the piece quickly perishes when Talma (Mr. George Grossmith) gives him a prolonged lesson in impressive attitudes – a scene of which it is impossible to tell whether its intention is satire or farce. The gallery, giving it the benefit of so uncomfortable a doubt, laughed enviably. The rest of us politely went down with the ship.

9 NOVEMBER 1934, THE TIMES

It Happened to Adam by David Boehm

DUKE OF YORK'S THEATRE

MRS. SLOAN   May Whitty
BRUCE CAMPBELL   Basil Radford

Though it would be pleasanter to leave this play unnoticed and so be the sooner rid of the taste of it, it is perhaps necessary to mention its subject and a few of its more conspicuous incidents. It concerns a young man, reputed to have won a Nobel Prize, who has written five volumes on the love-life of the lower organisms. The completion of the sixth is delayed by the effect on his nerves of an unsatisfied "instinct to mate." This instinct he sets out to satisfy, aided by the advice of others – of his butler, who chooses a plain secretary as candidate for his master's addresses; of a "man of the world" who, having given a lesson in technique, supplies by telephone a subject for experiment; and of a professional wrestler whose suggestions lead to the appearance of the Nobel prizewinner in wrestling costume and to his combat with the lady of his heart. The dialogue that accompanies the action draws a great part of its supposed humour from the relationship between the behaviour of men and women and that of organisms ungenerously called "lower." The actors and actresses play with professional skill and have laughter as their reward, if laughter springing from such material may be so regarded.

Hamlet by William Shakespeare[2]

NEW THEATRE

HORATIO	Jack Hawkins
GHOST	William Devlin
CLAUDIUS	Frank Vosper
LAERTES	Glen Byam Shaw
POLONIUS	George Howe
HAMLET	John Gielgud
GERTRUDE	Laura Cowie
OPHELIA	Jessica Tandy
ROSENCRANTZ	Richard Ainley
GUILDENSTERN	Antony Quayle
FIRST PLAYER	George Devine
SECOND PLAYER	Sam Beazley
FORTINBRAS	Geoffrey Toone
A COURIER	Frith Banbury
OSRIC	Alec Guinness

I s it a cold tribute to an actor to say that his Hamlet in the theatre gives pleasure of the same quality and measure as a private reading of the play? It should not be, for in a man's library is given his ideal performance, free of physical impediment; and Mr. Gielgud's playing is, for one spectator at least, this performance's precise equivalent. To others it may well seem too little spectacular, too curbed in its emotional display; but, indeed, Hamlet is not a flaunting part, though it is often so treated; it is not designed to provoke hot tears and shouting but to penetrate the soul by way of the intellect; and the first merit of Mr. Gielgud's interpretation is that it does not throw up passionate mists with which to conceal confusions. From the chill, ironical menace of its opening to the fierce attack of the play-scene and the terrible rage at the burying of Ophelia it pursues its argument with a brilliant lucidity. Nothing is smudged or doubtful; everything is as decisive as the line in the pencil-drawing of a master.

The consequence is that the problems of Hamlet's indecision resolve themselves. What held him from action was not fear, not some obscure disease of the will, but a quick intellectual apprehension of the event. Deep in his mind was knowledge of action's futility. To say that he would have acted if he had been bolder or stronger or more naturally human is to miss the point; he would have acted if he had been less intelligent. This is the seed from which the varied beauty of Mr. Gielgud's performance springs, and this is why it is completely satisfying to the mind – so satisfying in its

---

2   Because of its distinction the whole cast is given although not all are mentioned in the review.

application to the instance of Hamlet that imagination springs, as it does in a reading of the play, from the melancholy particular to the tragic universal. In this sense, the performance is deeply moving. It has the influence of a sky from which storm after storm has passed away, leaving a final and absolute serenity.

That one actor's performance should have this effect is made possible by the cast that surrounds him. Of these only one is at fault, and, indeed, the fault is not in her acting. Miss Jessica Tandy's appearance and temperament, the almost aggressive sprightliness of her, run contrary to Ophelia; but Mr. George Howe's Polonius, not a buffoon but an unconscious wit, Mr. Vosper's dark portrait of the King, Miss Laura Cowie's Queen – a little stupid as Hamlet's mother was – Mr. Hawkins's Horatio, and Mr. Devlin's Ghost are very distinguished company. Motley's setting is, in most scenes, beautiful if examined, and has the supreme virtue of submitting itself to the play.

2 DECEMBER 1934, THE NEW YORK TIMES

The Gielgud Hamlet

That dramatist, Shakespeare, whom we are so often accused of neglecting, once more claims this week the whole attention of the English theatre, for John Gielgud, now his own director, has appeared as Hamlet, and his performance is of such a rank as will entitle it to be remembered and debated for many years to come. He has played Hamlet before, but this performance is new, freshly considered and evidently strengthened by the actor's maturing powers.

To those who remember Forbes-Robertson's Hamlet, which I unfortunately do not, there appears, I believe, a certain coldness in Mr. Gielgud's treatment. The difference is, first of all, a difference of voice. Though I did not see Forbes-Robertson in this particular part, I know his voice well enough; it has, even now in his old age, an extraordinary richness and subtlety; there is emotion in the very sound of it, a sweetness and tenderness which, independently of the meaning of the words spoken, may, if the hearer does not keep a very careful guard over his intellectual integrity, bring tears to the eyes. It follows that, when the words were Hamlet's, Forbes-Robertson must have been able to ring the heart of his audience. Mr. Gielgud makes no attempt to do anything of the kind.

His own voice is beautiful and flexible, but it is – if I may so express the difference between him and Forbes-Robertson – without emotional resonance. To him the great soliloquies are not recitals on some angelic organ but the natural language of the mind, and he treats dialogue – with the exception of two passages – with faultless intelligence and vitality. I have never before heard the rhythm of verse and the naturalness of speech so gently combined.

The passages in which something is lacking are those in which Hamlet's tenderness towards Ophelia should be manifest and, for very different reasons, Hamlet's address to the players. These passages, above all others in the tragedy, require of Hamlet a human warmth which may suggest that likeable aspect of him which Godfrey Tearle, when he played the part, so happily revealed. Mr. Gielgud's Hamlet is not by any of the standards of plain judgment or affection a likeable man; sensitive, brilliant, pitiable, admirable, sometimes even lovable – all this he is, but not likeable. He is too singular, too aloof.

The wildness of his grief at Ophelia's grave is a magnificent surprise; we have not felt before that the girl is of any profound interest to him except as an integral part of his intellectual scheme. Other sentiments may exist between them, but not affection, not tenderness, nothing so warm or so simple that the heart of such a girl as Ophelia might mistake it for love. A part of the cause of this negative impression may be in the present Ophelia, for Miss Jessica Tandy is miscast.

Ophelia was modest, filial, submissive, unarmoured against the world; Miss Tandy, who made her reputation as the girl in *Mädchen in Uniform*, is an extremely accomplished young actress, but she is "modern," she is "up and coming"; half her charm is in her cheekiness. The scenes between her and Mr. Gielgud always seemed to me to be a little at cross-purposes. As for the address to the Players, I have no wish to insist upon it. The fault, if fault it was, is of no great importance and may have sprung from the nervousness of a first night. Mr. Gielgud seemed to me here to ride too high a horse, to treat the Players too much as if he were Dryden delivering a closely argued lecture in dramatic poesy; but this is a small matter.

What is, to me, a great matter is that this Hamlet gave me, as no Hamlet has ever done outside my own library, complete intellectual satisfaction. Here in the flesh was the creature of my own most secret imagination, differing only in this – that I have a certain reserved affection for my own Hamlet – while Mr. Gielgud's is aloof from affection. But he brings to the stage a miraculous and unprecedented lucidity of mental process. It has always seemed to me that the key to Hamlet's behaviour is to be found in his speech about Fortinbras and his armies – a speech that it is an astonishing habit of actors to omit.

Although there are indications that Hamlet was a good sportsman and certainly a fine fencer, he was not at any time what is ordinarily called "a man of action" – that is, a lover of action in whom action created singleness of mind. Nor, I think, was he of a highly imaginative or poetical temperament, though the peculiar Renaissance twist of mind which prevents him from killing Claudius on his knees lest the victim should go to heaven has in it more than a touch of imaginative fantasy. But the basis of Hamlet was his intellect.

The effect of Mr. Gielgud's treatment of Hamlet as an "intellectual" is to illumine the whole play. One has an impression, not of studying a masterpiece entangled by doubt and tradition, but of watching a new play instantly comprehensible and coherent. There is a fine King by Frank Vosper, a skilfully stupid Queen by Miss Laura Cowie and a most brilliant Polonius by George Howe. If I see a better performance of the play than this before I die, it will be a miracle; the only evident flaw is Ophelia.

21 DECEMBER 1934, THE TIMES

The Scarlet Pimpernel
A film from Baroness Orczy's novel

PRODUCED BY ALEXANDER KORDA
DIRECTED BY HAROLD YOUNG
LEICESTER SQUARE THEATRE

SIR PERCY BLAKENEY	Leslie Howard
LADY BLAKENEY	Merle Oberon
CHAUVELIN	Raymond Massey
THE PRINCE OF WALES	Nigel Bruce
ROBESPIERRE	Ernest Milton

To have been for many years an adherent of the Scarlet Pimpernel is to have the best of excuses for a mild confusion of his many adventures. Was there not a famous drive with Lady Blakeney inside the coach and Sir Percy on the box? Where is it? Or does that belong to another part of his chronicle? No matter. Hero though he is, he has not the classical rank of Mr. Pickwick to make passionate textualists of us all, and what matters, when he comes to the screen, is that he shall be, in his hours of ease, an elegant fop, a boon companion of the Regent, a lazy, posing, worthless fellow whom his wife can justifiably despise, but, in his bursts of secret activity, a gallant adventurer who, in impenetrable disguises, thwarts the villainous Chauvelin and snatches lovely French aristocrats from the guillotine.

Mr. Leslie Howard is all this and more. First, he is the old hag who drives the Tournay family through the barriers of Paris in a cart; then, in London, the empty-headed dandy whom all but the knowing contemn; then, dandy and strategist rolled into one, he is engaged in a battle of wits with Chauvelin. Miss Merle Oberon, who persistently resembles Miss Merle Oberon, may not be everyone's notion of a lady of fashion at the close of the eighteenth century, but she gives a sharp emotional twist to the tale when Chauvelin, by threatening her brother's life, drives her into betrayal of the unknown Pimpernel; and there, bless him, is Sir Percy feigning sleep in the library at midnight and there is the abominable Chauvelin allowing his prey to escape once more. But for a moment only. Soon the pursuit begins. The scene shifts to Boulogne. Lady Blakeney is there in an endeavour to save the man she loves and has unwittingly betrayed. But Sir Percy is well able to look after himself. Chauvelin traps him; the struggle between the two – Mr. Raymond Massey a dark, complacent menace at the table and Mr. Leslie Howard giving to effrontery a final romantic polish – is the best of the good things in the film; and behold, in spite of all the revolutionary platoons that surround the *Lion d'Or*, the Scarlet Pimpernel and his lady are away in their frigate and Chauvelin is indefinitely imprisoned in the basement.

Our own idea of Chauvelin was of something more moth-eaten than Mr. Raymond Massey can accomplish, but a frowning, swaggering villain serves almost as well, and there are a dozen other good performances to support Mr. Howard's – conspicuously Mr. Nigel Bruce's Regent and Mr. Ernest Milton's brief but impressive sketch of Robespierre. The sequence of the story might be better than it is; it has a tendency to hop, rather than flow, from scene to scene; but the spirit of the book is in it, its guileless adventure unspoiled by any of the so-called improvements which a less discreet studio might have invented.

22 JANUARY 1935, THE TIMES

Othello by William Shakespeare

OLD VIC

RODERIGO	Alan Webb
IAGO	Maurice Evans
OTHELLO	Abraham Sofaer
CASSIO	Leo Genn
DUKE OF VENICE	Cecil Trouncer
DESDEMONA	Vivienne Bennett
EMILIA	Mary Newcombe
BIANCA	Irene Palmer

Except to very pious bardolators, for whom Shakespeare can do no wrong, *Othello* is a teasing play – so magnificent, so wise, and even so true in many things, yet, in the ingenuities upon which its motive of jealousy is built, so unpersuasive. The Moor's concluding explanation of himself – thrust in, one would hazard, that Shakespeare might reassure Shakespeare – makes things worse, not better. This man, we are told, is

... Not easily jealous, but being wrought

Perplex'd in the extreme;

yet this is he who strangled the wife he loved without confronting her with Iago or Iago with Cassio. And unless we are prepared to fall back upon the desperate supposition that Iago was a creature possessed, for whom evil was for its own sake a good, we listen with something more than idle curiosity when Othello exclaims: –

Will you, I pray, demand that demi-devil

Why he hath thus ensnared my soul and body?

This time Shakespeare makes no final essay in analysis. "Demand me nothing," says Iago, "what you know you know. From this time forth I never will speak word." The incredulous spectator is left to make what he can of it.

To make what he can of it in the end, as the actors, cloaking the incredible in a pageant of words and concealing the major untruth in a thousand glittering truths, have been making what they can of it from the beginning. In a special sense, their task in this play is to suspend unbelief, and at the Old Vic they come very near to success. The four principal parts, considered collectively, have not within our recollection been better performed. Mr. Leo Genn's Cassio is simple and thoroughly likeable as that soldier should be; Miss Vivienne Bennett, though her expression is sometimes too hard and she lacks the exaltation of love, speaks her lines with excellent understanding and music; Mr. Alan Webb and Miss Mary Newcombe give good account of Roderigo and Emilia; and still Iago and Othello remain. It is almost possible to believe in Mr. Evans's Iago without running away into diabolism. The man has a kind of vile gaiety, a bragging way of parading his cunning that makes vanity the acceptable poison of his soul. The portraiture is brilliantly clear and firm; it may not answer all questions about Iago, but it stills them.

And Mr. Abraham Sofaer's Othello is a structure of the greatest intricacy and intelligence. At first what he seeks its lucidity and a firm establishment of Othello as a man of tenderness and reason; then, at Iago's prompting, madness comes upon him, not in a flood of rhetoric, but like a slow poison that at last seizes his brain. In the scene of the killing Mr. Sofaer exhibits the defect of his merits; not wishing to foam at the mouth, he is a little too cold; his love for Desdemona is perceptible in his deed, but does not shine through it. Apart from this, his performance is masterly, alike in its unsurpassed use of language and in the flowing urgency of its thought.

15 FEBRUARY 1935, THE TIMES

Barnet's Folly by Jan Stewer

HAYMARKET THEATRE

HANNAH MUDGE	Muriel Aked
GEORGE GROWSELL	Jan Stewer
LUCY LANNACOT	Mary Jerrold
MARK LANNACOT	Herbert Lomas
RICHARD BARNET	Reginald Tate
ELIZABETH BURRIDGE	May Agate
HETTIE BURRIDGE	Judy Hallatt

From time to time it happens that three hours of humorous life in Loamshire set the citizens of London guffawing in their stalls; and, indeed, a stall or a seat in the pit is a very convenient place from which to observe the activities of that prosperous county. To live in it would be a different matter. One cannot live on a farm where the cook and the cowman have a joke in every line, where even the visitors cannot open their mouths without uproariously entangling a couple of proverbs, and where, after fate has cruelly struck the farmer down, there is such sparkling unanimity among the hearts of gold. When the farmer, counting the loyal heart-beats of his retainers and gratefully observing the virtue of his wife and daughter, declares – in case the moral should not be plain to urban minds – that good most marvellously springs from evil, and when, at the last moment, he receives a letter that offers him the tangible salvation of £30,000, one would, if resident at Melston farm, sing a little hymn and return to the bleak reality of Baker Street by the Metropolitan Railway.

But viewing these things from a stall at the Haymarket, one is content. There have been many rural fantasies with worse and fewer jokes. There has been none with a less doubtful moral. The thing, in brief, is good in its own kind, with a workable fable, a pleasantly mixed drollery, a cheerful sentiment, and a competent performance. Miss May Agate succeeds even in making a character out of the lady with the villainous proverbs; Miss Muriel Aked, dry and commanding, and the author, a stubborn charmer of cows, play ingenuously together; Mr. Herbert Lomas – though even in Loamshire no actor can get away with all this good farmer's emotional decoration – gets away with a creditably high proportion of it; there are two little spurts of feeling ably communicated by Mr. Ralph Michael and Miss Judy Hallatt; and, as the heroine, Miss Jane Harwood has a lightness and steadiness of touch which keep her part on the plane of comedy and will serve her equally well in other counties than this. Their combined entertainment highly pleased their audience, and, indeed, there are many advantages in Melston Farm as long as one doesn't intend to live there.

4 APRIL 1935, THE TIMES

The Old Ladies
adapted by Rodney Ackland from Hugh Walpole's novel[3]

NEW THEATRE

MRS. BLOXHAM	Beatrix Feilden-Kaye
MAY BERINGER	Jean Cadell
LUCY AMOREST	Mary Jerrold
AGATHA PAYNE	Edith Evans

The lodgings of the three old ladies are in a draughty, dilapidated house in Polchester. By virtue of Motley's extremely skilful design the bleak little hall, the rickety staircase, and the three bed-sitting-rooms all lie open to view. Each room describes its inhabitant. In the foreground, on the level of the hall, is the cheerful neatness of Mrs. Amorest, a pink-cheeked widow with the gentle

---

3   Of this review James Agate wrote to the Editor of *The Times*: "this is the most brilliant piece of writing which has appeared in connexion with the theatre within recent years and the high watermark of the craft at the present day."

self-assurance of an easy conscience and a courageous, simple mind. In the curve of the staircase is the pale, indeterminate gentility of Miss Beringer, a timid creature whom life has starved and who responds to Mrs. Amorest's neighbourly kindness not with warmth, for no warmth is left in her, but with an agitated, chattering gratitude at which a part of the audience laughed until even they perceived the icy tragedy of it. And on the first floor, at the back, in a room dripping with highly coloured shawls and fringes in the midst of which, telling the cards of her Gypsy ancestors, Mrs. Payne sits in her rocking chair, a sprawling woman like a fierce and raddled toad.

Mrs. Amorest invites the others to a little party on Christmas Eve. Out of her poverty she has bought them presents and on the table has set up a tiny, glittering Christmas tree. Miss Beringer is delighted, and Miss Jean Cadell, brilliantly discovering a schoolgirl's excitement in this old hunted woman, chatters and giggles and hesitates until one's heart would break. Miss Mary Jerrold, the hostess, calm and plump and wistful is meanwhile drawing a portrait less spectacular, but in its nature more endearing and in its restraints as subtle. And down the stairs, supporting on the banisters her monstrous weight, comes Mrs. Payne. Mrs. Amorest, not being afflicted by nervous imagination, treats her with the tolerant affection that she lavishes on all the world, but poor Miss Beringer is with reason terrified. Mrs. Payne says little or nothing. Colour and glitter arouse in her a silencing lust. Her black, sodden eyes glare at the Christmas tree; her head becomes fixed, her bloated body seems to swell and loosen, her hands are flaccidly covetous. When at last the party is over and, on her way upstairs, she is shown the piece of carved and glowing amber that is Miss Beringer's dearest possession, her longing is directed towards it and her implacable cruelty towards its owner. The story of the play has still to be told – how Mrs. Payne won the amber by a process of mental torture that drove Miss Beringer to collapse and death – but, in a sense, it is all told when Miss Edith Evans first sees the object of her desire. Her back is towards us; she is powerless to act with her face; but the wrench of that gross body, the horrible greed of the uplifted arm and hand are enough. The theme of menace and suffering is stated; what follows is a poignant elaboration of it.

That the play is comfortable, no one need pretend; its life's blood is cruelty and terror, and they are not comfortable things; but its life is abundant, its impact continuous, and its performances, orchestrated by Mr. Gielgud, collectively flawless. And Miss Evans's own performance is something more. It is creative and cumulative – a slow nightmare of *macabre* genius. The body, the eyes, the hands are terrible enough, but the mouth wears the very shape and colour of the mind's disease. The whole figure, in its stained and mountainous velvets, is like some insane doll that increases continuously in physical stature and spiritual decay.

The Flying Trapeze
by Douglas Furber from the book by Hans Müller

MUSIC BY RALPH BENATZKY AND MABEL WYNNE
DANCES BY FREDERICK ASHTON
ALHAMBRA

The pleasures of this entertainment are, above all else, pleasures of the eye. The music is good in its own kind – that is to say, it neither moans nor whimpers but has a genuine and sensuous gaiety; the chief performers – Miss Ivy St. Helier with the dash and swagger of a circus proprietor, Mr. Jack Buchanan as trapeze-artist and wide-eyed hero, Mr. Fred Emney as comic master of the ceremonies – have material enough to exhibit their form, and a heroine, eupeptically girlish and a trifle too exclamatory even for such a piece as this, is represented at any rate with a cheerful skittishness by Miss June Clyde. The clowns, particularly Mr. Richard Hearne, are amusing, agile and not raucous; there are two sketches above the average – an operatic burlesque and a droll imitation by Mr. Emney and Mr. Buchanan of a ventriloquist and his doll; and such side-shows as are provided by the Su-Yee troupe of acrobats and by Gudzow's *haute école* fit satisfactorily into this remarkable circus's rehearsal (Act I.) or gala performance (Act II.). But what gives distinction to the evening – so rare a distinction that even those to whom clowns and acrobats mean little may have delight in the Alhambra – is the combined work of Professor Stern as designer, of Herr Charrell as producer, and of Miss Pearl Argyle as *première danseuse*.

The stage lies open, uncurtained. Its shape is circular for the good reason that it is the ring of a Parisian circus. Upstage, above the entrance to the ring, is the orchestra-box, and on either side are the seats of the spectators. The date is, vaguely, 1860, and it is the Empress of the French who occupies the stage-box and, with her ladies-in-waiting, forms a lovely detached group. In the scheme of colour reds are dominant – and with what subtle variants Professor Stern plays upon them! To any eye accustomed to the tangled, clashing, formless tinsel of many English *revues*, it is a pleasure to submit to the coherent design of a single artist. Here, too, is tinsel; that, indeed, is part of the charm, for, if you are decorating a circus, the thing must glitter, must flash, must have a certain theatrical aggressiveness. The spectator is entitled to feel, not that he is in a temple dedicated to the Muses, but inside an inspired wedding-cake made by the fairies in a moment of recklessness. This Professor Stern has achieved, and to this Herr Charell, by the massed movement of his people and the dissolving of design into design, has brilliantly contributed. ...

Golden Arrow by Sylvia Thompson and Victor Cunard

WHITEHALL THEATRE

LADY HARBEN	Helen Haye
PHILIPPE FAYARD	Cecil Parker
SEBASTIEN LEE	Denys Blakelock
RICHARD HARBEN	Laurence Olivier
FANNY FIELD	Greer Garson

This lamentable youth, who represents England at Belcarno, has nothing to recommend him except that he, in turn, is represented by Mr. Laurence Olivier. All that he does, from his loud and languishing flirtation in the Ladies' Gallery of the House to his reconciliation with his mistress in the lounge of an hotel, is to the discredit of his intelligence – everything except his desertion of the lady in whose grip we leave him. She is American and persistent. Deserted, she climbs over the balcony, dangles from it and screams. Rescued, she chooses as her travelling companion a French politician, chastily dupes him, and so reaches Belcarno and a postponed altar. She is Miss Greer Garson, who has at any rate a lively impudence of manner, and is accompanied in her travels by Mr. Cecil Parker, Mr. Denys Blakelock, and Miss Helen Haye, all of whom can give point to a "line." Other excuses being inadequate, the piece may be supposed to exist for the sake of its "lines." Many of these have the verbal neatness which may pass for wit between smoking-room and alcove, but it is a pity that our audacious statesman, if he must be daring in Latin, should be tripped by a quantity in his fourth word.

1 JUNE 1935, THE TIMES

Night Must Fall by Emlyn Williams

DUCHESS THEATRE

MRS. BRAMSON	May Whitty
OLIVIA GRAYNE	Angela Baddeley
HUBERT LAURIE	Basil Radford
MRS. TERENCE	Kathleen Harrison
DAN	Emlyn Williams

Mr. Emlyn Williams is blessed, as his name implies and his work has proved, with a Celtic imagination, which means, on this occasion, that his interest in murder is not the same as his interest in a crossword puzzle. As dramatist and as actor he has chosen to live inside the murderer's mind and to communicate his experience in a play that combines suspense of plot with genuine imaginative tension.

His story is extremely simple. A girl has been killed in the Essex wood on the outskirts of which Mrs. Bramson has a bungalow. Mrs. Bramson is an ill-tempered, self-pitying old woman who bullies her niece and her servants, lives unnecessarily in an invalid's chair, and keeps large sums of money on the premises. A young waiter from the local hotel in which the murdered girl was staying has no difficulty in flattering himself into Mrs. Bramson's confidence. He makes a virtue of her pretended ailments, fetches her shawl, wheels her chair, and charms her with his false and sprightly manners until she dotes upon her Dan with a blind, hungry doting. Her niece, on the contrary, is at once suspicious of him. She perceives that he is evil, that he is eaten up by vanity and by a passion for self-dramatization, and is led by fragments of evidence to knowledge that he is a murderer. She knows this; she knows also that, in time, he will make old Mrs. Bramson his second victim: but, in the midst of her terror and loathing, she is fascinated by the man who exists, suffering and perhaps spiritually innocent, within this arrogant, vain, play-acting shell.

The dramatist does not force the event. Once or twice Dan comes very near to detection and is saved by the glibness of his own tongue and by the girl's sudden impulses to help him; but the fate inherent in his own character is allowed to operate in such a way that, though the killing of the old lady is a very skilful piece of dramatic narrative, the interest of the play, even at the crisis of its action, is less in such things as cushions, paraffin, and hooting owls than in the imaginations of the protagonists. The only weakness in the writing is in its humorous sops. Its servant girls are, as tricks of the theatre, successful comic relief, and no doubt the play will be the more popular for their sakes, but Mr. Emlyn Williams could have dispensed with them. Their aim is directly at the audience, as the aim of the other persons of the drama is not. The murderer, Mrs. Bramson and her niece are drawn with the faithful economy of an artist. Dame May Whitty gives a rare authenticity to the old woman's doting vanity, and discovers a natural terror in her end. Mr. Williams himself lays open Dan's mind with a discretion and vision that yield a cumulative excitement that is the opposite of sensationalism, and Miss Baddeley's study of the girl has the very rare power of enabling the audience to grow in understanding of her, and to be more deeply interested by each expansion of their knowledge.

15 JUNE 1935, THE TIMES

Anything Goes by Guy Bolton and P. G. Wodehouse

LYRICS AND MUSIC BY COLE PORTER
PALACE THEATRE

BILLY CROCKER	Jack Whiting
RENO LAGRANGE	Jeanne Aubert
HOPE HARCOURT	Adele Dixon

A large and glittering liner in mid-Atlantic, eastward bound with a most fortunate list of passengers. Several of them are in disguise, one has many disguises, and the rest – though, as far as their consciences are concerned, they have nothing to conceal – change their frocks with the generous frequency that is expected of Mr. Cochran's Young Ladies. The ponderous clergyman with the floppy feet and the small half-brother of a machine-gun always at hand is Dr. Moon by courtesy, a crook by profession, and Mr. Sydney Howard in fact. His method of befriending our hero, who has no ticket, no money, but the lady of his heart on the passenger-list, is to lend him the ticket and passport of Public Enemy Number One. The confusions, the arrests, the escapes, the confessions, and the romantic triumph of this adventurous young man are represented by Mr. Jack Whiting with the dash and energy that have made American playboys what they are. Meanwhile the scenes change, the ladies dance, the audience leans back to enjoy itself and the moon shines as requisite.

The entertainment has the form and fable of a musical comedy but the gloss and snap of a *revue*. Mr. Sydney Howard has been given a genuinely absurd character to play with, and discovers, in the benign good-nature of a crook who can never reach the head of his criminal profession, an excellent opportunity for his clowning. Miss Jeanne Aubert has a harsh swagger of her own which most brilliantly drives her songs home; Miss Adele Dixon responds gracefully to the Atlantic moon; and there are a dozen performances, all fitting neatly into their places ... But the point of the evening is not in its individual performances but in its collective speed and economy. Nothing lasts too long. A song, a scene, a group of costumes makes its mark and is gone at precisely the moment when, in a less well-regulated entertainment, it might have begun to drag. Neither the wit nor the decor is above a high average of its kind, but the entertainment as a whole has a gleaming smoothness that is, perhaps, best expressed as the difference between what the programme calls a "satin swim suit" and what, in the days of a different technique of musical comedy, would have been described as a bathing-dress.

Murder in the Cathedral
Mr. Eliot's play

The Festival of Music and Drama, organized by the Friends of Canterbury Cathedral, began on Saturday, and will continue throughout the present week. A new play, *Murder in the Cathedral*, by Mr. T. S. Eliot, was performed during the evening in a setting designed by Mr. Laurence Irving to accord with the existing decoration of the Chapter House. The action, which is accompanied throughout by the tragic comments of a chorus of Canterbury women, describes Becket's return to England, his resistance to the persuasions of four Tempters, who represent the innermost working of his own mind, his death, and his murderers' attempt to justify their action. The play is an exposition, in Becket, of the nature of saintliness, and contains an urgent suggestion that the problems by which he was beset are present to-day. In form it is something between a Morality and a chronicle play, the use of introspective symbols being subtly interwoven with a simplified historical narrative.

Recognising the necessities of the dramatic medium, Mr. Eliot has put away from him, except on rare occasions, the use of private symbols and has written in a way that may be generally understood. There are certain passages of which, though the meaning is plain, the aesthetic purpose remains obscure – namely, those in which Mr. Eliot employs a limping jingle that reminds the hearer of nothing so much as the "book" of a pantomime. In some instances the intention appears to be satirical, the speaker (for example, one of the Tempters) being made to use language which, though its argument is serious, argues against itself by its sound: –

> And later is worse, when men will not hate you
> Enough to defame or to execrate you,
> But pondering the qualities that you lacked
> Will only try to find the historical fact;
> When men shall declare that there is no mystery
> About this man who played a certain part in history.

But sometimes the same jingle is used when there can be no satirical intention – perhaps simply to avoid stateliness of phrase in connexion with commonplace subjects. The Archbishop, encountering the murderers, says to his priests: –

On my table you will find
The papers in order, and the documents signed.

Why, here, the rhyme? And, when a Tempter says: –

Hungry hatred
Will not strive against intelligent self-interest

– on what system of prosody is the statement divided into two lines?

These are surviving mannerisms. For the greater part of the play Mr. Eliot has succeeded in combining lucidity and precision with an uncommon vigour of language – a fresh vigour that fully justifies his departure from the customary forms of dramatic verse. The Chorus is never a group of women dully chanting. Taught by Miss Fogarty how to use Mr. Eliot's rhythms, it has at once dramatic and intellectual impact. Beckett himself has a corresponding freedom from stately monotony. As represented by Mr. Speaight he is extraordinarily rich in spiritual vitality, and one has an impression, particularly when he preaches his sermon on the nature of peace and the nature of martyrdom, of being admitted to his mind and of seeing the world with his eyes. Over modern religious drama there is often spread a kind of pious mist, timid and thickly traditional. This has been cast off. Mr. Eliot's writing and Mr. Martin Browne's production are continuously keen and clear, but it is, perhaps, worth remarking that the peril to Mr. Eliot's dramatic method is in his rhymes, and that its merits most movingly appear in the prose sermon and in those passages of verse that are direct in their attack and are not twisted to irony or humour.

22 AUGUST 1935, THE TIMES

Full House by Ivor Novello

HAYMARKET THEATRE

LOLA LEADENHALL	Isabel Jeans
FRYNNE RODNEY	Lilian Braithwaite
LORD HANNINGTON	Hubert Harben

Once she was a dazzler in pink crêpe de Chine who has so far mounted the theatrical ladder that she was permitted, during the run of *The Bell of Somewhere-or-Other*, to announce in song and dance that she was "the pick o' the bunch." Mr. Novello not being in the cast, and there being no piano on the stage, only Mr. Hubert Harben's modest hum could give us an idea of this rash ditty which, 25 years ago, stirred the heart of Lord Hannington. Now she is Mrs. Rodney, a scatterbrained widow, still wearing (as she is careful to tell us) pink crêpe de Chine, though invisibly, and, it is to be presumed, a few yards of baby-ribbon to decorate her ever-youthful soul. Lord H. is President of the Divorce Court. When asked by Mrs. Rodney what time it is, he replies that for him it is 25 years ago. It is not surprising that the lady bridles a little.

But the play, though shoddy enough, is not exclusively concerned with this lamentable romance. It tells also of how Mrs. Rodney, with the guileless innocence that is her reputed charm, converted her house into a gambling club by forging the police permits; how Lord Hannington, with the assistance of comic policemen from the music-halls, improvised a raid to check her dangerous career; how his daughter, Lady April, came, was smacked, but conquered, and how all the other members of Mrs. Rodney's household made their little jokes, languorous or coy. "Does he breed horses himself?" someone asks; to which Mr. Novello's dashing wit replies: "No, he is a bachelor." This exchange may suffice as a tribute to the dialogue's earnest endeavour to entertain.

Of the acting in such a piece little can be said. The creatures of the stage are manipulated puppets with all their wires visible. In the circumstances Miss Isabel Jeans and Miss Heather Thatcher did what may be done, forcing a laugh from one line, dropping it, and hastening on to the next promising sally. Mr. Harben conducted his courtship without conspicuous embarrassment, and Miss Lilian Braithwaite, having to represent a woman with no quality but silliness, missed none of her opportunities. It is surprising that Mr. Novello should not have perceived how dull stupidity can be. Perhaps he mistook it for lightness of heart.

14 SEPTEMBER 1935, THE TIMES

The Harlot by Alfred W. Paxton

ARTS THEATRE

This, as its title will suggest to the experienced, is sentimental drama about a mother's love. Rose was married to an Army officer named John. They had a baby of the same name. On papa's thirtieth birthday they gave a dinner party to which were invited the officers of the regiment and their wives. First the Colonel, a bad, bristly man with an eye for any lady but his own and a Latin tag always ready to temper his abrupt seductiveness. Although the scene was dated 20 years ago, this officer, expeditious in this as in all else, was wearing the ribbon of the 1915 Star, and when a bleeding corporal hastened in with rough news from the frontier Colonel Blakeley lived up to his reputation for speed. Leaving his whisky and soda, or peg, on the table, he and his officers (including John, who took with him a miniature of his wife as a talisman) strode out to repel the enemy, who seem to have been by this time not far from the back garden. In eight hours they were back again, the battle won, leaving their dead (including John) on the field and finding the Colonel's whisky still on the table.

Six months later, Rose, with her baby, was desperate in Bombay. At all costs little John must go to Eton, for it would leave its mark on him for life, but little John's grandfather, a niggardly peer with a rich epistolary style, would not receive child and mother as well. "What can I do?" said Rose. Margaret, her faithful maid, being a Scot, reassured her with two lines of a hymn, from which she understood that Providence, if given time, would perform wonders, though mysteriously.

The wicked Colonel was quick on his cue. He would educate little John if she –. The honest woman hesitated. Should she accept a fate worse than death or her infant a school worse than Eton? While she stood in doubt Margaret's cheerful hymn rose from the pantry, reminding her that even the amorous Colonel, though moving in a mysterious way, might be an instrument of Providence. So began her self-sacrificial descent, which ended 20 years later (prologue and epilogue) in Shanghai. Here one night she had her recompense. A young man (Eton and Oxford) visited her, not professionally but to chat, as young men will, of his mother, believed dead. Fortunately he was carrying the miniature. There was no doubt about his identity – and never had been since the play began. The company did what was possible, and the audience, adapting their humour to the heroic circumstances, enjoyed themselves.

24 SEPTEMBER 1935, THE TIMES

Peer Gynt by Henrik Ibsen

TRANSLATION BY R. ELLIS ROBERTS, MUSIC BY GREIG
OLD VIC

PEER GYNT	William Devlin
ASLAK	Alec Clunes
SOLVEIG	Vivienne Bennett

The special fascination of Ibsen's *Peer Gynt* lies not in its occasional satire on the Norwegian people, but in its impulse as poetic narrative and personal confession. Wicksteed said, and Archer approved his saying, that *Peer Gynt* is an embodiment of "the poverty of spirit and half-heartedness that Ibsen rebelled against in his countrymen." There is justification for this. Peer is often seen to be guarding his lines of communication and refusing decisively to commit himself; but this is not the predominant impression that he leaves on a spectator's mind. What strikes one is not so much poverty as pride of spirit, not timidity (though timidity is present) but the arrogance of an imagination that has not learned to be humble. *Peer Gynt* is a dramatic essay first on the spiritual perils of self-dramatization; second, on the agony of the man who, inwardly desiring it above all else, cannot accomplish the supreme imaginative act of self-loss. This is the significance of Solveig, who is for Peer the death of self from which renewal springs.

It follows that the play is to be regarded less as a satire hostile to Peer than as a heroic poem on the struggle of man for redemption, and that whoever performs the part must contrive, while illustrating the follies and vanities of Peer's behaviour by the way, to communicate his essential nobility and the presence of a divine spark within him. He is to be pitied, not despised; loved, not hated. To consider him otherwise is to range oneself with those dullards at the wedding who mock his errant imagination and against his mother, Ase, who, reproving his wilfulness and extravagance, yet loved the spiritual impulse that they so often falsely translated into action.

...

18 OCTOBER 1935, THE TIMES

Romeo and Juliet by William Shakespeare

NEW THEATRE

CHORUS	John Gielgud
TYBALT	Geoffrey Toone
BENVOLIO	Glen Byam Shaw
CAPULET	Frederick Lloyd
LADY CAPULET	Marjorie Fielding
MONTAGUE	H. R. Hignett
LADY MONTAGUE	Barbara Dillon
PRINCE OF VERONA	Alan Napier
ROMEO	Laurence Olivier
PARIS	Sam Beazley
NURSE	Edith Evans
JULIET	Peggy Ashcroft
MERCUTIO	John Gielgud
FRIAR LAURENCE	George Howe

The saying that any performance of this tragedy must depend, in the last analysis, on the temperamental fitness for their parts of the actors playing the lovers is not so platitudinous as it sounds. Mr. John Gielgud's production has much grace and distinction, but its principal fascination is that in Miss Peggy Ashcroft's Juliet art and temperament seem perpetually to be moving hand in hand. Her performance is memorable for the exquisite naturalness with which it holds the character to the plane of poetry. She is helped to this effect less by her power to feel and express the refinements of the verse than by the temperamental sympathy which enables her to preserve the spirit of childhood in the girl who has suddenly become a woman miraculously deep in love. The warmth, the capacity for feeling and for imparting happiness which belong to the woman are beautifully conveyed, but whether ecstatic on the wings of passion or distractedly rushing to death this Juliet is never far from childhood.

Here, as Miss Ashcroft presents her, is a child who in love, and in nothing but love, is a woman; she has not had time to think, only to feel; and the depth of that feeling is everywhere implicit in a performance which may falter whenever Shakespeare entangles it in a difficult wordplay but never loses its poetic reality. It is the actress's inspired insistence that Juliet makes no such strides into womanhood as Romeo makes into his suddenly attained manhood that keeps unsullied her share of the silver-sweet dialogues in the moonlit garden and heightens the poignant beauty of Juliet's end. The petals have hardly opened when the flower is crushed. Mr. Laurence Olivier, on the other hand, is temperamentally ill at ease with Romeo. He shows us none of those marvellously quick accelerations of which an actor must be capable who plays a part that seems to have been written in sudden flashes of illumination. Through all the critical scenes he moves a little heavily, failing in the early Euphuistic passages to sound the underlying note of character which is there to reveal the man who will meet his fate full face, responding but stiffly to Juliet's impassioned advances and discovering his natural powers as an actor only in the torch-lit tom, and then it is too late.

Mr. Gielgud's production is admirable in the picturesqueness of its setting and costumes and especially admirable in its arrangement of curtains. Running diagonally towards a penthouse they allow the scene-shifters to work on one segment of the stage while the players are acting on another, and the consequent swiftness makes vivid the contrast between scene and scene which is Shakespeare's most obvious technical device in this tragedy. The Italiante Mercutio, who turns to politeness his dying 'A plague on both your houses!' is Mr. Gielgud's own. Miss Edith Evans's Nurse is a separate Joy. She is not satisfied merely to speak the jokes, but shows a quick and glowing apprehension of the personality to which the jokes belong. The Nurse is as much alive on the realistic plane as Juliet is on the plane of poetry. Mr. Geoffrey Toone's Tybalt gives this butcher of silk buttons something more than mere bluster, and Mr. Frederick Lloyd greatly humanizes Capulet.

20 OCTOBER 1935, THE NEW YORK TIMES

Peer Gynt Back Again

A NEW TRANSLATION OF IBSEN'S PLAY MAKES AN APPEARANCE IN LONDON

...

It remains true ... that any verse translation which follows Ibsen at all closely must reduce the stature of the play. The reason is a simple one – that Ibsen wrote in a tripping, rollicking meter which, though acceptable to the Norwegian ear as a means to communicate high and even tragic emotion, is not acceptable to ours. In English the lilt gives to the verse a comic and sometimes a trivial overtone, for our tragic convention in the theatre is rooted in five iambics, whether rhymed in heroic couplets or preserved in the Shakespearean blank. And yet, what is a translator of *Peer Gynt* to do? A version in prose or in blank verse might well be a greater work of art than any available translation, but it would be too far from Ibsen. The dilemma is not avoidable. In all the circumstances, Ellis Roberts's work is probably as good a translation as may be hoped for.

There arises, then, the problem of how to treat the play. Who is Peer Gynt? What did he stand for in Ibsen's mind? It is necessary, first of all, to accept the fact that Ibsen, in this matter, was not consistent, and that to attempt to reduce these rambling adventures to a logical symbolism is to fall into all the crimes of pedantry. But there is one question to which the actor who represents Peer must discover a clear answer. Is Peer, at root, a heroic and pitiable figure or is he the butt of satire, intended to be mocked and despised? There are many commentators of authority who take the latter view.

Ibsen, they say, was satisfying his Norwegian compatriots; Peer is to be shown as vain, unscrupulous, shallow, above all as a man who is forever securing his lines of retreat and refusing to commit himself. For evidence they point to the scene in which Peer is mocked as a compromising shipowner who makes profit by the double export of heathen idols and Christian missionaries. This evidence is very strong, but it is to be remarked that here and elsewhere, whenever Ibsen is personally and violently satirical at Peer's expense, the play deteriorates. It becomes narrow, provincial, bitter, and its greatness fails.

A play, like a man, is best known and judged by the good in him – not merely on grounds of charity but on grounds of essential truth. What is best in *Peer Gynt* is the scenes in which Peer himself, for all his extravagance, is lovable or pitiable. Then Ibsen writes like a God and not like an ill-tempered schoolmaster. Nothing of enduring value in life or in art springs from a sneer. From love – yes; from hatred – yes; these are radical passions; but not from a sneer.

For this reason I believe William Devlin's interpretation of the part to be fully justified. Mr. Devlin is a very remarkable young man – and he is very young. Some months ago he gave a performance of King Lear which I described at the time. He has not the vocal range for the scenes on the heath; he ranted then and lost his control of the stage; but the rest of his performance had an astonishing beauty and power. By age and appearance he is better suited to Peer, and his attack on the part is deeply moving and impressive. Without blunting the edge of the satirical passages, he yet treats Peer as primarily a heroic and tragic figure – the man of brilliant and sometimes disordered imagination struggling through life for self-realization.

Ordinarily it is said of *Peer Gynt* that its lesson is that love is all. This is too vague. What I understand it to mean is that the supreme good is singleness of mind and permeability of spirit, and the supreme suffering self-division and hard-heartedness. Solveig is, for Peer, the breast on which his eyes may be hid, the lap on which he may rest, the absolute singleness to which, through many battles, he has not the courage to surrender himself but to which he comes at last.

29 NOVEMBER 1935, THE TIMES

Romeo and Juliet by William Shakespeare

NEW THEATRE

TYBALT	Harry Andrews
BENVOLIO	Glen Byam Shaw
CAPULET	Frederick Lloyd
LADY CAPULET	Marjorie Fielding
MONTAGUE	H. R. Hignett
ROMEO	John Gielgud
PARIS	Sam Beazley
PETER	George Devine
NURSE	Edith Evans
JULIET	Peggy Ashcroft
MERCUTIO	Laurence Olivier
FRIAR LAURENCE	George Howe

In this memorable performance of *Romeo and Juliet* Mr. John Gielgud is now Romeo and Mr. Laurence Olivier Mercutio. Apart from this exchange of parts, the production is, in the main, what it was when first discussed in these columns on October 18. Those whose memory carries them to Mr. Gielgud's production of the tragedy for the Oxford University Dramatic Society, in which Miss Peggy Ashcroft and Miss Edith Evans first played Juliet and her nurse, may with interest extend their comparisons. They will observe, first, that Miss Evans has broadened her treatment, permitting personal mannerisms to appear in it which are not to its advantage, though they have no power to prevent her portrait of the old woman from being one of the most theatrically effective, and certainly the most amusing, of modern times; and they will notice also that, though Miss Ashcroft still fails in self-discipline and becomes emotionally entangled when she hears of Tybalts's death and Romeo's exile, her weakness in this passage and in the potion-scene is less conspicuous than it was, while all the former virtues of her performance have been multiplied. In the scenes of love, she has an extraordinary freshness and a brilliant power to preserve Juliet's girlhood through her passion. It is a lyrical performance, as moving as a spring morning and for the same reason. There are several minor sketches of distinction among which Mr. Lloyd's Capulet and Mr. Devine's Peter may be remarked. Mr. Olivier's Mercutio has a splendid dash and swagger; never was a man so nearly mad and so well pleased with himself, intoxicated with the light and heady wines of genius. And the whole production moves apace – even the fights, which have an uncommonly persuasive clash and dexterity.

The special interest of Mr. Gielgud's work is that he has deliberately avoided what would have been, for him, the easy way to succeed in it. He is, thank heaven, a naturally romantic actor; he might, if he had pleased, have exaggerated Mr. Gielgud and, by this simple process have set the gallery in an easy blaze. But he is, happily, an artist, and has chosen a more difficult way, proving Romeo in the poetry of character rather than proclaiming him in the extravagance of personal affectations. Romeo's thought and nature appear at once, even in the early, difficult couplets, and are continually elucidated afresh, so that, when enchantment comes, reason and knowledge support it. There has seldom been better proof that, in acting, austerity of method and warmth of effect may run together. When the enchantment is established it is complete, and one remembers – how rarely does that remembrance spring from the stage! – that this supreme tragedy and the Sonnets were written by the same man.

27 DECEMBER 1935, THE TIMES

Peter Pan by J.M. Barrie

THE LONDON PALLADIUM

PETER PAN	Nova Pilbeam
CAPTAIN HOOK	George Hayes

At this stage of the play's history it is convenient to forget the implications of its sub-title – "the Boy who wouldn't grow up" – and to consider *Peter Pan* simply as a children's entertainment about pirates and redskins and wolves and an elaborate game of make-believe in the Never-Never Land. That the piece has this year been extensively recast provides a good and welcome reason for discussing the performance rather than the play itself. There is a new Peter in Miss Nova Pilbeam, who at once makes it clear that she has, in common with Miss Jean Forbes-Robertson, the merit which, in general, distinguishes good Peters from bad – that of taking the part seriously and of distinguishing its peculiar swagger from the self-conscious mincing of a principal boy in a pantomime.

...

Miss Pilbeam's performance is vigorous and clear-cut. One does not feel of her, as one did of Miss Forbes-Robertson, that this is her natural part, that she is living it rather than playing it; she is not, in the same almost mediumistic sense, abandoned to it; but she *acts* it with genuine ease and grace, her mind moves a little in advance of her words, she has the right appearance and that air of excitement and stress by which one knows that Peter is neither plain fairy nor ordinary boy.

10 AND 14 JANUARY 1936, THE TIMES

To-Night At 8.30: Three Plays by Noël Coward

THE PHOENIX THEATRE

The entertainment consists of three pieces. *Family Album* is a funereal jollity with music. The scene, dated 1860, and charmingly decorated by Mrs. Calthrop, is a background to a family of that period, weeping over their dead father and swerving, in Mr. Coward's most uncomfortable manner, from sadness to fooling, from fooling to sentimentality, and from sentimentality to high-jinx with the butler. To be on the safe side, the tears are sugared and the sentiments acidulated, but when, at length, all is said and done, the apologies to *Bitter Sweet* are found to be insufficient.

The Astonished Heart is at any rate a serious attempt to write a serious play, which, though its title is from the Bible, might well have taken its text from Shakespeare's sonnet on lust. Mr. Coward's purpose is to exhibit the tyranny of the body over the mind and the humiliation of a spirit tormented and confused. He himself is the husband; Miss Leggatt, with feeling and distinction, is the wife; Miss Gertrude Lawrence is the woman whose subject he becomes. The writing and performance are successful up to a point; they created genuine nervous tension that is clearly related to the tension of tragedy; but tragedy, though strained for, does not come. Mr. Coward's people of the theatre can quarrel brilliantly, can play upon each other's nerves, and communicate their jangled distress, but they do not suffer. They cannot contain themselves to suffer. They are too active, too glib, too adroit, too easily poured out – above all, too conscious of their audience. As a work of art, the play falls short. Miss Lawrence lying on her face on the floor and Mr. Coward leaping from the balcony have not the dignity of tragic climax. But the thing is courageous and not frivolous, not written to a popular formula. At one moment, when Mr. Coward carefully looks at his face in the mirror before going to his death, it has a genuinely imaginative pang.

But the theatrical success of the evening belongs without question to *The Red Peppers*, a music-hall pair, in their dressing room and on the stage. Here, with quarrels and back-chat, Mr. Coward the dramatist is comfortably within his range, and Mr. Coward, the actor and, above all, the dancer, knows how, with Miss Lawrence, to make the most of his own swift nonsense. It was a robust end to an otherwise slim or perilous entertainment.

* * * * *

Mr. Coward's second batch contains nothing of the same experimental interest as *The Astonished Heart*, but is remarkably firmer and more assured than his first. The opening piece, *Hands across the Sea*, is an instance of his special genius for organized irrelevance. Two people from Malaya, whom Piggie Gilpin met (and forgot) during a recent journey through the world, call upon her in London. She believes them to be two other people whom also she met (and forgot) during the same journey, and we are presented with the confusions of her mind, of her friends, of her drawing-room, of her perpetual telephone, and with the inability, at once bland and insane, of everyone present to talk or think of any subject continuously or to be silent at all. Mr. and Mrs. Wadhurst (from Malaya) are tossed like sticks on Miss Lawrence's foam of chatter, while Mr. Noël Coward, her naval husband, musically rules the waves. As a piece of production it is, technically, of the utmost brilliance; as an entertainment, in its own kind frothily faultless.

Fumed Oak, described as "an unpleasant comedy," threatens at first to be Mr. Coward's earliest contribution to the Manchester School. During the opening scene he eats Mr. Gow's gloomy breakfast in Mr. Gow's gloomy home, while his wife, his mother-in-law, and his daughter whine, bicker, and disregard him. In the evening he comes home from his shop, a worm desperate and resolute, and, to the astonishment of his womenfolk, turns. He has saved £572. He is going, he will never come back, and the women, who are bitterly capable of it, can look after themselves. To all this Mr. Coward, in a make-up of seedy canary, gives a twist of his own, lending to the domestic manners of South London and to a moth-eaten shop-walker that alertness of humour and impudence of attack which he commonly reserves for Mayfair. The merit of the play is, precisely, that being descriptive rather than satirical, it is yet description from a new point of view – as though Wilde had retouched something of Gissing's – and that its entertaining insolence makes irrelevant for the time being the narrowness of its sympathy. Seen in retrospect it is little more than the old aspidistran sneer, but while it lasts it has an admirable comic rhythm which Mr. Coward himself conducts; Miss Lawrence as a snarling shrew, Miss Leggatt as a grandmother, and Miss Moya Nugent as a snivelling schoolgirl representing meanwhile the now subverted regiment of women. The odd thought is that, if the schoolgirl had wept and not snivelled, the piece might well have insisted upon becoming a tragedy.

Shadow Play, like *Family Album,* is one of Mr. Coward's musical experiments. The only way in which to suggest what he is driving at is to say that, feeling like the rest of us, that the naturalistic convention is often inadequate to the emotion of love, he has applied his own remedy. The escape, we know, is through poetry, whether it be Shakespeare's or Strindberg's or Turgeniev's – poetry whether in verse or not. When Mr. Coward wants to imply the love underlying the bitter quarrel that we witness, he searches his lovers' past with dance and song. The song is adequate to a *revue*, the dance is charming, the whole thing is moonily pleasant to watch. It is, in brief, good enough in its sentimental kind to suggest that Mr. Coward is striving for something more than popular sentimentality and is genuinely struggling towards a new convention. Here the odd thought is that, if he would but bend his mind to the words of his songs, he might achieve it, but it seems that in a song, any adjective will pad a line for him and any rhyme will serve. As it stands, *Shadow Play* is nothing but a decoration; one lyric that was a poem might have made it the forerunner of a new *genre*. Can Mr. Coward write a lyric that is not what a musical-comedy programme calls a "lyric"? The oddest thought of all is that he, in all else so elaborate a craftsman, in this seems not to care.

31 JANUARY 1936, THE TIMES

The Dog Beneath the Skin
by W. H. Auden and Christopher Isherwood

WESTMINSTER THEATRE

WITNESSES	Gyles Isham
	Veronica Turleigh
JOURNALISTS	John Glynn-Jones
	Desmond Walter-Ellis
GRABSTERN	Stefan Schnabel
POET	Robert Eddison

One is made aware by the moral earnestness of the two commentators or "Witnesses" that Mr. Auden and Mr. Isherwood have propaganda up their sleeve, but let it be said at once that this has not prevented them from writing an entertaining *revue*. And lest it should be supposed that this is backhanded praise aimed against their earnestness, let it be added that when they speak their minds and, in the comments of the Witnesses, point the moral of their satire, they do so in passages which – whatever one may think of their political implications – are often genuinely eloquent and seldom wilfully freakish.

They have invented a little legend which sends a young man and a dog (in the skin of which a lost baronet is concealed) on a journey through the contemporary world. This world, as they see it, is a "racket" or conspiracy among men to avoid facing the evil truth and taking action to remedy it. The evil has its origin in their separation from nature and from the ancient discipline of nature over man. Man by his inventions has become master of nature and is terrified by his own mastery. Being afraid, he submits himself wildly to false gods – to dictators or to priestly men of science, to rich men or to the Press. Or he seeks to escape – in eroticism, mediaevalism, art, asceticism, faith, even in invalidism. All these are bitterly assailed in little scenes which have generally an ingenuity of rhyming contrivance and a naivety of thought that combine to keep the stage amusingly alive. The lunatics, rejoicing in their leader, Mr. Stefan Schnabel, as a rich man misunderstood, Mr. Glyn-Jones and Mr. Walter-Ellis as journalists eagerly engaged in boiling themselves harder and harder – these go to prove that Mr. Auden and Mr. Isherwood have acquired the brighter arts of pamphleteering. Towards the end the dog comes out of his skin to preach and the Witnesses tell us with summary solemnity where civilization does, or should, get off. We are to "repent, unite and act" to destroy a social system in which love is governed by money. This stage of the proceedings is a trifle embarrassing, but how easily this form of embarrassment might have occupied the whole evening and how long an immunity there is to be thankful for! The "unity" for which the authors ask is presumably a corporate state of the Left. Why, on their own spiritual principle, it is more desirable than the corporate state of the Right which they satirize is not explained; but those who are glad to see satire and entertainment combined and who, without being Communists, reasonably share many of Mr. Auden's hatreds, need not fear, while enjoying his entertainment, that their liberties will be subverted by it.

12 FEBRUARY 1936, THE TIMES
MR. CHAPLIN'S NEW FILM

Modern Times

WRITTEN, DIRECTED, AND PRODUCED BY CHARLES CHAPLIN
TIVOLI THEATRE

Not a voice is heard nor a rasping note – until Mr. Chaplin sings a song of which the charm is that its words have been forgotten. There is, inevitably, a musical accompaniment, and there is, from time to time, a variety of mechanical noises – for this Tramp's adventures are chiefly among machines – but there is no dialogue. In the absence of it the screen appears to have come into its own again. The relief of a silent film – or, rather, of a film in which supplementary sound is rightly used and no attempt is made to borrow the methods and submit to the *tempo* of the theatre – is equivalent to relief from prolonged toothache. And this remains true though Mr. Chaplin's film is by no means faultless in its own kind.

Its fault consists not in its detail, which is brilliant, but in its lack of form. Though its many incidents are strung upon a thread of satire which is evidently intended to give unity to the story, the satirical thread is extremely weak, and if, for a moment, Mr. Chaplin's invention slackens, the whole film instantly sags, for it has no shape, no narrative expectancy to sustain it. But this, one exclaims, might go on for ever! Charlie in a factory, screwing innumerable screws; Charlie in prison; Charlie in a department store; Charlie in a shack – Charlie always innocent and always the victim of the fuss, the false efficiency, the abrupt, illogical tyrannies of contemporary civilization – it is, in many of its parts, entrancing, for this is a man of genius in his own fantastic world;

but, until the end comes with Mr. Chaplin and Miss Paulette Goddard setting out on a new adventure, there is no promise of a conclusion, and the essence of a good story is the expectation, the assurance of its end.

Mr. Chaplin begins as one of a row of mechanics whose job is to tighten bolts as they pass in an endless chain. They are quicker than his spanner, and, if one eludes him, he leaps after it as an obsessed kitten spins after its tail. Into his factory comes a hopeful traveller with a mechanical device for the rapid feeding of operatives and so for saving the time customarily wasted in the dinner-hour. Mr. Chaplin is chosen as the subject of experiment. He is set in the feeding chair. Soup is poured, food is propelled, into his mouth; a corn-cob is revolved, like a barber's machine-brush under his nose; the apparatus goes mad, as machines will, and humanity, in the person of Mr. Chaplin, has a nervous breakdown. So to hospital. So, with variation of detail, to prison, from which, to his profound regret, he is released upon a bleak, noisy, friendless world.

A world, however, in which he finds a friend, a *gamine* pilfering bread and bananas on the water-front, a dark, active, dancing waif – Miss Paulette Goddard. Mr. Chaplin's immediate concern is to get back into a comfortable prison, and his attempts to do so – the meal that he blandly refuses to pay for, the cigars that he picks from a tobacconist's stall with his right hand while the policeman is engaged with his left – are among those details of fantastic invention that are the making of the film; far better than his adventure with Miss Goddard in a department store, which drags, and at least the equal of his later escapades which bring him at last, as a waiter and a singer in cabaret, to a restaurant in which Miss Goddard is the dancer.

Here Mr. Chaplin is at the top of his form. The roast duck and *Chianti* that he carries across the dancing-floor are whirled away in the dance, and when at last the opportunity comes to him, as a singer, to retrieve his shattered fortunes as a waiter, the cuff, on which the words of his song are written, being, like his memory, detachable, becomes detached. He is lost, paralysed, ruined; but, at the sight of Miss Goddard, he opens his mouth and sings. Not English, not French, not Italian, not Spanish – and yet, under the sublime influence of the Jabberwock, all of these. What he sings is the national anthem of those who builded the tower of Babel, and it is sung with an *élan*, a kind of dashing pathos, that is Mr. Chaplin's own. There are *longueurs* in the film for two plain reasons: that it has no story to give coherence to its incidents, and that, in so far as it is a satire on modern civilization, its satire is not determined enough; but it has Mr. Chaplin's abiding genius for fantastic detail and for seeing the common happenings of life not so much through a distorting glass as through the other end of truth's telescope.

Pride and Prejudice
from Jane Austen's novel by Helen Jerome

ST. JAMES'S THEATRE

MR. BENNET	Athole Stewart
MRS. BENNET	Barbara Everest
JANE BENNET	Dorothy Hyson
ELIZABETH BENNET	Celia Johnson
MR. DARCY	Hugh Williams
MR. WICKHAM	Anthony Quayle

The Janeites are at any rate given no opportunity to be insulted. The poor mummers could not have invaded their garden with a more cautious, a more discreet, one would almost say a more timorous, step. Mr. Rex Whistler has put them in his very best clothes; even the tight white legs of the men are consistently white and tight. As they advance through the garden they politely draw attention to as many of Jane's flowers as possible, transplanting them now and then, it is true, but with reverent care. Not all the flowers can be exhibited and admired. Mr. Collins's proposal has to be paraphrased, but that, it may be whispered outside the garden gate, is because Mr. Collins's proposal did, even in the book, err a little on the side of – but this is no place for heresy.

The mummers' treatment of Mr. Darcy's affair is easier to criticize. The letter is gone – that letter by which Miss Austen opened Elizabeth's eyes, and, for lack of it, Miss Jerome has been driven to highly unorthodox expedients by which, first, to explain the misunderstanding and then to explain it away. They made a muddle of the last act, with everyone being hurried off the stage as soon as he is on it, so that everyone else may have a chance to explain what has happened to Lydia, or why Wickham was wicked, or how Jane's intentions were misunderstood. Elizabeth, it will be remembered, felt, after reading that letter upon which the plot hangs, that "Jane's feelings, though fervent, were little displayed, and that there was a constant complacency in her air and manner not often united with great sensibility." That is Darcy's pardon as the letter is his excuse. The theatre, denied both the letter and Elizabeth's thoughtful comment, has its work cut out to do better than propel her into Darcy's arms.

...

Still, even the propulsion is extremely polite. The real difficulty of an adaptation of *Pride and Prejudice* is not the difficulty, common to all borrowings from classical novels, of avoiding vulgarity and anachronism or of transferring the anecdote from one medium to another. Here the common errors have been decently shunned and the anecdote is told with good faith. The acting is, for the most part, just, true, and as little excessive as circumstances permit – Mr. Athole Stewart a charming Mr. Bennet, very close to the mark; Miss Dorothy Hyson a Jane, not perhaps "complacent," for she is seen only in her least complacent moods, but a gentle allurement to Bingley; and the younger gentlemen, Mr. Hugh Williams and Mr. John Teed, as good as the compression of their opportunity allows. Mr. Collins is played for farce, but Miss Austen here shares the blame; Lady Katherine, too, and this is not Miss Austen's fault; and there are adroit sketches by Mr. Deering Wells and Miss Joan Harben. But it remains true that the essence of *Pride and Prejudice* is that it is not a demonstrative book, while acting is nothing if not a demonstrative art. The moment anyone conspicuously *acts* – as, for example, when Mrs. Bennett trots about the stage – the irony cries out "Look at me!" and the natural effect of the dialogue is swamped. It is as if the passages in the novel that some editor had thought exceptionally amusing were underlined in red. And that is reason the more for admiring the delicacy of Miss Celia Johnson's treatment of Elizabeth. There could be no higher test of theatrical tact, and Miss Johnson survives it. Every true Janeite has his own idea of Elizabeth, and it may not agree with Mrs. Johnson's portrait, but every Janeite who is not stony hearted in his prejudice will rejoice in a substitute so alive, so unforced, so intelligent and unaffected.

6 MARCH 1936, THE TIMES

Rosmersholm by Henrik Ibsen

CRITERION THEATRE

MRS. HELSETH	Esmé Church
REBECCA WEST	Jean Forbes-Robertson
RECTOR KROLL	D. A. Clarke-Smith
JOHANNES ROSMER	John Laurie
ULRICH BRENDEL	Walter Piers
PETER MORTENSGARD	Wilfred Grantham

This great play of a period not our own, springing from a set of values not ours and warring against prejudices that the years succeeding it have dissipated, is to-day without the challenge that once redeemed its gloom; so that to us, now, its gloom, though wrongly, seems deliberate, and the mill-race into which men and women throw themselves has lost its power as a symbol. The fault is not in the play, which is a masterpiece, but in ourselves – that we are too near to it. We must bide our time until it regains its impact, as certainly it will.

Meanwhile, there is nothing to do but to observe those splendours in it which assure it survival, of which the chief is the stilled passion of Rebecca West. The Rector Kroll, also, is an astute study of conservatism, and Mr. Clarke-Smith, one would have imagined, was brilliantly cast. This is an actor who, in parts grave or gay, seems never to fail; he has a range and accomplishment extremely rare in the theatre; and if he failed as Kroll it was for one reason only – that, under the rule of some obsession or some compulsion, he was playing the part faster than human being can play it. Of that there is no more to be said; it is one of the freaks of the theatre to be recorded and forgotten. Mr. Wilfred Grantham gives a cruel, brittle study of Mortensgard; Miss Esmé Church, as the servant, has a naturalism and simplicity that are useful ballast to the play; Mr. Walter Piers as the old scholar, Brendel, gives to each of his interventions a value in itself and another value as a contribution to the play's structure; and Mr. John Laurie, though his Rosmer has too feverish a pitch and lacks the justification of Rebecca's adherence, gives to his part a compensating intellectual tension and emotional stress. Apart from all this, and whatever estrangement a modern audience may feel from the play itself, there is a performance of the part of Rebecca West which gives to this production exceptional authority. There have been occasions in the recent past in which it has seemed that Miss Forbes-Robertson was sacrificing the power formerly hers to a kind of garish looseness. She has now recovered herself. Her austerity and her power to communicate passion without display have returned. To each word and each phrase she gives a perfect lucidity; nothing is squandered, nothing done for easy effect. The mind of Rebecca West glows through her language as the mind of Juliet glowed through one of her earliest performances on the stage. In its response to emotion and in its intellectual coherence this is acting of the first rank.

10 MARCH 1936, THE TIMES

Hedda Gabler by Henrik Ibsen

CRITERION THEATRE

MISS TESMAN	Esmé Church
GEORGE TESMAN	Walter Piers
HEDDA GABLER	Jean Forbes-Robertson
JUDGE BRACK	D. A. Clarke-Smith
EILERT LOVBORD	John Laurie

"I didn't think of that!" says Hedda, when she has been made to understand that the pistol, which she gave to Lovbord, may be identified as her own, and scandal be the consequence. Upon her failure to "think of that" depends Brack's triumph, for his recognition of the pistol puts her in his power, and her death, which gave Ibsen what, clearly, he intended to be an inevitable curtain. The whole of the last act springs from Hedda's having failed to "think of that," and this failure in a woman so astute and so fearful of scandal is incredible. But in this play Ibsen must have his effects – at all costs. The first dangerous sign of over-emphasis is Hedda's insistence that she is bored. With the power of genius to communicate mood, Ibsen has already made clear the whole nature of her boredom; then, with disastrous cancellation of genius, he states again and again what is already known. The burning of Lovbord's manuscript is worse. We know well enough why Hedda is tempted to destroy it: it is, in the language of Ibsen's own symbolism, "the child" of Lovbord and Mrs. Elvsted. If she took it from the desk, put it upon the fire, and silently watched it burn, the emphasis would be complete; but Ibsen is not content – she must shriek his symbol at the flames. Again and again throughout this piece he has refused to let well alone, with the consequence that a tragedy is unevenly daubed with the colours of melodrama. The play is made enthralling by the weight of its passion and by the impetus – not the persuasiveness – of its story-telling, but none is harder to preserve from the laughter that falls against the dramatist's intention.

It is the special merit of Miss Irene Hentschel's production that it does save the play from this. The way of salvation is to give the audience every legitimate, and almost legitimate, opportunity for laughter that can be wrung from the text – in brief, to use the ironic comedy of the first two acts for all, and more than all, it is worth. Acting on this principle, Mr. Walter Piers gives a fat, almost farcical portrait of Tesman, and somehow contrives to preserve the character's integrity. Mr. Clarke-Smith, as the villainous Brack, bravely responds with comedy in a lighter vein, and Miss Forbes-Robertson, without sacrificing the tragic intensity of Hedda, plays her scenes of raillery with a devilish skill of tone and continuance that are compensation for the hysterical outbursts to which Ibsen afterwards condemns her. Ingenious though all this is and fresh though the light may be that it throws on the play, it remains true that it is a redistribution of Ibsen's own emphasis. It does much to recommend the piece to a modern audience and to save its errors from ridicule, but it does so by changing the play itself. This may be observed in the light of contrast if Miss Esmé Church is carefully watched in the relatively small part of Miss Tesman. It is faultlessly done and it is pure Ibsen. The result is a solidity and assurance found nowhere else. The old lady is quietly alive; the rest are acting.

13 MARCH 1936, THE TIMES

Lysistrata by Aristophanes
English version by
Reginald Beckwith and Andrew Cruickshank

THE GATE THEATRE

LYSISTRATA	Joan Swinstead
CALONICE	Sylvia Coleridge
MYRRHINE	Susan Taylor
LAMPITO	Molly Francis
WORSHIP	Ian Dawson
CINESIAS	Reginald Beckwith

The writers of this new version of the *Lysistrata* have not considered it part of their duty to expurgate Aristophanes and those who prefer him expurgated had better look elsewhere. The rest of us may enjoy his wit in the happy knowledge that these translators, rightly perceiving that the play itself strides easily from 412 B.C. to this year of peace, have nowhere pressed his moral or paraded themselves in smart anachronisms. They have translated freely, but they have, in spirit, translated. The result is a pointed and dashing comedy, and not what might so easily have been thrust upon us – a shabby little *revue*, masquerading under a great name.

In the casting of the play Mr. Norman Marshall has made a clear distinction between Lysistrata herself, who is a leader, an originator, a Shavian creature, and her accompanying women of whom the essence is that they are the wives of their husbands. If the leading part were played more winningly or more sensuously than it is the edge of the women's defiance would be blunted and Aristophanes be robbed of the seriousness that is the salt of his jest. It is precisely the touch of Major Barbara that Miss Joan Swinstead gives to Lysistrata which preserves the play's balance and makes possible the delightful mingling of wisdom and fooling that distinguishes the concluding peace conference. Round her the action naturally groups itself; her women, Miss Sylvia Coleridge, Miss Susan Taylor, and Miss Molly Francis, are her active and entertaining supporters; and when exiled mankind intervenes in the person of Mr. Ian Dawson, the Probulus, or Mr. Reginald Beckwith, the disappointed husband, they also, because Lysistrata herself has established the comic integrity of the play, are fooled with reason and not dully or loosely as victims are in farce. In one matter only is weakness conspicuous: where Aristophanes is plainly looking for the rough humours of slap-stick, the English production lacks spontaneity. The old women and the old men do not always come off. But that is, perhaps, inevitable. Nothing on earth is harder to translate from language to language or from age to age than clowning. Witness, the troubles of Dogberry and his fellows. No one is to be blamed. The play hangs fire for a moment, and proceeds. For the greater part of the evening it moves with remarkable ease and freshness, and, for all its phrases that invite a censorious blue pencil, without a shadow of corruption on its wit.

Spread it Abroad by Herbert Farjeon
Music by William Walker

SAVILLE THEATRE

To encounter genuine wit and character in a *revue* is to be in danger of praising it extravagantly. It is as if, in the midst of what, in another place, would be called a bevy of dumb blondes, one were to meet a lady with individuality, a sprightly humour, and, be it added, an edge to her tongue. Now and then, for a moment, the sparkle goes from her conversation; sometimes, as in a *ballet* called *Four Winds*, she attempts something a little beyond her range; and once, even with the collaboration of Mr. Nelson Keys and a lighthouse, she misses her target. But one has to seek in memory even for these momentary weaknesses. The entertainment as a whole has gaiety, point, and form.

One of the best songs of the evening, a comment by Mr. Lyle Evans on the taste of smart audiences, was so fiercely aimed that the present audience shifted a little, but the rest of the satire being farther from home was received with delight – an encouraging sign, for the curse of *revue* in London has long been its timorous insipidity. Mr. Nelson Keys as an Italian barber, instructing his customer in strategy; or with Miss St. Helier in a group of imitations or in a skit on an operatic dressing-room; Mr. Nelson Keys, coming to every sketch as if the freshness and sting of it were to him an adventure, is the core of the entertainment. Miss Dorothy Dickson, though sometimes charged with sentiments too pretty, gives charm to them and an edge to her livelier opportunities; Miss Hermione Gingold, Mr. Walter Crisham, and Miss Tessa Deane variously contribute to the evening's minor pleasures; and Miss Ivy St. Helier, whether in solitary splendour or in partnership with Mr. Keys gives to each of her sketches a special quality of her own. Her sentimental dressmaker is a lesson in adroitness – what a disaster it might have been and how good it is! It is refreshing to see an actress who is an actress control the stage, direct her material, and *use* her audience. *L'Absinthe* is a little masterpiece, worthy of its setting.

Baby Austin by B.C. Hilliam

STRAND THEATRE

HENRY NORTHORPE	Bromley Davenport
GEORGE PHELPS	Aubrey Mather

The chief entertainment of the evening is preceded by Mr. Edward Cooper, who is proved by subsequent events to have been himself the chief entertainment of the evening. These events include a baby left upon the doorstep of a guest-house, a maiden who is accused of and admits being its mother, an infantile prattler for whom this sacrifice is being made, a youth whose detective enthusiasm leads him astray, and a dear old lady whose intuition insists upon the heroine's self-sacrificial virtue. All this in a thin atmosphere of farce without a sparkle of wit to recommend it. Once a window-curtain fell upon Mr. Aubrey Mather's head; once Mr. Bromley Davenport informed an elderly lady that she had nothing to fear from him; there were equivalent jokes on the subject of baths, and there was a servant who, when crossing the stage, was told to pick her feet up and obeyed.

During the intervals one distinguished member of the audience read a humorous journal, which, with enviable foresight, he had brought with him. A man who takes Mr. Punch with him to the first performance of a dull farce is a prophet of his needs. He deserves his smiling consolation and the envious glances of the unprovided.

24 APRIL 1936, THE TIMES

Parnell by Elsie T. Schauffler

GATE THEATRE

KATHERINE O' SHEA	Margaret Rawlings
MRS. BENJAMIN WOOD	Marda Vanne
CAPTAIN WILLIAM HENRY O' SHEA	James Mason
CHARLES PARNELL	Wyndham Goldie
WILLIAM EWART GLADSTONE	Arthur Young
MONTAGUE HARRISON	Laurier Lister

The value of this piece, which tells the story of Mrs.O'Shea from her first meeting with Parnell to his fall and death, does not arise from its political interest but from a special quality of its romantic narrative and from the power of its three chief performances, those of Mr. Goldie, of Miss Marda Vanne as Mrs. O'Shea's shrewd old aunt, and of Miss Margaret Rawlings as Katie O'Shea herself. Spectators whose memory carries them back to Gladstone may well feel that the play has been misnamed when they discover that the political background is but summarily sketched, but, when once they have accepted the selective limits that the dramatist has imposed upon herself, they will find that, within them, the storytelling is honest and that the play is neither a belittling of great men nor a vulgar travesty of history.

Much of history is omitted; some is compressed; but Parnell's fascination as a leader of men is clearly indicated in a performance to which Mr. Wyndham Goldie, tall, dark, and bearded, brings a genuine power of evocation, and in which he survives with high credit a perilous associative challenge. The dramatist's and Mr. Arthur Young's sketch of Gladstone, however incomplete it may seem to those who have his full stature in their minds, has, within the frame of the divorce-suit and its consequences, discretion as well as liveliness, and, in so far as it is by implication critical, is critical of policy, not of personal honour. For these reasons it is to be hoped that the ban which now lies upon the play may not permanently withhold it from a larger stage. Mr. Norman Marshall, greatly assisted by the dresses of Motley, has made gallant use of his resources, but it is no joke to produce at the Gate Theatre, a combative meeting of the Irish Party in Committee Room 15.

But the play is one that survives hardship, for it describes a man and woman in whom love is not a contemptible and cowardly greed but a single-minded passion. Its simplifications are sometimes those of naivety rather than of penetrative insight; but it has remarkable tautness of narrative and the power to cast upon the theatre that spell which, for a little while, can give to playgoing the excitement that a story has for a child, the rare thrill of self-loss. Such plays are the joy of actors, and the performance, in this instance, though it lacks poise and finish in some of the lesser parts, gives in general a warm response. Mr. James Mason plays O'Shea too continuously on a single note, but Mr. O'Rourke in his humour, Mr. Lister in his unaffected naturalness, and, particularly, Miss Marda Vanne in the dry precision of her wit all distinguish themselves.

The representation of Mrs. O'Shea, together with that of Parnell, is deeply moving and brilliantly accomplished. In her unforced and gentle opening Miss Margaret Rawlings establishes the integrity of her character. There, as a painter may enrich his monochrome with various colour until his whole canvas glows, she reveals the qualities of this woman – her intuitive shrinking from O'Shea, her sudden entrancement by Parnell, her mingling of the utmost tenderness with an unswerving and, at root, an unselfish passion – all this within the compass of a part which, in retrospect, is seen never to have made a spectacular claim or to have received spectacular treatment. Seldom in recent years has an actress given a performance in a leading part not in itself of the first order so fully persuasive in reason and so steadily illumined by the faith, not the pretence, of romantic passion. Her timing, her grace of movement, and her variety of tone spring from devoted craftsmanship; while the warmth and – for those who can understand the word in its application to passionate acting – the modesty of her performance are, in their reactions upon each other, a rare enchantment. The suffering of this Parnell and this Katie O'Shea is felt to be not so much the penalty of their love as the proof of it; and to say this is to mark a distinction between genuine romance, that is at once pitiable, enduring, and proud, and the hoax of love that can feed only on easy fortune and starves in the first hostility of circumstance.

21 MAY 1936, THE TIMES

The Seagull by Anton Tchehov

NEW THEATRE

IRINA ARCADINA	Edith Evans
CONSTANTIN TREPLEF	Stephen Haggard
PETER SORIN	Frederick Lloyd
NINA	Peggy Ashcroft
ILYA SHAMRAYEF	George Devine
MASHA	Martita Hunt
DORN	Leon Quartermaine
BORIS TRIGORIN	John Gielgud
MEDVEDENKO	Ivor Barnard

The play produced by Komisarjevsky

When, as a consequence of this performance, Tchehov is established as a popular dramatist in England the high-noses will begin to turn away their timid heads. The loud shrill voice of denigration will arise in the more sensitive drawing-rooms to declare that there is too much moonlight and music in the opening, too much veneration for Turgeniev throughout, and that the over-romantic scoundrel is – to use an expressive Americanism – as "phoney" as Lamartine himself with his lake and his love. And such love! Is it not individualistic and contemptibly *bourgeois*? Has it any useful political significance? These questions will begin to be asked with becoming solemnity by those whose rule for the judgment of a work of art is that its merit varies inversely with its popular success.

It is, therefore, necessary to say – what might otherwise have been taken as read – that *The Seagull* is among the supreme masterpieces of the theatre, having, particularly in the first two acts, a fluidity and ease that by their perfection make the heart turn over. To these qualities are added, as the play advances, the terrible insight into human weakness that has created the scene of Arcadina's clinging to her unwilling lover, and the superb pity that enabled Tchehov to reach, without strain, the tragic climax of the last act. It is the more necessary to insist upon the play's greatness and upon its passionate effect in the theatre because there are certain aspects of the present performance of which it must be said that they are unsatisfying. One of them is a question of personal interpretation. If we say that Trigorin has always seemed to be a man of more humour, more substance and of less finicky precision that Mr. Gielgud allows, Mr. Gielgud is entitled to reply that he sees him, not as genius that has missed its aim, but as one who was in essence nothing else than a mechanical *dilettante*; and certainly, on his own lines, Mr. Gielgud plays the part with rare accomplishment and satirical grace. The difficulty of accepting Miss Evans's Arcadina is more stubborn. There are two aspects of Arcadina – the peacock and, at any rate in effect, the dove.

Miss Evans is all peacock – as such, magnificent, a cruel, swaggering figure of fantastic selfishness, but nothing in her performance hints at the source of Arcadina's power over men – over her lover, over her son – with the result that her compulsion of Trigorin in the third act is only angry and vile, lacking that element of persuasive pity with which Tchehov enriched it and made it credible.

All else remains for praise and gratitude. Mr. Haggard's Constantin, not clearly defined at the outset, has the uncommon gift of silent passion at the end. Mr. Lloyd's Sorin, Mr. Barnard's Medvedenko, Mr. Quartermaine's cool sketch of the philosophical doctor, and Miss Martita Hunt's control of Masha's hysterical suffering are all sensitive responses to the dramatist's genius for secondary parts. Miss Ashcroft's Nina has an enchanting freshness in the early scenes, and her tragic return has the supreme quality of being indeed not the coming of a stranger, but the return of the girl we have known, changed by suffering but not obliterated by it, so that what she was is visible always through what she has become.

21 JUNE 1936, THE NEW YORK TIMES

Of A Hit Called The Seagull

The great popular success of John Gielgud and Peggy Ashcroft in *Romeo and Juliet* has established a fashion at the New Theatre, with a consequence which until a few months ago would have been scouted as incredible by those who believe that one must always play down to the public. This "incredible" consequence was the sight of an immense queue of playgoers standing for hours, or perching themselves on camp stools, in the hope of gaining admittance to the first night of Chekhov's *The Seagull*.

It is true that what the English public has always cared for is acting. You may say that they had come to see Gielgud and Ashcroft as, in the past, they came to see Irving and Terry. But Chekhov! It was not long ago that many members of the Stage Society, feeling that they were being insulted in their intelligence or that their legs were being pulled, solemnly marched out of the first performance of *The Cherry Orchard*. And now here is that offending dramatist choking pit and gallery in the Charing Cross Road.

Soon, for this very reason, the sons and daughters of the high-noses who marched out of *The Cherry Orchard*, will turn against Chekhov. They will turn against any dramatist who draws the town, any actor whose stage is larger than a postage stamp, any poet whose poems are read. At the moment they are occupied in sneering at A. E. Housman because his lyrics, like Shakespeare's, can be and are sung. Soon they will sneer at Chekhov, formerly their idol, because to see his plays is no longer an exclusive ritual. A high-nose is a man who hates all art that is loved by more than two or three persons gathered together in one dustbin.

Here the production is by Theodore Komisarjevsky, who, thank heaven, has played with Chekhov no tricks of stylisation. The garden scene beside the lake is, as it should be, in the spirit of *Les Sylphides*; the trees are trees, the music across the water is sweet and clear and a hump-backed bridge is cleverly used for romantic and satirical silhouette. The later interiors are unobtrusively naturalistic. This is what Chekhov requires – either unforced naturalism or no scenery at all except a table and a chair. He is one of those dramatists who, like Shakespeare, seldom fails to paint his own scene verbally, but, because it is nowadays less affected, I prefer an easily naturalistic setting to no scenery at all.

Above all, no tricks, no "productionism." Chekhov is a great master. The producer's job is not to repaint the picture or daub his own signature over it, but to illumine it and give it a frame. There was a time when Mr. Komisarjevsky was given to spectacular tricks. He has matured; this work is admirable.

Formerly Mr. Gielgud himself played the young man, Treplef, now represented by Stephen Haggard. I do not regret that on this occasion he has preferred Trigorin, for an actor of his quality must experiment and Mr. Gielgud is entitled to a change from romantic ecstasy. His treatment of the popular, weak, vain novelist is precise, restrained and fresh; for all that, I believe Trigorin to have been miscast. There are three men in England for this part – Alan Napier, if what one wants to emphasize is Trigorin's potentiality as an artist and the nervous delicacy of his manners; Ion Swinley, if one wants the artist again and a clear indication of Trigorin's almost magical power over women; and D. Clarke-Smith, if the artist, though still clearly suggested, is to be out-weighed by a worldly, cynical, rakish and brilliantly stated romanticism.

The fault in Mr. Gielgud's interpretation is that he suggests that Trigorin's claim to be an artist was essentially false. It is true that Trigorin has been corrupted by the vanities of success, but the tragedy of the man is gone if we are not compelled to believe that there was in him something to corrupt. If he was not at root a genuine artist – and Chekhov seems in fact to have had Turgeniev in mind – his speech to Nina on the agony of being a writer, and on the joy within the agony, becomes empty rhetoric instead of one of the most searching analyses of genius in all literature. Mr. Gielgud has underestimated Trigorin.

Miss Edith Evans's Arcadina has greatly pleased critics, who see here a one-way part – a flamboyant study of selfishness, vanity and greed. If Arcadina stands for no more than that, there is no fault to be found in Miss Evans's highly coloured, peacocklike performance. But it must be remembered that, vile woman though Arcadina was, she did not always appear to be vile. It was her attraction as well as her persistence that enabled her to drag Trigorin away from the much younger Nina; and there must have been a charm, a gentleness in some of her moods that caused her son Constantin, though he feared and despised her, to love being bandaged and cared for by her hands. Any clever actress can suggest the vileness of Arcadina; Chekhov hands it to her; but a great performance of the part would communicate, as Miss Evans never does, the woman's fitful and deceptive charm.

In spite of these defects we are given a memorable performance of a masterpiece. Miss Ashcroft's Nina, young and fresh at the outset, young and tragic at the close, is stable in essential character and marvellously progressive in experience. The performance is as deep in feeling as it is lovely in intellect. The minor characters – among whom Frederick Lloyd, Leon Quartermaine and Ivor Barnard win the chief honours – are so well done and so guiltless of selfish caricature that they never impede, but continually contribute to, the play's distinguishing virtue – its oneness, its fluidity.

12 JULY 1936, THE NEW YORK TIMES

Salute to an Actor

It was, I believe, no more than a coincidence that Heinrich Schnitzler came to England for a holiday at a time which enabled him to direct the production of his father, Arthur Schnitzler's play, *Professor Bernhardi*, at the Embassy Theatre. Certainly the coincidence was fortunate, for he found in rehearsal the actor, Abraham Sofaer, who could play the part of the Jewish doctor better than anyone else in England.

Mr. Sofaer's position in the theatre is of unusual interest. He has all the qualities of an actor – imagination, vitality, bodily grace, an expressive face, and intuitive control of gesture, a voice of the greatest beauty and power. He speaks verse as no other English actor – not, excepting Gielgud – can speak it, so using its music to clarify its meaning that, under his control, even the language of Biron in *Love's Labour's Lost* comes to the audience with unfading lucidity.

Yet I think I do him no injustice in saying that, in the public eye, he has never held the place he deserves among the leaders of his profession. The reason is his appearance, which, though handsome, is so pronouncedly Oriental as to limit the range of his parts. Six years ago he appeared in New York as Isaac Cohen in *The Matriarch*; I am not aware that he is otherwise known in the United States. Here, though he has played with success in pieces of all kinds, he is chiefly known, as far as leading roles are concerned, as a Shakespearean actor. The reason is the simple one that, while Shakespeare created Shylock and Othello and even Iago, who may be cast as an Oriental, if you please, modern playwrights, unless they want an Oriental villain for a thriller, generally write for Occidental leads. *Professor Bernhardi* provides Mr. Sofaer with an opportunity that he has long deserved.

The play, though it has been performed only once before in England, and then privately, is familiar to students of the theatre; but it has a special and renewed interest at the present time. It opens with a scene in which a Jewish director of a Viennese hospital refuses to allow a priest to have access to a dying patient. He says that the patient is happy, that she does not know she is dying, that the priest's arrival would put into her the fear of death. At this point, I think, Schnitzler missed an opportunity.

Because he was writing as an anti-clerical Austrian, he never allows the Catholic point of view on this incident to be represented; instead, he hurries on to the consequences of the incident itself, showing how from so small a seed there sprang up a forest of intrigue.

Once launched on this subject, he has the courage to examine it in all its aspects, and the play becomes, not simply a piece of Jewish and anti-clerical propaganda, but a genuine study of differing sets of values. Bernhardi himself is by no means exempt from criticism; his stubborn refusal to compromise in little things, his fanatical lack of proportion, his special variety of spiritual pride are set out side by side with the excessive desire of priests and politicians to excuse their immediate failures or weaknesses by saying that it is often necessary to subordinate the means to the end. Schnitzler is not impartial; he has his own prejudice and does not conceal it; but his satire is by no means undistributed.

The result is a play of rare balance and subtlety and one that rewards every perceptive delicacy of the players.

21 JULY 1936, THE TIMES

The Seagull

TRIGORIN   Mr. Swinley

Mr. Gielgud having left the cast, Mr. Ion Swinley's appearance as Trigorin at the New Theatre provides an exceptionally good reason – if anyone should need a reason other than the play's own beauty and merit – to visit *The Seagull* again. Mr. Gielgud, with the admirable justification of thus avoiding the obvious "Gielgud part", left the young and romantic Constantin to Mr. Stephen Haggard, who, it may be added, now represents him with much clearer definition than on the first night, and accepted for himself the difficult hesitations, the profound self-analysis, the unstable charm of Arcadina's lover. Though Mr. Gielgud's treatment of the part was at once interesting and distinguished, its effect was to give to Trigorin an air of being almost a charlatan and to deny to him altogether the quality of artist which, one supposes, it was Tchehov's purpose to exhibit in the tragic circumstance of weak betrayal and gradual decay. This quality Mr. Swinley preserves through all Trigorin's failures and shams, and his performance is, in consequence, the more complete, the truer, and the more moving.

The great speech in which Trigorin describes an imaginative writer's inability to escape from his knowledge that all he sees – even a cloud shaped like a grand piano – is stuff for his pen, and all experience, even the most deeply personal, material for his art, was delivered last night too slowly, but even so it was impressive as Mr. Gielgud's delivery of it was not – impressive because Mr. Swinley used it to give utterance to a genuine artist's struggle with himself. Once this truth was established, the whole part, and indeed the whole play, was informed by it. When Trigorin was overwhelmed by Arcadina, when he was accused of being the lover of two women at once, when he used Nina and betrayed her, he was not simply a weakling or a cad; he suffered and communicated his suffering so that it might be understood. Partly perhaps for this reason, partly because the production as a whole has matured, several other performances have been enriched and none has deteriorated. Miss Evans has brought a new tenderness to the second act. Miss Ashcroft's beautiful portrait of Nina has found new strength in the contrast of her return, which is now played with a fresh edge and fierceness. Mr. Frederick Lloyd, Mr. Quartermaine, and Mr. Barnard are as good as ever, and Mr. Swinley's Trigorin refreshes a play that is itself a masterpiece.

23 AUGUST 1936, THE NEW YORK TIMES

Why Not a Holiday from The Bard?

The performances of Shakespeare that are being given this summer in the Open Air Theatre at Regent's Park prompt in me the heretical thought that not only the English but perhaps the English-speaking peoples would benefit by a holiday from Shakespeare, and that, in the end, Shakespeare would benefit accordingly. Not that *A Midsummer Night's Dream* was not a charming entertainment on green grass, with trees and bushes as its background, but even under the sky there is nowadays an atmosphere of piety and good works about Shakespearean productions which is cramping and destructive.

If any man says that one's object ought to be to get the populace to Shakespeare at any cost and in any mood, he is, I think, wrong. The value of poetry is not instructive. You cannot make people receive its value as you can make them wet by turning a hose onto them, for the value of poetry consists in an interaction between poet and audience, just as love consists of action and response between man and woman. The poet impregnates his audience. His function is not to imagine for them but to cause them to imagine for themselves. And if they come because they are brought, or because they consider it their duty, or in the spirit of those who assist in the organization of charity, little good can come of it. That is why I suggest a holiday from Shakespeare.

Even in Regent's Park, where there is no playhouse to rent and no fantastic salaries are paid, Shakespeare, it seems, cannot stand by himself. Mr. Sydney Carroll had to issue "an appeal" to safeguard his season from loss, and the government department in charge of the parks had to grant Shakespeare specially favourable terms. He received, in effect, a subsidy because he was Shakespeare. I believe it would be better to let him vanish from all stages on which he does not pay his way. This is not inconsistent with a belief in the private patronage of living, and sometimes even of dead, artists.

Shakespeare stands in a category by himself. He has been consistently thrust down the people's throats for years. They have been taught that there are two classes of poets – Shakespeare and the rest, which is an extravagant way of asserting his ascendancy.

By treating him as a god, an institution, a subject for schools; by pulling his plays to pieces line by line, and examining each word in the spirit of jealous inheritors disputing a will; by organizing, in Stratford, annual festivals with processions and banners and ambassadors and feasts, we have represented the greatest of our dramatists as a bore.

People have heard him so much in season and out of season that, unless they are drawn by a desire to see Gielgud as Hamlet or Romeo, they fight shy of Shakespeare, or go, if they go, in the spirit of a weary family herded into the customary pew in church. And they pay as those do who put coins into a collecting bag. Men receive knighthoods for their services to Shakespeare.

What is needed is a little healthy hunger for Shakespeare. It will never be felt as long as the diet is compulsory. The first step is to drop him clean out of school curriculum except proportionately with other artists. Let the pupils be told something of Leonardo for a change. At the same time, let us cease to subsidise Shakespeare, directly or indirectly. Half my dislike of the proposal for a state-endowed National Theatre in England springs from my assurance that it would become a Shakespeare Admiration Society.

I want the next generation to be given a chance to come to him fresh, to discover his genius anew, to interpret it on terms of their own secret lives. I want them to be allowed, when they are young men and women, to think their own thoughts about him, so that they may fall in love with him as they may now fall in love with Marvel or Shelley or Byron. You cannot fall in love with the Statue of Liberty or Nelson's Column, and the bardolators have made Shakespeare into that. A poet is barren unless we love him; he has nothing to give except to the hungry.

15 OCTOBER 1936[4], THE TIMES

Antony and Cleopatra by William Shakespeare

NEW THEATRE

CHARMIAN	Margaret Rawlings
IRAS	Rosalind Iden
CLEOPATRA	Eugenie Leontovich
ANTONY	Donald Wolfit
ENOBARBUS	Leon Quartermaine
POMPEY	Ion Swinley
OCTAVIUS CAESAR	Ellis Irving
OCTAVIA	Vera Poliakoff
MENAS	Lawrence Anderson
SOOTHSAYER	George Hayes

---

4   James Agate wrote to C. M. the following day: "In the matter of last night, I don't know where you have been for your holiday. If the Dolomites, then hurrah for those protuberances! We are all thanking you for an article whose outspokenness Sparkenbroke would have deplored."

Hospitality and inclination alike suggest that the least said about this travesty of Cleopatra the better; but the interests of the theatre in England must not be allowed to suffer for the susceptibilities of any actress, though she be a guest, and when a performance in a great classical part is dull, pretentious, and for the most part incomprehensible, it is necessary that criticism should say so. The part of Cleopatra was written in English and in verse; Mme. Leontovich has neither. A phonetic script would be needed to describe what she makes of the great speeches, but plain lettering may serve to illustrate her difficulties.

> O weederdee dergarlano devar
> Desolderspo lees falln: yong boisenguls
> Alefnow wimen.

Whoever, reading that once in a perpetual *tremolo*, can interpret it as: –

> O, wither'd is the garland of the war,
> The soldier's pole is fall'n: young boys and girls
> Are level now with men.

may attend this performance in peace. Those who do not welcome the task of lightning translation will understand that when Cleopatra was at last dead and Charmian's superb farewell broke in upon the spiritless babble of her mistress, Miss Rawlings, who has verse and voice and a flashing command, fairly swept the stage. And Charmian's is a small part. Mr. Quartermaine, with more opportunity, ran away with the play. Why? Partly on his own high merit, his quickness, vitality, and humour, but also because Enobarbus stands much apart from Cleopatra and is not, like this poor Antony, everlastingly beset by her.

The same is true of Caesar, to whom Mr. Ellis Irving gave uncommon liveliness and dignity. So, in lesser parts well played, Mr. Anderson's Menas, Miss Poliakoff's Octavia, Mr. Hayes's Soothsayer. But who plays with this Cleopatra is lost, for she is so occupied by her own vain struggle with the text which, like her fantastic skirts, is for ever getting in her way that she cannot listen to or understand anyone else, and Mr. Donald Wolfit, who has the equipment of a good Antony, and proves it on occasions, finds himself, in passionate scenes with the Queen, one of two vocal islands apparently without communication.

Nor are these difficult circumstances Shakespeare's only rival. M. Komisarjevsky, doubtless in his pursuit of a "synthetic" theatre, has decided to treat *Antony and Cleopatra* as if it were a cross between a *ballet*, an operetta, and a *revue* at the Folies Bergères. The dresses have little to recommend them but a tinsel splendour. The set is so designed that, during the opening of the monument scene, none of the players is visible from the advanced stalls. The order of the scenes has been changed – for example, Charmian and Iras open the play, presumably on the music-hall principle that the house must be "warmed" for the star's entrance. One receives the impression that, in M. Komisarjevsky's view, nothing is so important as his lighting operations. The stage pales and darkens, smiles and gleams, glows and flashes so often and so restlessly that the whole emphasis is on the electrician. Seldom has a play been so tormented and twisted and stifled or a work of genius been so casually scorned.

31 OCTOBER 1936, THE TIMES

Murder in the Cathedral by T.S. Eliot

DUCHESS THEATRE

THOMAS BECKET	Robert Speaight
THIRD KNIGHT	Norman Chidgey
FOURTH KNIGHT	E. Martin Browne

After many performances at the Mercury Theatre and in America, Mr. Eliot's play is now to be seen within a few yards of the Strand – a remarkable and welcome instance of the truth that more mistakes are made in underestimating than in overestimating the discernment of the public. By ordinary standards this is by no means an easy play. Its intellectual argument is extremely close; it throws out no sops to the unintelligent; its convention is unnaturalistic, and so, to most playgoers, unfamiliar; but it stands for these very reasons that might have seemed to imperil it, and perhaps because of its piety.

It has been so often discussed that fresh analysis would now be inappropriate. The play has lost none of its freshness of attack, and what at first seemed examples of wilfully spectacular scansion and rhyming are now softened by time. Mr. Robert Speaight, who sometimes became too slow during the long run at the Mercury, has regathered the spirit of his delivery, and his representation of Becket, particularly when he preaches, is full of persuasion and fire. Mr. Norman Chidgey and Mr. Martin Browne distinguish themselves among the Knights, and the Chorus, though not simple enough in the design of their dresses, have greatly added to their force and cohesion since the first performance in Canterbury. Whether the altar, with its electric candles, is a valuable addition may be doubted; it introduces a note of toy-like naturalism which conflicts with the play's austerity of style.

Parnell by Elsie T. Schauffler

NEW THEATRE

KATHERINE O' SHEA	Margaret Rawlings
MRS. HAMISH	Marda Vanne
PHYLLIS	Barbara Cochran
MRS. BRIDGET BLAIR	Tosca Bissing
WILLIAM HENRY O' SHEA	Glen Byam Shaw
CHARLES STEWART PARNELL	Wyndham Goldie
THOMAS MURPHY	J. A. O'Rourke
WILLIAM EWART GLADSTONE	Arthur Young
MICHAEL DEVITT	Harry Hutchinson
MONTAGUE HARRISON	Laurier Lister

It is illuminating to reflect how seldom one encounters on the stage, as one does here, a man and woman of intelligence and breeding, deeply in love – as distinct from the customary cats on slightly expurgated tiles or a flurry of kittens prematurely escaped from their basket. *Parnell* swept its audience because it is neither trivial nor callous nor adolescent; it is first-rate storytelling, and conveys an unfailing impression that Parnell and Mrs. O'Shea are indeed lovers wrapt in their own experience, not exhibitionists whose heaven is the proscenium arch. In brief, it has persuasion, wit, and pulse; and it is further memorable in that Miss Margaret Rawlings's portrait of Mrs. O'Shea, which has none of what Mr. Shaw once called "the ordinary theatrical splashes and daubs of passion," yet marvellously communicates the entrancement of this woman's life.

The play was delayed by the censorship on technical, not moral, grounds. Far from having been watered down, it is strengthened by revision. The beauty of scenery, costume and lighting has its reward on a large stage, and the whole cast, under Mr. Norman Marshall's direction, responds to its extended opportunity. Of the wit Miss Marda Vanne has the share of a brilliant and benevolent lioness. The humour divides its honours between the Irish warmth of Mr. O'Rourke and the icy puritanism of Miss Margaret Webster. Mr. Byam Shaw's O'Shea combines an engaging swagger with the temperament of a husband whose telescope is now at his seeing and now at his complacent eye. Mr. Lister represents Parnell's secretary with charming and discreet awe; Miss Barbara Cochran, Miss Bissing, and Mr. Hutchinson fit admirably into the pattern; and Mr. Arthur Young has added dignity and fire to his sketch of Gladstone.

A magnificent appearance and an authority at once personally overpowering and publicly aloof were needed to suggest Parnell, and Mr. Wyndham Goldie has them both. He makes Parnell's ascendancy persuasive, particularly in the battle of

Committee Room 15, and, in his scenes with Mrs. O'Shea, he holds the stage with Miss Rawlings. This is to say much, for her performance has extreme subtlety and power. It was received at first, as challenge to the highest honours always is, with attention eagerly critical; then, as the action progressed, with self-loss in a compelled and delighted illusion; and, finally, when the curtain had fallen, with a momentary hush, as though applause itself were spell-bound, and a shout, that was almost a cry, of recognition and relief. That recognition comes when it comes best to genuine artists, not by chance, suddenly, when they have not the equipment to proceed, but at the instant of maturity. In her, youth and experience are matched, and none can doubt her range. She has the gleam and vitality of a Goya. Her whole movement vibrates to her thought; her hands speak; her repose is absolute; and she has a voice – almost a double voice – that can pass, within the compass of a phrase, from the lightest spring of the mind to a deep, final tenderness and an indomitable courage. *C'est cette voix du coeur qui seule au coeur arrive*, said Musset of Malibran 100 years ago. Last night an audience, profoundly moved, heard it again

7 NOVEMBER 1936, THE TIMES

French Without Tears by Terence Rattigan

CRITERION THEATRE

KENNETH LAKE	Trevor Howard
BRIAN CURTIS	Guy Middleton
THE HON. ALAN HOWARD	Rex Harrison
M. MAINGOT	Percy Walsh
LIEUTENANT-COMMANDER ROGERS	Roland Culver
DIANA LAKE	Kay Hammond
JACQUELINE MAINGOT	Jessica Tandy
KIT NEILAN	Robert Flemyng

The villa Miramar in the South of France is fortunately not at all what one fears it may be. Not a cocktail is to be found in it, not a croupier, not a false pearl nor a decayed princess – not even a pet dog. What everyone is doing, or failing to do, is to learn French, and Monsieur Maingot presides over his assembled pupils with earnest affability. In giving lessons he is assisted by his daughter Jacqueline, at once sparkling and modest. Of the young men, Brian, too, is sparkling but not modest, Kit is a charming fool who needs three acts in which to discover that Jacqueline is in love with him, Alan is the governing droll, and Kenneth – well, Kenneth is Diana's brother. And who is Diana and what is she doing here? Not learning French. She is the drawling mischief in the bathing-dress and in Miss Kay Hammond.

The catalogue would now be complete if the Navy had not been forgotten. Commander Rogers, studying for an interpretership, is the most grave and guileless of Diana's victims. The dramatist and Mr. Roland Culver make the most of him, pulling each of his sea-legs in turn, until at last through his folly salvation comes and the truth is made known. For Diana – to use a word politer than Mr. Rattigan's – is a minx; she is a beguiler of men to no purpose – for which there is scarcely a word impolite enough. And yet such is the mood of the play and the neatness and lightness of Miss Hammond's performance that the word minx shall serve, for what we are concerned with is a world in which nothing matters except to be entertained. The entertainment, in its own frothy kind, is beyond question. Mr. Rattigan writes a sly, cool, and delightfully opportune dialogue; Mr. Rex Harrison has most of it to manipulate and manipulates it with casual adroitness; Mr. Guy Middleton is wickeder and Mr. Robert Flemyng softer and Mr. Percy Walsh has all the advantages of French, but it is Mr. Harrison who controls the game. A very amusing game it is, and the more remarkable in that its excursions into sentiment, for which Miss Jessica Tandy is responsible, are so smooth and carefully proportioned that they do not break the form.

2 DECEMBER 1936, THE TIMES

Waste by Harley Granville-Barker

WESTMINSTER THEATRE

WALTER KENT	Stephen Murray
AMY O'CONNELL	Catherine Lacey
RUSSELL BLACKBOROUGH	Cecil Trouncer
HENRY TREBELL	Nicholas Hannen
SIR GILBERT WEDGECROFT	Harcourt Williams
LORD CHARLES CANTILUPE	Gibb McLaughlin
CYRIL HORSHAM	Felix Aylmer
JUSTIN O'CONNELL	Mark Dignam

It would be to flatter ourselves to suppose that the subject of this play has become out of date since Mr. Granville-Barker discussed it in his original version of 1906. Trebell is robbed of great political opportunity by a threat of scandal in his private life and by the use which those of his colleagues who are opposed to him make of that scandal. The thing was true in Gladstone's day, was true 20 years later, and is true now, and Mr. Granville-Barker's approach to it is at once so steadily objective and so keenly critical that there is nothing in his play – except the unhurried distinction of its dialogue and its air of being set in a politer and more leisurely world than ours – to date it back 30 years.

The pleasure that it gives is of a kind nowadays rare. The scene opens in a country house with the hostess, Lady Julia Farrant, playing Chopin to her guests. As soon as conversation begins one is struck instantly by its point, its careful lightness, the shrewd restraint by which its meaning is declared. These people are talking, not gabbling; this dramatist is making use of each phrase to tell his story, to illumine his characters; nothing is haphazard or fluffed. So it is when the narrative is further developed. When Amy O'Connell, full of bitter self-pity, comes to tell Trebell that she is with child by him, and, in honesty and egoism, is unable even to pretend that he loves, or has ever loved, her, Miss Catherine Lacey and Mr. Hannen are given a scene brilliantly taut, of which they faultlessly make use, Miss Lacey here particularly distinguishing herself by the ruthless insight of her portraiture – an insight that would entitle her to play Madame Bovary if it had been for the theatre that Flaubert wrote. And when Amy O'Connell is dead and there are the consequences to face or shirk, Mr. Granville-Barker keeps the same grip on his politicians. Mr. Felix Aylmer leads them, a model of cool detachment – not a cynic but an unsparing realist; Mr. Cecil Trouncer supplies without excess the contrasted crudeness of an ambitious party hack; Mr. Gibb McLaughlin gives a genuinely persuasive sketch of Cantilupe's icy scruple; and Mrs. O'Connell's fanatical husband is drawn with remarkable mediaevalism by Mr. Mark Dignam – a stained-glass window astonishingly come to life. Through it all Mr. Hannen carries the weight of the play. He has the fire to suggest Trebell's imaginative power and the balance which enables him to distinguish Trebell, as Mr. Granville-Barker distinguished him, from the common political dreamers of the stage. It is a little odd to find men and women dressed as they are dressed to-day debating a world in which no political issue is more perilous than Disestablishment. For that reason the costume of 1906 would have been an advantage, but for that reason alone.

4 DECEMBER 1936, THE TIMES

O Mistress Mine by Ben Travers

ST JAMES'S THEATRE

MAX	Pierre Fresnay
SOPHIA	Yvonne Printemps
NELSON	Frederick Cooper
MATTERBY	Frederick Lloyd
MRS. QUILL	Kathleen Harrison
THE KING	Austin Trevor

The National Anthem, played before the rise of the curtain, was applauded in all parts of the house.

The play is a very light Ruritanian comedy, telling how Queen Sophia of Ardenburg (Mlle. Printemps) is rescued during a revolution by Max (M. Fresnay) and brought by him to his flat in Mayfair. Concealment is difficult, for the fugitive Queen has a habit of singing in her bath and even of running out of it, ravishingly betowelled, into a crowded drawing-room. Max's country cottage is no more secure a refuge, but they make the best of it until the reported success of the Ardenburg royalists sends Mlle. Printemps to the cottage door, tearfully (but in good voice) singing farewell to love. But there is another act – time enough for the royalists to be overthrown and the Queen to be released from her patriotic duties. Indeed a thin piece, but with some of the merits of its kind. The sentimental passages are fortunately brief; one can put them in brackets and wait until Mlle. Printemps is free to frivol again. She and M. Fresnay play their parts with a kind of cynical ease that makes them appear to be more witty than they are; Mr. Austin Trevor, Miss Helen Haye, and Mr. Frederick Cooper subscribe to the same effect; and but for one lapse of memory, so serious that it almost brought the curtain down, the play would have had throughout a silky smoothness to recommend it. But neither the narrative nor the dialogue has the elegance of Mlle. Printemps's last frock – a charming thing which it is a relief to praise wholeheartedly. Besides, a critic is bound to refer to it who, without feminine aid, guessed the maker of it in the dark, and, when the lights (as Mlle. Printemps would say) "confirmed him," patted himself and the Faubourg St. Honoré on the back.

6 JANUARY 1937, THE TIMES

"Hamlet" In Full by William Shakespeare

OLD VIC

HORATIO	Robert Newton
CLAUDIUS	Francis L. Sullivan
LAERTES	Michael Redgrave
POLONIUS	George Howe
HAMLET	Laurence Olivier
GERTRUDE	Dorothy Dix
OPHELIA	Cherry Cottrell
FIRST PLAYER	Marius Goring
PLAYER QUEEN	Stuart Burge
A MESSENGER	Crichton Stuart
FIRST GRAVEDIGGER	Frederick Bennett
OSRIC	Alec Guinness

Special performances of *Hamlet* unabbreviated have been given in the past, but the opportunity provided by the Old Vic's courage in putting it on for a run is exceptional and extremely well worth taking. The play begins at seven and, excluding intervals, occupies less than four hours, and this without a sign of rush or gabbling. In fact the effort of response is less now than it is when *Hamlet* is cut, for the stress of bridging gaps is absent and Shakespeare, who as a craftsman knew when to ease and when to tax his audience, is allowed to tell his story in his own way. The consequence is a feeling of spaciousness and of being led, not driven.

Mr. Tyrone Guthrie's production and Mr. Battersby's scenery strengthen this effect. The built-up stage is simple and without affectation; changes of place are clearly indicated by the use of various curtains; and the grouping, particularly in the burial of Ophelia, makes impressive use of different levels. Ophelia herself errs on the side of the grotesque; the Queen, for reasons not to be defined except at length, seems often to be consciously outside the play as though she were aware of being in costume; but the standard of performance, even in the lesser parts, is high and there is one Messenger, who announces Laertes' revolt with such vivid assurance as sends everyone to his programme to note an actor in Mr. Crichton Stuart. Mr. George Howe, whose Polonius has earned him distinction in the past, gives again the right edge of wit to the old man's likeable folly; Mr. Robert Newton's Horatio, though a trifle lacking in solidity and too highly strung, is spoken well and with understanding; Mr. Francis Sullivan, except when he allows a final sentence to drop as if it bored him, is a good King whose mind is clearly outlined; and Mr. Frederick Bennett makes sense – and not incoherent comic relief – of the First Gravedigger.

The Hamlet is original in the best sense – namely, that Mr. Olivier has neither imitated others nor wildly defied convention, but has looked for himself in the part and for the part in himself. The performance has its limitations and they are personal ones. In general, it is too light; in particular scenes it gives an impression of a man little engaged in intellectual struggle and dominated by emotional impulse. But though when Hamlet comes upon the King at his prayers and in other solitary passages of equal subtlety the character slips from Mr. Olivier's grasp, he brings to many of his personal contacts – with the Players for example or, in a different kind, when he comes to the Queen – a natural energy and a special tenderness of sympathy that are his own. This is not an intellectually brilliant Hamlet, but it combines its intelligence with grace in an unusual degree, and serves well as the centre of a production of which the conspicuous merit is that it never drags and is full of vitality.

12 FEBRUARY 1937, THE TIMES

As You Like It by William Shakespeare

NEW THEATRE

ORLANDO	Michael Redgrave
OLIVER	Valentine Dyall
CELIA	Marie Ney
ROSALIND	Edith Evans
TOUCHSTONE	Frederick Lloyd
LE BEAU	Robert Eddison
FREDERICK	Neil Porter
DUKE	Harvey Braban
JACQUES	Leon Quartermaine

This was an evening that will be remembered among the rewards of criticism, for even where a playgoer may dissent from Miss Edith Evans's interpretation of Rosalind he may enjoy the tussle of disagreement with one who proves herself again and again a masterly executant. That praise of her may be understood, it is necessary to say first of all that Miss Evans's appearance does not naturally cast her for Rosalind; she has to make, to create imaginatively, a boyish – or a girlish – lightness and impudence that another might bring to the stage with her, or, in Shakespeare's day, with him; and she does create the impudence and lightness; she can move like an arrow, she can roll over on the ground in a delight of comedy, she can mock and glitter and play the fool with a marvellous ease and grace; and if the boyishness – or girlishness– is not there, it is because she has decided to reject it in favour of a feminine guile that is her own edge to the part – her deliberately implied and original criticism of it. And there lies the key to criticism of her performance. Upon one who feels of Rosalind that, within all the dazzle of her pretences, there was a girl in love, Miss Evan's re-creation of her may produce such an effect as might be made by a translation of a Shakespearean lyric into the verse of Corneille. But even this criticism must itself be qualified at one point. When Miss Evans was at the Old Vic she missed (in the view of one who will not exclude passion from Rosalind) the vital transition after Orlando's exit in Act IV, Scene 1. Rosalind, disguised as a boy, has been pulling Orlando's leg. When he is gone, she cries: "O coz, coz, coz, my pretty little coz, that thou didst know how many fathoms deep I am in love!" At the Old Vic Miss Evans spoke even that lightly, mockingly – consistently, that is, with her whole sharply ironic and anti-romantic interpretation of the part. Suddenly, last night, she said it with passionate feeling – brilliantly and splendidly right – but, for those who see a lyric in Rosalind, too late!

But for a summary of her whole brilliance, see that leg-pulling of Orlando. If ever the scene is to be better played, may we live to see it! The flash, the tenderness, and the exalted spirit of it are astonishing and are to be discovered not here only, but wherever the authenticity of Rosalind's love is not deeply challenged. Much of this is made possible by Mr. Redgrave's Orlando, which is more romantic than Miss Evans's Rosalind, but fully responsive to her wit; by Miss Marie Ney's enchantingly precise Celia; by Mr. Quartermaine's Jacques, as light as good wine; and by a *décor* and production which – if again one is to welcome eighteenth-century formalism into Arden – have a rare decorative charm. But everything stands or falls by the view one takes of Rosalind, for Miss Evans is the centre about which all things move. The audience was delighted, and with reason; the thing is aflame with invention. If only, through all the surface comedy, the fathoms beneath were always kept within the reach of imagination!

Macbeth by William Shakespeare

O. U. D. S.

MACBETH	John Featherstone Witty (Exeter)
MACDUFF	Michael Denison (Magdalen)
BANQUO	Willoughby Gray (Hertford)
LADY MACBETH	Margaret Rawlings

The stage of the New Theatre is very large; for an undergraduate performance the auditorium is much too large; the Oxford University Dramatic Society has, so to speak, been required to swell; and, to make a long story short, Mr. Hugh Hunt, the producer, has had his work cut out. It is to be remembered that he, his cast, and his scenery have access to the theatre for the first time only on the day before production. Nothing, therefore, can fairly be said about details of lighting and arrangement, but, in view of the difficulties, extreme simplicity is the safest rule, and this production attempts too much. Certain scenes – Lady Macduff with her child, the witches at their cauldron, and others more populous – are tucked away in small illuminated alcoves or caverns; a great part of the stage is occupied by a long slope on which important scenes are played; and one receives an impression of a broken and often remote action, the ordinary fore- stage level not being used enough. Mr. Hunt's purpose is clear. He has aimed at giving the play a special pulse by long movements on his slope and across his fore-stage and by the swift outbreak of action now in one cavern, now in the other. But for such experiments an undergraduate cast is not the material. What is needed is a smaller theatre with easier entrances and exits, not more than two stage levels, plain lighting, plain curtains, and Shakespeare's words. Amateurs are not happy when, with armour, pennons, and Viking beards, they go mountaineering in the doubtful dusk.

But an O. U. D. S. performance is never dull. Something remarkable always turns up – Miss Evans's Nurse, for example, in *Romeo and Juliet* – and this year there are two things memorable: first – and for this we are greatly indebted to Mr. Hugh Hunt – the establishment of a genuinely interesting relationship between Banquo and Macbeth; secondly, a Lady Macbeth by Miss Margaret Rawlings so original in conception and so steadily and clearly supported in execution that, in different company, it would rank among the great performances of the part, and even now must produce a lasting effect on criticism of it.

Banquo is played by Mr. Willoughby Gray with excellent spirit. Almost alone, he is master of his beard; his words spring from him, their meaning instantly clear. Mr. John Witty, moreover, is at his best in his scenes with Banquo. His convention, as Macbeth, is heavier and more rhetorical than Miss Rawlings's; he fails to receive from her and is sluggish in response to her rhythm; but among his peers he is more at ease, and together with Mr. Willoughby Gray he does succeed in making it clear that Banquo, not only as a consequence of the weird women's prophecy, was a menace to Macbeth, who continuously feared the rivalry of this more direct and less divided nature. This relationship is of great value for its light on Macbeth himself and because it establishes a clear line in a play of which Dr. Johnson said that "it has no true discrimination of character." Apart from this, the warriors in the present performance give only too much support to Dr. Johnson. Mr. Maurice Williams's Malcolm has life and feeling; Mr. Michael Denison, though he looks little older than one of his own slaughtered chicks, speaks Macduff's words simply and allows Shakespeare to do the rest; but no one else conspicuously holds his audience.

Miss Rawlings, therefore, like Mr. Hunt, has her work cut out. Lady Macbeth is a short part, but fortunately much of it is independent of thanes and the mufflement of beards. Miss Rawlings makes two things clear at once – that this woman has loved her husband and that she is not a monster but a human being. Imagination of Duncan's murder, when it comes, is strange to her, foreign to her previous imagining of herself. She drives Macbeth, but not as a monster of crime whose murderous way is simple; to steel him she must continually steel herself; and, when the thing is done, she would be done with it. The fire of her determination is spent; she is now prisoner of the tragedy, not one who thirstily adds blood to blood;

Nought's had, all's spent,
Where our desire is got without content.

Already she is emptied of the fiend, and when Macbeth contemplates the destruction of Banquo and Fleance– "there shall be done a deed of dreadful note" – she replies: "What's to be done?" with the terrible broken weariness of a spirit tormented. This is the turning point in Miss Rawlings's performance. By it, so early, the sleeping-walking scene is foreshadowed, and that scene, when it comes, is made not a passage of rhetoric, not a set piece, but, detail for detail, a re-enacting of the original crime, and beyond that, a summary of this woman's nature. What is to be remembered in this performance is that its terror springs from reason, and its beauty, not only from the magic of words, but from the communicated agony of a woman whom fate has trapped. The part of Lady Macbeth is commonly thought of as a group of spectacular scenes. Now she is the imaginative blood of the whole play; the development of her life is felt to be not fragmentary but continuous; she speaks sometimes with a brilliant lightness and speed; always, until her burden breaks her heart, she has the resilience of nature; at last, when all is done, darkness overwhelms her as the rush of great seas overwhelms a ship defeated.

Twelfth Night by William Shakespeare

OLD VIC

ORSINO	Leo Genn
VIOLA	Jessica Tandy
SIR TOBY BELCH	Laurence Olivier
MARIA	Ivy St. Helier
SIR ANDREW AGUECHEEK	Alec Guinness
FESTE	Marius Goring
OLIVIA	Jill Esmond
MALVOLIO	John Abbott

There are certain Shakespearean questions that one would give much to have answered. For example, when Duncan came to call, where was the thane of Cawdor? Again, is it possible that, in the title of the present play, we have an authentic utterance of Shakespeare? As a tedious rehearsal drew to an end, did the fellow responsible for getting out the bills come to him and say: "But I must know – what is the title of this piece?" And did the dramatist (*petulant*) reply: "Oh, call it *Twelfth Night* or what you will"? The commentators will tell us, with one eye on the sonnets, that he was punning on his own name, and they may be allowed to think so if they will answer another question: how did Viola and Sebastian happen to be dressed precisely alike? *Twelfth Night*, in the matter of plot, is an extremely entangling play, but what an enchanting entanglement.

Mr. Tyrone Guthrie has used Miss Jessica Tandy, who is normally Viola, to represent Sebastian also, wherever the young man appears separately from her; and, where at the end the two are on the stage together, Miss Tandy, as Sebastian, is embracing Olivia at one moment, and, as Viola, is chattering to the Duke at another, while an interchangeable double flits about the stage under cover of masking gentlemen in cloaks. It is ingeniously done and was worth trying again, but, in fact, it emphasizes the entanglement. No matter: in all else the production is smooth and graceful and gay, and has enough in it that is conspicuously good to make this a performance of the play that is uncommonly well worth visiting.

There is a pleasant Sir Andrew by Mr. Alec Guinness, on the quiet side of Aguecheeks; an Olivia by Miss Jill Esmond that is sometimes too prancing and skittish but improves on acquaintance; and a Maria by Miss Ivy St. Helier, which is a trifle disappointing because too determinedly girlish, but is nevertheless interesting, odd, and controversial. Mr. Marius Goring is a good, bitter clown whose fierceness deepens the collour of Malvolio's imprisonment, and Miss Tandy's Viola, which has vivacity and sharp intelligence, lacks chiefly feeling, and lacks it, not because Miss Tandy misreads the part, but because her voice is shallow to the verse. But there are two outstanding performances. Mr. Laurence Olivier has transformed himself as Sir Toby. Only by a gleam of teeth is he now and then recognizable. The gait is that of Mr. Barrett of Wimpole Street if Cedric Hardwicke had drunk the porter; the voice is that of an old, raddled knight – Belch, in brief; and the incidental acrobatics are a dream of humorous timing. And Mr. John Abbott's Malvolio, shaky only at the opening of the letter scene, is what the heathen imagine the Foreign Office to be – with an added touch of the Senior Common Room. Halfway through the letter scene he turns the whole character to pity – the pity that one has for the disappointment of dupes; hope and vanity shine in his foolish and yet intelligent face; and the way is prepared for his downfall. The reference, of course, is no longer to the Foreign Office, but it is impossible to escape a happy impression that this Malvolio owes his peculiar moderation and assurance to a diplomatic training.

27 FEBRUARY 1937, THE TIMES

The Ascent of F6
By W.H. Auden and Christopher Isherwood

MERCURY THEATRE

| MICHAEL FORSYTH RANSOM | William Devlin |
| THE ABBOT | Evan John |

Embedded in its doctrine this play contains a fable that is in itself interesting and coherent. The dramatists need not blush to find themselves story-tellers, however doctrinal their chief purpose may be, for it is a rule common to authors, teachers, and politicians that they must not bore their audience, and the tale of Ransom's ascent of a mountain peak serves well to hold attention to the stage and to prepare the mind to receive instruction. Ransom is by nature a leader of men, who hates the motives that cause others to accept his leadership and praise his achievements. When he is invited by his brother, a prosperous member of the Government, to lead an expedition to F6, his intuition is to refuse, for he distrusts the political motive underlying the invitation and fears his own corruption by the idea of power. He goes nevertheless, and achieves what is, for him, a success spiritually barren. On the way he has gained insight into his comrades – the sketches of whom are rich in character and of genuine dramatic value – and he has learned from an Abbot on the great glacier what his alternative course might have been.

The action is complicated by the observations upon it of a suburban couple, who are adroitly used as chorus; by the intervention of Ransom's mother, whose symbolic significance is clouded by the fact that many of her words are sung and cannot be distinguished; and by snatches of satire at the expense of conventionally minded men of wealth, which have the disadvantage of being themselves common form in pieces of this kind. The real interest of the play lies in its working out, through the medium of a persuasive and unaffected performance by Mr. William Devlin, of the dramatists' theory of power. The Abbot gives the key to it. He points to the vanity and peril of achievement, and sets out as alternative the surrender of the will. Does this apply only to individual achievement and individual will, or do the dramatists extend their doctrine to a surrender of the collective will also? If not, the discovery they have made is, as yet, but a halt on a long and familiar journey; but it is an extremely interesting halt, neither combative nor arrogant. The whole play seems to be written less with the desire to wound and contemn than to understand. It is tentative, and that is its value.

24 MARCH 1937, THE TIMES

The Taming of the Shrew by William Shakespeare

NEW THEATRE

CHRISTOPHER SLY	Arthur Sinclair
LUCENTIO	Alec Clunes
TRANIO	Anthony Ireland
BAPTISTA	George Howe
GREMIO	Frederick Lloyd
KATHARINA	Edith Evans
HORTENSIO	Ronald Simpson
BIANCA	Elspeth Duxbury
PETRUCHIO	Leslie Banks
TAILOR	Frank Napier

If there is a paradise for producers, *The Shrew* is a producer's paradise. Here they may take – and Mr. Claud Gurney has taken – all the liberties they pine for with less danger of being frowned upon than in any other play of Shakespeare's. So long as the piece goes with a swing, none but the dustiest greybeard will be a stickler for the text. Cut the Pedant from Act IV, scene 2, introduce Christopher Sly to play the part, and who cares for the confusion if it but give us a little more of Mr. Arthur Sinclair. Or throw in a ballet or two and who will complain that Will Shakespeare's versatile hand has seemingly been turned to *revue*? Even the appearance of a pantomime horse in a leading part with a scene to itself and curious interventions in others must not – on conservative grounds – make us hold up shocked or indignant hands.

> O happy horse, to bear the weight of Katharine!
> Do bravely horse! For wot'st thou whom thou movest?

But horse, dancers, scenic elaboration, tricks, quirks, and fancies, though they are not to be rejected from this play for reasons of purism, are to be judged by the answer to one question only: do they lighten the action, free the intrigue, make swift the entertainment, or do they cause it to drag?

The answer is, in this instance, that though Miss Zinkeisen's decorations are a delight to the eye, her costumes splendid, her columns beautiful, her distant prospects charming, there is too much marching about of gloriously dressed servants visibly performing the job of scene-shifters, and that, though Mr. Gurney's inventions are fun as separate turns – the *ballets* pretty and the horse a cheerful one – collectively they become a delay and a bore. If *The Shrew* is not taken at pace, it is lost, and these interruptions, instead of lightening the movement, weigh it down.

That said, let the virtues of the entertainment have their turn. There is scarcely a part in it not well performed. Among the smaller and the middle fry may be observed a blessedly clear-cut Tranio by Mr. Ireland, a Bianca gracefully sketched by Miss Duxbury, a neat Hortensio by Mr. Ronald Simpson, a Tailor endowed by Mr. Frank Napier with an eloquent face, and a Lucentio so good that even this intrigue becomes gay and smiling when Mr. Alec Clunes is on the stage. Passing from the small fry, recognize a whale of a Katharina by Miss Evans – an odd performance, heavy – too heavy, too sullenly dead – while the taming is in process, as if Katharina were not potentially charming but a leaden scold, then suddenly, when the taming is complete, dazzling. "A woman moved is like a fountain troubled" – when she comes to that Miss Evans is at the height of her powers, but the performance as a whole is not among her best, the early Katharina, astonishingly in so great a comedy actress, lacking the comic fire. But the Petruchio – granted that in conformity with the production it is to be fantasticated – is flawless. Mr. Leslie Banks has an impetus, a dash, a lightness of attack that carry the play through all obstacles, preserving it as a fierce, swift piece for the theatre, and saving it from being the pageant with clowning that it now and then threatens to become.

20 MAY 1937, THE TIMES

The Constant Wife by W. Somerset Maugham

GLOBE THEATRE

MRS. CULVER	Helen Haye
CONSTANCE MIDDLETON	Ruth Chatterton
JOHN MIDDLETON	Cecil Parker
MARIE-LOUISE DURHAM	Eileen Peel
BERNARD KERSAL	Cyril Raymond

How pleasant it is to write again that dramatist's name at the head of a notice! How pleasant it is, one is compelled to add after the experiences of the last few weeks, to write a dramatist's name at the head of a notice! *The Constant Wife* has not become a masterpiece with the passing of the years. It is still too rigid a statement of a case. If the life of men and women may be compared to the sea, Mr. Maugham's representation of it in this piece resembles a little too closely a group of neat, efficient, well-controlled reservoirs to which the sea is admitted for inspection and analysis. In the sea and in the reservoirs is the same water; Mr. Maugham's enclosures contain the genuine stuff, with as much buoyancy and even more glitter than the irregular ocean; what one misses is the moon and tides, the currents that cross or intermingle, and – dare we say? – the poetry of life which, though it may be a part of illusion, is for that very reason a part of truth and a part that Mr. Maugham's realism takes too seldom into account. But when that has been said one can sit back comfortably and count the benefits that Mr. Maugham provides. Of these three are remarkable: he has a story to tell; he has something to say which (leaving out the moon and counting the sixpences) is both entertaining and, so far as it goes, true; and he can write. He can turn a phrase, a scene, an act. He writes so well that actresses who, like Miss Helen Haye, have the edge of comedy to their speech are at a premium, and gabbling, which is almost a mercy in many other plays, would be criminal in this.

The case he has to state is set out by Constance. When she finds that her husband has been unfaithful to her, she is complacent and herself remains chaste – the first because she is no longer in love with him or he with her, the second because she will not be unchaste until she is economically independent of him. The argument is presented without didacticism, with excellent wit, and with the cool detachment that is the dramatist's own. The performance is not all that it was when the play first appeared, chiefly because Miss Ruth Chatterton, though she has the sense and spirit of the part, appears unfinished among an English company, her timing and intonation being different from theirs; but Mr. Cecil Parker and Mr. Cyril Raymond have the dryness and control that Mr. Maugham's comedy requires, Miss Eileen Peel cleverly avoids over-emphasis in her sketch of the silliness of Marie-Louise, and Miss Helen Haye (quietly) has a field-day. There is not a flutter of emotion in the evening, though love – or something related to it – is the subject discussed. That is Mr. Maugham's limitation, but it is a limitation deliberately self-imposed, and it produces the opposite virtues of a style unswervingly directed to its purpose and as brilliant as it is hard.

27 MAY 1937, THE TIMES

He Was Born Gay by Emlyn Williams

QUEEN'S THEATRE

FRANCIS	Harry Andrews
MISS MASON	Gwen Ffrangçon-Davies
LEWIS DELL	Glen Byam Shaw
LADY ATKYNS	Sydney Fairbrother
SOPHIE RAFFERTY	Carol Goodner
MR. LEROY	Frank Pettingell
MASON	John Gielgud
LAMBERT	Emlyn Williams

This is one of those occasions on which criticism does not stand about talking, but rubs its eyes and withdraws hastily with an embarrassed, incredulous, and uncomprehending blush. What made Mr. Emlyn Williams write this play or Mr. Gielgud and Miss Ffrangçon-Davies appear in it is not to be understood. About the time of Waterloo a young music master, known as Mason, is employed in the Dell's household at Dover. He is, in fact, Louis XVII of France, but a lady spoken of as his sister is anxious to conceal the proofs of his descent and to keep him in safety and concealment. In this plan he might have acquiesced if another and more flashing lady (Miss Carol Goodner) had not spurred his ambition, and her plan might have succeeded if it had not been thwarted by an agent of Louis XVIII and a glass of poison.

All this would have been very well if it had been treated either seriously or with the dash and glitter of sword and cloak. Alternatively, the farcical passages about two other claimants to the Throne of France might have carried the piece if it had been a farce, and Mr. Williams and Mr. Pettingell between them do succeed in making the opening of the third act a little comfortable. But when for long, long passages of rhetoric Mr. Gielgud whimpers childish memories of prison, or, in flowing periods, spreads emotional tremors over the beloved scenery of France, or, while reading aloud a proclamation of one of the imposters, droops into dreaming retrospect of the glories and the flunkeys of Versailles, one holds fast to the arms of an astonished stall and prays that no one will laugh out loud before it is over. It is, however, fair to add that no one did, Mr. Gielgud's prestige having the effect of a sermon; that Miss Elliott Mason and Miss Sydney Fairbrother obtained laughter where it was intended; and that the soft music (off) was composed, to provoke in the Dauphin sad memories of a gilded babyhood, by Mozart.

The Great Romancer by Jules Eckert Goodman

NEW THEATRE

IDA FERRIER	Coral Browne
VICTOR BRUN	Eric Portman
ALEXANDRE DUMAS	Robert Morley
ADAH ISAACS MENCKEN	Carol Goodner

Other things being equal, what is it that makes one biographical play a cheerful prospect, and another, before the curtain rises, indubitably dull? The answer is that the immortals are divided into three classes: those whom one would like to meet at supper – for example, Byron; those whom one would like to meet on the stage – for example, Dumas; and those who, perhaps by no fault of their own, exude, as they wander among the shades, the odour of tediousness. No one, as Lewis Carroll knew, would be pleased to meet Edwin and Morcar. '"Ugh!' said the Lory, with a shiver, when their names were mentioned, and the Mouse, to make it plain that his list of bores was not exhausted, hastened on to 'Stigand, the patriotic Archbishop of Canterbury, [who] found it advisable –'

'Found *what*?' said the Duck,

'Found *it*,' the Mouse replied rather crossly." All of which is only a way of saying that, though the play's title is a little awkward, and though they will rhyme his name with Bloomer, Dumas *père* is one of those people who give promise of a warm evening.

And not the father only, but the son, and de Vigny and Dorval and Adah Isaacs Menken. What a galaxy! And what costumes! There is a dressing-gown of de Vigny's that is itself a justification of Dorval's infidelity to Dumas, and there is a dress (and a hat) of the Mencken's in which Miss Carol Goodner, appearing for a moment at the end of an act, proved to the world how rich, how generous, and how exasperating the management of the New Theatre can be. It is true that, when next she appears, it is in white petticoats and cerulean stays, but even so – how can men have the heart to drop the curtain on that face and that hat? Still, it gives one something to chatter about in such a way as may perhaps indicate to the discerning that, though this history of Dumas, his ghosts, his collaborators, his duns, and his ladies, is a rambling tale about nothing in particular, it provides an affable, amusing evening in the tradition of the cheerful rattle.

It will, in fact, be better than it is when it has learnt to rattle with less persistence. The first act is deafening. Everyone is so determined to exhibit the bohemian vitality of the Dumas household that everyone shouts its roof off. Even Mr. Morley himself is swept up in the storm. The evening owes much to him. If he did not play the part with a dashing emphasis on the charm and energy of Dumas, we should have been given time to question the reason of the dramatist's portrait, and that would never do; but, even so, there is no disadvantage in varying the speed of energetic charm; there are lulls in all the more discreet whirlwinds. ... But there is something odd about a play that begins again and becomes a new play when Miss Carol Goodner comes on at the end of the second act. She has no need to fight for emphasis. She has it in her voice, her presence, her natural grace on the stage. As soon as she appears the audience begins to collaborate with her – an actress who, even when she has a part no more important than this, gives to it the distinction of a minor work of art.

22 JUNE 1937, THE TIMES

Victoria Regina by Laurence Housman

LYRIC THEATRE

LORD CONYNGHAM	Allan Aynesworth
VICTORIA	Pamela Stanley
PRINCE ALBERT	Carl Esmond
LADY JANE	Penelope Dudley Ward
DUCHESS OF SUTHERLAND	Mabel Terry-Lewis
EARL OF BEACONSFIELD	Ernest Milton

The Lord Chamberlain's license having been granted to it, Mr. Housman's play on Queen Victoria, first seen long ago at the Gate Theatre, was publicly performed last night in the presence of the Duke and Duchess of Kent.

It opens with the arrival of Lord Conyngham and the Archbishop of Canterbury at Kensington Palace to inform the Princess of King William's death and of her accession; it ends on the day of the Diamond Jubilee, having given, in seven intervening scenes, a sketch of the personal history of the Queen. It is a sketch at once candid and affectionate, giving a clear impression of the early doubts and the final security of the reign, and making of the ruler herself a study not indeed complete, but so balanced in its selection and so genuinely progressive in its development of character that it gives the satisfaction of completeness. If this is not all of history, neither in effect is it history falsified.

Miss Pamela Stanley is the core of the play, and no account can be given of it except in terms of her performance. What in this is surprising is that it seems less at ease when the Queen's years are within range of the actress's own than it is in full maturity and in old age. The accession scene is prettily done, but it is the wit and authority of Mr. Allan Aynesworth's Conyngham that here make all else seem a trifle amateurish. The Queen's proposal of marriage has still something more of the stage than of Windsor in it, and the pleasure of this encounter is in observing the likeness and the grace of Mr. Carl Esmond's opening as Prince Albert. It is, in fact, Mr. Esmond who has the honours in the three passages that follow – a domestic note on Prince Albert shaving, another on Prince Albert's tact in finding a way through the Queens wilfulness, and an account of the attempted assassination in 1842.

Then follows what is in many respects the best of the play – a story of the Queen's too-swift jealousy and of its appeasement. It is a beautifully written and deeply moving scene. Miss Penelope Dudley Ward, as the suspected girl, has schooled herself to a Victorianism both fiery and discreet; Miss Mabel Terry-Lewis represents the Duchess of Sutherland with faultless poise; and Miss Pamela Stanley, now magnificent in the dress in which she is holding her Court, begins to come into her own – perhaps because now for the first time the Queen's emotion is openly and passionately expressed. From this point onward the portrait steadily deepens.

In 1861, under the threat of war with America, Miss Stanley's Victoria, in gait, in voice, in a greater deliberation of movement, takes on new strengths, to which, in a meeting with Beaconsfield 16 years later, is added a new tenderness and a discerning irony that mark a genuine insight into old age. This scene is, perhaps, a little over-written. Disraeli was flowery, but was he as flowery as this? Mr. Milton gives an admirable portrait of him which suggests his influence on the Queen and the extravagance of his genius, but Mr. Housman seems here to be painting the waistcoat. It is a slight defect, and does little to weaken the impression of the evening as a whole – an impression, greatly helped by the richness and variety of Mr. Rex Whistler's designs, of a brilliant pageant, quick in emotion, but as restrained as it is just.

29 AUGUST 1937, THE NEW YORK TIMES

Juno and the O'Casey

James Agate has lately said that Mr. O'Casey's *Juno and the Paycock* is the greatest play written in English since the days of Queen Elizabeth. When first I saw this pronouncement I was astonished, but reserved judgment for the good reason that I had in my mind no clear impression of *Juno and the Paycock* on the stage. In criticism these isolating superlatives are to be distrusted. It is rash to say that any play is "the greatest," for it cannot properly be compared with pieces not in its own kind. How is *The School for Scandal* to be matched with *The Dynasts* of Hardy or *She Stoops to Conquer* with Shelley's *The Cenci*?

It seems to me reasonable to ask whether O'Casey is, as a dramatist, superior to Synge, for there is between them a visible relationship of substance and manner, but to put O'Casey at the top of the post-Elizabethan group and to imply that Shelley, Shaw and Sheridan must stand lower is, I think, to behave like a rash and uncharitable schoolmaster who decides to give one prize and one only, though some of his pupils do mathematics and some Latin and some dancing, and cannot justly be compared except within their own classes. Is the good boy of the dancing class "greater" than the best scholar in Greek? Is Mr. O'Casey's prose to be preferred to Shelley's verse? But perhaps it is unjust to put too much logical pressure on Mr. Agate's superlative. Let us rather welcome enthusiasm when it appears – and when it appears to be justified.

Juno and the Paycock has been revived in full state at the Haymarket. The leading Irish players are there – Arthur Sinclair, Sara Allgood, Maire O'Neill. My memory of the piece, except in print, was so dim that I went to this performance with a fresh, open and eager mind, and greatly enjoyed it, particularly the third act, but nothing in it shook my opinion that *Within the Gates* is, in poetic intensity, in depth of vision and in originality of treatment a formidable advance on the earlier play. It might have been expected that those parts of *Juno and the Paycock* which are directly concerned with the tragedy of the Irish rebellion would by now have become stale; but this is not so. In all its tragic aspects – the shooting of the son, the wretched collapse of the father's boast, the betrayal of the daughter, the mother's suffering at the hands of fate – the play is keen and alive.

Suffering gives an edge to Mr. O'Casey's genius; he writes of it from within himself and sometimes poisons it with his innermost hatreds; it is always his own, unborrowed, not visibly derived. His comedy, even at its best, has not the same freshness. It is good, but good within a clearly established convention of the Irish theatre. There is, for example, in this play a scene in which, the family and two visitors being gathered together, they proceed to sing songs to one another. The mother and daughter's duet is pleasant and creditable; the male visitor's attempt is funny because he has neither memory for the words not ear for the music; the female visitor's contribution is a music-hall short. In brief, a prolonged series of variety turns, during which the play is allowed to stand still. And it is to be observed elsewhere in the piece that its humour again and again depends not upon the point but upon the pointlessness of what is being said and upon the mere loquacity of the speaker.

This is a legitimate form of humour; it bores me a little because I am not Irish; but it is in Ireland a legitimate and approved form against which there can be no critical complaint. I wish only to point out that it is conventional and in a sense local. It has neither the universality nor the originality of Mr. O'Casey's tragedy. For this reason the first two acts of *Juno*, which greatly depend on it, though good entertainment, cannot, I think, sustain the claim to greatness which is established by the tragic third act.

That in the long run *Juno and the Paycock* will rank with *The Playboy* as a piece for the theatre or that it will be remembered as a work of art when the *The Cenci* is forgotten I find it hard to believe. Mr. O'Casey's strength is in his power to carry his audience to the heart of a tragic symbol and to compel their imagination not only to receive but *bear again* the essence of his despair. When he writes tragedy he is what great artists must always be – a sower of seed that will bear new fruit in every generation. Now and then he poisons his seed with a specialized political bitterness, but when his tragedy has its origin in pity for mankind and not in hatred for particular men or groups of men it is beyond question tragedy of a very high rank.

Richard II by William Shakespeare

QUEEN'S THEATRE

KING RICHARD II	John Gielgud
JOHN OF GAUNT	Leon Quartermaine
HENRY BOLINGBROKE	Michael Redgrave
THOMAS MOWBRAY	Glen Byam Shaw
DUCHESS OF GLOUCESTER	Dorothy Green
DUKE OF SURREY	Antony Quayle
DUKE OF AUMERLE	Alec Guinness
GREEN	Denis Price
BUSHY	Harry Andrews
DUKE OF YORK	George Howe
QUEEN	Peggy Ashcroft
EARL OF NORTHUMBERLAND	Frederick Lloyd
BISHOP OF CARLISLE	Harcourt Williams
A GARDENER	George Devine
SIR PIERCE OF EXTON	Harry Andrews

If this production were defective, criticism might yet be tempted to soften its defects and over-praise it, for the season that it begins – a season of great plays, each put on for limited and guaranteed runs – is one upon the success of which much good in the theatre depends. Its failure would give disastrous opportunity to those who cry that the living theatre is a sick man that cannot save himself. Fortunately it is too good to fail. There is no danger of over-praising it.

The key to Mr. Gielgud's interpretation of the part is in Richard's speech when, after his abdication, he has considered his mirrored face and thrown the glass to the ground: –

'Tis very true, my grief lies all within;
And these external manners of laments
Are merely shadows to the unseen grief
That swells with silence in the tortured soul.

All his playing is a movement towards this climax, and, after the fall, a spiritual search beyond it. Some have objected to Mr. Gielgud's more recent acting that he has become increasingly inclined to emphasise his mannerisms. It is, therefore, of the first importance to say clearly that this performance of Richard is not only more mature, but simpler in construction, than his performance of the same part years ago at the Old Vic. In certain passages, before the rebellion has brought misfortune on the King, a wish to indicate his frailty of character and, perhaps, his personal charm, leads Mr.

Gielgud into a smiling that is too frequent, and gives an impression of contrivance; but even these scenes are not mannered; they are played with a rare directness and integrity, so that the growth of the man in his despair of this world is felt to be a real growth, and the petulance of the beginning and the splendid agony of the end are linked each to each by early hints of a splendour within and by late reminders of a weakness not, even in prison, wholly transcended.

Of Miss Ashcroft it is enough to say that in this play she accepts a small part and plays it with admirable grace. The whole production is distinguished by the excellence of its proportion. The opening is made lively by the Mowbray, at once violent and secretive, of Mr. Glen Byam Shaw; by the fierce Surrey of Mr. Quayle; by Miss Dorothy Green's keen note on the Duchess of Gloucester and by Mr. Michael Redgrave's introduction to a study of Bolingbroke so steady and lucid that, when at last he is silent on his throne, the silence is illumined by knowledge of him – his ruthlessness, his uncertain desire to be honest, his conflicting conscience. There is a rich, heavy Northumberland by Mr. Frederick Lloyd; a sketch of York by Mr. George Howe lighted by a perceptive wit; and studies of Gaunt and Carlisle by Mr. Quartermaine and Mr. Harcourt Williams that are fresh within the tradition. In sum, a beautiful, carefully studied and extraordinarily complete performance of the play – as alive and well-balanced as any we may reasonably hope for in our time.

22 SEPTEMBER 1937, THE TIMES

Pygmalion by George Bernard Shaw

OLD VIC

ELIZA DOOLITTLE	Diana Wynyard
COL PICKERING	Mark Dignam
HENRY HIGGINS	Robert Morley
MRS. PEARCE	Dora Gregory
ALFRED DOOLITTLE	Jay Laurier

To say that Eliza Doolittle is the deuce of a problem of casting and acting is to invite Mr. Shaw to appear from Olympus with assurances that of all the women of his theatre she is the simplest. So, in a sense, she is – which is why she is such good company; but she is also, like all good Cockneys, an eel with a kick in her tail and actresses with the quality of eels are not easily come by. Eliza was by nature quick on the rebound, taut, wiry, a fighter. For that reason an actress who is not naturally persuasive in the first two acts cannot by miracle or by accomplishment be fully persuasive in the remaining three. That, under the influence of Higgins's lessons in elocution, Eliza has become outwardly a fine lady does not solve the actress's problem. Once an eel always an eel, and contrariwise. And Miss Wynyard is not an eel. Nothing else can be said against her performance. It is charming, witty, and extremely entertaining. It is, moreover, studied with unusual care – the movement of hands and body, the droop of despair, the cry of triumph, every detail of the performance has the support of reason. But it remains a delightful *tour de force*. Just as in the first act what we see is mimicry of a flower-girl, so later in the play, it is mimicry of a flower-girl mimicking a lady of quality. The flick of the tail is never fully spontaneous. One feels of Eliza that, if she were cut into six pieces, each would retort vigorously and at once – and love it. One feels of Miss Wynyard in the part – well, that, though she is giving as clever and amusing a performance as any she has given, she was not born to play it.

But that does not prevent her from being, by her accomplishment and grace, the centre of as good an evening as the Old Vic has for a long time provided. Mr. Morley takes Higgins a trifle slowly; he is not enough intoxicated by his rhetoric; but his grave deliberateness has remarkable compensations in giving new point to old lines, and he has an admirable collaborator in Mr. Mark Dignam. Miss Dora Gregory gives a genuine cut to Mrs. Pearce's dignified tolerance; she is a monument of middle-class morality unbending slightly to freakish genius; and Mr. Jay Laurier, as Eliza's father, has many of the superbly eel-like qualities that were in her glorified. The time that has passed since the performance at Buxton has enabled Mr. Guthrie's fresh and inventive production to be brought to the Old Vic in a perfection of ripeness.

10 OCTOBER 1937, THE NEW YORK TIMES

More on Time and Mr. Priestley

Both in *Time and the Conways* and in his more recent piece *I Have Been Here Before*, Mr. Priestley is uncommonly modest in his claims. The nature of Time has become for him an absorbing interest and what he wishes to communicate through the medium of the theatre is precisely that interest and no more; he does not pretend to be announcing a final – or, I think, even a provisional-truth. In brief, he has discovered that Time can be used conveniently as a theme for the kind of play which, at present, he wants to write – a play, that is, with metaphysical implications but with a persuasively naturalistic setting.

Instead of the masks, the poetic prose and the group-symbols by means of which some of our younger dramatists seek to express metaphysical ideas, he, though claiming an airy territory at least as wide as theirs, will keep his feet on earth. The contest of style is not new and is for that reason the more interesting. The young poetic symbolists have their origin in Strindberg's *Dream Play*; Mr. Priestley's inspiration is in Strindberg's so-called "naturalistic" dramas or, even more clearly, in Ibsen's *The Master Builder*. This is not the place in which to examine the two methods at length. I will discuss Mr. Priestley's; the other, for the present, only by implication.

The outstanding advantage of Mr. Priestley's style is its lucidity. It is, of course, not true that the best art is that which can be most easily understood. There are certain themes so profound, so unfamiliar or so complex that a simple statement of them is impossible and the artist who treats of them is always in danger of being called "obscure" by seven-eighths of the world. This accusation he can afford to disregard. His first duty is to express the truth that is in him and to express it whole; he is under no obligation to sacrifice any part of it so that what remains may be comfortably assimilated by dull minds. But it is his duty also to express his truth with the greatest lucidity consistent with the nature of that truth. The more difficult his subject the more strenuous must be his labour for precision. To be vague as a means of avoidance is to be a charlatan.

Aware of this, Mr. Priestley is extremely careful to keep his outlines clear, so careful that the opposite peril of rigidity immediately presents itself. I mean rigidity of idea, not stiffness of theatrical treatment, and it is right to say at once, in parentheses, that, philosophy or no philosophy, *I Have Been Here Before* is from first to last good theatre with none of the heaviness or diffuseness that is sometimes a defect in *Time and the Conways*. That said we may return to what I have called his rigidity of idea and to the dramatist's battle with and his victory over it.

He is telling the story of a German man of science, Dr. Gortler, who comes to an inn on the Yorkshire moors in pursuit of his theory of Recurrence and Intervention. Gortler, in a waking dream, has plunged into what we call the future, and there has met a bitterly unhappy girl and her young husband and has been informed of their past. They had met in an inn on the Yorkshire moors, he a young schoolmaster on holiday, she at that time the wife of Walter Ormund, a rich man older than herself. They had fallen in love and run away together. Ormund, a man of unhappy temperament, had committed suicide, thus bringing scandal, poverty and bitterness to them and to vast numbers of people indirectly dependent on him. Dr. Gortler has come to the inn to see this fatal drama enacted, for it is his belief that we live the same lives over and over again, moving as it were in a spiral groove. Having, in his dream, watched the sequel to the tragic story of the girl, the husband and the schoolmaster, he has come to witness the story itself and, if he can, to intervene upon it.

This notion that our lives repeat themselves in spiral grooves is one which, it seems to me, ought not to be pressed too hard. One can too easily pick holes in any strictly logical interpretation of it. At best, it is a metaphor possibly suggestive of truth, and to treat it as if it were itself truth is to commit the sin of rigidity that I have spoken of. Nor is it of profound importance to explain why we experience sometimes the sensation expressed in the poem of Rossetti that gives the play its title. If this were really what the play is about it would be of no more interest than the scores of plays which are given an artificial twist of oddity by the appearance of some mysterious stranger or by the theory of some learned professor. But Mr. Priestley's work has a quality of its own that sets it apart from other plays of theory-spinning and of the occult.

The truth is that though the hard precision of Dr. Gortler's theorizing about spirals and time-grooves will cause many people to discuss the play as if it were, in essence, scientific, it is not scientific at all, but mystical and intuitive. If the spirals and time-grooves were its core, it would be of little value and there are moments when Mr. Priestley himself seems to overestimate their importance. It is not they that give life to the play, but two things to which they are no more than a metaphorical adjunct: first, the sense of fate in the minds of the people of the play and, second, Gortler and Priestley's sudden emancipation from the rigid form of the time-groove theory.

At the moment when the young wife and the schoolmaster are about to run away and the husband to kill himself, Gortler tells Ormund that he can get out of the time-groove by an exercise of will. This truth can be expressed without reference to time-grooves. It is the truth of the Gospels, of Socrates and of Tolstoy that by an act of creative imagination a man may be born again. It is, as Tolstoy would not admit at the end of his life, the justification of art; it is, as Tolstoy knew well, the reason against despair and the assurance of redemption. Its statement in the third act of a modern play, its acceptance by a man whom Mr. Wilfrid Lawson in a brilliant performance has shown to be an inhabitant of hell, its coming from the lips of Dr. Gortler, who has hitherto been playing about with time-grooves, fairly lights the theatre's stage.

Time-grooves are no more than pseudo-scientific jargon for destiny. It is not the niceties of theory that make the play, but Mr. Priestley's power to show a group of un-fantasticated human beings who, with their feet on earth, are yet continuously aware of the spiritual forces surrounding them. If he could have done this and expressed his spiritual idea without using the pseudo-scientific framework of Gortler's theories, the play might have been a masterpiece. As it stands, it is an oasis for which theatrical travellers have every reason to be thankful.

31 OCTOBER 1937, THE NEW YORK TIMES

London Views a National Theatre

LONDON, OCT 15

So far as I am aware, no new appeal has recently been issued in America by the committee which has for so many years been attempting to establish a national theatre in England. Unless such an appeal is issued, it will be unnecessary to trouble readers of *The New York Times* with a general discussion of the whole problem. There has, however, recently sprung up in England a fierce national theatre controversy, provoked by the committee's purchase of a site in the museum district, upon which they propose ultimately to build. Having purchased the site, which is itself greatly open to criticism, they have remaining the equivalent of about $375,000, which is obviously so much less than the sum which will be required for building and endowment that either a new appeal or the intervention of the State will be necessary if the work is to proceed.

In the controversy which has engaged the newspapers during the last few weeks, all the old questions have been debated over again – questions of control, policy, of the wisdom or unwisdom of State endowment, of whether a new building is necessary at all, and if so, whether the building should precede the establishment of a company of actors or the theatre be built round a company already in existence – and one new element has been introduced into the discussion. It has been said again and again that in fact a national theatre already exists in the Old Vic – Sadler's Wells organization. This claim may lead to misunderstandings, and a preliminary discussion of it may clear the ground.

To say that the Old Vic at present fulfils all the functions that are ordinarily associated with the idea of a national theatre is to make for it an unreasonable claim, but it is certainly arguable that in the Old Vic organization there exists, as a living entity, the nucleus from which a national theatre might develop. It is, in the first place, a theatre which has been partly endowed by voluntary subscription and has, to that extent, been freed from the stress of commercial competition. Because it receives no subsidy from the State, it is free from parliamentary interference and is, therefore, regarded with affection and not with suspicion among the English, who have an intuitive distrust of any artistic organization that is not "free."

At the same time, it is so well run and so widely supported that during its more recent seasons it has paid its own way, and any further endowments which are given to it will not be absorbed by footing a bill for current losses, but will be spent in paying off reconstruction debts and in further capital development. Here, then, is a living unit which may, perhaps, be compared with Molière's company of players, for whom the Comédie Française was established, and from whom the whole French system of subsidised theatres has sprung.

For us closely to imitate the French system would be pedantic folly. The genius of our theatre is different from that of the French theatre, the mood and purpose of our audience are different from the purpose and mood of French audiences. If we are to have an endowed theatre on a large scale, whether it be called national or not, and whether or not it receives a State subsidy, it must take its shape from the special attitude of the English public toward the drama, and a very fair indication of that attitude may be found in the audiences at the Old Vic.

Within my own recollection the Old Vic was a theatre which provided rather indifferent performances of Shakespeare at low prices for an audience drawn almost entirely from the poorer part of London. It was at that time in no sense national. Very few people from the West End ever visited it, salaries of actors were extremely low, production costs were kept down to a minimum and the general standard of performance was more pious than exalted. Since that time its development has been astonishing, and the cause of its development has been the peculiar quality of Miss Lilian Baylis's management.

Miss Baylis is, above all else, a "character." At first nights she appears on the stage wearing the cap and gown of an honorary M. A. of Oxford and with the appearance not of a theatrical manageress but of an extremely energetic and benevolent schoolmistress addressing her affectionate pupils. So far as I am aware, she has not, and has never been, a profound theorist, either on the text of Shakespeare or methods of producing Shakespeare. She is in no sense a theatrical stylist, and, though the Old Vic is undoubtedly hers, it is not hers in the sense in which the Moscow Arts Theatre was Stanislavsky's or the Théâtre Libre, Antoine's.

She has the peculiar power, which seems necessary to all great enterprises in this country, of seeming to the general public to do very little and yet of drawing more and more experts in every branch of the theatrical art into her devoted service. She would not have this power if she herself were not devoted to what she considers to be "the cause," which, in her case, means the service of Shakespeare and the education of the people to appreciate him. Somehow she has drawn into the Old Vic one young actor and young actress after another, who has made a name there, has afterward increased in repute in the West End and has returned to her service as a star, accepting something incredibly less than a star salary.

Not only this, but wherever one goes in the theatrical world, whether it be among very young people starting in their profession, or among established leaders of it, one finds that it is everywhere regarded as an honour and almost a necessity to prestige, to become a member of the Old Vic company. A woman who can endow her organization with such a spirit as this, and at the same time allow it to develop beyond her original Shakespearean intentions to include other classical and even modern plays is a unique figure in the English theatre and one whose powers it would seem a folly to neglect in any attempt that may be made to extend a system of theatrical endowment in this country.

Miss Baylis, in a recent speech, said, "I don't care a dash for a national theatre," and implied quite clearly that in her view the Old Vic was a national theatre. And so it is, in a sense. But Miss Baylis herself, in one of her less abrupt moments, would probably freely admit that there is a long gap between the Old Vic as it exists today and the ideal of an endowed theatre in its full development. The point I wish now to make is that, whether this full ideal is approached through the Old Vic or independently, it will probably never be attained in England except by a process of gradual development from a living company under the control of a dictator of a peculiar kind – a kind of which Miss Baylis is one example, and Mr. Norman Marshall, who controls the Gate Theatre, another.

The dictator who is going to succeed in the English theatre is something very different from the man devoted to a particular aesthetic style, who is sometimes able to establish a great theatrical movement in Russia, in France or in Germany. What is needed in England is neither a tedious committee which appoints a theatrical director to work under its orders, or a purely artistic and executive genius such as Stanislavsky; but rather a man with a wide general idea, a power to resist specialization and cranks, and an intuition which enables him to make others work for him – in brief a loose dictatorship not restricted by rigid theory, and therefore not of a kind to unite against it all those forces which in England, whether in the theatre or elsewhere, are inclined to combine against anything that can be called pedantic discipline.

Apart from anything else that can be said against the existing national theatre committee and its schemes, it is clear that it has made at the outset a psychological error. It has given Englishmen the impression that it wishes to impose something upon them for the improvement of their minds. They are, therefore, in stubborn revolt. Miss Baylis entertained her public first and taught them imperceptibly, with the result that she has now at her disposal a theatre burning with vitality, whose name springs to everyone's lips whenever a national theatre is mentioned.

8 NOVEMBER 1937, THE TIMES

It's You I Want by Maurice Braddell

CAMBRIDGE THEATRE

SHOLTO DELANEY	Seymour Hicks
MELISANDE MONTGOMERY	Jane Carr

The revival of this farce is an opportunity to signal the jubilée of Sir Seymour Hicks. It is not so much that he still runs indefatigably from door-to-door, releasing husbands, concealing wives, and providing beautiful ladies with refuge in the fire-escape, as that he is able, in the midst of it all, to show himself as a great actor, unique in his kind. The hardest-faced frowner upon farces can have delight in this performance, and there is scarcely an actor, and certainly no critic, who may not learn from it. For example, Sir Seymour perched on a sofa-arm in the ecstasies of love, finding that he has his feet free, acts with his feet, and a more brilliantly expressive piece of acting is not to be found in the theatre. "Oh," says the grave young man, whose idea of acting is to droop mumblingly in his corner, "oh," says he, "but that is just Hicks." But it isn't. It is one of the ways of life and mobility on the stage. It is one of the ways of making love. And if what is in question is not the genius of acting but this play only, the answer is still the brief rhyme: –

Doors six;
One Hicks.

9 NOVEMBER 1937, THE TIMES

Ghosts by Henrik Ibsen,
in an adaptation by Norman Ginsbury

VAUDEVILLE THEATRE

REGINA	Sylvia Coleridge
ENGESTRAND	Frederick Bennett
PASTOR MANDERS	Stephen Murray
MRS. ALVING	Marie Ney
OSWALD ALVING	Clifford Evans

"Adaptation" is so dangerous a word when applied to Ibsen, and Mr. Ginsbury's work gives to the play so different a tone from that given it by Archer's, that for a moment one distrusts him. Has he been playing tricks with the text? Reference to Archer at several points that seemed questionable acquits Mr. Ginsbury, and he is entitled to the more credit – a credit shared with Miss Church's production and Miss McArthur's designs – for having given to *Ghosts*, while remaining faithful to it, more spring than we have known in it before. It is, in its writing, a heavy play with a heaviness that is by no means of the essence of great tragedy; it has none of *Hedda Gabler's* varying light and none of the *Master Builder's* passionate impetus; the outbreak of fire gives a forced emphasis to the end of the second act, and Ibsen has been so interested in Mrs. Alving that he has oddly neglected Regina, who might have quickened the pulse of the narrative. Terrible, powerful, and unrelenting though the play is, it depends too much on its study of Mrs. Alving, and is not, as a dramatic unity, among Ibsen's masterpieces.

Everything, or almost everything, depends on Mrs. Alving, but before discussing Miss Marie Ney's performance it is right to say that she is uncommonly well supported. Though later in the evening he becomes a trifle monotonous, Mr. Stephen Murray does what may reasonably be done with the tiresomeness of Pastor Manders. Mr. Frederick Bennett gives colour and a controlled humour to Engstrand; Miss Sylvia Coleridge plays Regina well enough to make one wish that Ibsen had developed the part more fully; and, except in one outbreak which he takes at too high a pitch, Mr. Clifford Evans gives a magnificent study of young Alving, showing him not as a whining degenerate in whom the adoration of life and the sun is a contradiction, but as what Ibsen intended him to be – a creature of natural splendour and vitality, as his father was in his youth, for whom disease has, therefore, a multiplying horror.

In the midst of this group is Miss Ney, her Mrs. Alving is an ageing woman, in manner naturally austere. The treatment of the part, except in its climaxes, is deliberate, rational, precise, unspectacular – one may say even cold. But this quality of coldness springs from Mrs. Alving's own past when, as she herself perceives, she was burdened by a sense of duty and yielded herself too little to the joy of living. Miss Ney appears to have built her interpretation on this confession. Everything seems to spring from it – her repressed passion that gives force to her early scenes with Manders, her terror when she first sees life repeating itself, her fierce battle against despair when life is ruined in her son. The part may be played in hotter blood, but not with more persuasive analysis or more profound suffering. The performance is memorable as much for its feeling as for its intellect.

Mourning Becomes Electra by Eugene O'Neill

WESTMINSTER THEATRE

CHRISTINE MANNON	Laura Cowie
LAVINIA	Beatrix Lehmann
HAZEL NILES	Jean Winstanley
CAPTAIN ADAM BRANT	Reginald Tate
BRIGADIER-GENERAL EZRA MANNON	Mark Dignam
ORIN MANNON	Robert Harris

Mr. O'Neill's trilogy, which is, perhaps, the highest of all his titles to fame, has for years been denied to London, and is now at last to be seen. It is long; one may argue that it would, in fact, have been a greater work of art if it had been shorter; but let us take it, without quibbling, for what it is – an enthralling narrative, a profound piece of psychological inquiry, and a tragedy that is to be discussed only in terms of the masterpieces of the theatre.

It tells of the Mannon family, who lived in New England in 1865; of how hatred and the power of their dead was a perpetual curse upon the living; of how Christine, the mother, poisoned her husband for her lover's sake; how the daughter Lavinia, using her brother Orin as her instrument, pursued Christine to her death; and of how at last Lavinia and Orin, haunted by their own guilt and possessed by the spirits of their dead mother and father, were driven into fearful loves and hates – Orrin to die by his own hand, Lavinia to live on alone in the house of their doom.

The story reaches back, in retrospect, beyond the generations represented on the stage, and the parallel with Greek legend may be traced to Iphigenia. Mr. O'Neill even introduces groups of people whose comments suggest that he had the Chorus in his mind, but he makes little use of them – too little; they are the weakness that might have been the final strength of his play. But except a certain forcing of the theme in the third part there are few other weaknesses. Mr. O'Neill's Fate works through character and heredity. To make this plain he relies much upon physical likeness – a dramatist's demand to which it is hard for flesh-and-blood actors to respond. Miss Beatrix Lehmann, though Lavinia wear her mother's dress, cannot grow into a resemblance of Miss Laura Cowie, but by her and by the whole Mannon tribe the difficulty is courageously faced; the perpetuation of an evil and pervasive spirit is communicated; and the play stands, not only as brilliant narrative but as an expression of those spiritual forces that were evidently, in Mr. O'Neill's mind, that narrative's essence. Imagination, evoked by the facts, runs out beyond the facts. The play is alive in the sense that it gives life to the spectator's imagining and causes it to become the dramatist's ally.

The cast has been stirred by so splendid an opportunity. Miss Laura Cowie has not the fierce flame that should burn in Christine, but, within this limitation, her performance is of high accomplishment. Mr. Reginald Tate, as her lover, has an admirable ease, followed by a tormented sense of being in a trap – the part being, as he treats it, a genuine development. There is a fine sketch of the stiff, tragic, General by Mr. Mark Dignam, a useful note on a young girl by Miss Jean Winstanley, and a study of the haunted Orin which reveals new depths in Mr. Robert Harris, who, without for an instant deserting the naturalistic plane, suggests with extraordinary skill the agonized division of this young man's mind as he finds himself turning into the father whom he hated and feared.

Miss Beatrix Lehmann's performance is a temptation to write an essay, so elaborate is it, so finished in detail, and yet so firmly simple in its outline. There are passages in which it is physically a trifle too rigid; this stiffness of body is intended, and has reason behind it, but is carried too far. In all else Miss Lehmann's study of the beating down of this determined girl by fate – a fate that dwells in her own blood – is of the highest rank. There is a terrible darkness behind its flame, and, when the flame is quenched or hidden, it burns by its iciness.

24 NOVEMBER 1937, THE TIMES

Robert's Wife by St. John Ervine

GLOBE THEATRE

SANCHIA CARSON	Edith Evans
MISS ORLEY	Edith Sharpe
THE REV. ROBERT CARSON	Owen Nares
THE BISHOP OF WINTERBURY	David Horne
MRS. JONES	Margaret Moffat
JUNE HARVEY	Ann Farrer
MRS. ARMITAGE	Margaret Scudamore

This, certainly, is a play about something, and that, in the first place, is a reason for gratitude. While telling the story of Robert Carson, a parish priest, and his wife, Sanchia, a doctor in command of her own clinic, and observing the clash between the professions of two sincere human beings who love each other, it is an opportunity for Mr. Ervine to discuss a multitude of subjects – the Church, pacifism, the Sixth Commandment in its relationship to war, to the absolute ideal of doctors and to the Sermon on the Mount, with more than a note on those who are, or conceive themselves to be, pioneers, and on the efficacy of personal self-sacrifice in remote causes. Mr. Ervine has never been a quibbler, and so long a list of subjects might lead to a fear that in writing a serious play, he has mounted a tub. On the contrary, he is elaborately careful to give points of view not his own, and even in the instance of a violently pacific undergraduate, who is the weakest in his gallery of portraits, he has fought a gallant battle to represent an opponent with sympathy. The result is a genuinely serious play – that is to say, a play that discusses subjects worth discussing and makes an unremitting attempt to arrive at the truth of them. Prejudice is there, or the thing would not be a play, and certainly not Mr. Ervine's, but when we remember what Mr. Ervine thinks of men who smoke in theatres the moderation with which, as an artist, he approaches the controversies of the soul is a blessed astonishment.

There are periods, particularly in the second act and to a less degree in the first, when the narrative halts for the discussion and the play is in great danger. Not that the discussion is not good and sane and provocative; Mr. David Horne's Bishop, who often presides over it, is a humane and intelligent creature with enough limitations to make him interesting; but the argument is inclined to wander, to seem to lose direction, and the underlying story of Robert and his wife is not, at that point, of an intensity that holds the stage. Perhaps the key to this trouble is that for two acts Mr. Nares has little chance to deepen his study of the parson and that, during the same period, Miss Evans, in playing her comedy scenes, had last night a tendency to sacrifice variety to strength of tone.

As soon as Robert and Sanchia are in deep trouble, the play's whole movement becomes stronger and swifter. One may still wish that the choice had not been between a clinic and a deanery, for, as Sanchia does not fail to point out in an unanswered comment, Robert might save souls as well in a parish church as in a cathedral. With this qualification the contest is well-balanced, and the problem is solved, not with adroitness only, but in a way that increases our knowledge of and liking for the husband and the wife. Miss Edith Sharpe's intervention, as a woman who has loved the vicar all her life, is admirably restrained and simple; there is a hard, dry, and skilful portrait of a poor parishioner by Miss Margaret Moffat, a neat piece of cup-and-saucer comedy by Miss Scudamore, and an effectively unpretentious sketch of a young girl by Miss Ann Farrer. But what lifts the play at the end and earns for it the applause it received is the tact and feeling of Mr. Nares and the sudden gracious tenderness of Miss Evans, who shows then for what transition and what contrast she was playing, perhaps too stridently, in the earlier passages of her performance.

The School for Scandal
by Richard Brinsley Sheridan

QUEEN'S THEATRE

LADY SNEERWELL	Dorothy Green
SNAKE	Alec Guinness
JOSEPH SURFACE	John Gielgud
MARIA	Rachel Kempson
MRS. CANDOUR	Athene Seyler
CRABTREE	George Howe
SIR BENJAMIN BACKBITE	Glen Byam Shaw
SIR PETER TEAZLE	Leon Quartermaine
ROWLEY	Harcourt Williams
LADY TEAZLE	Peggy Ashcroft
SIR OLIVER SURFACE	Frederick Lloyd
MOSES	George Devine
TRIP	Ernest Hare
CHARLES SURFACE	Michael Redgrave
CARELESS	Harry Andrews

M r. Tyrone Guthrie holds us in debt for so much pleasure and so much to admire in his past work that to be in fundamental disagreement with his whole method and purpose when he produces *The School for Scandal* is a misfortune. It is unfortunate, first of all, because it robs an evening in distinguished company of most delights except those of controversy, and it is just to say at once that the many who may agree with Mr. Guthrie on principle will find his work as entertaining, capricious, novel, ingenious, decorative – or what you will – as we consider it misguided. To disagree with him is a misfortune also because it may lead criticism to be unconsciously unjust to players whose duty it has been to conform. But the issue is simple. If *The School for Scandal* is rightly to be treated as an elaborately stylized musical comedy, if all its characters are to be treated as stage groups forever posing and bowing, if Charles Surface is to skip to prove his vitality and exits are to be made dancingly, hand in hand, to music – if in brief the emphasis is to be neither on the dialogue nor the character nor Sheridan but on pattern-making and elegant diversions, then all is well. If not, not.

Three instances will serve. The drinking scene begins with general music and the song "Here's to the maiden of bashful fifteen" is thus summarily disposed of. The same scene ends with those who have taken part in it mincing musically off the stage for all the world as if they were the back row of a chorus. The play ends with what is ordinarily called in pantomimes "the whole company" skittishly dancing. At last they come down-stage in a compact group, smiling over one another's shoulders, to enjoy, on a darkened background, the benefit of a light concentrated upon them as the curtain falls. What is Mr. Guthrie aiming at? Ballet? And even if, in this connexion, ballet be a politer word than musical comedy, why is Sheridan of all men considered to be in need of so much fantastication?

Mr. Gielgud and Miss Ashcroft accept Mr. Guthrie's ruling, and those who likewise accept it will think their performances delightful; they are, indeed extremely accomplished. Mr. Leon Quartermaine conforms without being overwhelmed, and the result is a good Sir Peter slightly embarrassed. Nothing will make Sir Oliver into a *ballerina* and Mr. Frederick Lloyd keeps his feet successfully and entertainingly on earth until, in the romp of the last act, they lift him off it and whirl him about the stage. Charles Surface is given liveliness, but a too artificial liveliness, by Mr. Michael Redgrave. "Too artificial"? There, perhaps, injustice to the actor is creeping in; Charles, too, must dance to the general tune. Miss Dorothy Green steers Lady Sneerwell firmly through all her difficulties, loyally preserving both her place in the decoration and the integrity of her part. Only Mrs. Candour appears to have much to gain – though she also has much to lose – by the oddities of the production, and Miss Athene Seyler, frisking, big-eyed and brilliantly emphatic, is in her element – but still not in Sheridan's.

27 NOVEMBER 1937, THE TIMES

Macbeth by William Shakespeare

OLD VIC

DUNCAN	Neil Porter
MALCOLM	Niall MacGinnis
MACBETH	Laurence Olivier
LADY MACBETH	Judith Anderson
BANQUO	Andrew Cruickshank
MACDUFF	Ellis Irving

It is partly a consequence of a lucid production by M. Michel St. Denis and greatly to the credit of Mr. Laurence Olivier that, in this performance of the play, Macbeth himself remains the pivot of the action and the centre of speculation. Miss Judith Anderson plays Lady Macbeth with tautness and energy but seemingly with a confusion of purpose. Her opening suggests that she is to be considered as a woman of blood, needing no stimulus to deeds of blood, yet on the night of the murder she plays the part with a smiling unsteadiness as though she intended to imply that Lady Macbeth was drunk. Either reading may be defended, though defence of the second is dangerous, but they are not easily reconcilable. Later, when blood leads to blood, and Lady Macbeth is shaken, Miss Anderson's performance becomes more persuasive, but if, as we believe her to be, she is right here, her rightness contradicts the eager, natural villainy of her opening. In any case, her performance is one that is watched from the outside; even in the sleepwalking scene it fails to communicate the emotional stress that it describes.

An uncommonly good Porter by Mr. John Ray, a keenly imaginative Banquo by Mr. Andrew Cruickshank, and two valuable and steady performances of Duncan and Macduff by Mr. Neil Porter and Mr. Ellis Irving are the chief minor supports of the evening, but its outstanding merit is Mr. Olivier's Macbeth. Sometimes still he misses the full music of Shakespearean verse, but his speaking has gained in rhythm and strength, and his attack upon the part itself, his nervous intensity, his dignity of movement and swiftness of thought, above all his tracing of the process of deterioration in a man not naturally evil give to his performance a rare consistency and power.

...

12 DECEMBER 1937, THE NEW YORK TIMES

Mourning Becomes Electra

In England to dine well and at leisure is, for better or for worse, part of the whole ceremony of playgoing. It is this, more than anything else, which has prevented so long a play as Eugene O'Neill's *Mourning Becomes Electra* from being produced here until this week. Anmer Hall, who has long pursued an adventurous policy at the Westminster Theatre, has now put it upon his stage. With two short intervals it lasts from 7 o'clock until soon after 11 and for this reason alone it may be prevented from transfer to a larger theatre. It has, however, enjoyed so profound a success in its present home and is so well performed that such a transfer is by no means impossible and is greatly to be hoped for.

It has for so long been familiar to playgoers in the United States and has been so well and so elaborately discussed there that a full-length criticism of it now might be out of place and I shall content myself with indicating what its impact has been upon English audiences. We are a conservative people, in whom the classical tradition is still strong, and the challenge to Greek tragedy implied in Mr. O'Neill's structure and title might well have been expected to create prejudice against his work.

This is, in fact, by no means the case. His trilogy falls short of the full stature of the corresponding Greek legend chiefly because it does not conclude in that spiritual appeasement which, in the classical original, was at once an implication of the pity complimentary to the terror of the gods and the means by which the audience was enabled to relate the tragic action before their eyes to a cosmic reality outside the special instance of the legend. Mr. O'Neill's story ends, as it begins, in a condition of pathological neurosis. It is, therefore, much narrower in its scope and of less spiritual force than the classical plays to which, in subject, it is related. Nevertheless, within its own boundaries, it is a profoundly impressive and moving play.

To the mind of one who reads it without having seen it on the stage a doubt immediately presents itself whether, in his emphasis upon physical likeness as a means of suggesting the power of fate and blood upon the Mannon family, Mr. O'Neill is not asking more of the theatre than it can give. He suggests that the faces of many of his characters should be like "life-like masks" with a strong resemblance to one another, and it is of the utmost importance to his theme that, as the daughter, Lavinia, grows older, she should come to have a close resemblance to the mother she hated and feared.

Such resemblances, unless masks are actually used, are extremely hard to obtain in the theatre, and I will confess that when I read the play some years ago I felt that the difficulty was well-nigh insuperable. It has certainly not been fully overcome. Miss Beatrix Lehmann, who gives a brilliantly taut and impressive representation of Lavinia, has not, and cannot, be made to have any physical resemblance to Miss Laura Cowie, who makes of Mrs. Mannon a large and voluptuous woman, differing radically in type from the thin and nervous hardness of Miss Lehmann.

But such is the power of genuine imaginative acting that Miss Lehmann goes far toward bridging the gap, and is greatly assisted by the way in which Mr. Robert Harris, whose performance in this play puts him in the front rank of young and serious actors, enables Lavinia's brother Orin to grow, scene by scene, into such a man as his father, General Mannon, is known to have been. From Mr. Harris's and Miss Lehmann's work one does receive a genuine impression of the possession of living beings by the spirits of the dead, and to acknowledge this is to recognize that Mr. O'Neill has, at any rate, not so far overestimated the powers of the stage as to lose, in the theatre, the main thread of the theme.

It may with reason be argued that the people he represents are all pathological "cases" and that, therefore, the spiritual generalizations that he wishes to imply do not necessarily follow the premises. But there is no doubt either of the accuracy of his psychological observation or of his success as a story-teller. For the reasons I have already suggested, his play is not comparable, except in outline, with the Greek original; but it is, in its own right, a powerful and brilliant piece of the theatre, which holds its audience spellbound and causes their imagination to flow out from it in a way which is nowadays one of the rare experiences of playgoing and is always among the most unmistakable signs of a major work of art.

You Can't Take It With You
by George S. Kaufman and Moss Hart[5]

ST JAMES'S THEATRE

This is, presumably, the end. Mad families and incoherent dialogue have had their day. Mr. Kaufman and Mr. Moss Hart have carried them to an extreme of dismal incoherence, have mixed with their extravagance a little sob-stuff about the rich employer's son and the gallant typist, and have converted the stage into a madhouse of irrelevant bad manners unseasoned by wit. With the best will in the world, one can find little to commend in the play except its brevity, which the clock surprisingly proves.

A Midsummer Night's Dream
by William Shakespeare

OLD VIC

THESEUS	Gyles Isham
LYSANDER	Stephen Murray
DEMETRIUS	Anthony Quayle
BOTTOM	Ralph Richardson
SNUG	Frederick Bennett
OBERON	Robert Helpmann
TITANIA	Vivien Leigh

So that no later discussion of detail may cause any doubt in the minds of those who wish to be enchanted, let it be said at the outset that this is an enchanting performance of the play. The word "enchanting" is not vaguely used as an adjective of general praise, but to mean that the stage ceases altogether to be self-consciously theatrical, that a spell descends upon it, that illusion is complete, and that the fairies are the fairies that one expects to leap out of the air. Mr. Messel's designs, Miss Ninette de Valois's choreography, and Mr. Tyrone Guthrie's production have combined in the waving of a single wand.

Oddly enough, Mr. Guthrie in a programme-note gives elaborate reasons for the production's being "early Victorian." This, he says, "has not been arranged merely to

---

5   C.M. wished to confine his review of this play to "You won't want to". The play was showered with honours in New York and has frequently been revived.

be amusing," but in an attempt to make union between "the words of Shakespeare, the music of Mendelssohn, and the architecture of the Old Vic." He seems to have felt either that someone might lift a brow over his pretty-prettiness or that someone else might accuse him of monkeying with the text. But *A Midsummer Night's Dream* is not *The School for Scandal.* In one the form is loose and asks for inventions; in the other strict, forbidding all but its own. To one ballet is appropriate; to the other, not. And as for "period" – who cares in this Athenian wood? Shakespeare and Mendelssohn, in the world of pure imagination, which is to be distinguished from the comedy of manners, are artists independent of what is fashionable, what is "contemporary," what is early Victorian or up to date. What matters is that the other contributory artists – Guthrie, Messel, de Valois – should exercise their own imaginations freely. They can call the result "early Victorian" if they will. Perhaps it is, if you think in those terms, but it appears as one of the loveliest, most magical, and least affected productions of the play that the stage has seen for many years.

...

Miss Vivien Leigh, who looks extremely pretty, and at the opening of her performance promises a genuine firmness in her verse, is as yet a trifle nervous of Titania's authority. But there is an end of complaint. Even those who are not naturally enthusiastic about Shakespearean comics may be delighted by the vivacity of Mr. Ralph Richardson's Bottom, and the special drollery of Mr. Frederick Bennett's Snug. When they and their companions pass from rehearsal to performance they combine with Mr. Guthrie's inventions – which here are at their best – to give as entertaining a version of the interlude as we remember. The flying fairies seem not to be on wires but in sweeping flight. White muslin, pink roses, silver crowns, moonlight and wings – is it necessary to count the early "Victorian" constituents? These *are* fairies and there's an end of it or rather a beginning, for air and imagination are full of them. And the production yields, moreover, a discovery. It will be useless in future for Mr. Robert Helpman to pretend that he is exclusively a dancer of the first rank. Certainly his dancing gives strength to his Oberon; he glides into imagined invisibility; but that is not all: his verse sings with his thought, his Oberon flashes with power, and presides, as Oberons do rarely, over the whole magic of the wood.

16 JANUARY 1938, THE NEW YORK TIMES

Mailed Fists Across The Sea

THE LONDON FAILURE OF "YOU CAN'T TAKE IT WITH YOU" AGAIN BRINGS UP THE QUESTION OF ANGLO-AMERICAN TASTE

In nothing are people so divided as in their sense of humour, and no division between the American and English peoples is harder to define than this. *Room Service*, in spite of a heavy first act, promises to succeed in London, but if *You*

Can't Take It With You is successful, first nights cease altogether to be pointers. Not that the Kaufman-Hart play was received with hostility. Hostility in our theatre, except for reasons of personal or political partisanship, has almost ceased to exist. We take everything lying down, and that, precisely, is how the Kaufman-Hart play was taken.

If the position is to be understood, it must be understood first of all that there is in England a snobbism which requires fashionable, or would-be fashionable, people to applaud American humour when they can. They imitate your slang; they borrow your wisecracks; they are afraid, like the people in the story of the Emperor's new clothes, to confess that a great part of your language, when applied to farce, is incomprehensible to them. In brief, they are favourably disposed.

But *You Can't Take It With You* was too much. A considerable portion of the cast was English. Some of the trouble may have its origin there, but by no means all. The story, as presented to us, appeared tediously sentimental. A poor girl becomes engaged to a rich young man. Their romance is threatened by the social differences between their families, but the girl's philosophical grandpapa persuades the rich young man's father that money and social position are of less importance than he had believed, and so all is well.

At this point one begins to perceive why, in England, this tale is dull. The social differences are meaningless as presented to us, for, though a list of the clubs to which the rich father belongs is read out, the man himself is as much a vulgarian as the poor family with which the dramatist proposed to contrast him. Of this, the dramatist may say that they were aware. Probably they intended to be satirical at the rich man's expense. But in England that explanation is unavailing. All the people in the play, rich and poor, are utterly foreign to us, except, perhaps, the old grandpapa, who is recognizable as an old-fashioned stage-type of the kind that Horace Hodges made familiar.

The girl who wishes to be a ballet dancer, the father who makes fire-works, the mother who taps out plays on a typewriter with the hysterical futility of a cat licking a fur glove, the heroine who, in the English performance, appears to have no individuality at all – these people seem to have no link connecting them with that life of which farce is, or should be, a recognizable distortion and fantastication. I am willing to be told that the fault was in the English company, and many critics have laid all the blame on their shoulders, one saying that the trouble with this play is that you can't take it with you – across the Atlantic. But even an American company would, I believe, have been in difficulties here.

Room Service is in a different world. It is a fantastic projection of something known and comprehensible. One of the people in the Kaufman-Hart play keeps snakes in a glass container; another dances on all occasions; a third for no reason in particular, brings a grand duchess to supper; and an unexplained woman is found drunk on a sofa. They would have been as humorous and as understandable if one had kept lions in a basket, another had walked on her hands, and a third had had three heads and a monkey's tail.

But the people in *Room Service* begin on the map of experience and, as the degree of fantastication increases, move continuously toward its edges. They move fast and wittily – and in a way that never depends for its effect on shades of social difference incomprehensible in England. *Room Service*, though wildly foreign in many respects, is within our reach. *You Can't Take It With You* might have been written about the inhabitants of Mars.

29 JANUARY 1938, THE TIMES

Three Sisters by Anton Tchehov
translated by Mrs. Constance Garnett

QUEEN'S THEATRE

OLYA	Gwen Ffrangçon-Davies
MASHA	Carol Goodner
IRENA	Peggy Ashcroft
TCHEBUTYKIN	Frederick Lloyd
BARON TUSENBACH	Michael Redgrave
SOLYONY	Glen Byam Shaw
VERSHININ	John Gielgud
PROZOROV	George Devine
KULIGIN	Leon Quartermaine
NATASHA	Angela Baddeley
FEDOTIK	Alec Guinness
RODDEY	Harry Andrews

There was a time when Tchehov's work was treated, in manner as well as in spirit, as though it were undiluted and gloomy tragedy, with two unfortunate results – first, that the lighter passages of his dialogue appeared to be the prattle of madmen; second, that his tragic essence, which is not dark and stormy but has the implicit melancholy of a clear night at the end of summer, was not translated to the stage. There is a danger that, in reaction from this error, modern production may move too far, through ironic tragi-comedy, towards farce, and it is a relief to find that, except on rare occasions, M. Michel St. Denis's interpretation holds the balance with sensitive accuracy. Aiming above all at liveliness, he is inclined to obscure by grouped movement certain passages of sentiment, and there is a different failure of intensity in Vershinin's first declaration to Masha; but on the whole the production is as sane and unaffected as it is beautiful.

The company act together in rare concord and with such remarkable unselfishness that their work may be praised collectively without the pains of a selective catalogue. Mr. Gielgud is persuasive and unmannered; Miss Ffrangçon-Davies and Miss Ashcroft are so faultlessly in the composition that their honour consists partly in Masha's allowed emergence from the sisters' group, Miss Goodner giving a performance which, though never assertive, draws the mind to it by its passionate reserve and repose. Mr. Frederick Lloyd and Miss Angela Baddeley distinguish themselves in lesser parts; there is a brilliant portrait of Tusenbach, full of imagination and humour, by Mr. Michael Redgrave; and Mr. George Devine, whose control of the lighting – particularly in the garden scene – is among the production's chief assets, contributes a growing and deepening study of Prozorov, the girls' brother. In all the company, only Solyony seems out of drawing, having been driven beyond eccentricity into madness. The rest move and live with a rhythm that gives the effect, not of lives photographed, but of life distilled.

5 FEBRUARY 1938, THE TIMES

Henry Irving

An actor depends for his immortality on his influence and his legend. Even Henry Irving, the centenary of whose birth falls to-morrow, could not leave behind him, as painters and writers may, anything material of his art. To-day there are still living many who remember and some who worked with him; while they continue, he endures in their memory, and all may hear of him from them at but one remove. That remove is one too many, for no art loses more by report than the art of acting; there is no means of reproducing it; and the presence of Irving on the stage, which was his essence, is even now almost lost. But his "legend" exists powerfully; and if we ask why his more than other men's, and in what precisely that legend consists, we may approach through him a livelier understanding, not of him only, but of the stage as it was and as it has now become.

It sounds paradoxical to say that he was not a popular actor, but it is true that he was not easily and in his nature popular. Tales of the early struggles of the famous are almost common form; but there is a distinction between an easily acceptable man's fight against adverse circumstance and the different battle of such public figures as Irving or Disraeli, or of such a woman as Yvette Guilbert, the very nature of whose genius stands between them and swift recognition. Those whose achievement, whether as actors or as democratic politicians, greatly depends on their personal contact with human beings in mass, attain success most easily if their talent includes, as Ellen Terry's did, that gift of never offending which, in the superlative degree, is called charm – the gift of putting up no one's bristles and of winning, together with appreciation from the discerning, the slack tribute of mediocrity unchallenged and undisturbed: "Oh, isn't he a *nice* man!" Or "Oh, isn't she *sweet!*" Often for a player to receive this tribute is a sign of mediocrity in himself. Certainly it was not Irving's way to triumph. At first almost everything he did was accounted wrong, affected, mannered; every one of conventionally sound judgment must have counselled him to conform and compromise, to remember what the public wants and what it will "stand for." He did not abate his genius, but persisted in his "affectations" and "mannerisms" until their rightness in him was perceived, and the groundlings idolized what in any other man all their tastes and timidities would have led them to contemn. He is spoken of as the "first knight of the stage" and much has been said, and with justice, of his power to raise the status of his profession; but that service was perhaps more questionable than it appears to be, for the coming together of drawing room and green room is not an unmixed advantage to either. Irving's chief title to remembrance is his victorious genius for self-vindication as an artist, of which our own players, who are often too polite, and our own audiences, who are still inclined to prefer the mildness of concession to the rash and stormy independence of genius, would do well to take note.

Whether Irving would have won his battle now as he did then is a question the answer to which must reflect the changed conditions of the stage and of public taste. The plain answer is almost certainly "yes"; any other would be a denial of faith in the essential timelessness of genius; and Irving would have known how to redirect his attack, for he was "crafty." The word is Ellen Terry's, and no portrait of him is more persuasive, as none is more discriminating, than hers. What emerges strikingly from it is his special aloofness, his inability to pat the world on the back or stroke its prejudices, whether as man or as artist. When in 1895 he met his company in Montreal, he hated "shaking their greasy paws." He was "quiet, patient, tolerant, impersonal, gentle, *close*, crafty – tolerant," it is to be presumed, in the sense of that other and colder word "indifferent" that Ellen Terry more than once applies to him. He was "incapable of caring for people"; he had "a lack of enthusiasm for other people's work or indeed for anything outside *his own* work." When his friends helped him – "No word from him, however! Is it shyness? Indifference? Anger? What? I rather think self-consciousness by indifference out of conceit!" And yet she says: "Concentration has achieved results. He is a wonderful man He is great. Constantine, Nero, Caesar, Charlemagne, Peter, Napoleon, all "Great," all selfish, all, but all "INTERESTING.". Ellen Terry writes the word in capitals, and it stands to-day as the key to the Irving Legend. He had all the qualities which cause the public to hate and resent an artist; he had the two qualities which, in the end, invariably subdue them. He was inhumanly concentrated on his work, and he was "interesting."

We have passed now into a different age and a different theatre. After a violent reaction against actor-managers and an equally violent swerve towards productionism and "mass-drama" it is beginning to be understood that the virtues of genuinely collective acting do not necessarily imply the enslavement of individual genius, and the qualities that made Irving great, which may be called "selfishness or mannerism" if one pleases, are in fact the qualities which make acting itself "interesting." Acting is not conformity to drawing-room prejudice; it is not always comfortable; it is, at its highest, a flame, a barb, a challenge, a command to the imagination; it is, as art, alive because it is more intense than life. There is something of madness in it, the splendid, liberating madness of a dream so vital that, when we awake from it, the world's sanity seems drab and unreal. It was Irving's power that he gave such acting to the stage. It will be the immortality of his legend to inspire it.

9 FEBRUARY 1938, THE TIMES

Othello by William Shakespeare

OLD VIC

RODERIGO	Stephen Murray
IAGO	Laurence Olivier
OTHELLO	Ralph Richardson
CASSIO	Anthony Quayle
MONTANO	Michael Goodliffe
EMILIA	Martita Hunt
DESDEMONA	Curigwen Lewis
HERALD	Jack Merivale

Everyone knows his own Iago; he is universal because disputable; because one interpretation is right, another is not for that reason wrong. There is none of Shakespeare's people whom criticism must approach in the theatre with a more receptive mind – and this openness should be the more carefully preserved when the actor's execution of his own purpose is so brilliant as Mr. Olivier's. He plays the part for comedy. There is no suggestion that evil is this man's good, no hint of spiritual possession or, alternatively, of the tragic pressure of intellectual intrigue. This is a rattling Iago, an undergraduate at his pranks, at his best when playing a practical joke on Roderigo, seemingly unaware of the existence of a devil, whether as tempter or ally. On these lines the interpretation is sparkling, and Mr. Stephen Murray's Roderigo aptly supplements it. Those who cry out for novelty – for any novelty if it be but lively and accomplished – will be satisfied, but this Iago seems to be very distantly connected with the tragedy of Othello.

Othello and Iago are linked. Mr. Richardson is made to seem heavy by this gadfly about him, and is further handicapped by Desdemona, at once arch in manner and lifeless in intonation, of whom it is best to say – since Miss Curigwen Lewis has elsewhere shown merit – no more than that she has been miscast. There is an admirable Emilia by Miss Martita Hunt, and in Mr. Jack Merivale a herald who speaks conspicuously well. The movement of the stage, if we accept Mr. Guthrie's purpose to squeeze comedy out of everything, is inventive, quick, and ingenious; but the collective performance gives an impression of trickiness, the majestic splendour of the piece is gone, and Mr. Richardson, whose scene before the epilepsy is magnificently played, is found before the end to be fighting a solitary and losing battle.

22 FEBRUARY 1938, THE TIMES
DISNEY'S FILM

Snow White and the Seven Dwarfs

At first they were called "moving pictures," and the name was good, for it contained in it the principle of what might have been, and may still become, an art. They became moving photographs, at the outset silent, then speaking, and in spite of the attempts of a few experimental artists who employed silhouette and other graphic methods, the cinematograph became a trade, sometimes still of value in its uses of photography and in the opportunities it gave to film actors of the quality of Chaplin and Garbo, but divorced – as we may believe Leonardo would not have allowed it to be divorced – from the individualism of the pencil. So long as films remain silent – and it is significant that Chaplin has allowed them, so far as he is concerned, to persist in silence – it seemed that the camera's speed and brilliance would at any rate provide its own compensation for the pencil's disappearance. The coming of the conversational sound track made difficult, if not impossible, the natural development of the cinematographic medium on lines not entangled with naturalism. Films, as such, lost their way, and became in effect mechanized plays, deadened by the absence of direct contact with an audience and by the studios' method of non-continuous production. Throughout this long process of the cinematograph's deterioration as an art and its growth as a form of mass production, Mr. Walt Disney almost alone has been a link between modern commerce and the art of "moving pictures." That he might not lose touch with the "trade," he has hitherto devoted himself principally to the making of specialised "shorts" intended primarily to provoke laughter, but in making such pieces as *The Three Little Pigs* he has again and again proved that his genius lies less in broad farce than in free fantasy, and has led many admirers of his work to hope that he would someday free himself from the dictation of the box office and produce the fairy story that was in his heart.

This he has now boldly attempted. The emancipation is not complete. The same roughness of humour which marred the lovely miracles of his tale of the Ark enters now and then into his treatment of Snow White's seven dwarfs. The drawing of their faces is coarse and fleshly; they are faces designed to appeal to the easy humour of fat men in their stalls, not the authentic faces seen by Snow White, by children, and by lesser creatures of imagination. Snow White herself, that enchantment in rags, has been given by Mr. Disney a face which is unworthy of the legend – a rigidly "pretty" face, with scarlet lips and gaping eyes of the kind that one may find any day in the comic-strips. So far Mr. Disney has compromised. The fat men in the stalls would say that this Snow White was pretty, and it would not occur to them that there was something too violent and crude, something too much of the music-halls, in the faces of the dwarfs. But there compromise stops. The rest is magical, and entertainment for men and children which is not only without equal, as entertainment in the history of the films, but is, in itself, an act of liberation. "The total cost," we are proudly told, "exceeds £250,000." That is the only misfortune. If Mr. Disney's film could have cost less there would have been more hope of its exercising an immediate influence on film production. As things are it may remain unique unless Mr. Disney himself provides successors to it. Even so, it is an adventure, and the more valuable when it is understood to be pioneer work in its own kind. In his next story Mr. Disney will probably have treated his lady's face with the same delicacy that he has now given to his drawing of her body. The minor defects in Snow White will have gone, and its virtues, now conspicuous in the use of animals, of fantastic scenery, and of magical metamorphosis, will have advanced.

The first and outstanding virtue of the present film is that it plays no tricks with the story. The Wicked Queen, jealous of Snow White's beauty, commands her death, but the appointed murderer has not the heart to kill her, and the terrified girl runs through a forest filled with the images – the staring eyes, the clutching branches – of her own fear. Suddenly, when she falls exhausted, the friendliness of the forest appears. A host of animals and birds – fawns, rabbits, squirrels, what you will – become her escort to refuge in the dwarfs' house, and the dwarfs, returning at night from their diamond mine, terrified at first by the monster sleeping in their beds, uncover her, and are themselves happily enslaved. And when the Wicked Queen, changing herself into a witch, is persuading the guileless Snow White to eat a poisoned apple, the alarm of the animals, their haste to summon help, their dragging home of the unsuspecting dwarfs, their twitter of panic and sympathy, has in it the quality of Mr. Ralph Hodgson's poem on Eve. The witch's flight and death; the dwarfs' and the animals' mourning for the sleeping beauty whom they believe dead; the animals' delight – a faultless mingling of humour and sentiment – when, after Prince Charming's kiss, Snow White sits up and rubs her eyes – all these things are but instances of a continuous series of scenes which give one an impression, not of being the observer of a trick, but of being transported into the heart of a midsummer night's dream. It is said that 2,500,000 drawings were needed and that 570 artists were employed. The effect is of the labour of one man, still sometimes a little timid of seriousness, but with an unequalled power to give at once unity, lightness, and feeling to a work of art for the screen. The idea, which some have had, that Snow White is in any part unsuitable for children is incomprehensible. It is as suitable as the Brothers Grimm, and it does marvels with animals that belong, not even to fairy tales, but to the imagining that springs from them.

...

The Case of Miss Tempest

LONDON, FEB 18

The case of Marie Tempest is the most mysterious in our theatre. Since the celebration of her stage jubilee she has been made a Dame of the British Empire – an honour which in women corresponds to that of a knighthood in men, and, for better or for worse, sets upon her achievement the seal of official recognition. Everyone regards her as the grand old lady of the English stage, and, although the attendance of royal personages at a first night is extremely rare, Queen Mary was in a box when Marie Tempest reappeared this week at the Haymarket.

How well she deserves her honours I have pointed out again and again in these articles. As an actress in comedy, and particularly in light comedy, she has unrivalled technical equipment and authority. What is mysterious about her is that she will give so little scope to her powers. Her range is narrower than that of any other actress of comparable repute. Within my recollection she has never attempted a classical part or any part, except Catherine of Russia, that has not been strictly a "Marie Tempest part," nor can I remember any play in which she has appeared, except *Hay Fever* and *The First Mrs. Fraser*, that has made any claim to be a work of art, even in the frivolous kind.

The result is that no first-night is harder to discuss than a Marie Tempest first night. *Mary Goes to See*, by Rosemary Casey and B. Iden Payne, is no exception. It is the story of an abrupt and flippant woman who visits her brother's household in America and finds it dominated by his brother's wife, an earnest and insincere creature given to Beauty and Good Works. Marie Tempest upsets all this woman's plans and frees everyone from her tyranny. It is all too easy. Difficulties exist only that Marie Tempest may have the glory of flicking them aside; actors and actresses exist only as tributaries; the play exists as a setting to the Marie Tempest part.

In psychology, development and manner it is a part that she has played a hundred times before – the victorious charmer for whom Providence created a troublesome world that she might set it right. There is nothing to be said about it; nothing new is attempted, no risk is taken. To watch the performance, which in itself is brilliantly competent, is as exciting as watching a good workman lay down his thousandth length of railway line. If Marie Tempest were capable of no more than this, we should, perhaps, be grateful to her for recognizing her limitations, but she has always led us to believe, by flashes perceptible even in the midst of routine, that her range is much greater than she herself allows.

...

Power and Glory by Karel Čapek

SAVOY THEATRE

PROFESSOR SIGELIUS	Felix Aylmer
DR. GALEN	Oscar Homolka

At last a play on war with a mind behind it – a play, let it be said at once, with one dangerous flaw, but nevertheless a play at once impassioned and intelligent with two outstanding merits: that it is not propaganda for any party, and that it is, in essence, the act of a man who seeks no cheap applause for himself by screaming against war, but is content to kneel before the idea of peace and ask others to kneel with him.

The flaw consists in Herr Čapek's having allowed the mechanics of his plot to distort the presentation of his idea. He is telling the story of a humble doctor in a totalitarian State who, having discovered a cure for a plague that threatens the life of mankind, refuses to share his knowledge with others, or to use it to save any but the humble and poor, except on condition that the nations of the world bind themselves to a lasting peace. Baron Krug, the maker of armaments, being himself stricken with the plague, is driven by fear to accept the doctor's conditions, and finding that he has not the power to stop the manufacture of arms, kills himself. The dictator, having launched an aggressive war, is, in his turn, persuaded by fear of the plague to reverse his policy and summon the doctor to his aid. In both these instances there is no genuine change of heart or persuasion of intellect. The dictator, it is true, justifies his change of policy by persuading himself that God has so commanded him, but in fact both he and the Baron Krug are impelled by fear for their own skins.

If Herr Čapek intended to say no more than that men may be turned from war by personal cowardice, we mistake his purpose. The plea is more general and more powerful and is sustained by a rare force of ironic feeling. There are a dozen signs that the dramatist had it in his mind to write a play on the great theme of the power of a single-minded man to influence the world. Only the exigencies of the plague-story have given to the discussion a dangerously crude and melodramatic twist.

The real merit of the play appears in its treatment of three characters – those of the doctor, of the dictator, and of a bleakly unimaginative and vain professor of medicine, whose sycophancy is brought to bear on the scene with a brilliant emphasis by Mr. Felix Aylmer. The doctor and the dictator are represented by Mr. Homolka himself. His portrait of the dictator, abrupt, hysterical, self-deluding, but no fool, is a highly skilled variant of a model now familiar. His study of the little stubborn, hunchbacked doctor is something much more – a deeply memorable performance which, without struggle for spectacular effect and by plain adherence to the dramatist's own vision of the character, brings to life a man obsessed by the sanity of peace, an unselfconscious martyr, a natural saint. It is a portrait magnificent in its lovable moderation and gives to the play of quality of wisdom that outweighs all its minor defects.

20 APRIL 1938, THE TIMES

Coriolanus by William Shakespeare

OLD VIC

MENENIUS AGRIPPA	Cecil Trouncer
CAIUS MARCIUS	Laurence Olivier
SICINIUS VELUTUS	Stephen Murray
JUNIUS BRUTUS	George Skillan
VOLUMNIA	Sybil Thorndike

Coriolanus is very rarely performed, and one may reasonably believe that, if Shakespeare's name were not attached to it, it would not be performed at all. The story of a patrician general who, to avenge his exile by an ungrateful mob, led a foreign army against Rome ought to be a sufficient peg for Shakespeare to hang his genius on, but for some reason he has taken little trouble with it. Coriolanus himself, with his warrior's vanity, his loathing of the common people, his arrogance, energy, and charm, is a crude skeleton of what might have been a great Shakespearean character; but Shakespeare has put no flesh on the bones.

Among the minor characters there is here and there a greater liveliness. Volumnia, Coriolanus's commanding mother, is given by Dame Sybil Thorndike a touch of refreshing and satirical humour, but it is in the main a heavily statuesque part; and all Mr. Trouncer's boldness in caricature is needed to keep old Menenius alive. Shakespeare has not troubled with them. He has not troubled even to write the lyrical interludes or the great passages of meditative or rhetorical verse that are the saving of other lesser plays of his. He seems to have written *Coriolanus* at breakneck speed and to order, without finding in it a spark to kindle his fires. Again and again opportunities appear for an outbreak of his genius. He shrugs his shoulders and plods on with his narrative.

There is only one thing to do: keep up the pace and beat the drums – and this Mr. Casson's production does vigorously. The humour, fortunately not of the riotous kind, is used for all it is worth, Mr. Stephen Murray and Mr. George Skillan winning credit for the Tribunes and Mr. Trouncer contributing a full share of what entertainment there is. Coriolanus himself is played by Mr. Olivier not as a rhetorical creature only, but with a genuine wit. Nothing can discover great depth in the part, but Mr. Olivier's sensitiveness to its comedy prevents it from being dull.

The Merchant of Venice by William Shakespeare

QUEEN'S THEATRE

ANTONIO	Leon Quartermaine
BASSANIO	Richard Ainley
GRATIANO	Glen Byam Shaw
LORENZO	Alec Guinness
PORTIA	Peggy Ashcroft
NERISSA	Angela Baddeley
SHYLOCK	John Gielgud
PRINCE OF MOROCCO	Frederick Lloyd
LANCELOT GOBBO	George Devine

Half enchantment, half tragedy, an entanglement of two stories different in kind, *The Merchant of Venice* is an invitation to the trickiness of producers of one school and to the dull, scholastic traditionalism of another. Here it moves effortlessly and without affectation between the two extremes, labouring nothing, fantasticating nothing, allowing Shakespeare to have his own way in the story-telling and leaving in the end the faultless, the rare, the only true impression – that of a fairy-tale that swings to character as a beautiful ship swings to the wind. Even the caskets, those plagues of reason, are treated with such gay simplicity and lightness that no one need be troubled by them, and a performance that is not tedious in its casket-scenes is a performance indeed.

How much of all this is due to Miss Ashcroft shall appear presently. Consider first the smaller fry and proceed to her by way of Shylock. In the first place, there is a Lorenzo by Mr. Alec Guinness who gives reason to Jessica's truancy and lifts the final scene to an unspectacular, meditative, star-struck beauty that takes the breath away. Mr. Richard Ainley's Bassanio is superbly decorative and well spoken, if sometimes too consciously romanticized; Mr. Glen Byam Shaw gives a fine dash of impulsive folly to Gratiano; and Miss Baddeley's Nerissa is as entertaining in her silences as she is graceful in her speech. In the midst of these Mr. John Gielgud moves with the wisdom and assurance of a man who knows his way and is content not to proclaim himself that Shakespeare may be the more lucidly interpreted. The performance may be said to lack "body"; it is nowhere majestic; it has no outstanding splendours of rage; but it is for that reason the more consistent – a portrait of a man whom one is invited neither to pity nor to hate, of an unlikeable and mean creature whose faults are yet not the deliberate crimes of a mere villain but the result of a determination to have what is considered a legitimate revenge. The fireworks of the part are sacrificed to Mr. Gielgud's conception of the truth of it, and so clearly does he establish his truth that a new Shylock emerges from his playing.

What is more, this is a Shylock who deliberately abstains from capturing and so unbalancing the play. Belmont is not overwhelmed by Venice and Portia is permitted to rule in her own country. Miss Ashcroft rules it with magic, giving Portia a miraculous youth, her sweetness, her wise gravity, her underlying spirit of laughter; carrying the court scene with a natural ease and humour, converting the whole part into a lyric and giving to the play a freshness such as we do not remember having seen upon it before.

24 APRIL 1938, THE NEW YORK TIMES

The Circus Has Come To (London) Town

LONDON, APRIL 8

An acute and stinging review, *Nine Sharp*, by Herbert Farjeon, is filling the Little Theatre for the good reason that there are brains behind its satirical fooling. One of its most entertaining turns is a skit on what in England is called continuous review, which does indeed deserve to be satirised. Continuous review in London corresponds roughly to a burlesque show in the United States and has certain affinities with the Folies Bergères or the Concert Mayol in Paris, but it has distinguishing characteristics of its own which are an expression – perhaps the oddest – of the British spirit of compromise.

The compromise springs from three facts: first, continuous review is expected to exhibit considerably more of the feminine figure than is ordinarily exhibited on our stage; secondly, the censorship is to a great extent verbal and, though it may permit a certain freedom in the matter of costume, would fall heavily upon any sketch in which the dialogue was alarming; thirdly, the lower middle-class, who are the chief patrons of continuous review, have extremely powerful inhibitions or hypocrisies on the subject of nakedness itself.

The result is that the entertainment has to be planned in such a way that those who wish to do so may call it light-hearted and innocuous, while those whose pleasure is to feel that they are wickedly daring may not be too gravely disappointed. In practice, the struggle to ride every horse at once produces the strangest mixture between the clean dull fun of a concert in a village hall and the drearier exhibitionism of a second-rate Parisian review designed for Anglo-Saxon tourists. The general impression given by many of the turns is of a group of tired parish workers who, in an embarrassed determination to be cheerful, have unaccountably removed a great part of their clothing.

The satire in *Nine Sharp* emphasises this effect of weariness, and weariness is not to be wondered at. It is not that the young women who take part in these continuous entertainments are necessarily overworked, if we reckon their labour in hours. I believe that the terms of their employment are carefully safeguarded and that, in the material sense, they are well treated. In any case, I have little sympathy with those whose only idea of improving the state of an employee is to shorten his hours of work.

Twelve and even sixteen hours a day is not too much if the work is of a kind that one can be interested in and proud of, and on which progress is possible. Work is painful only when the worker is bored by it, and these girls must be unspeakably bored. Many of them have no accomplishments at all. They are required neither to sing, speak nor dance. They stand about in their gauze and spangles – the human furniture of the stage. Sometimes they walk a little; sometimes they wave their arms to alter the folds of the gauze; but for the greater part of their time they are inert flesh.

Their boredom is communicated to any imaginative member of the audience, for their work is humiliatingly inferior to that of a painter's model. A model may wear no clothes at all, which is a thousand times better than the ridiculous and timid self-consciousness of a showgirl's costume. A model, if she has a trained intelligence, can use it inventing poses, holding them as no amateur can, and being of genuine value to the artist for whom she works.

A good model is keen on her job; she is not, and has no reason to be, ashamed of it. But these inert showgirls are doing work of so drab and valueless a monotony that it is a disgrace, not to them but to the civilization that permits it. The point is not whether they wear much or little or nothing. The questions to ask are: Is the result beautiful? Are they exercising the human skill of mind or body? Are they serving any useful or artistic purposes? If not, what right have we to employ human beings in this way?

The root of the trouble in these continuous reviews is in the dull timidity of their compromises. Sometimes a good comic man appears; sometimes an adroit juggler; sometimes a dancer of some merit. In these things the reviews are comparable to the ordinary music halls and raise no questions peculiar to themselves. But if, in addition to ordinary music-hall turns, they intend to have scenes conspicuously less dressed than usual, they should design these scenes on a consistent and intelligent principle, and they should give those who take part in them an opportunity for talent.

As it is, these scenes are dully and lugubriously exhibitionist. A vocalist sings a song, while elsewhere on the stage another girl slowly parades in or out of her gauze. Or a man plays the piano while four showgirls stand about on the platform behind him. There is a lamentable separation between plain, flat exhibitionism and any kind of theatrical skill. If the women are to be undressed, let it be so, but let them justify their presence on the stage by something else than this.

Banana Ridge by Ben Travers

STRAND THEATRE

ELEANOR POUND	Kathleen O'Regan
MASON	Basil Lynn
SUSAN LONG	Olga Lindo
WILLOUGHBY PINK	John Robertson Hare
DIGBY POUND	Alfred Drayton
JONES	Robert Flemyng
CORA POUND	Carla Lehmann
JEAN PINK	Constance Lorne
WUN	Ben Travers

Many years ago Sue was only a landlady's daughter, and the young officers billeted on her home did not neglect her charms. There were several of them – enough to supply her own and her son's needs ever since, and to leave over two possible fathers, a large one represented by Mr. Alfred Drayton and a small one who is Mr. Robertson Hare. Allies in little else, they are determined to rid themselves of Jones, their possible son, and it is Mr. Robertson Hare who acts, so to speak, as the forefront of the battle. Somewhere in the Malay States he cultivates rubber and is condemned to take Jones as his assistant. What happens need not trouble us. Nothing matters except that before the right father is found for the young man and all the ladies, suspicious or adoring, are satisfied, each after her own manner, everything that happens – the squirting siphon, the returning mamma, the storm, the fire in the bungalow, the plague of mosquitoes – is part of an ingenious conspiracy of fate to trouble Mr. Alfred Drayton and Mr. Robertson Hare.

The farce lacks one thing only – a fresh farcical idea. The problem of doubtful paternity is a little stale, but fortunately the treatment is not. Mr. Travers is one of the few writers of farce who, not content with a multiplicity of doors, takes the trouble to invent characters for the people who come and go through them. Even the ladies have individualities of their own – Miss O'Regan an Irish determination, Miss Constance Lorne a smouldering Scottish fire, Miss Carla Lehmann a clearness of outline very grateful in one who might have been a farcical *ingénue* and no more, and Miss Lindo a rare humour and tact in dealing with Sue's not easily sympathetic demands. Mr. Robert Flemyng, too, as the young man whose existence is the cause of all the trouble, plays with just enough seriousness to establish Jones's title to curiosity on his own account and enough lightness to make him a foil for his elders. And it is the elders who make the play – Mr. Drayton, who by deadly, accurate timing can make the house laugh by the toss of his head or a flick of his fingers, and Mr. Robertson Hare, a natural clown with a genius for turning pompous solemnity to ridicule and a gift of scurrying about the stage as if all life were a rabbit warren and he the king of the rabbits. They make an almost faultless pair, never obviously feeding each other and yet contriving to give an impression that their absurdities are complementary.

4 MAY 1938, THE TIMES

You Never Can Tell by George Bernard Shaw

WESTMINSTER THEATRE

VALENTINE	John Wyse
WILLIAM	Stanley Lathbury
MRS. CLANDON	Gillian Scaife
GLORIA CLANDON	Lydia Sherwood
BOHUN Q.C.	Mark Dignam

Here is young Mr. Shaw, in the year of calm 1896, paddling in the revolutionary shallows, and paddling with a blessed willingness to laugh at opponents without necessarily chopping off their heads. No doubt, at that time, there were many to be shocked or alarmed. No hero! No heroine! The lady is separated from her husband and no moral indignation about it! Gas and dentistry on the stage! It is not improbable that in the year 1899, when at last the play was given performance by the Stage Society, a section of that advanced and august audience hesitated to laugh at *You Never Can Tell*. Even in those days you never could tell, though the piece was called "pleasant," when the Shavian paddler would cease from paddling and go in off the deep end.

A perilous young man, but what a story-teller when he had a story to tell! No one, when light-hearted, ever had (or has) a more brilliant lightness of heart. Witness Valentine the dentist, who was once Mr. Granville-Barker and is now Mr. John Wyse; Valentine, that technician of romance who by the exercise of his skill pricks all the bubbles, and yet, because he is experiencing as much of chemical passion as Mr. Shaw permits to mankind, continues to blow them. Mr. Wyse misses some of Valentine's intellect but none of his spirits; the rapier is not as keen as it might be, but it flashes. And there is not a person in the play who has not begun to take on him or herself the glamour of immortality. Mr. Lathbury is a drier waiter than most, but a credit to the part; the affable William will survive. So will Gloria and her mamma, the heart and the head (sometimes as happily mixed as they are in Mr. Shaw himself) of advanced feminism. Miss Gillian Scaife has almost too much heart for Mrs. Clandon, but the brains are there as well, and when she goes off dancing one remembers how to waltz. Miss Lydia Sherwood is a brilliantly trained and erring Gloria, a *bombe surprise,* a warm heart and an icily educated mind. Of all the rest, a good company, Bohun Q.C. must have his praise, Mr. Mark Dignam building for him a new monument of ferocious affability. How good the play is and how alive and how fortunately produced by Mr. Macowen in the dress of the period. But did dentists, in that year of dark dignity, wear white coats?

12 MAY 1938, THE TIMES

People of Our Class by St. John Ervine

NEW THEATRE

LADY MARCH	Mary Jerrold
MAJOR-GENERAL SIR GREGORY MARCH	Nicholas Hannen
ELSPETH ALDERNEY	Athene Seyler
EDGAR MARCH	Raymond Francis
SHENA MARCH	Ursula Jeans
HENRY HAYES	Bernard Lee

Mr. Ervine, wishing to say that divisions of class must, ought, and anyhow will be over-written by courageous people determined to marry, and wishing also to issue the customary warning to stubborn parents, tells how Shena March, daughter of Major-General Sir Gregory March, forced her father's hand in the matter of Henry Hayes, son of the butcher and now the chemist's assistant at 70s. a week. She might, indeed, have married without her father's consent or she might have waited until she came into £3,000 which he was bound to release when she was 30, but neither alternative suited her book. Whereupon, on the advice of a racy maiden-aunt (Miss Seyler without much to do but doing it faultlessly) Shena improved a little on Jude' s Arabella, and came back one day from a doctor in Exeter to announce that she was with child and that the Major-General must choose to be the grandfather of a bastard or to hand over the money. Miss Ursula Jeans plays the part with so much balance and good sense and so accurate a picking of her way through its emotion that she preserves what in the theatre is called "sympathy" with the girl and at the same time implies Mr. Ervin's open-eyed criticism of her; and Mr. Bernard Lee, steady, likeable, unassuming and yet firm when attack is necessary, correspondingly weights the scales in favour of the chemist's assistant. But there is a crudity in the last act that defies all their attempts to make it fully persuasive.

Everything is accounted for. Mr. Ervine is much too adroit to leave loose ends or to come to the stage unprovided with an answer to every question. Even the dull people – Mr. Hannen's crusty and violent papa baffled by the antics of modernism or Miss Jerrold's mamma who keeps her head and says she's silly and turns out to be wise – even these are likeable, and at the height of a quarrel Mr. Ervine preserves an impression that he is patting them all on the back with a benign and tolerant hand. But the baby is a little too simple a weapon; the £3,000 is too obvious a counter; the opposition collapses too abruptly; and one feels a Mr. Ervine is having it too much his own way – a way carefully planned but not the way of mankind in emotional conflict.

There is trouble, too, in the opening, not because Mr. Ervine is unsympathetic towards the young people he introduces then – on the contrary he does his utmost to discover merit in them – but because this pulmonary essay on "modernism" in general too long delays the main attack, and because one is left unsure of the date. What is the date of the action? A girl in shorts, whom one would guess to be 24, is said to have been 15 when the War ended. That puts the play at 1927, but it has appearances of the present day and one looks in vain among Mr. Ervine's chromium-plated youth for the recent revival of primness and chaperonage that is the latest embarrassment of parental life. But between the chromium-plate and the drastic baby there is a firm and advancing second act, and there is throughout a good humour and a liveliness of dialogue that entertains the house and goes far to silence criticism ... Mr. Francis, as a weakling young man, remarkably distinguishes himself, and enables Mr. Ervine to prove that, though we may doubt his strategy now and then, he is among the most skilful tacticians of the stage.

24 MAY 1938, THE TIMES

Yvette Guilbert

FRENCH SONGS AT WIGMORE HALL

Yvette Guilbert, who has attained to such eminence that one may omit all title but her name, gave at the Wigmore Hall yesterday a recital of French songs ranging from the tenth to the eighteenth century, and to-morrow will give another under the general title *Femme dans la Chanson*.

This is the year of her stage jubilee. Though it is certainly one of the advantages of age to have heard her in her youth, let no one who did so abstain from hearing her now. She is by all reckoning a supreme artist. What the years may have taken from her voice, they have given again abundantly in wit, tenderness, experience, and depth of understanding, and it was not at any time to hear Melba that one went to hear Yvette Guilbert.

English audiences, particularly well-behaved English audiences not blessed with much saving Celtic enthusiasm, are notoriously dumb. At pantomime-time our comedians sweat exceedingly in an attempt, little rewarded, to urge people to sing with them. Who else in the world but Yvette Guilbert, with one superb gesture – that "giving," outward gesture of both hands which is her own – could sweep the Wigmore Hall into song?

> *C'est le mai,*
> *C'est le mai,*
> *C'est le joli mois de mai!*

sing the grave and stately ladies. *C'est le mai!* sing the gay maidens. *C'est le joli mois de mai!* shout the cheerful gentlemen, young and old. The English forget their self-consciousness and dream that the Wigmore Hall is a *café-concert*. And yet, looking back over the programme, one perceives how great Yvette Guilbert's development has been and how wide her range has become – from *Le Prisonnier de Kerloan* to the enchanting tale of the sailor, *sur le Pont de Nantes la la*, who had a reasoned preference for brunettes, or from *Le Retour du Marin* to the profound and moving miracle of Sainte-Berthe. Through it all Yvette Guilbert's power of narrative never fails her, nor that quality in her art which strikes and gives and makes alive. She is to-day the standard by which the work of a *diseuse* is to be judged.

1 JUNE 1938, THE TIMES

Spring Meeting by M. J. Farrell and John Perry

AMBASSADORS THEATRE

In County Tipperary enough of the eighteenth century survives to enable servants to be something more than answerers of bells and carriers of trays – more, too, than what the fashionable English theatre has made them: comic relief on stilts. In Sir Richard Furze's house, at any rate, they are as large as life and as companionable as Mr. Arthur Sinclair. The odd thing is that there are so few of them about – Johnny Mahoney, the superb James himself, and that is all. One feels that the place would have been lively with chattering maids and old nurses and grooms and stable boys, all of them, in effect, members of the household community. However, old James is a host in himself, Johnny Mahoney has the right kind of argumentative laziness, and they may be accepted as representative of the servants' hall. The point is that, in this piece, the servants do come out of the servants' hall, and no one, thank heaven, is in the least surprised or shocked.

No doubt the manners of the Furze household are twisted a little towards farce, but not nearly so far as some may imagine who only England know. Those of us who have encountered in Wales houses in which Tchehov would have been at home or have heard George Moore discourse on County Mayo need mix no astonishment with our delight when James, the butler, obeys old Bijou Furze with patient courtesy at one moment and orders her to bed the next; or when he asks permission to plant himself in an armchair and talks to Joan, the elder daughter, as if he were her father; or when he decides whether Baby, the younger, is to have a glass of brandy or wear her fur coat. Is there exaggeration of his humour, his familiarity, his wisdom? Perhaps; but it is a portrait continuously related to Nature. The dramatists know their subject and Mr. Arthur Sinclair knows his job.

The romantic story is much like other stage-stories in its mechanism – how the daughters obtain husbands, how a smart lady from outside cajoles their miserly but affable father into arranging the necessary settlements, and how everyone is happy in the end. Mr. Roger Livesey, Miss Carey, Miss Chancellor, and Miss Zena Dare do very competently what there is to be done with this aspect of the tale, but they and the play itself are at their best when they are more concerned with manners than with plot. For what distinguishes this piece from most theatrical contrivances is the blessed fluidity; the ease, the warmth of its social background. To this Miss Rutherford's half-mad, horse-racing spinster contributes much. Mr. Roger Furse's scenery is admirable, and Mr. John Gielgud has given a faultless pattern to his production. The piece is a cheerful entertainment from whatever point of view one regards it, and was deservedly applauded; but its special claim is that this "mad family" isn't mad at all but happens to be composed of individualists – that is to say, of men and women and butlers of original quality who are not forever wondering what the sixth form would think of them.

5 JUNE 1938, THE NEW YORK TIMES

Mr. and Mrs. Lunt in London

The coming of the Lunts is very good and very bad for us – bad, at any rate, for those unthinking disparagers of our native product who assume that all the American Theatre is as good as this and that our lamentably contrasted average makes backwoodsmen of us all. Thank heaven that, in New York itself, the Lunts are exceptional and *Amphitryon 38* an exceptional play, for they appear among us like some sudden and brilliant dish that makes tedious our daily theatrical bread.

Are we, by the standards of American criticism, unorthodox in thinking that what is here chiefly to be observed is the miraculous duet, and that the nature of the miracle is not precisely an equal partnership but the stimulus of Mr. Lunt and the response of Miss Fontanne. Mr. Lunt's Jupiter has finality and authority. No doubt, in Paris, the part was differently played, but while watching Mr. Lunt one does not bother one's head about Paris.

Miss Fontanne is in a different, a less authoritative category. She has an extraordinary charm of grace and lightness of touch. She attempts nothing that she does not succeed in enchantingly. There remains the knowledge that there are aspects of Girandoux's Alkmena that Miss Fontanne does not attempt – chiefly the impression that Alkmena might give, and Miss Fontanne does not, that she was a woman profoundly, passionately, even agonisingly in love with Amphitryon. Miss Fontanne has chosen to smile at this aspect of Alkmena and yet there are moments when she says simply that she loves her husband or that she wakes beside him sometimes on the shock of fear that he may be dead – moments that are poignant beyond smiling and that contain a passion that no lightness of touch can communicate.

In brief, Miss Fontanne acts faultlessly within certain definite limitations; these limitations are self-imposed, deliberately and discreetly chosen. How wise she is not to overstep them, not to pretend to an original authority which is not a natural part of her superlative talent! But there it is. Mr. Lunt is the sun, she the moon. The loveliest of all her accomplishments is that she recognizes it. It is Mr. Lunt who reveals that Girandoux's play is something much more than a "smart" or a "sophisticated" or an "amusing" enchantment of a classical legend.

First of all, it is still pure legend. Girandoux is guiltless of the easy trick – which belongs to review workers, not to serious artists – of getting a laugh by guying Olympus with pert modern illusions. The play is neither a skit nor a pamphlet but what a legend should be – a philosophic parable, applicable to gods and men at all times and of all ages, told in this instance on the tradition of high comedy.

Mr. Richard Whorf's Mercury is a brilliantly ironic and rhetorical contribution to the Lunt-Fontanne duet. Few actors nowadays have the power or the courage of rhetoric. In England Esmé Percy has it, Ralph Richardson on occasion; among women, Edith Evans and Margaret Rawlings. But Mercury would be hard to cast among us and Mr. Whorf's brilliance must share the Lunts' credit for as exciting an evening as we have had in the theatre for many seasons.

10 AUGUST 1938, THE TIMES

As You Like It by William Shakespeare

THE OPEN AIR THEATRE

JAQUES	Philip Merivale
ORLANDO	Geoffrey Edwards
TOUCHSTONE	Billy Leonard
ROSALIND	Gladys Cooper
CELIA	Sylvia Marriott
PHOEBE	Thea Holme

This was certainly not a fortunate performance of *As You like It,* but the Open Air Theatre works in difficult conditions and it is best to believe that, as time passes and more of the players become familiar with their words, virtues will emerge that are not now apparent. Yesterday afternoon the handicap of words was, in many instances, destructive. A Touchstone without fluency is a bore, and Mr. Billy Leonard could make nothing of the part. Even more serious was the effect on Rosalind, for Miss Cooper was driven to eke out memory with a violence of emphasis and a soaring extravagance of gesture that caricatured her own swashbuckling conception of masculine disguise. Mr. Geoffrey Edwards spoke well, but was too brittle an Orlando, from whom the sap seemed to have been drained off by his melancholy. There was a charming Phoebe by Miss Thea Holme, a good and lively Celia by Miss Sylvia

Marriott, and an uncommonly interesting Jaques by Mr. Philip Merivale, whose thought had evident spring in it throughout all his set speeches. But the production is not yet together, and criticism of individual performances, whether favourable or unfavourable, may well be revised by those who go to Regent's Park in a few days' time.

24 AUGUST 1938, THE TIMES

Tobias and the Angel by James Bridie

THE OPEN AIR THEATRE

TOBIT	Eliot Makeham
TOBIAS	Romney Brent
RAPHAEL	Robert Eddison
RAGUEL	Stephen Murray

It is very rare that a play of genuine quality gives an impression that it is sprung from a mood of happiness. There are many that the dramatist evidently enjoyed writing, and many others that are in themselves high-spirited and induce high spirits in their audience; but who, as he watches even *As You Like It* or *Twelfth Night*, would wager that they were the product of happiness in Shakespeare's mind? *Tobias and the Angel* is remarkable in this, and the happiness in it is more fully communicated in the open air than, in the past, it has been within the walls of a theatre. One may wish for better and fewer dancing-girls, for they have a tendency to break the simplicity and directness of the narrative. They are tinsel, and the first merits of the play is that, though it risks the perils of fantasy, it preserves an evenness of treatment and a saving gravity in its smile.

It is, too, a little disconcerting at first to find that Tobias is American, but Mr. Romney Brent justifies himself by an admirable ease in his humorous approach to the young man's adventures. Mr. Stephen Murray gives a pleasant fuzziness to old Raguel; Mr. Eliot Makeham though he misses a part of Tobit's spiritual strength, gives the imperturbable and unworldly cheerfulness that is at any rate a mirror of the spirit; and Mr. Robert Eddison, modest of angelic splendours, yet preserves a dignity within a light treatment of the part. This is a good and peacefully minded play, which Mr. Frank Birch, in his production, has carefully and rightly withheld from farce. It is, moreover, a play of a kind that the Open Air Theatre does well to produce, for it is a piece of adventure and free imagining, and depends very little on the tension of phrase to which an unconfined stage is always dangerous.

Factual Note on **She, Too, Was Young**

The writer finds himself this week in a position of embarrassment. Apart from a musical piece at the Hippodrome there has been but one opening – that of a play called *She, Too, Was Young*, by Hilda Vaughan and Laurier Lister, at Wyndham's. Hilda Vaughan bears by marriage the name that appears at the foot of this article. I am therefore precluded, in New York as I have been in London, from criticizing her work, but I should fail in my duty as a theatrical correspondent if I did not mention it, for it has received a unanimously favourable press and is filling its house.

The plain facts are these: its scene is a country house during the 1870s. Its story is of a girl who, prevented by her mother from marrying the man she loved, almost married another who loved her, but was enabled at the last moment to fulfil her own romance. Its theme, traced through three generations, is the relationship of mother and daughter. Its method is never to guy Victorianism but faithfully to reproduce it and to allow its tragedy and comedy and absurdity to appear naturally in a mirror which, without distortion, reflects its manners. It gives opportunity for a beautiful and unusual decor and for a group of carefully balanced performances by Mr. Edmund Gwen, Miss Marie Ney, Miss Ann Todd and Mr. Esmé Percy.

The audience on the first night paid it the unusual tribute of renewing their applause after the national anthem had been played. Unless the United States are more romantically minded than I suppose them to be, it may not be as well suited to American as to English audiences, for its pace is leisurely, its emotion seldom emphatic and its ending happy. These are the simple facts. It is not possible for the husband of half-the-author to say more without launching into criticism.

Dear Octopus by Dodie Smith

QUEEN'S THEATRE

CHARLES RANDOLPH	Leon Quartermaine
DORA RANDOLPH	Marie Tempest
HILDA RANDOLPH	Nan Munro
MARJORIE HARVEY	Madge Compton
KATHLEEN KENTON	Muriel Pavlow
CYNTHIA RANDOLPH	Valerie Taylor
NICOLAS RANDOLPH	John Gielgud

HUGH RANDOLPH	John Justin
BELLE SCHLESINGER	Kate Cutler
GRACE FENNING	Angela Baddeley

The fourth generation – or can we have lost count, and is it the fifth? – remains unseen and unheard in the night nursery, but the other three are all present and correct. They are assembled to do honour to Charles and Dora's golden wedding, and all the honours are done. In the first act the Randolphs assemble and explain themselves in the hall; in the second, laid in the nursery, they explain themselves in greater detail, recalling the past, remembering the feel of the rocking-horse's mane, listening to Miss Tempest sing a duet with her most gifted grandchild, and, later in the evening, drifting in from the dance downstairs; and in the third act they drink the family toast, proposed by Mr. Gielgud, and the lady companion is sought in marriage by the eldest son – Mr. Gielgud again. There are, indeed, plays by Tchehov with no more story than that.

From this it is not to be concluded that Miss Dodie Smith is even winking an eye at Moscow. She has a style of her own and she is true to it, striving always to extend its range. What she is aiming at here is not narrative or close, individual portraiture, but a collective study of an English family, exceptional only in its size, and the subject is one that gives opportunity to her talent for observation. It is important to notice that she is now less concerned with superficial detail than she was, and much more courageously willing to hold the stage without interrupting herself with easy laughter. Not yet courageous enough. Still, after a girl has played a scene of suffering, Miss Smith will send her out on an "exit-line" about hens. Still the love-story is rounded off in a brief final scene without fire or love in it. And still, in quest of variety – or is it in distrust of her audience? – Miss Smith can cap a genuinely moving passage with two-dimensional sentiment that even Mr. Quartermaine and Miss Tempest cannot make welcome. But none of these objections would be raised against Miss Dodie Smith if her uncommon and increasing value did not make her defects astonishing. If one were not continually expecting from her the play she always just fails to write, it would be easy to sit back and enjoy *Dear Octopus*, rejoicing in its many merits.

Its definition of character is clear, its dialogue easy, and its sympathy with its people genuine. Though the part is Miss Tempest's, grandmamma is the least attractive of the group, but even she comes out of her type in her understanding of her prodigal daughter. Among the others it is inevitable to select. Mr. Gielgud, Miss Nan Munro, and Miss Angela Baddeley draw their sketches with accuracy and decision. Miss Kate Cutler plays a harsh part and Miss Annie Esmond a gentle one with equal distinction. There is a portrait of a very young girl by Miss Muriel Pavlow that has a sensitiveness and vision that strike at the heart, and one of the Randolph daughters is played by Miss Valerie Taylor. How little, how faultless, how profoundly moving! This is what Miss Dodie Smith can write if only she will – and Miss Taylor will interpret her. There is a scene between Miss Taylor and

Miss Pavlow that shines from the play. This and the whole of Miss Taylor's superb performance are enough to give distinction to the evening.

24 SEPTEMBER 1938, THE TIMES

Good-bye, Mr. Chips
by James Hilton and Barbara Burnham

SHAFTESBURY THEATRE

MR. CHIPS	Leslie Banks
MR. BLAKE	Michael Shepley
MR. WETHERBY	Charles Quartermaine
MR. UPTON	Godfrey Kenton
MR. TEMPLE	Ronald Simpson
KATHERINE	Constance Cummings

It needed an honest and quiet play to hold an audience last night and the audience was continuously held from the day on which Mr. Chips, a young man of 22, took preparation for the first time in the Big Hall at Brookfield until, as an old man, he retired and, as an older, returned to service of the school during the War, and, in extreme age, went to sleep in his chair. His adventures by the way are exceptional only in the quality given them by his character. He marries and deeply loves a young and beautiful wife; she dies in childbirth. He is accused of being old-fashioned by an innovating headmaster and invited to resign; he quietly survives his accuser.

He teaches Latin while the bombs drop, steadying the nerve of his class by directing them to appropriate passages in Caesar. Slowly he becomes at Brookfield – what? The easy word is an "institution," but it is too pompous to serve Mr. Chips. He becomes that extremely rare being – an imaginative, an unspectacular, a great schoolmaster.

There is one point in the play at which his capacity for greatness is attributed to his modest notion that he is of all ordinary men the most ordinary. On that subject one might argue for a year. It is simpler to agree with his wife's more direct tribute to him when she says that he is "pure in heart." Miss Constance Cummings's share in the action is not extensive, for Katherine dies young, to be seen again only in a brief vision, but her performance is faultlessly judged, and we remember her gentleness and wisdom, as Mr. Chips remembered them, when she has been long absent. There are a dozen sketches of boys and masters – conspicuously those of Mr. Simpson, Mr. Shepley, and Mr. Godfrey Kenton – which assist the portraiture of Chips by supplying a background of a school at work, but it is Miss Cummings who, by a light she throws on the whole action, contributes most. But her work and the work of all the others is subordinate to Mr. Banks's. The extraordinary virtue of his performance is its patience. How easy, in the early scenes, for the unimaginative to wish for more emphasis, more display, and how splendidly, as scene follows scene, does Mr. Banks's method justify itself! The play is episodic but one receives a genuine and satisfying impression of the passage of time. Preserving always the constancy of his spirit, the outward man changes, and, through these changes, his constant nature becomes more and more recognizable and to be loved.

7 OCTOBER 1938, THE TIMES

The White Guard adapted by Rodney Ackland from the Russian of Bulgakov

PHOENIX THEATRE

ALEXEI TURBIN	Michael Redgrave
NIKOLKA TURBIN	Basil C. Langton
YELIENA TALBERG	Peggy Ashcroft
VIKTOR MYSCHLAJEVSKY	George Devine
LARIOSSIK	Stephen Haggard
VLADIMIR TALBERG	George Hayes
ALEXANDER STUDESINSKY	Glen Byam Shaw
LEONID SCHERVINSKY	Marius Goring

Those of us who have for years been asking for continuity of policy in the theatre have good reason to welcome the experiment began by Mr. Bronson Albery and M. Michel Saint-Denis at the Phoenix Theatre last night. The company is of genuine quality, the plays promised for the future – *The Cherry Orchard*, *Uncle Vanya*, *The Wild Duck*, and half a dozen others – are of the first rank, and the piece chosen to inaugurate the season has a high reputation in Soviet Russia and is of uncommon interest.

The oddity of *The White Guard*, if considered as a Soviet play, is that it is concerned with a group of men and a woman who in 1918 were opposed to the Bolshevist regime and is by no means abusive of them. They are in Kiev, serving the Hetman of the Ukraine who was put in power by the Germans after the revolution. Deserted by their German allies, they are overcome by an independent revolutionary, Petlura, who in his turn is defeated by the Bolshevists. Through all their changes of fortune, the White officers whom we are watching change little. One receives an impression of sadness, weariness, disorganization, fecklessness, fatalism, and courage so mingled that the nature of these men establishes itself in the imagination. They remain foreign, but they cease to be strange. And the drifting, casual story is told in a style of which it is scarcely an exaggeration to say that it reveals a new aspect of comedy.

The White Guard has, in common with many Russian plays, and a few Irish, the gift of using comedy and tragedy as a compound, but it has also a special quality of its own that may best be described as a mingling of sadness with gaiety – the gaiety not of defiance or despair but of the spirit that is made light by the knowledge that it has no more to lose. Miss Ashcroft has this gaiety in perfection. Where Yeliena is there is peace, says one of the officers, and she does very beautifully communicate the radiance springing from the character – communicates it the more clearly because with so complete an absence of solemn intensity. Laughter, irresponsibility, even a little absurdity appear in Miss Ashcroft's performance, and the work of all the others is complimentary to hers. Mr. George Hayes and Mr. Marius Goring decorate their portraits with fantasy; Mr. Basil Langton and Mr. Glen Byam Shaw keep a little closer to naturalism; Mr. Stephen Haggard is a laughable and pathetic sprite let loose; Mr. George Devine and Mr. Michael Redgrave give to the piece its background in suffering and courage. But no performance can be confined within a couple of adjectives. They are like shot silk, revealing continually fresh lights, fresh colours. It is true that when it is done the play is seen to have been thin in substance. It describes much and tells little. But its manner, its performance, and M. Saint-Denis's production are enchanting, and the more enchanting because they are so unforced, so little mannered or self-conscious.

16 OCTOBER 1938, THE NEW YORK TIMES

London after the Armistice

LONDON, SEPTEMBER 30

With trenches dug in all the parks, the fleet mobilized and the whole population served with gas masks, there has been in England this week little care for the theatre. Day by day opinion has hardened, and, in the manner of the English, opinion has become less excited and more determined. Those of us who served from the outset in 1914 recognized the symptoms. There was this distinction – that, in 1914, there was a mood of elation; the fixed, steely and unhysterical purpose of the English did not come until later; but on Wednesday, Sept. 28, we had already reached the condition of mind in which, about the middle of 1915, we settled down to an indefinite war, put all thought of yielding and all thought of personal happiness from our minds, and went steadily on into the darkness the only end of which should be victory.

The cloud appears now to have lifted. Agreement has been reached at Munich – on what terms we do not yet know. War with the dictatorships has been, at any rate, postponed – whether to their advantage or to ours, only those who have a complete knowledge of our relative preparedness can decide. But England has learnt a lesson. A foreign nation does not drive us into gas masks and drag our Prime Minister to and fro across the world for nothing. We shall presumably not too eagerly disarm again. Meanwhile the theatre may proceed.

There were to have been two openings this week. One, having gone as far as dress rehearsal, was postponed, but, if Germany has not changed her mind meanwhile, will take place in a few days. Nothing is more surprising than the notion, continually recurrent across the Rhine, that England is without a democratic ideal worth dying for, that she is decadent, and that, when hit, she will not hit back. Last time this notion possessed Berlin, we fought for four years. This time we mobilized the fleet, dug trenches and removed all our children into the country. Therefore, until the notion possesses Berlin again, we are graciously permitted to bring our children home again and to explain to them how ardent is the German desire for England's friendship. And we may go to the theatre instead of a dug-out.

But how is one to write of the theatre in such a week as this without a hypocritical detachment? The only piece inviting comment is Jeffrey Dell's *Official Secrets* of which it is enough to say that it is an efficient spy play with an ingenious plot and rather more characterization than is customary in spy plays. In normal circumstances, it would have succeeded as a neatly contrived and unexacting entertainment. What its fate has been this week, I dare not guess. Even the greatest successes in London have been playing to dwindling audiences, which is not surprising while all trains and all roads are packed by the evacuation.

Presumably the English will now return to their own city and, in the interests of European peace, say no more about it. But the way to persuade this decadent people to shake you by the hand is not to drag their King from Balmoral, their Prime Minister to Berchtesgaden, Godesberg and Munich, and drive their children from their homes with the threat of bombs. We should remember this, but meanwhile the theatre may proceed.

21 DECEMBER 1938, THE TIMES

Under Suspicion
by Leslie Harcourt and Basil Dearden

THE PLAYHOUSE

DETECTIVE-INSPECTOR ARMITAGE	William Fox
BARNEY STEVENS	Walter Fitzgerald
LUCILLE	Patricia Hilliard

> Who is this man the coppers seek
> And colleagues call the Boss,
> Who gives the slip to Armitage
> And double-crosses Cross?

Beneath our Barney's waterproof
Is more than he concealed?
If the steel door were once thrown back
What truth would stand revealed?

How skilfully is Scotland Yard
Shown up by William Fox!
How neatly does Fitzgerald play
With pistols, proofs, and locks!

Miss Hilliard decorates the stage
And dazzles the police;
New York and Paris telephone
To complicate the piece.

With torture in the dark and bells
That ring when no one's there,
And poor professors gagged and bound,
And foolish clerks who stare,

The story ties itself in knots
For grim and guileless men
Who wonder what the others guess
For two whole acts; and then –

Wig after wig, a whole act through,
Falls blithley on the ground,
Until, ingenuously peeled,
The blessed Boss is found.

Peter Pan by J.M. Barrie

THE PALLADIUM

PETER PAN	Nova Pilbeam
CAPTAIN HOOK	Seymour Hicks
MR. DARLING	Antony Bushell
MRS. DARLING	Cicely Byrne
SLIGHTLY	Jimmy Hanley
TIGER LILY	Olive Wright
WENDY	Pamela Standish
SMEE	Charles Doe

The first thing to be said at the opening performance of this year's *Peter Pan,* which was given before a vast audience of London children on Saturday afternoon, is that, though illness had for the moment prevented Miss Forbes-Robertson from appearing – and all who have seen her in a part she has made her own were disappointed – Miss Nova Pilbeam, who took her place, and who has before played Peter in her own right, enabled that personal disappointment to be forgotten. She is an imaginative and vital Peter with an openness of manner that goes far to save the part from sentimentality. She has not that flamelike conviction which can subdue even the sceptical members of the audience, but she is firm and direct, she is not a "principal boy," and those who have a natural taste for peterism are delighted by her.

The play begins well in the nursery, where Mr. and Mrs. Darling have things to say which can be converted from embarrassments into assets if they are spoken, as Miss Cicely Byrne and Mr. Antony Bushell speak them, in a tone of matter-of-fact confidence. Barrie, in his nursery mood, needs to be left to himself. Emphasize his symbolical whimsies and all is lost; speak them plainly and all-or nearly all-is saved by a miracle and a hair's breadth. Nowhere is the peril greater than in the nursery, and Miss Pamela Standish's straightforward and unaffected Wendy shares with her mother and father the honours of surviving it. In any case, the position is saved as soon as the flying begins. The pyjamaed children kicking about in mid-air set the house laughing, and the tale is well in its swing.

And this year there is Sir Seymour Hicks's Hook to which to look forward. Mr. Handley's Slightly has character; Miss Olive Wright's Tiger Lily is clear and vigorous; the pirates are collectively good, though their singing does not always do credit to Mr. John Crook's music; and the lagoon scene, which it was once customary to omit, fully justifies itself. But what one waits for is the pirate ship. On Saturday, Sir Seymour was not in good voice, nor could his following of the text to be called slavish. In these circumstances – particularly when his face was not well lit or when a rascally pirate, in the lagoon scene, insisted upon standing between him and the limelight – some of his points were missed, but he has hit upon little pieces of business that are new and brings to his whole treatment of the part an inventiveness that revitalizes it. An audience of small children has much in common with a congregation of starlings; certainly they do not listen while the pins drop, and everyone in the company – even Sir Seymour, who can dominate anything not indomitable – has his work cut out. But an impression remained that, as the afternoons pass, the Hicks Hook, which is extravagant where others have been suave, will become memorable for its richness and its glorious absurdities. It goes all lengths; it may always produce, at the shortest notice, a gigantic spoonerism; it has the effect of a fantastic improvization; and the man who, in this play and in this year of grace, can make you wonder what on earth Hook will say next is something to be thankful for. Not, of course, that Sir Seymour would venture to gag. For him, as for all good peterists, the text is sacrosanct, but the faithful must be on tenterhooks.

26 JANUARY 1939, THE TIMES

Design for Living by Noël Coward

HAYMARKET THEATRE

GILDA	Diana Wynyard
ERNEST FRIEDMAN	Alan Webb
OTTO	Anton Walbrook
LEO	Rex Harrison

Mr. Coward is always at his best when he is fooling, though it seemed long ago, in the old days of *The Vortex*, that he might become a master of satire. Here is the mixture of satire with fooling that is his special talent and his particular confusion. Sometimes, while telling of a woman who loved two men and was loved by both, he says openly, through them, what he believes to be true; sometimes, he mocks at what he believes to be a lie; and the play, in these moments, is a serious play and deeply interesting. Sometimes, when the two men, abandoned by the girl, drink together in one of the most brilliant drunken scenes in the theatre, or when the same pair turn up in New York like a couple of music-hall comedians, Mr. Coward's dialogue dips and swings and glitters as though he were writing a dazzling farce. Both moods, the serious and the flippant, are good, each in its kind, but they are dangerously joined.

Suddenly Mr. Coward, when discussing a theme that is after all related to the theme of Goethe's *Elective Affinities*, catches the eye of his fashionable audience, is embarrassed, and with a little shriek of surrender turns on the tap of flippancy. It is not a question only of mixing conventions; it is almost a question of running away. There is an instance in the final curtain, much debated in the past and explained by Mr. Coward in his preface. All the people concerned go off into a howl of laughter and the play ends. They are laughing at themselves. Very well: a dramatist may choose his own period of action; he's not required to solve all problems, to untie all knots; but he must not put up smoke-screens to cover his retreat from thought that he himself has challenged. The theme is not faced; the subject is not worked out.

For these reasons, the play is disappointing. It remains, in the aggregate of its parts, good entertainment, though with a bitter taste and sometimes with a callow "daring." Miss Wynyard and Mr. Anton Walbrook are not perfectly cast. She has a lovely grace and a tenderness that goes far to vindicate Mr. Coward's serious passages, and she is gloriously gay when Gilda is not bitter; but she has not the dragging sharpness – like the drag of a slate-pencil on a slate – which Gilda's harsher flippancies require. Mr. Walbrook is amusing with Mr. Harrison, but too heavy on Mr. Coward's difficult passages of sentiment. Mr. Harrison is nearest to what seems to have been the author's intention – dry in tone, light-hearted in manner, not altogether without feeling – and there is a performance of precise and flawless judgment by Mr. Alan Webb.

1 FEBRUARY 1939, THE TIMES

The Importance of Being Earnest
by Oscar Wilde

GLOBE THEATRE

JOHN WORTHING, J. P.	John Gielgud
ALGERNON MONCRIEFF	Ronald Ward
CANON CHASUBLE, D. D.	David Horne
MERRIMAN	Felix Irwin
LANE	Leon Quartermaine
LADY BRACKNELL	Edith Evans
THE HON. GWENDOLEN FAIRFAX	Joyce Carey
CICELY CARDEW	Angela Baddeley
MISS PRISM	Margaret Rutherford

Opening the program of the first of eight matinées of this comedy, the playgoer was put into good humour by the discovery that, beside the present cast and preceding it, was printed the original cast of 1895. It is worth printing again for history's and for courtesy's sake: –

JOHN WORTHING, J. P.	Mr. George Alexander
ALGERNON MONCRIEFF	Mr. Alan Aynesworth
CANON CHASUBLE, D. D.	Mr. H. H. Vincent
MERRIMAN	Mr. Frank Dyall
LANE	Mr. F. Kinsey Peile
LADY BRACKNELL	Miss Rose Leclercq

HON. GWENDOLEN FAIRFAX	Miss Irene Vanbrugh
CICELY CARDEW	Miss Evelyn Millard
MISS PRISM	Mrs. George Canninge

Can you beat it? as they say in that pithy country where our decadent language is not good enough. Certainly you cannot; but it remains possible to treat Wilde's comedy as a work of highly specialized genius, to play it in its period as we play, or should play, Sheridan, and not to mock it, not to rag it, not to maul it as a twentieth-century joke. Now, for the first time within our experience, it is being given in its own tradition. The performance may be criticized in detail, but taken by and large it is the best that any but the most senior playgoers can remember.

There are certain qualities in a performance of *The Importance of Being Earnest* without which the performance is not. There are other qualities that are to be prayed for, but the absence of which is not ruinous. The necessary qualities are these and are present: that every phrase be spoken for its shape; that the impression be given that this fantastic language is the language naturally used by the ladies and gentlemen who utter it; that the wit appear to be sufficient unto itself, needing no barrage of grins to prepare its coming and no winking of the eye to emphasize its advance; and, finally, that everyone, whether their reported origin is Belgrave Square or Victoria Railway Station, shall appear to have been bred on the floodlit side of the Elysian fields. To all of which may be added, if the gods are uncommonly gracious, what is now a little lacking and may, perhaps, be called the Nausicaa-touch – the power of actors to persuade you that they are not consciously exchanging the most brilliant dialogue written for a hundred years, but are, like Nausicaa and her maidens, playing at ball, passing the time, wasting the time, all unconscious of the wily Odysseus.

Even this airy, responsive, ball-playing quality, which, the mandarins tell us, Alexander and Aynesworth had to perfection 44 years ago, may be added to the present production before the eighth *matinée* is out. As yet Mr. Ronald Ward is sometimes slow with Algy and Mr. Gielgud (until the third act warms him) indecisive in John Worthing's solemn, irritated, and indignant attack. But neither anticipates Wilde's wit; their performances are light, clear, and – how shall it be expressed? – above all, civilized; and Mr. Gielgud, in particular, has the special naturalism proper to the part – a naturalism that preserves, for example, a fine comedy in his appearance in mourning and delights the audience, but not with the extravagance of farce.

Miss Joyce Carey has not the resilience, the charming and absurd false-naivety of Gwendolen Fairfax, but Miss Angela Baddeley was evidently born when Wilde says she was – in 1877 – and has grown ever since in a perfect contradiction of naughtiness and innocence. Miss Prism is a gift to Miss Margaret Rutherford, and Canon Chasuble to Mr. David Horne, Miss Rutherford's bridling over the restored handbag, as if it were a favourite cat long lost and now astonishingly mewing in her lap, being as restrained and effective a piece of drollery as one could wish for. And there is Miss Edith Evans as Lady Bracknell, so born to play the part that even what may be called her mannerisms decorate it. Her appearance is masterly – perfectly upholstered, with a feminine art now lost, before and behind; and her voice is correspondingly upholstered so that every phrase, harsh or drawling, comes from the comfortable heart of Lady Bracknell's arrogance. A woman, of course, for the earnest to hang on the first lamp-post, but what a dying speech and what a superb corpse she would make!

1 FEBRUARY 1939, THE TIMES

Gas Light by Patrick Hamilton

APOLLO THEATRE

MR. MANNINGHAM	Dennis Arundell
MRS. MANNINGHAM	Gwen Ffrangçon-Davies
ELIZABETH	Beatrice Rowe
NANCY	Elizabeth Inglis
MR. ROUGH	Milton Rosmer

The purpose of this tale – a purpose brilliantly obtained – is to play upon the nerves of its audience. In this sense it is a "thriller," but it would be unjust to leave it in the same category with pieces that depend on groping hands and phosphorescent faces or, alternatively, on gangsters and G-men. Mr. Hamilton can write, and he obtains his effects by the imagining, and not by the trappings, of fear.

In a gas-lit house in Pimlico, towards the end of the last century, Mr. and Mrs. Manningham live unhappily together. She is miserably and abjectly grateful when he promises to take her to a play; she is wildly afraid when he accuses her of having moved a picture that she has not moved or having lost a bill that she knows was on her table an hour go. Soon it appears that he is trying to drive her mad by compelling her to believe in her own madness. Why? To be rid of her. Why does he wish to be rid of her? Because she knows too much. Of what? Who is he? Why does he occupy this particular house where, for the sake of her jewels, an old lady was murdered 20 years ago? Mr. Rough, a former detective, who visits Mrs. Manningham in her husband's absence, gradually reveals to us and to her the desperate plight she is in, and it is evidence of Mr. Hamilton's rare power to tell a story of this kind that, when she seems helpless and unprotected, the tension is painful, and when there is a reasonable assurance that help will come to her, the tension does not drop.

With a momentary exception at the end of the last act when emotion is forced and the forcing defeats its purpose, the play is written in a style of quiet observation that increases the effect of terror, and is performed in the same spirit. The sketches of servants by Miss Rowe and Miss Inglis fall into the general scheme. Mr. Rosmer, by the reassurance of his benign and incisive manner, keeps the story skilfully on this side of hysteria. Mr. Arundell, though he lacks the power to lend the murderer the deep terrors of imagination that might have proceeded from him, is adroit, silky, and cruel; and Miss Ffrangçon-Davies's performance is distinguished not only by the shiver of its little movements and the pale sickliness of its fears, but by what can only be called its natural control, which compels one to see Mrs. Manningham, not as a victim in a thriller, but as a living woman caught in a dark trap. The play is not, and is not intended to be, a comfortable one, but it has remarkable distinction in its own kind.

23 FEBRUARY 1939, THE TIMES

Johnson Over Jordan by J.B. Priestley.

NEW THEATRE

MRS. JOHNSON	Edna Best
ROBERT JOHNSON	Ralph Richardson

It is impossible in a few paragraphs driven by time to discuss Mr. Priestley's play with the elaboration that criticism of it requires. No one but a fool would venture to say of it briefly either that it is good or that it is bad, for it is a struggling, courageous play, an experiment exciting even in its failures. There is real danger of over-praising its gigantic ambition because ambition of this kind is greatly needed and is a profound relief from the easy trivialities of the theatre, and an equal danger, unless nice distinctions are made, of speaking too harshly of those crudities of treatment which – particularly in the last act – almost bring the piece to ruin. In fact it was not ruined. A magnificently buoyant and imaginative performance by Mr. Ralph Richardson sustained it, but it must be admitted that the fall of the last curtain and a kindly reception came like a rescue from long-impending shipwreck.

This is an account of the spiritual experiences of Johnson after his death. He is outwardly a commonplace, respectable man who began as a clerk, has made a moderate way in life, and leaves behind him a devoted wife and two grown-up children. The action begins with his funeral, and parts of the burial service periodically recur. Meanwhile we follow the adventures of his spirit. At first it is, in part, earthbound, obsessed by earthly fear and desire, particularly by care for money. Next, Johnson is shown, in a masked and fantasticated cabaret scene, indulging the cruelty and the sensuality that were probably suppressed in him during his life. Next, in an imagined inn to which Death directs him, he re-encounters those aspects of his life that have made it happy and illumined it, and so, liberated at last and with spiritual confidence recovered, is permitted to "depart in peace."

The purpose of the cabaret-scene is nothing less than to give an impression of hell. The masks, the dreadful aridity of bought pleasure, and a fiercely symbolic interlude in which Johnson bullies his own daughter in the belief that she is a prostitute do succeed intermittently in producing an effect of terror, but the cabaret is still too much like a cabaret, waves of the common boredom pass over it to the audience, and Mr. Priestley says more in one brief and noble soliloquy than in all the contrivances of dance and lighting and violence to which Mr. Basil Dean has devoted so much care. And the third act is endangered for a different reason. Here Johnson is re-introduced to the joyful memories of his life – his dead brother; the characters in fiction – Pickwick and Don Quixote – who affected his youth; an old clown, a famous cricketer, an admired schoolmaster; and is permitted to live again early and fragmentary moments of happiness with his wife. That these memories are, in themselves, commonplace, is by no means an objection to them, for Johnson was outwardly a commonplace man. The trouble is first that they are a string of incidents that do not contain the continuous impulse of drama; secondly, that their triviality, though justifiable in itself, mixes ill with the splendours of the Prayer-book; the styles of the parish magazine and the Burial service will not mix, whatever justification there may be, in the play's particular circumstances, for the naiveties of the parish magazine. But one hates to seem to speak even for a moment derisively of such a play as this. It gives Mr. Richardson a great opportunity and he carries all its burdens with spring and lightness. It is, moreover, a deeply serious, impassioned, and charitable attack upon a great subject, and that, in the theatre, is more than half the world.

13 APRIL 1939, THE TIMES

Of Mice and Men by John Steinbeck

GATE THEATRE

GEORGE	John Mills
LENNIE	Niall MacGinnis
CURLEY'S WIFE	Claire Luce

The strength of this play, which has won for itself a high reputation in the United States, lies not in any subtlety of thought, but in the plainness of its statement and in the impression it unfailingly gives of adhering to fact without embroidery or distortion. If it were to be compared with certain French plays that have been given at the Gate Theatre – with the work of Monsieur Mauriac, for example – it might appear young and crude, young aesthetically in its love of violence, and crude in the simplicity of its comment upon the nature of man; but such a comparison would be unjust to it, for Mr. Steinbeck's work is different from Monsieur Mauriac's, not only in treatment, but in purpose. His desire is, above all else, to stir his audience by direct and simplified narrative, to obtain his effects by the use of swift and vigorous dramatic outline.

He is writing of two Californian tramps, George and Lennie, who obtain work on a farm. Lennie is a good-natured giant with a sub-normal mind. His great strength is dangerous, for he is incapable of controlling it, and George has made himself responsible for this vast, babyish man. On the farm is a girl, the young wife of the

Boss's son, who, being lonely, seeks the company of the labourers, not wishing to stir desire or jealousy in them but inevitably doing so. Only the extreme directness of Mr. Steinbeck's writing and of Miss Claire Luce's admirable performance could make this character persuasive, and persuasive it is. That there will be a clash between Lennie and the girl is foreseen from the outset. Neither wishes harm to the other; neither loves or desires the other; when, at last they are alone together, the girl talks of her life and Lennie of his, neither listening to the other. It is a brilliant piece of dialogue and a good example of Mr. Steinbeck's method. Lennie touches her hair in curiosity, and his clumsy fingers become entangled in it. She cries out in fear, he, frightened in his turn, tries to stop her crying and breaks her neck by mistake. He escapes, is pursued, and, by the time his friend George finds him, has completely forgotten what he has done. He is happy, is looking forward childishly to the future, when George mercifully shoots him.

Mr. Niall MacGinnis performs the giant's part with the innocence of a flawless simplicity. Miss Luce brings to the girl an energy of attack and an emotional economy that are of great value to the play. The events in which they are concerned remain nevertheless open to the criticism that they are over-simplified, and it needs the sympathy and charity of Mr. John Mills's treatment of George to give the piece light and shade. George, whose single purpose is to save Lennie from himself, and who is to him at once nurse and brother and friend, brings to the tale a warmth and sentiment that are its salvation.

14 APRIL 1939, THE TIMES

A Woman's Privilege by Margaret Branford

KINGSWAY THEATRE

MR. HAYDON	Ralph Roberts
LILAH HAYDON	Phyllis Calvert
ANNE HAYDON	Rosemary Scott
BILL FERGUSON	John Penrose
JAMES E. QUIGLEY	Douglas Stewart
DAVID MARCHMONT	James Raglan

An uncommonly civilized and entertaining piece, evidently written by that rare specimen in the theatre, a gentlewoman who does read and can write. So good and, at the same time, so fluent is her dialogue and so shrewd her observation of character that an exceptional stiffness such as: "Please don't think it was jealousy that prompted the remark," is a momentary shock, and the use of the word "'phone" by a woman not of the flapper-carrier class leaps uncomfortably to the ear. In an informal proportion of the plays performed, "'phone" is both noun and verb in Tottering Towers, "like" is interchangeable with "as," and no one has heard of Scott. Mrs. Branford positively quotes him, and that is the least of her merits.

There are two sisters in the Haydon family, Lilah and Anne, and this is, on the surface, a tale of how Lilah everlastingly changes her mercenary mind, seizing and dropping first one man, then another, and of how, in the end, she is left digging for American gold. How easily such a piece might have been conventionally "tough," designed to shock by its crudeness! Instead, Mrs. Branford, remembering the classical models, has treated her theme as high comedy, sometimes fumbling a little with old papa, but not hesitating to draw Lilah a trifle larger-than-life, welcoming a chance to contrast a puppyish young man who is her dupe with a maturer being who sees through her, having the courage to give shape and balance to the scenes within the acts, and, above all, quickening her dialogue with a dry, easy wit that is worth a wilderness of wisecracks. And Lilah's sister, who might have been a dull foil, emerges as a woman in her own right, independent, of a firm but unassertive integrity, continuously entertaining because unfailingly true.

Miss Phyllis Calvert gives Lilah a sharp, determined energy; there are sketches of quality by Mr. Penrose as the unsmiling dupe, by Mr. Raglan as the undeluded critic, and by Mr. Douglas Stewart as the American; but the genuinely subtle performance of the evening is Miss Rosemary Scott's discreetly humorous treatment of Anne's open-eyed and yet unembittered observation. There are moments of awkwardness and inexperience in Mrs. Branford's piece; it is not a dazzlingly competent succession of pistol-shots; nor is it a masterpiece even in its own kind. But it has grace, humanity, and language; it looks contemporary life in the face; it gave continuous pleasure to its audience; and one can safely say of it what can be said of few of its rivals – that it would not have been written if Goldsmith and Sheridan had been drowned at birth.

21 APRIL 1939, THE TIMES

The Women by Clare Boothe

LYRIC THEATRE

MARY	Karen Peterson
LITTLE MARY	Joan Greenwood

Belonging not only to another continent but seemingly to another age, this is a crude, course narrative of the sexual jungle. The authoress makes no bones about it. The approved nail-varnish recommended by one woman to another is called "Jungle-red," and "jungle" is the dramatic and the moral key-word. And not only is the authoress candid but she is tolerably consistent. Now and then a few filial tears are dropped to dilute the play's raw spirit. The deserted wife's small daughter, known to the programme as Little Mary, creeps into mamma's bed, asks winningly to have her back scratched, and lets fall from her innocent lips what she has heard the wicked Crystal say on the telephone. Up jumps Mary Senior, exchanges her nightdress for a pink frock, and gallantly (as brave little wives should) snatches back the husband previously snatched from her.

But sentiment of this kind is brief and formal. For the most part the play is pure jungle – beauty parlours, "exercise salons," bedrooms, bathrooms, and jaded, arid dialogue by grim women about men and money and money and men. The 40 members of the cast, all-female, cannot easily be distinguished, for they have but two interests and discuss them in the same language, but, except where sentiment shows its unhappy head and causes embarrassment to Miss Karen Peterson, the general impression is of metallic competence.

30 APRIL 1939, THE NEW YORK TIMES

Steinbeck in London

Politics has called another halt to the theatre. Existing plays are struggling on, for the most part on reduced salary lists, and announcements of future productions are fewer than I have ever known them at this time of year. Outside London, festivals continue, as at Stratford, but in London enterprise is chiefly confined to the small subscription theatres, such as the Gate, where John Steinbeck's famous play, *Of Mice and Men*, has just been performed for the first time with Miss Claire Luce in the lead. It is understood that if the play should have a prolonged run, a substitute will have to be found for Miss Luce, whose other engagements hold her. We count ourselves the more fortunate to have been given an opportunity to see her, even for a little while, in her original part.

By the small, specialised and intelligent audience at the Gate, Mr. Steinbeck's work was received with discerned enthusiasm. Whether it would hold a wider public in England may be doubted, not because the English necessarily require a love-story but because a piece which introduces a girl into a group of men and excludes all expression of romantic sentiment is in danger of failing in England for precisely the same reasons which recommend it in America.

The emotional strength of Mr. Steinbeck's play is in the devotion of the two tramps, George and Lennie, a devotion brilliantly implied in a series of carefully planned understatements. Lennie, because he has softening of the brain, can speak only in brief, childish repetitions. George, though quick-minded and voluble, is in effect inarticulate, and it is fascinating to observe the skill with which Mr. Steinbeck, while permitting George none of the self-analysis of cultivated men and preserving his rough simplicities of a tramp, yet manages to convey the depth of feeling in the man. I am inclined, nevertheless, to believe that, even if the censorship's ban were removed, the English would admire the play, as an example of foreign method, rather than enjoy it.

It is, at any rate, remarkable that the limits set to Miss Luce's part came as a surprise to the English audience, and when, at the end, it was found to be indeed an un-developing part, except in the final retrospect before the girl's death, the effect was of disappointment. This was unjust to Mr. Steinbeck, and was afterward seen to have been unjust.

Nothing in his first or second acts suggested that the girl would ever exercise a deliberate influence on the action; she was drawn from the outset as a passive and static character, carefully subordinated to the independent drama of George and Lennie; and it is not until one realises this, and understands that Mr. Steinbeck's refusal to strike any romantic spark from her is his peculiar merit and integrity, that the special strength of his method is perceived. Miss Luce treats the part as it should be treated. Her emphasis is always metallic, not romantic. She makes no attempt, such as even a great actress of the romantic school might have made, to magnify this girl or to draw the play unto herself. She remains steadily a target, not an arrow, allowing the play to make its effects upon her, she exercising throughout a hard and brilliant constraint.

The positive, as distinct from the negative merits of the play, were made clear by John Mills and Niall MacGinnis as George and Lennie, particularly by Mr. Mills, who, with a thousand un-emphatic touches, none of them deliberately explanatory, used Mr. Steinbeck's dialogue to build up a portrait of a lovable man who probably believed himself to be a tough realist but who, in common with many who hold that belief, was at heart a dreamer of boyish dreams. The part is so truly written and so faithfully performed that when, at the end, George shoots his friend Lennie, deliberately, hopelessly and because he still loves him, what might have been a falsely symbolic or an arbitrarily melodramatic ending is neither of these things but falls into its place as natural and inevitable.

3 MAY 1939, THE TIMES

Third-Party Risk
by Gilbert Lennox and Gisela Ashley

ST MARTIN'S THEATRE

EDITH HARVEY	Gillian Scaife
LADY LAVERING	Ivy des Voeux
JOSEPH HARVEY	Waldo Wright
SIR DAVID LAVERING, M.D., F.R. C.P.	John Wyse
ANN MORDAUNT	Nora Swinburne
SYD	Ronald Shiner

A Harley Street doctor, angered by his wife's unjust suspicions is indiscreet enough to drive with Ann Mordaunt, one of his patients, to her country cottage. What would have happened if misfortune had not intervened the dramatists are clever enough to leave in doubt. The breach between Sir David and his wife is evidently not permanent. Miss Ivy des Voeux having been adroit enough to suggest affection within the lady's anger; but still Mrs. Mordaunt is pretty, she plays the piano, the cottage is faraway, and no one will ever be certain that Sir David, given time, might not have fallen from or to grace. As it is, he isn't given a chance. Before he reaches his destination he runs over a man, and before the man has been in the cottage three minutes he is dead. David and Ann's problem then becomes not how to subdue the flesh but how to get rid of the body.

Nothing would have been simpler than to carry it out and dump it in the ditch, but alas! It is the body of an escaped convict and the local constabulary is on its track. The sergeant comes, and when he has gone two hikers appear at the door, and when they have gone a policeman (looking for the convict) hides himself obstinately at the garden gate. Were ever lovers so embarrassed, or so protected, by the stubborn presence of a corpse? But it makes a lively and quickly moving second act with Mr. John Wyse and Miss Nora Swinburne twining themselves further and further into innocent entanglement and Mr. Ronald Shiner adding mysteriously a new complication. Ann goes off to London and David stays with the petrol tins, having decided, on the principle of roast pork, that the best way to get rid of the corpse is to burn down the house.

So to Harley Street. It is a pleasure to meet again Miss Gillian Scaife, Mr. Waldo Wright, and Miss des Voeux. It is a pleasure, too, to be assured, after a brief skirmish with Scotland Yard, that Ann and David somehow escaped from their entanglement. How they did so is a puzzle that experienced puzzlers must solve for themselves if they can, for we cannot help them. Perhaps the explanations button up, but they seem to gape a little. Not that it greatly matters except that it makes a disappointment of the last act, for this is a play that stands or falls by the contrivances of Act II, which are certainly ingenious, though sometimes a trifle ingenuous as well.

19 JUNE 1939, THE TIMES

The Greek Theatre

...

Founded in 1900 and reconstituted in 1930, the Royal Theatre is now among the most flourishing institutions of Greece. ... The classical and the modern drama of Greece and the whole theatre of Europe are included in its range; it has continually done honour to the work of Shakespeare, Sheridan, and Wilde; it has used to the full the opportunities which the climate of the Mediterranean and the surviving treasures of the ancient Greek theatre offer to open air performance; and it has courageously faced the problem set to modern producers by the special mingling, in classical drama, of religious and dramatic motive, of lyrical and narrative treatment, and the resulting mystery of the Greek chorus and Greek music. Those who saw, some years ago at Delphi, a production of *The Suppliants* of Aeschylus, which rightly treated it not as a crudely primitive play but as a link between a lyrical past and the individualized drama that was to succeed it, will know how careful the Greeks are of their own inheritance and how much we have to learn from their understanding of it; and their present treatment of the *Electra*, under the direction of M. Rondiris, will be watched with eager interest. That interest will be the greater because the gigantic part of Electra will be undertaken by Mme. Catina Paxinou. She comes to us with a reputation, won in such parts as Jocasta, Clytemnestra, Mrs. Alving in *Ghosts*, and in the plays of Wilde, which, unless we are to discredit the most discerning of our own countryman, entitles her to the highest rank.

For these reasons, and because there is in this country an affection for all things Greek, we may repeat Hamlet's welcome to the players. The British Council have done much to enable English actors to represent us abroad, have brought foreign companies here, and, with genuinely imaginative recognition of the theatre's part to increase mutual understanding between peoples, have steadily encouraged an interchange of the real values of civilization. None of their activities is more certain of endorsement by public opinion than the invitation which has brought the leading company of Greece to His Majesty's Theatre, for, proud though we are of our own dramatic tradition, we know its seed and that if there had been no Athenians there would have been no *Midsummer Night's Dream*. It has often been said by those who give little cause for gratitude that there is no gratitude between nations, and that they are bound together, if at all, only by a shifting and precarious self-interest. This is conspicuously untrue of the relations between Greece and England. The loveliest and most remembering complement that a Greek can pay to an Englishman is to welcome him as a countryman of "milord Byron," and it is often paid still, even to a lady, if she has hair of the right colour. The past is remembered in Greece as if it were to-day, and there is no traveller or seaman among us that has not a sense of home-coming in the Aegean or cannot say, among those home-islands, *Heureux qui, comme Ulysse, a fait un beau voyage*. What sane men live and die for had its origin in Greece and has its perpetuation in our liberties. The *Electra* and *Hamlet* are reminders of this. Not that the Greeks or we are likely to forget it.

20 JUNE 1939, THE TIMES
ROYAL THEATRE OF GREECE

Electra at His Majesty's by Sophocles

MODERN CRITIQUE BY J. GRYPARIS

ELECTRA	Catina Paxinou
CHROSOTHEME	Vaso Manolidou
CLYTEMNESTRA	Helene Pakpadaki

The Royal Theatre of Greece gave their first performance in London at His Majesty's Theatre last night. Tragedy, even Shakespeare's, has become in England a rare experience, and the *Electra* had upon its audience an effect not only of its natural power but of an extraordinary freshness. To the majority of those who heard it, Gryparis's modern Greek – and perhaps the Greek of Sophocles – was unknown, but throughout a continuous action of almost two hours the house was held by that silence of rapt attention which is distinguishable from the silence of courtesy. The first reason is that the production of M. Rondiris, under the general direction of M. Costis Bastias, has the effect of allowing the play itself, and not the imposed ingenuities of stagecraft, to be master of the stage. The Chorus, for the ancient uses of which there is no certain authority, is not employed as a background to the main characters nor as a self-assertive entity, but as a "lead" to Electra, as a means of convergence upon her, and instrument of unity; and the music of M. Mitropoulos, far from being, in the ordinary sense, an accompaniment to the words, is a rhythmic undercurrent to the whole dramatic movement, a link between the principal action and the choral comment, a response to mood. Elaborate though the production is in its study of collective movement and orchestrated sound, the impression it gives is of revealing the anatomy of the play, never of muffling it in hesitant decorations.

Except on rare occasions the divided chorus faces inward and up-stage, its attention on Electra, and, except for her joy in Orestes's return, which she clearly wishes to distinguish from all that precedes and follows it, Madame Catina Paxinou uses the forestage scarcely at all. That she abstains from it is a mark of her absolute confidence in her part and in her own powers. Employing none of the restless devices that are commonly used to "avoid monotony," she preserves in her position and in her gestures a passionate repose – a repose to which Madame Papdaki responds as Clytemnestra and which Madame Manolidou, sometimes a little disturbingly, rejects. Madame Paxinou needs no other variety than her voice and the astonishing expressiveness of her body. Whether she is bowed in grief while the messenger tells of the supposed death of Orestes, or is hurling defiance at her enemies, or is urging Chrysotheme to a boldness she dares not pursue, or, in response to the spring and vitality of M. Cotsopoulos's Orestes, is herself possessed by a brilliance of joy and hope, she proves herself again and again a majestic actress with that magnetism and, above all, that discipline which, in any mood, draws an audience to her and holds it in unfailing expectancy. If one may record a single impression as a summary of the impressions given by this production it is one of spiritual excitement. This was not a performance undertaken in pious devotion to a classical tradition. It was unforced, beautifully simple, and, with Mme Paxinou at the heart of the flame, burningly alive. ...

21 JUNE 1939, THE TIMES
ROYAL THEATRE OF GREECE

Hamlet by William Shakespeare

TRANSLATION BY B. ROTA

HAMLET	Minotis
POLONIUS	Jakobides
OPHELIA	Manolidou
GERTRUDE	Paxinou

A performance of *Hamlet* in modern Greek is very different in its effect on an English ear from a performance of *Electra*. At first one cannot help feeling for the familiar words and to some extent retranslating them. That they should be so familiar appears to be an advantage; the meaning is continuously clear; one knows at each instant precisely what the speaker is trying to express; but the advantage is not all on one side, for retranslation must always be a little out of step and response to the actor's attack and rhythm correspondingly weakened. It is a mark of the force of M. Minotis's performance that, before long, it bore down the quibbling desire to dig in the mind for Shakespeare's phrases, and established itself in its own right not as a line-by-line reading of the text carried in the English memory but as a vital interpretation of the part as a whole.

M. Minotis's particular strength rests upon two qualities – the intensity of his passages of fire and the contrasted lightness of his irony. Where the language is unknown and, therefore, the precise verbal emphasis cannot be estimated, one hesitates to question him on detail, but it appeared that the great soliloquies, magnificently though they were spoken, were sometimes too spectacular, too little a spontaneous product of the mind. In brief, M. Minotis seemed, in them, to be a trifle self-conscious; which is precisely what elsewhere he was not. His ironic play with Polonius has remarkable ease and wit; his scenes with Ophelia, often the most baffling in the play, have a splendid lucidity; and his passage with the Queen after Polonius's death has reason as well as terror. M. Minotis evidently responds strongly to the good in others. He happens to have in M. Sakobides a lightly and admirably drawn Polonius and, in Mme Paxinou, a superb Gertrude. She plays a great part of her scene with Hamlet with her back to the audience, leaving him his attack, responding in the turn of her shoulders, the movement of her dropped hands; then slowly turns to witness his discovery of the Ghost. This is a memorable climax of a production by which the Royal Theatre of Greece did honour to the play at his Majesty's last night.

27 JUNE 1939, THE TIMES

The Plough and the Stars by Sean O'Casey

Q THEATRE

THE YOUNG COVEY	Cyril Cusack
BESSIE BURGESS	Sara Allgood
FLUTHER GOOD	Brefni O'Rorke
MRS. GOGAN	Maire O'Neill

Though it is a tale of Easter week in Dublin, *The Plough and the Stars* was not at any time a propagandist or even a topical play, and the qualities of critical insight into the follies and heroisms of man which saved it from being so preserve it now from staleness. It is, indeed, an object lesson to imaginative writers who, wishing to use a contemporary scene and a controversial subject, find that what seems to be a work of art to-day is in peril of becoming stale journalism to-morrow. Mr. O'Casey faces this difficulty and overcomes it, not indeed by a romanticized avoidance of contemporary fact, but by penetrating superficial fact and ephemeral controversy and building his play upon realities underlying them.

These are his play's foundations, but what gives it its special vitality is less its content than its style. All the people who live with the Clitheroes in their tenement have an Irish eloquence, but it is more than Irish, it is O'Casey's own eloquence, used always with the central aim of poetic irony – and eloquence that can scarcely be overplayed. In this it resembles Shaw's; to be timid, to be afraid to fantasticate it, to subdue it to a rule of photographic naturalism is to throw away its rhythm, and it is only in its rhythm that its full meaning appears. For this reason Miss Allgood and Miss O'Neill are right to let themselves go, but it must be added that there are times when the company's slowness on its cues halts the eloquence and makes it seem artificial, or when even Miss Allgood herself is too heavy on her emphasis. Nevertheless this is a welcome revival of the play. Mr. Brefni O' Rorke distinguishes himself in a study of Fluther, which is as broad and free as you please, but remains a continuously ironic comment on the man it represents; Miss O'Neill and Miss Allgood act with a rich humour, and a genuinely evocative power; and the production, though not perfectly in time last night, survives the test of any performance of this play – it makes a single pattern of Mr. O'Casey's tragic and comic observations.

29 JUNE 1939, THE TIMES

Hamlet by William Shakespeare

LYCEUM THEATRE

HORATIO	Glen Byam Shaw
GHOST	Jack Hawkins
CLAUDIUS	Jack Hawkins
LAERTES	Harry Andrews
POLONIUS	George Howe
HAMLET	John Gielgud
ROSENCRANTZ	Andrew Cruickshank
GUILDENSTERN	William Gates
FIRST PLAYER	Marius Goring
GERTRUDE	Laura Cowie
OPHELIA	Fay Compton

The few performances that Mr. Gielgud is giving in London before taking his company to Elsinore will be memorable not for their own sake only but because they are the last that will be seen at the Lyceum Theatre. They are an honourable farewell, and are of the more interest because many of the players are already well-known in the parts they now maintain. The production, for which Mr. Gielgud himself is responsible, owes an acknowledged debt to Mr. Granville-Barker's preface, and has an excellent precision and lucidity. Motley's dresses are of rare beauty, and, if the architecture of the set appears a trifle spindly and unsupported, like poor Polonius on his weak hams, it is just to remember that at Elsinore, for which it has been designed, it will be backed by castle walls. There, moreover, it will be possible, as it is not at the Lyceum, to make full use of a projecting forestage.

In a discussion of the acting, it is no discourtesy to Mr. Gielgud to speak first of Miss Compton's Ophelia. Hamlet is so often the Prince alone that, when any other performance is unquestionably of the first rank, there is a remarkable gain in balance and unity. This is a magical Ophelia, at the outset young, simple, full of wonder, and yet not cold, and, in her madness, possessed of that coherence on a different plane from ours which is the genius of the scene. Miss Compton does not wander in vague pathos; her song, cut by the plain tone of her speaking voice, draws the imagination into Ophelia's mind and gives definition to her dreams. No other performance in the parts less than Hamlet's can be the equal of Miss Compton's, but Mr. George Howe's Polonius is brilliant and nimble, Mr. Jack Hawkins, a good King though a little slow, is a genuinely impressive Ghost, Mr. Glen Byam Shaw's Horatio is played lightly and well, while Miss Laura Cowie and Mr. Marius Goring take their opportunity to distinguish themselves.

Hamlet's first soliloquy was for a moment alarming. Perhaps because it was the first or because he was seeking the range of so large a theatre, Mr. Gielgud spoke it with the taughtness of a nervous driver at the wheel of a motor-car and, at the end, forced it. Now and then this unease recurred later in the play, particularly in one or two over-emphatic exits, but for the most part Mr. Gielgud's tension, which is extreme, was the natural tension of Hamlet's mind. Hamlet is presented not so much as a man ordinarily hesitant or weak but as a brilliant creature, naturally of a quick and even violent decision, who is here bound by particular mental cords. One of the delights of the performance is in the periods when these cords are loosed – either in the scene with the Players or in the passionate licence of Hamlet's attack on the Queen. Mr. Gielgud plays these scenes so well, each on its different plane, that the contrasted scenes, when the cords are fast upon him – in the great soliloquies, in his pitiful chiding of Ophelia, and in his discovery of the King at prayer – are themselves enhanced, and the whole reading of the part is given continuity and form. It is a beautiful, fiery, and, above all an uncomplacent performance, as rich in experiment as it is solid in achievement.

Note: this was Charles Morgan's last review for The Times before he was called to work in The Naval Intelligence Division of The Admiralty.

16 JULY 1939, THE NEW YORK TIMES

John Gielgud: The Melancholy Dane Again

The outstanding first night of the past week has been John Gielgud's production of *Hamlet*. With his performance of the part New York is already familiar, but now, in anticipation of taking his company to Elsinore, he has remodelled his treatment of the play, basing his interpretation of it very closely on Granville-Barker's preface. His own performance has matured and acquired a tension different in kind from that which it formally had. The original emphasis was upon Hamlet's infirmity of purpose, and this led Mr. Gielgud into a treatment which was in some respects oversensitive or, if one may use the phrase, over decorative.

The Hamlet we now see is naturally a much firmer and more resolute man, whose resolution has been temporarily shaken by the special circumstances in which he finds himself. It is thus possible for Mr. Gielgud to keep continually in view two interwoven threads of the part; first, the natural firmness and vigour which appear in the scene with the players and which are developed to the point of violence in the attack on the Queen, and, secondly, those passages in which Hamlet's natural character is twisted or subverted; for example, his agonized and unwilling cruelty to Ophelia and his profound spiritual confusion when he refrains from striking the King at prayer.

The production need not be discussed at length, because many of the players, like Mr. Gielgud himself, are already familiar in their respective parts, Miss Fay Compton being still the most moving and the most lucid Ophelia within my experience and Mr. George Howe repeating his distinguished interpretation of Polonius. Only a few performances of this revival are being seen in London before the company moves to Denmark, but these few will be memorable as the last to be given in the Lyceum Theatre before that great house, where Miss Fay Compton's aunt, Jessie Bateman, played Ophelia to Irving's first Hamlet, is pulled down.

There have been two other revivals of some interest, *The Ascent of F6*, by W. H. Auden, and Christopher Isherwood at the Old Vic, and *The Plough and the Stars*, by Sean O' Casey at the "Q" Theatre; and there has been one new play, *After the Dance*, by Terence Rattigan, which, because the author wrote "French Without Tears," the most successful farce of modern times in London, aroused before its appearance considerable eagerness and curiosity.

Mr. Rattigan has here turned resolutely away from farce and set out to write a serious play of discussion. He contrasts two generations, those who are now very young and those whose grown-up life was beginning during the last war. The nature of the contrast which he sees is, broadly stated, that the war generation wear over their seriousness a cloak of flippancy and over their deeper emotions a mask of indifference; while their successors, now in the early twenties, take themselves with open seriousness and even with solemnity and are always prepared, without preservation, to mount the moral high horse.

David Scott Fowler, who is brilliantly represented by Robert Harris, has been married for twelve years to Joan and they have, throughout their marriage, preserved a facade of flippancy which has actually prevented them from ever fully acknowledging their love for each other. The affectation has become in them almost a reality, with the result that David, hungry for a warmth of affection which his wife never openly gives him, and desiring, as a vain and thwarted man, an open recognition of his own worth, falls blindly in love with a girl, Helen, much younger than himself, who is skilfully presented to us, first as potentially a romantic heroine and then gradually as the opinionated and unconscious hypocrite that she is.

Mr. Rattigan is a little inclined, in working out the plot, to use incidents unpersuasively melodramatic. Here his theatricalism is over-deliberate and he gives an impression of forcing his material into unnatural shapes; but where he is quietly drawing his major characters, he reveals himself as a serious dramatist of genuine insight, who can write light dialogue that is never an interpolated comic relief, but is always contributory to our knowledge of the mentality of the speakers.

He has, too, the rare quality of not playing all his cards at once. Many characters in modern plays are static after the end of the first act. By the time the first curtain falls, we know all there is to be known of them, there are no surprises left, except such as may be provided by the twist of the action. Mr. Rattigan's people grow and change before our eyes, and their development is so truly traced that what is revealed of them in the third act is, when it comes, completely satisfying as a fulfilment of the hints given about them at the outset. For these reasons the play, though sometimes mechanical in structure, holds out a real promise that in Mr. Rattigan we have not only a successful writer of farce but a dramatist of serious consequences.

INDEXES

INDEX OF PLAYS AND FILMS

Charles Morgan: Three Plays

9781849431828

Includes the plays *The River Line*, *The Flashing Stream* and *The Burning Glass*

Charles Morgan (1894-1958) was a distinguished novelist before he moved onto stage drama, with his reputation as a major dramatist established by his first play, *The Flashing Stream*. Morgan was unique for combining the roles of principal dramatic critic of *The Times* with that of a practicing dramatist. *The Daily Herald* wrote that *The Flashing Stream* would 'indefinitely refute the old idea about the gulf between our preaching and the practice. It was hailed as 'a masterpiece' by the *Manchester Guardian*, and also drew praise from *The Telegraph* who noted that 'it handles a major problem of humanity with passion and intelligence'. The combination of serious themes with dramatic tension and masterly craftsmanship was continued in his other plays, *The River Line* and *The Burning Glass*, which are also included in this collection.

'Always a thrilling experience.' – Harold Hobson on *The River Line*

'Mr. Charles Morgan has written the play, not only of the year, but of the decade in which we live.' – Ludovic Kennedy on *The Burning Glass*

'Utterly gripping… wholly enthralling.' – Daily Telegraph on *The River Line*

'This overlooked classic is highly engaging… Like a fantastic Greek tragedy transposed to post-war Europe, *The River Line* works its themes of death, grace and regret to powerful effect.' – *Time Out London*

WWW.OBERONBOOKS.COM

Follow us on www.twitter.com/@oberonbooks
& www.facebook.com/oberonbook